*Palgrave Shakespeare Studies*

General Editors: **Michael Dobson** and **Dympna**

Editorial Advisory Board: **Michael Neill**, University Folger Shakespeare Library; **Lois D. Potter**, Univ **Grazia**, University of Pennsylvania; **Peter Holland**,

*Palgrave Shakespeare Studies* takes Shakespeare as its focus but strives to understand the significance of his oeuvre in relation to his contemporaries, subsequent writers and historical and political contexts. By extending the scope of Shakespeare and English Renaissance Studies the series will open up the field to examinations of previously neglected aspects or sources in the period's art and thought. Titles in the *Palgrave Shakespeare Studies* series seek to understand anew both where the literary achievements of the English Renaissance came from and where they have brought us.

*Titles include:*

Pascale Aebischer, Edward J. Esche and Nigel Wheale (*editors*)
REMAKING SHAKESPEARE
Performance across Media, Genres and Cultures

J. Bednarz
SHAKESPEARE AND THE TRUTH OF LOVE
The Mystery of 'The Phoenix and Turtle'

Mark Thornton Burnett
FILMING SHAKESPEARE IN THE GLOBAL MARKETPLACE

Lowell Gallagher and Shankar Raman (*editors*)
KNOWING SHAKESPEARE
Senses, Embodiment and Cognition

David Hillman
SHAKESPEARE'S ENTRAILS
Belief, Scepticism and the Interior of the Body

Jane Kingsley-Smith
SHAKESPEARE'S DRAMA OF EXILE

Stephen Purcell
POPULAR SHAKESPEARE
Simulation and Subversion on the Modern Stage

Erica Sheen
SHAKESPEARE AND THE INSTITUTION OF THEATRE

Paul Yachin and Jessica Slights
SHAKESPEARE AND CHARACTER
Theory, History, Performance, and Theatrical Persons

---

*Palgrave Shakespeare Studies*
Series Standing Order ISBN 978–1403–911643 (hardback) 978–1403–911650 (paperback)
(*outside North America only*)

You can receive future titles in this series as they are published by placing a standing order. Please contact your bookseller or, in case of difficulty, write to us at the address below with your name and address, the title of the series and the ISBN quoted above.

Customer Services Department, Macmillan Distribution Ltd, Houndmills, Basingstoke, Hampshire RG21 6XS, England.

*By the same author*

*MASTERS AND SERVANTS IN ENGLISH RENAISSANCE DRAMA AND CULTURE

*CONSTRUCTING 'MONSTERS' IN SHAKESPEAREAN DRAMA AND EARLY MODERN CULTURE

*SHAKESPEARE, FILM, FIN DE SIÈCLE (*co-editor with Ramona Wray*)

SCREENING SHAKESPEARE IN THE TWENTY-FIRST CENTURY (*co-editor with Ramona Wray*)

*FILMING AND PERFORMING RENAISSANCE HISTORY (*co-editor with Adrian Streete*)

THE EDINBURGH COMPANION TO SHAKESPEARE AND THE ARTS (*co-editor with Adrian Streete and Ramona Wray*)

*From the same publishers*

# Filming Shakespeare in the Global Marketplace

Mark Thornton Burnett
*Professor of Renaissance Studies*
*Queen's University, Belfast, Northern Ireland*

© Mark Thornton Burnett 2007, 2012

All rights reserved. No reproduction, copying or transmission of this publication may be made without written permission.

No portion of this publication may be reproduced, copied or transmitted save with written permission or in accordance with the provisions of the Copyright, Designs and Patents Act 1988, or under the terms of any licence permitting limited copying issued by the Copyright Licensing Agency, Saffron House, 6–10 Kirby Street, London EC1N 8TS.

Any person who does any unauthorized act in relation to this publication may be liable to criminal prosecution and civil claims for damages.

The author has asserted his right to be identified as the author of this work in accordance with the Copyright, Designs and Patents Act 1988.

First published in hardback 2007
First published in paperback 2012 by
PALGRAVE MACMILLAN

Palgrave Macmillan in the UK is an imprint of Macmillan Publishers Limited, registered in England, company number 785998, of Houndmills, Basingstoke, Hampshire RG21 6XS.

Palgrave Macmillan in the US is a division of St Martin's Press LLC, 175 Fifth Avenue, New York, NY 10010.

Palgrave Macmillan is the global academic imprint of the above companies and has companies and representatives throughout the world.

Palgrave® and Macmillan® are registered trademarks in the United States, the United Kingdom, Europe and other countries

ISBN 978–1–4039–9215–4   hardback
ISBN 978–0–230–39145–1   paperback

This book is printed on paper suitable for recycling and made from fully managed and sustained forest sources. Logging, pulping and manufacturing processes are expected to conform to the environmental regulations of the country of origin.

A catalogue record for this book is available from the British Library.

Library of Congress Cataloging-in-Publication Data

Burnett, Mark Thornton.
    Filming Shakespeare in the global marketplace / Mark Thornton Burnett.
    p. cm. – (Palgrave Shakespeare studies)
    Includes bibliographical references and index.
    ISBN 978–1–4039–9215–4 (cloth) 978–0–230–39145–1 (pbk)
         1. Shakespeare, William, 1564–1616–Film and video adaptations.
    2. English drama–Film and video adaptations. 3. Motion pictures and globalization 4. Culture and globalization. 5. Film adaptations–History and criticism I. Title.

PR3093.B87 2007
791.43'6–dc22                                                              2006050833

10  9  8  7  6  5  4  3  2  1
21 20 19 18 17 16 15 14 13 12

Transferred to Digital Printing in 2012

*To Louis Thornton Burnett*

# Contents

*Preface* viii
*List of Figures* xiv
*Acknowledgements* xvi
Introduction 1
1 Screening the Stage 7
2 Sequelizing Shakespeare 28
3 The Local and the Global 47
4 Racial Identities, Global Economies 66
5 Remembrance, Holocaust, Globalization 87
6 Spirituality/Meaning/Shakespeare 107
7 Post-Millennial Parody 129
Epilogue 158
*Notes* 167
*Bibliography* 193
*Index* 213

# Preface

To revisit *Filming Shakespeare in the Global Marketplace*, five years after the book's publication, is to take an opportunity to reflect on how the field of Shakespeare on film is changing. As the opening decade of the twenty-first century recedes, what might be termed a discipline of Shakespeare on film is firmly rooted in the educational curriculum. Shakespeare films are widely taught in schools, colleges and universities; indeed, they are increasingly the first port of call for a student encounter with the Bard. Most institutions will advertise a course or courses on Shakespeare and his film manifestations or Shakespeare and the history of adaptation. In terms of range and depth, criticism of Shakespeare films is entrenched: academic conferences boast dedicated sessions to the subject and feature *premières* of works intended for commercial cinema release. There are conferences devoted to the fortunes of a single play on screen, journals that run special issues on Shakespeare on film, and essay collections that, to illustrate a larger theme, showcase a contribution on a particular Shakespeare screen interpretation. Rapidly, but inexorably, Shakespeare films have assumed canonical positions, while commentary has developed in aspiration, volume and effect.

With time, the sample of work on which interest focuses shifts. Since the publication of this book, there have been additional entries in the genre of Shakespeare and film, entries which have taken us in some exciting and not always expected directions. *The Tempest* (dir. Julie Taymor, 2010) impressed on its release as an art-house, festival-pitched adaptation of Shakespeare's play characterized by an acute self-consciousness of its own representational methods, as revealed in purposeful applications of CGI and, in the director's words, a 'heightened expressionism'.[1] The film announces its distinctive take on the play by casting Helen Mirren as Prospera, a female mage composed of 'erratic fury, cruelty, maternal warmth, cold authority, and poetic inspiration', and adorning her in a striking shard-like glittering blue cloak.[2] Such colours belong with the film's rich palette, the Hawaii and Lanai volcanic locations providing browns, reds and oranges that both connote a raw environment and suggest explosive energies held imperfectly in check. Visually, *The Tempest* is a feast, from sepulchral, tenebrous interiors to snaky, smoky trails of vengeful energy scored across the skies. In keeping with an approach that plays up the metaphorical richness of a natural environment, Ariel (Ben Whishaw) is consistently linked to water and fire, the twin elements that define his condition. And, as befits a play that has been seen as imbued with colonialism, Taymor's *The Tempest* is permeated with reminders of empire and the ways in which imperialism inscribes itself on the bodies of its subjects. This is suggested not least in the shot of a dissolving hand-held sandcastle but also in the appearance of Caliban (Djimon Hounsou) upon whose scaly and mottled skin insults are carved. Oppressive linguistic histories take on adverse physical forms, ideas which are reinforced by a drum-laden soundtrack and the detail of the autochthonous, rocky home that Shakespeare's 'savage and deformed slave' inhabits. The work of an American director of theatre, opera, film and musical, *The Tempest* is a bold undertaking, rewriting gendered performance histories, summoning the legacies of the European lust for dominion, and extrapolating the Shakespearean word in feats of cinematic wizardry.

*Coriolanus* (dir. Ralph Fiennes, 2012), released two years later, is a gritty and discordant screen reading of Shakespeare's Roman play, noted for its evocation of a battle-torn landscape marked by apocalyptic primitivism. At once, the film would seem to gesture to recent conflicts – the war between Russia and Chechnya, the Arab Spring and the London riots, for example – as part of its anatomization of a society in decline and disrepair. More specifically, drawing on the associations of its Belgrade-set shooting location, *Coriolanus* summons the Balkan wars of the 1990s, finding in the fading communist constructions, new buildings, open boulevards and denuded topography of the Serbian capital apt architectural correlatives for the antagonism between the Romans and the Volscians.[3] Certainly, in the scene involving the fight between Coriolanus (Ralph Fiennes) and Aufidius (Gerard Butler), filmed among the collapsed staircases and flaking pillars of the abandoned Hotel Jugoslavia, a vivid sense of the tribulations of East European history is captured. Yet, in another way, *Coriolanus* is characterized by a predilection for conjuring images of *any* city-state in crisis: the tattoos and bandanas sported by the combatants point to no clearly identified constituency, and the clash of designer suits and combat fatigues would belong in a number of similarly afflicted environs. This city is nowhere and synecdoche, a further element of the *mise-en-scène* being the ways in which the war is envisaged as simultaneously possessed of a violent visceral materiality and a postmodern orientation. Here, the inclusion of fictional live streaming, photographs, and front-line reporters grants to the action scenes an unnerving quality and blurs the lines of representational distinction. The work of a British actor and director, *Coriolanus* is a mould-breaking feature that, mixing genres and recasting the ills of austerity, is highly attuned to its times.

Both films might be said to be global in tenor and style. According to Ralph Fiennes, director of *Coriolanus*, 'Rome' was envisaged as 'multinational, multi-lingual'.[4] An informing premise was that Shakespeare's 'Roman' play spoke eloquently to issues of deterritorialization and polyvocality. With *The Tempest*, director Julie Taymor, building upon the play's imbrications in the fate of the Globe Theatre, makes of Prospera's revels a heavenly extravaganza: as the signs of the zodiac fade in and out of view, circles and spheres revolve, telling images of old and new worlds. On the film's website other worlds are conjured: the menu, in the form of a compass, invites users to navigate, like any Renaissance adventurer, the different instantiations of the film, whether this is the gallery, the book or the music download.[5] Implicit is a choice – between themes but also between film modes. The user is granted powers of access as he/she explores various routes to *The Tempest* in the global marketplace.

As the content of what we examine in Shakespeare on film studies has changed, so, too, have the methodologies. In his preface to the published screenplay of his 1993 film adaptation of *Much Ado About Nothing*, Kenneth Branagh imagines the possibility of a 'Shakespeare film that belonged to the world'.[6] Branagh's more inclusive ownership of the genre has gained ground in recent years, although perhaps not quite in the way the auteur intended. There is now a greater interest in complicating the US–UK axis embodied in directors such as Taymor and Fiennes and in attending to other points of origin, sites of energy, types of Shakespeare film and, crucially, non-Anglophone productions. It is clear that, as we enter a period in which the Bard is expanding and diversifying as a global icon, a more nuanced and ambitious sense of the multifarious ways in which Shakespeare is screened inside and across nations and cultures is called for. In this way, we might be able to arrive at an ethically capacious grasp of a Shakespearean cinema that is for and of the world, that is 'not the other, but is us'.[7] *Filming Shakespeare in the Global Marketplace* is invested in that initiative, not least in its discussion of issues of globalization and their relation to films such as the Derry Film Initiative *Hamlet* (dir. Stephen Cavanagh, 2005), animated by its politically dissident use of the Irish language, and *In Othello* (dir. Roysten Abel, 2003), with its regionally-encoded alternations between Assamese and Hindi, but there are grounds for arguing that the examples privileged inside this methodological shift might extend further still.

Particular auteurs within the non-Anglophone Shakespeare on film genre are now enjoying visibility. French director Alexander Abela has

*Preface* xi

come to notice for *Makibefo* (1999), a Malagasy-language production which identifies itself via an on-screen translation of its title as a revision of *Macbeth*, and *Souli* (2004), a Malagasy and French language work advertised in the end credits as 'librement inspiré d'*Othello* de William Shakespeare'.[8] *Macbeth* the director takes to the Antandroy people of Faux Cap in the south-east corner of Madagascar; *Othello* he transposes to the fishing village of Ambola on Madagascar's western shoreline. Both films access Shakespeare via performative transplantation, which is defined, in the director's formulation, as the participation of 'individuals isolated from the rest of the world'.[9] *Makibefo* was enacted by fishermen and herdsmen, while *Souli* combined a professional, non-native cast with local players. The rationale was that, from a communal and intercultural experience, fresh readings of Shakespeare would emerge. The auteur is further glimpsed in the films in the reliance upon visual vocabularies, charms approximating the contents of the witches' cauldron in *Macbeth*, a pen and paper pointing to *Othello*'s absorption in stories, and a recurrent *zebu* or ox indicating a more general preoccupation with wealth and status. Distinctive to *Makibefo* and *Souli* is a combination of specific traditions and motifs and an overarching directorial vision, with the result that the Bard, in this particular manifestation, takes on a revealing collaborative significance.

If auteurs are privileged in such critical revisionism, then so, too, are certain nations and regional configurations. Complicating a US–UK trajectory is a focus on previously bypassed locations for Bardic encounters on screen, Latin America being a case in point. In films such as *Sangrador* (dir. Leonardo Henríquez, 2000), a Venezuelan adaptation of *Macbeth*, and *Huapango* (dir. Iván Lipkies, 2004), a Mexican adaptation of *Othello*, responses to mediations of Shakespearean metaphor are encouraged by the concentration on a localized *mise-en-scène*.[10] Emerging from a purposeful utilization of distinctive environments (the Huasteca region of northeastern Mexico and the Venezuelan Andes), the plays' allusions to animals are indigenized to highlight shifting praxes of power, sexuality and prestige. Such reworking carries a political charge: *Sangrador* and *Huapango* offer trenchant critique by exploiting recognizable typologies of character, such as the romanticized brigand (Max/Macbeth [Daniel Alvarado] is a mountain bandit) and the *jefe* or chief (Otilio/Othello [Alejandro Tomassi] is a cattle rancher), identifying the political and postcolonial determinants of their acts of national self-expression. Where *Sangrador* uses *Macbeth*'s alliance with political tragedy to reflect upon Venezuelan militaristic authoritarianism, *Huapango* pushes the black–white racial dichotomies of *Othello* to test the ties that bind ethnicity and conquest. In both films, *Macbeth* and *Othello*

– rewritten – expose the intricacy of the connections running between established institutions and the popular imaginary in modern Latin America.

Belonging with that broader embrace of non-Anglophone Shakespeare film is an examination of productions the pairing of which demands interpretive and conceptual readjustment. *As You Like It* (dir. Kenneth Branagh, 2006) pitched itself as an English pastoral comedy transformed into a 'dream of Japan', but this is not an isolated example, other filmmakers having lent the tragedies a more thorough-going 'Asianized' treatment. A recent collection of essays places in juxtaposition the Indian film, *Maqbool* (dir. Vishal Bhardwaj, 2004), an adaptation of *Macbeth*, and the Chinese feature, *The Banquet* (dir. Xiaogang Feng, 2006), which demonstrates many affinities with *Hamlet*, so as to tease out their mutually constitutive characteristics.[11] In each film instance, a cultivation of authenticity is a translation strategy: *Maqbool* feeds Scotland's internecine conflicts into a carefully composed rendition of Mumbai's underworld, while *The Banquet* unfolds in China's Tang dynasty period, indicating historical distance via a rich array of oriental objects and accoutrements. Psychic tension is a watchword. For, in *The Banquet*, the action hinges on a vexed triangulated relationship involving Wu Luan/Hamlet (Daniel Wu), his stepmother-lover, Empress Wan/Gertrude (Ziyi Zhang), and Emperor Li/Claudius (You Ge), which means that desire is constantly in play; by contrast, *Maqbool*'s equivalent entanglement is demonstrated in the erotic frisson that runs from Maqbool/Macbeth (Irfan Khan), the right-hand man of drug-lord, Abbaji/Duncan (Pankaj Kapur), to Nimmi/Lady Macbeth (Tabu), his patron-boss' mistress. Bonds of familial and political loyalty collide with each other even as they are also contested. Thematic frictions are shaped by each film's 'look', whether this is the kinaesthetic sumptuousness of *Maqbool*'s song and dance sequences or the aesthetic grandeur of *The Banquet*'s filmic properties – bright unfurling fabrics, jade carvings and elaborate statuary. Like some of the other film tragedies discussed in this book, *The Banquet* matches Fredric Jameson's discussion of how a 'nostalgia film' approaches 'the "past" through stylistic connotation, conveying "pastness" by the glossy qualities of the image'.[12]

Such a film imaginary, reified or otherwise, is available to interested parties in outlets other than a conventional release. For, surpassing even the less secure place of 'Hollyworld' as a representational machine and the diversification of Shakespeare film languages, is the movement from cinema to the new media. Thanks to its replication on YouTube, the six-minute 'short', *Romeo & Juliet* (dir. David Lachapelle, 2005), which is discussed in this book, enjoys a life more active and interactive than any other distribution idiom. YouTube, more broadly, plays an important role in determining criteria of reception and appreciation. Blogging and social networking are growing as conduits through which an academic community makes sense of itself, while multimedia platforms, in their pedagogical deployment, are reinventing Shakespeare screen canons and refining interpretive practices. The online Shakespeare film not only asks challenging questions about value, quality and exemplarity. It also insists upon fresh methodologies suited to addressing the 'Shakespeares' of cyberspace.[13]

What does the future hold? In a reflective piece on the genre of Shakespeare and film, Ramona Wray anticipates reacquainting ourselves with the archives (going back to 'lost' or occluded examples), which might entail corresponding interdisciplinary developments, an attention to citation, rehearsal and context, and an investigation into filmic afterlives.[14] In pursuing these and other endeavours, we will, I think, both challenge and broaden existing networks of dissemination and arrive at a knowledge and appreciation of Shakespeare on film that admits of world-wide depth and diversity. If some of the newer film examples sketched in this preface prompt us to entertain a generous sense of Shakespeare, they also encourage a process of watching and writing in emergent and as yet untested ways. An experience of Shakespeare films understood and articulated according to an expansive purview allows for exchange; it liberates arguments about what Shakespearean cinema is and yet might be; and it forces us to reflect on pertinent questions of fidelity and authorship, authority and evidence. Exposed to Shakespeare in a range of guises, we critics and teachers learn and grow not only by scrutinizing currently available methodologies, but also by accepting an invitation to pursue comparative analyses.

Mark Thornton Burnett<br>Belfast, 2012

# List of Figures

| | | |
|---|---|---|
| Figure 1. | *Get Over It* (dir. Tommy O' Haver, 2001) culminates in the climactic production of *A Midsummer Night's Rockin' Eve*. Courtesy of Jerry Ohlinger's Movie Material Store, New York. | 18 |
| Figure 2. | Storyboard illustration from *Much Ado About Nothing* (dir. Kenneth Branagh, 1993). Courtesy of the Kenneth Branagh Archive, Queen's University, Belfast. | 40 |
| Figure 3. | Design sheet for *Hamlet* (dir. Kenneth Branagh, 1997). Courtesy of the Kenneth Branagh Archive, Queen's University, Belfast. | 51 |
| Figure 4. | The protagonist (Ethan Hawke) as auteur in *Hamlet* (dir. Michael Almereyda, 2000). Courtesy of Jerry Ohlinger's Movie Material Store, New York. | 53 |
| Figure 5. | Storyboard illustration for Fortinbras's takeover in *Hamlet* (dir. Kenneth Branagh, 1997). Courtesy of the Kenneth Branagh Archive, Queen's University, Belfast. | 55 |
| Figure 6. | Commemorative programme for the European première of *Hamlet* (dir. Kenneth Branagh, 1997). Courtesy of the Kenneth Branagh Archive, Queen's University, Belfast. | 61 |
| Figure 7. | O (Mekhi Phifer) parades the broken basketball hoop in *'O'* (dir. Tim Blake Nelson, 2001). Courtesy of Jerry Ohlinger's Movie Material Store, New York. | 74 |
| Figure 8. | Shylock (Al Pacino) and Tubal (Allan Corduner) contemplate their inimical environment in *William Shakespeare's 'The Merchant of Venice'* (dir. Michael Radford, 2004). Courtesy of Jerry Ohlinger's Movie Material Store, New York. | 90 |
| Figure 9. | Ray (Bruce Davison) reflects upon an abandoned landscape in *The King is Alive* (dir. Kristian Levring, 2000). Courtesy of Photofest, New York. | 112 |
| Figure 10. | A typical fantasy sequence from *In Othello* (dir. Roysten Abel, 2003). Courtesy of Amit Bhatia and ANB Motion Pictures. | 142 |

Figure 11. Sheeba/Desdemona (Sheeba Chaddha) produces a  154
rose during the concluding moments of *In Othello*
(dir. Roysten Abel, 2003). Courtesy of Amit Bhatia
and ANB Motion Pictures.
Figure 12. An announcement for Kenneth Branagh's projected  162
film of *Macbeth*. Courtesy of the Kenneth Branagh
Archive, Queen's University, Belfast.

# Acknowledgements

I owe primary thanks to two institutions which have generously funded my research, made available precious time and provided material resources. Queen's University, Belfast, granted me a semester of study leave, and the Arts and Humanities Research Council provided an additional semester away from teaching and administration under its one-year research leave scheme. Queen's University has been equally supportive in the form of grants from the Publications Fund, the Research and Travel Fund, and the Vice-Chancellor's Fund. I am also grateful to the British Academy and the International Shakespeare Association for supporting attendance at three overseas conferences.

At Queen's, I have been fortunate in my Deans and Heads of School, Ellen Douglas-Cowie and Hugh Magennis respectively, and in colleagues who have offered friendship, advice and counsel: they include Fran Brearton, Marion Campbell, Richard English, Adam Hansen, Nigel Harkness, Eamonn Hughes, Edel Lamb, Debbie Lisle, Jaime Lizardi, Naomi McAreavey, Michael McAteer, Des O'Rawe, Andrew Pepper, Daniel Roberts, Satia Roberts, Isabel Torres and Harvey Whitehouse. I have had many stimulating conversations about Shakespeare and film with Adrian Streete – to him I am particularly obliged for his collegiality and companionship. Carolyn Jess-Cooke, too, has taught me much about the subject.

Further afield, I am grateful to John Joughin for the title, and to Richard Burt, Kevin de Ornellas, Kate Chedgzoy, Peter Donaldson, Susanne Greenhalgh, Peter Holland, Russell Jackson, Doug Lanier, Courtney Lehmann, Kenneth Rothwell and Peter Stoneley for conversations and courtesies. Sam Crowl has been a significant source of instruction and encouragement, and Robert Shaughnessy has been importantly facilitative.

Different versions of some of these chapters have been given as papers at Belfast (Renaissance Spaces and Margins Conference and Research Seminar), Bermuda (Shakespeare Association of America), Brisbane (World Shakespeare Congress), Dublin (Research Seminar, University College), Galway (Research Seminar, University College), Geneva (Literary and Economic Signifiers Conference), London (*Hamlet* on Screen Conference, Shakespeare's Globe, Renaissance Endings Conference, Roehampton University, and Research Seminar, Royal Holloway College),

Minneapolis (Shakespeare Association of America), Rouen (Shakespeare on Screen Conference) and Stratford-upon-Avon (International Shakespeare Conference and Thursday Seminars). I would like to thank the audiences on those occasions for their informed attention, the organizers of the conferences at which I spoke, and the colleagues who invited me to address their staff and students. In particular, I am greatly obliged to John Brannigan, Susan Bruce, Dan Carey, Ewan Fernie, Sarah Hatchuel, Jane Kingsley-Smith, Kate McLuskie, Nathalie Vienne-Guerrin and Valeria Wagner.

I would like warmly to thank Kenneth Branagh for the donations that constitute the Kenneth Branagh Archive at Queen's: in this endeavour, Tamar Thomas has also been keenly instrumental, as have Sarah Hatchuel and Jude Tessel, who, through Ken's Friends, selflessly and generously refines and augments our holdings. Kenneth Branagh is also to be thanked for agreeing to be interviewed for this book, for giving permission for the reproduction of the cover photograph and for inviting me to an advance screening of *As You Like It*. At HBO, Susanna Felleman, Mark Hoerr, Dana Scroggins and Glenn Whitehead were active behind the scenes for arranging for additional cover image permissions. Press officer Sara Keene and US agent Judy Hofflund were no less helpful here, and Liz Corbett and Bryce Dallas Howard enabled the final stages of securing rights to proceed unhindered. Others in the film trade have been interested and unsparing with their time, including Amit Bhatia of ANB Pictures and Stephen Cavanagh of the Derry Film Initiative.

Throughout, Paula Kennedy has been a model editor. I am obliged, too, to Michael Dobson and Gail Kern Paster for their scrupulously productive readings and criticisms as readers of the series to which this book belongs. A previous incarnation of chapter 3 was published in *Shakespeare Survey*, 58 (2005), pp. 185–98, and I am grateful to Cambridge University Press for permission to reproduce that material. Richard Dutton, Sarah Hatchuel, Diana Henderson, Jean Howard, Willy Maley, Andrew Murphy, Frank Tomasulo, Nathalie Vienne-Guerrin and James Welsh suggested or commissioned previous written efforts in the area, and I am indebted to them for providing those formative opportunities.

To Ramona Wray there goes a special debt of thanks. She provided invaluable reflections on, and insights into, how the manuscript might be improved: without her the book could not have been written. This book is dedicated to my son, who every day brings joy.

# Introduction

Most obviously an extension to and effect of the potential embodied in technology, globalization in the late twentieth and early twenty-first centuries has promoted fresh forms of electronic imperialism which have enabled trade to be conducted without immediate recourse to the boundaries of nation-states or territorial conglomerates.[1] In a recent discussion, 'What is Globalization?', the theatre historian Gary Jay Williams defines this phenomenon in terms of material and cultural products:

> Globalization is ... A.T.M.s on every street corner in every wealthy city in the world. It is Japanese Toyotas manufactured in Tennessee, Nike shoes made in Southeast Asia, and computers made in China using U.S. Microsoft programmes. It is the rock musical *Bombay Dreams* and India's 'Bollywood' films for international audiences.[2]

His description evokes the ways in which globalization exists in an evolving state inseparable from the circulation of commodities and capital. It emphasizes that the global scene is as much characterized by processes and movements – the ascendancy of the corporation, the dominance of world factories, changes in the composition of labour and unheralded population shifts – as it is by goods and properties.

Such has been the impact of technology world-wide that, possibly because of the speed of transmission of information, time and space are often experienced as compressed or telescoped: actions, bewilderingly and excitingly, operate 'at a distance'.[3] It is unsurprising, then, that the world appears to be both a more heterogeneous space and a more homogenized locale. 'Globalization', writes Jan Aart Scholte, introduces a 'single world culture' and increases 'cultural diversity' at one and the same time.[4] As Rob Wilson and Wimal Dissanayake state, the 'space of cultural production and national representation ... is simultaneously becoming more *globalized* (unified around dynamics of capitalogic moving across borders) and more *localized* (fragmented into contestatory enclaves of difference, coalition and resistance) in everyday texture and composition'.[5] On the one hand, then, globalization allows for bonding and interconnectivity; and, on the other, policies of integration dislodge, divide and even eradicate the indigenous. One consequence of inhabiting a world that pulls in contrary directions is the evolution of a split or inchoate sense of self. The ownership of more than one national or cultural attachment entails a 'globalization of biography', a 'personal life' which involves transgressing barriers and meshing identities.[6] Hyphenated and, on occasions, hybridized identities are symptoms of a world in which a particularized attention is now paid to race and religion, ethnicity and difference. Even as globalization has celebrated the vitality of cultural, spiritual and ethnic modes of belonging so has it functioned to foster ideologies that reinforce conservative politics and generate terrorism and xenophobic conflict.[7] In part this can be traced to the fact that, in globalization, the nation is no longer the first point of contact; rather, supranational fields of collectivity are becoming the norm, activities that take place without borders are rising, and social spaces that take little account of historical perimeters comprise the new geographies.[8] Globalization has indeed generated a smaller world, but one more enlarged in scope, complexity and power than ever before envisaged.

*Par excellence* the expression and prime exemplar of a market mentality and economy, globalization, as Michael Walsh writes, grants to the international market an all-encompassing prominence, while the marketing of global products, according to Richard Langhorne, has permitted stocks, currencies, banking and securities to distinguish themselves as multinational entities.[9] Among the various markets that globalization both targets and incarnates, 'Hollywood', or 'Hollyworld' as it has sometimes been labelled, is arguably the most pre-eminent.[10] However it is conceptualized and indeed located, the Hollywood film industry enacts a pivotal part in screen entertainment, as a power in its own right and as a force against which other film organizations agitate to defend and distinguish themselves. This supremacy of position and influence may be accounted for in terms of the successful mastery of another typifying dimension of globalization practice, identified by Fredric Jameson as 'the export and import of culture'.[11] Hollywood studios have historically invested in the cachet of American symbolic registers as well as quality production values and, more recently, in the importance of a horizontal and vertical expansion programme that has encompassed agreements with independent producers, the securing of foreign investment and the development of international distribution markets.[12] As a result, the American film industry has turned 'itself into the focal point of [one of] the highest growth sectors in the American and global economies', with Hollywood owning between 40 and 90 per cent of the films screened throughout the world.[13]

In the late twentieth and early twenty-first centuries, Shakespeare's cultural capital has meant that, particularly on screen, he has become a presence newly minted as a market asset in the global economy, not least because his name is associated with forms of value and because he is seen to embrace the particular and the universal spectrum on which the transactions of globalization depend. As Peter Donaldson states, 'Shakespeare seems to have an ever more natural, self-evident role to play as a symbol of ... world-wide networks'.[14] It was perhaps inevitable that, after a pause in the 1970s and the 1980s, Shakespeare should gravitate again to Hollywood, and vice versa, and many of the films discussed in the present work are so-called 'Hollywood' productions. This book understands the multiple relationships between the filmed Shakespeare and the global marketplace by utilizing a logic that prioritizes theme and content, form and context. It argues that Shakespeare films, produced on both sides of the millennium, engage with globalization as a subject of enquiry in refractions of the pressures and processes of their own global environs. It enlists globalization as a mechanism through which the concerns, generic choices and intertextual trajectories of the filmic Bard might be illuminated, not as an imposed template but as an active participant in the assessment of preoccupations that have a global purchase. This is a study which places in the spotlight global flows, media technologies and questions of difference as they play out in the screen constructions that are 'Shakespeare'. Discussion concentrates on Shakespearean issues of national and religious affiliation, impersonation and performance, as they are in turn inflected and transmuted by global exposure. In doing so, the films reveal themselves as acutely responsive to their own marketplace location, self-consciously contemplating Shakespeare's status as an icon moulded according to the dictates of world consumerism and late capitalist modalities of consumption.

'By 2000', observes Bruce McConachie, 'Disney ... controlled much of Broadway'. 'Viacom', he adds, 'was also a player'.[15] Taking as its point of reference the ownership of some forms of theatrical practice by global corporations and the challenges this poses to traditional forms of performance, chapter 1 focuses on a series of recent filmic and televisual productions that construct the enduring stability of Shakespearean theatre. Culminating in Shakespearean stagings of complementary kinds, these works affirm the socially and personally applicable meanings of Shakespeare across a range of contexts. At the same time, although ostensibly pitched against Hollywood, such a filmic re-creation of theatrical power entails a corresponding acknowledgement that existing methods of Bardic transmission and dissemination must modify and merge in the light of global realities. Integral to the global reach and cultural influence of film is the capacity of the Hollywood-inspired production to authorize a proliferating series of versions of itself. Chapter 2 addresses *Much Ado About Nothing* (dir. Kenneth Branagh, 1993) and *William Shakespeare's 'A Midsummer Night's Dream'* (dir. Michael Hoffman, 1999) by way of sequelization, which, as Carolyn Jess-Cooke argues, is central to the ideologies of 'repetition' and 'compulsion', 'continuation' and 'interaction', that justify and support the budget-determined economy.[16] Interestingly, both films offer gendered reflections on questions of reproduction and technology, and are of a piece in endeavouring to free Shakespeare from the baggage of earlier readings and inscriptions. Yet, in undertaking this mission, and in underscoring the functions of a marketable Shakespeare, the films give credence to the antagonisms that bedevil any attempt to turn the Bard into cinematic material. In a spirit of homage, Hoffman's film looks to Branagh for authenticity, but this move is simultaneously undone by the discovery of a vexed relation to the model of inspiration and to the textual 'original'. The global qualifications of Shakespeare are, in this instance, an agent of anxiety as much as a spur to reanimation.

Conversations taking place between Shakespeare films are extended in chapter 3, which considers recent screen outings of *Hamlet* and *Macbeth* along the axis of a global/local dialectic. Inside these tragedies on film, it is suggested, homogeneity, although a narrative concern and a mode of representation, never exorcizes the lure of heterogeneity, which is repeatedly summoned with spectral specificity. Hence, film versions of *Hamlet* conjure ghosts of Ireland as ciphers of longing, nostalgia and desire, while screen treatments of *Macbeth* amplify echoes of Scotland to romance the regional and put forward dissident positions. The local, the chapter concludes, works most powerfully as a vehicle of historical particularity, as an instrument of opposition to corporate hegemony and as a counterpoint to Shakespeare's status as a transnational voice. What is 'local' is, as Shakespeare film understands it, frequently deemed attractive or contestatory because indivisible from what is 'different'.

Chapter 4 develops the connection, arguing for an approach to *Othello* (dir. Oliver Parker, 1995) and *'O'* (dir. Tim Blake Nelson, 2001) that eschews a merely topical line of enquiry and privileges instead an arena in which broader intersections between race, identity and difference are held up for scrutiny. Concentrating on markers of black and white, the chapter considers the ways in which a representation of hybridized selves lies at the heart of the films' explorations of the shifting contours of a globally racial experience. In keeping with trends in globalization, race in *Othello* and *'O'* is erased even as it is prioritized, particularly in scenes that testify to the controlling power of those mediatizing instruments through which identities and identifications, and spectacles of performance, are communicated. The visibility of race as a category of interpretation, and the concomitant effects of the Shakespearean imprimatur, are in part determined by reflections on, and an engagement with, globally dictated representational mechanisms.

A related discussion, which attends to the historical and political ramifications of notions of affiliation and attachment, is offered in chapter 5. In the context of the recent global Holocaust commemorations, *William Shakespeare's 'The Merchant of Venice'* (dir. Michael Radford, 2004) is seen as striking an uneasy balance between aestheticization and anaesthetization. Or, to put it another way, the film invests in a distancing idealization of the early modern period *and* a grammar of appalled Holocaust memory. For the Holocaust, the chapter argues, configures *The Merchant of Venice*'s traumatic sub-texts: it is the unspeakable and often unspoken world event of the twentieth century that shapes and manipulates this statement's use of documentary modes, elevation of a redemptive Jessica and victim-conscious exposition of the central protagonist. As a result, a Shakespearean play often seen as impossible to film is granted an appositeness that intersects with both the defining moments of the past and present concerns.

To *The Merchant of Venice*'s insistence that there may yet be poetry after the Holocaust can be added the contention of *Macbeth in Manhattan* (dir. Greg Lombardo, 1999) and *The King is Alive* (dir. Kristian Levring, 2000) that new types of spirituality can be accessed via global transformations. Extrapolating the enabling cultural dimensions of globalization, chapter 6 details these films' absorption in a Shakespearean sacrality that returns to correct gaps and transgressions in situations of waste and abandonment. Dispossession in primeval and unorthodox environs is the prompt for summonings of Shakespeare's spiritual utility, to the extent that forms of postcolonial justice and global expiation, which allow for release and enlightenment, are facilitated. In terms of the continuing reinvention of his ideological instrumentality, then, Shakespeare appears as by no means exhausted. Far from precipitating a Shakespearean apocalypse, or a drying up of the wellsprings of his relevancies, the marketplace of film, it is suggested, has enabled a global penetration of the Bard's constructed powers and pertinences.

A similar claim can be made for parodic versions of Shakespeare produced in the post-millennial period which, in chapter 7, are assessed as sites of political critique, as transnational creations whose importance resides in their capacity for pointing up global inequities. Itself a type of global flow or movement, the modern manifestation of parody dispassionately illuminates the particular workings of capital, the fraught realities of border zones and the cultural mutations of American imperialism, as is testified to in the chapter's readings of a range of 'world' films, *The Street King* (dir. James Gavin Bedford, 2002), *In Othello* (dir. Roysten Abel, 2003) and *Romeo & Juliet* (dir. David Lachapelle, 2005). Parody, in fact, is emblematic of the operations of Shakespeare in the global economy as a whole, since it highlights the ways in which new elaborations of Bardic meanings always emerge from the old. This process is not so much linear or consistent as it is constant, evolving and circulating: it is akin to a cultural flux in which Shakespeare is constituted as a guardian of entrenched positions and as a looser configuration associated with adaptation, intervention and play. Within that paradigm, Shakespeare films demonstrate conflicted investments in notions of history, place and the simultaneous diminution and enlargement of the cultural sphere. They rehearse linguistic 'originals' in order to demonstrate their having been superseded by a twentieth- and twenty-first-century vernacular, casting an ironic glance at the ills of recent global developments without necessarily agitating to replace them with a 'Shakespearean' manifestation of the social and cultural dispensation. The films investigated in this book perform more than one task, initiating and sequelizing, authenticating and demythologizing, looking outwards and inwards, and emptying out the regional as they restore the local within a grammar of the global. They straddle the spectrum of informed observation and ideological avoidance, fresh felicities and old truths, inimical realities and longed for utopias, thereby clarifying the global Shakespearean marketplace as a resolutely contemporary if unpredictably postmodern experience.

# 1
# Screening the Stage

In the period following the Second World War, described by Samuel Crowl as the 'great international phase' of 'Shakespeare's absorption into film by directors as diverse as Laurence Olivier, Orson Welles, Akira Kurosawa, Grigori Kozintsev and Franco Zeffirelli', there often obtained a relatively conservative relationship between theatre and film.[1] Screen realizations of the plays tended to emerge from or base themselves on previous productions, translating into film a theatrically-oriented methodology. In the wake of mediatization and globalization, and alongside corresponding changes in the performance event, however, the Shakespearean filmic–theatrical relationship has taken on a greater complexity. The last twenty years bear witness not only to an unravelling of the filmic–theatrical connection but also, intriguingly, to the emergence of filmic representations whose narratives prioritize theatrical shows and stagings of Shakespearean texts. Films as different in date and provenance as Peter Weir's *Dead Poets Society* (1989), which concludes with a school version of *A Midsummer Night's Dream*, and Roysten Abel's *In Othello* (2003), which explores a Delhi-based English theatre company's fractured relationship with Shakespeare's play, typify the tendency and form, and join other works which take as a central premise the mechanics and the processes of Shakespearean performance. Within this genre, amateur and professional groups feature. Action is oriented towards the climactic event of an opening night; and Shakespeare is the dramatist whose works are selected for production, with the result that fragmented quotations from and allusions to the plays abound.

Concentrating on Kenneth Branagh's *In the Bleak Midwinter* (1995) and James Callis and Nick Cohen's *Beginner's Luck* (2001), independent

British features that enjoyed a limited theatrical release, Roger Goldby's *Indian Dream* (2003), a television drama first aired on BBC2, and Tommy O' Haver's *Get Over It* (2001), a successful and Miramax-backed Hollywood 'teen picture', this chapter examines mutually entertained motifs of Shakespearean performance, arguing that the films display vexed and unresolved attitudes towards the relations between cinema, theatre and the global scene. To the Shakespeare productions with which each film culminates, specific narratives are attached. *In the Bleak Midwinter* concerns the attempt to stage *Hamlet* in a disused church, while *Get Over It* details the efforts of Berke (Ben Foster) to join his school production of *A Midsummer Night's Dream* as a means of rekindling a relationship with Allison (Melissa Sagemiller), a former girlfriend who is also in the cast. The fictional imperatives governing the action of *Beginner's Luck* centre on an unsuccessful theatre company's touring production of *The Tempest*; the circumstances surrounding the participation of Surender (Christopher Bisson), a young Indian teacher, in an English village production of *A Midsummer Night's Dream* involve his escape from a detention centre. Despite the fact that the playing space is understood in plural ways in these films, they come together in coding Shakespeare as a repository of enduring values that can be accessed through performance. In so doing, they offer a nostalgic construction of the Bard in the theatre as a vehicle for personal and social redemption. More specifically, key to filmic constructions of stage production are the ways in which they enable romance and personal growth, learning and cultural reformation, with the dramatist envisaged as a point of communal stability in the midst of competing art-forms. The traditional resonances of theatre, and its historical association with forms of communion, are placed in an oppositional juxtaposition with the inconstant operations of the global marketplace, a procedure linked to the ways in which 'memory practices', because of their 'temporal anchoring', implicitly 'contest the myths of cybercapitalism and globalization and their denial of time, space, and place'.[2] Assumptions about the plays' continuing relevance, however, as mediated through film, interact with anxieties about Shakespeare's marginal place in the contemporary mindset and contradictory reflections on the comprehensibility of his work. As a result, *In the Bleak Midwinter*, *Beginner's Luck*, *Get Over It* and *Indian Dream* ultimately debate the utility of the staged Shakespeare, ruminate on the processes of his appropriation and acknowledge that the historically rooted status of his word may need to adapt.

# I

The proliferation in Shakespeare films of a stage subject coincides with an anxiety that the institution of theatre is in crisis, aptly summed up in Caridad Svich's statement that 'theatre in its most traditional sense has stopped speaking to its immediate culture'.[3] Theatre suffers from being seen as an increasingly irrelevant art-form. As a result, the place of the stage has been compromised, with plays and players, in Baz Kershaw's formulation, having become a 'marginal commodity in the capitalist ... marketplace'.[4] In this process, only those institutions which present material geared to the tourist and heritage industry tend to be profitable, and even their limited success often depends on subsidies.[5] Although in the western world huge diversity in theatrical practice can be identified at the national and geographical level, innovation and development take place alongside the gradual shrinkage of an already decentred audience, within the framework of a funding recession for the arts and in the face of the loss of many playing venues.[6] Performance is now found in factories, railway stations and warehouses. In this regard, it is revealing that, in all four films under consideration, Shakespearean production takes place extra-theatrically. The woods that feature in *Indian Dream* as part of the amateur theatricals of the fictional English Sedgton, and the high school hall that appears in *Get Over It* as a rehearsal and production space, are more traditional performative realms. In contrast, *In the Bleak Midwinter* and *Beginner's Luck* reveal the extent to which Shakespeare, at the whim of market forces and economic vicissitude, becomes a transportable theatrical property.

*Beginner's Luck* spotlights playing locales that are eclectic or ultimately non-existent. A seedy Soho club presided over by the foul-mouthed and violent Prospero figure, 'Magic Bob' (Steven Berkhoff), is the only place where the Vagabond Theatre Company production can initially secure a booking. Magic Bob's announcement that the 'adult stuff' can be found 'upstairs' while the 'culture' is to be enjoyed 'downstairs' offers a parodic impression of the spatial banishment of Bardic theatre. Reinforcing the notion of cultural doubling, the film frequently intercuts scenes of Mark Feinman (James Callis) dreaming about staging Shakespeare with media insets of his successful *alter ego*, Andrew Fontaine (Christopher Cazenove), portentously publicizing his critically acclaimed *Tempest* production. The juxtaposition points up the fact that Fontaine has mastered the relationship between performance and technology to emerge as a theatre practitioner on a global scale. As such, he commands the staging of Shakespeare in time and space. By contrast, Mark, the recent school-leaver and would-be director, can only fantasize about the transnational and publicity-aware circuits of exchange that typify Fontaine.[7] Because of his mastery of the media and his *auteur* name, Fontaine is empowered to precede the Vagabond Theatre Company to the *Théâtre Obscur* in Paris, thereby assuming the group's place and consigning Mark to the 'obscurity' he had hoped to avoid. Consequently, the Vagabond *Tempest* is ousted to a void in the theatrical system. Honouring in their substitutions and represented practices the conventional homes of performance, *In the Bleak Midwinter*, *Beginner's Luck*, *Get Over It* and *Indian Dream* simultaneously conjure theatre as an aspirational realm, as an ideal that is present by virtue of its absence. Symbolically and ideologically, theatre – as an edifice or a building – is unattainable, remaining only at the level of projection or desire.

What unites these films' playing spaces is their gravitation to staging the Bard, suggesting that the separation of the theatrical into different sites, and the acknowledgement of the fractured condition of the playing institution, do not preclude a corresponding dismantling of the prominence of Shakespeare as a performative property. Although the continuing authority of the Bard is attested to by such initiatives as the RSC's 'Complete Shakespeare' season of 2006, Shakespeare production generally is more often linked, in Robert Shaughnessy's words, to a conservative 'poetics of spatial and narrative coherence' and a declining cultural elitism.[8] But, in the films under discussion, Shakespeare becomes the *raison d'être* of an alternative performance poetics, filling the gap vacated by a traditional theatre and bringing to the space of production a particular significance. The various filmic narratives refract the ways in which globalization has been both detrimental for traditional theatre and enabling for broader forms of performance and the orientation and content of the performative product. 'Alternative theatre' companies have been encouraged to develop; multi- or intercultural productions are fast establishing themselves as the norm; and mixed-media creations (defined by Philip Auslander as 'events combining live and mediatized representations – live actors with film, video, or digital projections') have disrupted older boundaries and fostered cross-disciplinary dialogue.[9] The plays glimpsed in these films suggest just such innovations in artistic practice – a species of performance that is appealing not least because it is globally recognizable.[10]

*In the Bleak Midwinter*, *Beginner's Luck*, *Get Over It* and *Indian Dream* all represent their Shakespearean choices as self-evident, as abundantly obvious and as in keeping with the particularities of what are very different institutional/personal settings and locations. For both the 'luvvie' thespians of *In the Bleak Midwinter* and the frustrated kids of *Get Over It*, Shakespeare is the unquestioned first port of call, even if his work is thrust on them by the symbolic authorities of director and drama teacher. *In the Bleak Midwinter* is voluble about what drives Joe Harper (Michael Maloney), the film's backward-looking actor and theatre director, to produce *Hamlet*. His choice of an old-spelling edition of the play for rehearsal belongs with the film's comic investment in pretension, self-regard and a bourgeois cultivation of Shakespeare's importance. Emerging from the film's pseudo-anterior orientation is its 'nostalgic invocation', in Kathy Howlett's words, 'of a great and distinctly English theatrical tradition'.[11] This is seen nowhere more obviously than in the scenes in which Henry (Richard Briers) and Terry (John Sessions) appear as Henry Irving and Ellen Terry, self-consciously modelling themselves on their namesakes. *In the Bleak Midwinter* here stages a temporal double-take, for in the productions of Irving and Terry, according to Russell Jackson, audiences were granted 'a window onto the romantic past ... and ... reassurance that certain human and, specifically, national values could still be cultivated and recalled amidst so much rapid change'.[12] The effect of Henry and Terry's impersonation points up the vanity of the theatrical practitioner, but also suggests the ways in which a local history of staging Shakespeare might operate as a source of sustaining memory and replenishing stability.

The applications of history are also elaborated as supporting the production of *A Midsummer Night's Dream* in *Indian Dream*, although in this television film an English past becomes the means to confront a postcolonial present. For both Surender and Rajiv (Nitin Ganatra), the Indian village doctor, the attraction of the production is Shakespeare's mediation of, and indissoluble connection with, an unchanging heritage. 'I love this play', states Surender, 'and performing it on a midsummer night's eve in an English village is like a dream for me'. The play operates like the photographs of Sedgton pastoral scenes so precious to the accidental tourist – projections of a 'dream' of England mediated through an unquestioning reliance on the 'mother country'. Similarly, for Rajiv, the village is 'everything that's great about England ... civilized, polite, and with a long and rich history'. W. B. Worthen writes that 'a Shakespeare play ... can ... evoke the pastness of ... values, behaviours [and] subjects in the present action of performance'.[13] Certainly, for the doctor, Shakespeare is imagined as a route to assimilation in a place where, despite his pivotal role, he continues to feel like an outsider. Types of Lysander and Demetrius in *A Midsummer Night's Dream*, Surender and Rajiv fight not for possession of a woman's body but for the ownership of Shakespeare's symbolic resonances, working under the illusion that Puck, the role they both covet, is the key to cultural acceptability.

The Shakespeare-as-passport motif is invoked in a variety of ways. For Mark in *Beginner's Luck*, Shakespeare is the guarantor of a species of global domination in which the place of origin is incidental: 'the plan was simple', he remarks in the opening voiceover, 'we would establish ourselves in London, then we would roll on to Edinburgh, then with the money we made we'd take Paris, and from Paris the world was our oyster'. Appropriately mixing a language of militaristic conquest and maritime metaphors in keeping with the themes of *The Tempest*, the announcement discovers Mark as agitating to colonize through art, to assume control via the commercial and transnational power embodied in Shakespeare's word. In *Beginner's Luck*, however, confidence in the Bard's appeal is accompanied by anxiety about his comprehensibility. 'Upon closer inspection', states Mark, '*The Tempest* proved to be completely indecipherable', the sobriety of the realization wonderfully undercutting the initial espousal of Shakespearean power.

The admission is of a piece with a host of related filmic recognition scenes in which the use-value of Shakespeare is seen to be hampered by the works' impenetrability. 'I'm understanding about every word of this shit', Berke's ironic assessment in *Get Over It* of his first reading of *A Midsummer Night's Dream*, sets the tone for the actual performance, where cultural unintelligibility is the backwash against which the text must strive to assert itself. The opening song – 'Did you ever read a Shakespeare play, / And never understand a word they say? / Well tonight we're gonna make things clear, / 'Coz Shakespeare's dead, but we're all here' – implicitly associates Shakespeare with an extinct mode of entertainment and identifies the actors as charged with renewing and explaining his scripts for a modern audience. In its articulation of anxieties about Shakespeare, *Get Over It* joins company with other films in which a preoccupation with a distant and unmanageable Bard is paramount. Even for the theatre professionals of *In the Bleak Midwinter*, Shakespeare is not necessarily the default position. '[Your audition speech] doesn't have to be Shakespeare', Joe tells the would-be members of his cast, demonstrating an understanding that Shakespeare's customary place in theatrical culture is accompanied by a reputation for interpretive difficulty.[14] Modified and repeated across the films, Joe's statement bears witness to a self-consciously thematized Bardic demythologizing even as it seeks to install the utility of Shakespearean authority. In fact, what ultimately compromises Shakespeare, according to these films, is not so much an inexplicable internal dynamic as a collocation of external forces that impinge on the likelihood of the work achieving a greater visibility. The films' conjuring of theatre in the marketplace links to recent work on the impact of mass media technologies on traditional performance, the pressures posed by global products that, in a competitive ethos, enjoy a particular pre-eminence and advantage.[15] In recent studies, theatre is positioned as an implicit and explicit rival with such forms as television, film, video, DVD and the world wide web. The result is that the 'liveness' of the theatrical event – its simultaneous presence and ephemerality – has been first threatened and then overtaken.[16] Arguably it is because the theatrical moment is not strictly reproducible that it has been sidelined by modes of reproduction more adept at accessing and mediating 'reality'. Because theatre constitutes 'a unique economic event in every performance, indigenous, place-bound, and indivisible', it does not obviously participate, as Dennis Kennedy contends, in 'late monopoly capitalism', which trades on economic networks that transcend 'national borders' and the power of 'global corporations'.[17] 'Nobody wants to see Shakespeare', explains Javaad (Jean-Yves Berteloot), a French theatre practitioner in *Beginner's Luck*, '[everyone is] at the movies having a good time or watching porno films'. Occupying the negative binary of an arrangement that judges his plays incompatible with cinema and the sex industry, Shakespeare is judged to be hopelessly out of touch with the realities of modern commerce: the joke is that even in France, historically a second home to Shakespeare and supporter-preserver of the arts, there is no truck with 'culture'. *In the Bleak Midwinter* plays a variation on the point. Tom's [Nicholas Farrell] request that, as Fortinbras, he be allowed to 'rip [my] shirt off and abseil down from the organ' (p. 31) represents an obvious parody of a melodramatic filmic convention, but simultaneously suggests that Shakespeare is forever positioned in a losing relationship to Hollywood and to cinematically-tutored audience requirements. Courtney Lehmann instructively argues that 'the "bleak truth"' of Branagh's film is that it is impossible to '"relate to" Shakespeare in a society saturated by ... mass media and the mighty seduction of the spectacle'.[18] Hence, when Molly (Hetta Charnley), the catering manager, imagines instructing the 'kids' to '[turn off] *Mighty Morphin Power Rangers* and come and watch a four hundred year-old play about a depressed aristocrat' (p. 23), she invokes an American television action show that, modelled on a syndicated Japanese series and internationally exported, implicitly mocks philosophical Shakespearean heroes at the same time as it detracts attention from English stage traditions. As *In the Bleak Midwinter* understands it, the problems that accrue from the encounter with Shakespeare are the products of the rise of multinational conglomerates that cast England – and Shakespeare – into the shade. *In the Bleak Midwinter* discovers both the country and its art as pincered between more powerful global entertainment entities which span the east/west divide, with Shakespeare typifying the marginality of theatre and the powerlessness of national interests.

## II

In such a dichotomy, efforts to understand the Bard, as each of the films suggests, are represented as productive in terms of self- and social awareness. In the encounter with Shakespeare, characters are stimulated to recognize and locate in the process of performance meanings that touch their lives and those of their communities. Theatre, despite – because of – its waning cultural purchase, becomes an instrument of self-illumination as well as a force for the 'greater good'. Typical is the vision which opens *Beginner's Luck*: 'in my dream [of an] ... island', Mark tells us, 'I am following something, but I don't know what it is'. That 'something', it is implied, will enable Mark to find direction and purpose, and, since the dream is of Shakespeare's *The Tempest*, it is via an experience of the play that the discovery process will unfold.

Vital for signalling that *In the Bleak Midwinter*, *Beginner's Luck* and *Get Over It* constitute trajectories concerned with the drive to self-understanding is the films' deployment of the retrospective form. Taking as their points of departure types of Shakespearean epilogue, all three contemplate the fictions of their respective pasts in such a way as to offer a paean to the affirmatory nature of theatrical involvement. 'If you want to be successful ... you'll have to be lucky', Mark's voiceover intones, the statement functioning to generate audience anticipation of a serendipitous narrative outcome. Throughout, documentary-style insets in *Beginner's Luck* feature rosy reflections on the production endeavour, much in the manner of a 'docudrama', a television 'film ... that dramatizes actual events or an actual person's life with fictional devices'.[19] *Beginner's Luck* consistently incorporates pseudo-footage: the successful documentary being pedalled, within the fictional narrative of the film, concerns the experience of the less successful stage *Tempest* production. Similarly, Vernon's assumption of adult responsibility in *In the Bleak Midwinter* is bound up with a separate plotline concerning his off-screen filmmaking enterprise. Although we never see his footage, it is clear that the invented process of its compilation has been productive. Performing a similar operation is the epilogue to *Indian Dream*, which, recuperating conflict to bolster a linear development of story and character, illustrates how far the chief players have come. Whether prologue or epilogue, both work to provide an interpretive framework within which previous events can be assessed and measures for resolution might be appreciated.

These films take as their thematic focus, then, not so much Shakespeare as the process of the encounter with his relevancies. Fictionalized types of *Looking for Richard*, Al Pacino's 1996 documentary about the endeavour to stage and comprehend *Richard III*, *In the Bleak Midwinter*, *Beginner's Luck*, *Indian Dream* and *Get Over It* underscore the virtues of the performance event in the same moment as they draw attention to the importance of the activities that surround it. The parallel with Pacino's film suggests that Shakespeare has shifted ground in the light of contemporary experimentation with media and genre. It is less the discovery of the 'truth' that matters, it seems, as the effort to unravel what the Bard's work embodies.

This particular filmic grouping discovers the phenomenon of Shakespearean performance as one means whereby insights are gained and individual improvement is secured. Learning trajectories are repeatedly represented as evolving inside productions of the drama; or, to adopt Wolfgang Iser's formulation, cinema functions to illuminate the ways in which Shakespeare, having been 'remembered' via theatre, 'becomes open to new' and productive 'connections' and 'correlates'.[20] Enlightened by a version of Lysander's lines in *A Midsummer Night's Dream*, therefore, Berke in *Get Over It* admits that he has been 'half asleep / half awake' (IV.i.144) to Kelly's charms. Here, the film's title is indicative, for 'to get over it' implies both an animal-like means of sexual congress and the process of recovering from a broken relationship.[21] Resembling a more forgiving Prospero, Mark in *Beginner's Luck* realizes that he needs to lose inflexibility and reconstitute himself to avoid psychological shipwreck. And, acting on the recuperative powers of *Hamlet*, the whole cast of *In the Bleak Midwinter* is represented as waking up to miraculous transformations: among other instances of personal triumph, Joe puts his depression behind him and Vernon (Mark Hadfield), through his documentary about the production, relinquishes his 'child actor' (p. 9) stigma to emerge as *auteur* of his own life. Abundantly on display is a jettisoning of delusion and an embrace of knowledge, a movement away from self-destruction and towards creativity and reparation. In other words, these films essentialize Shakespeare in seeing his drama as stagings culminating in awareness and integration. As much as these films are distinguished by postmodern orientations, then, so are they committed to a critically anterior construction of a liberal humanist playwright who can be positively recycled.

Clearly apparent in all four films is a construction of theatre as a site of refinement, reformation and possibility. *Indian Dream*, for instance, plots a recuperative narrative around Surender's joining the production of *A Midsummer Night's Dream*. Initially, because Surender represents 'the history that happened elsewhere, overseas, his postcolonial, migrant presence does not evoke a harmonious patchwork of cultures, but articulates [a] narrative of cultural difference'.[22] 'He's an asylum seeker', David (Anthony Calf) exclaims, 'If we let him into our play, we might as well put a sign up saying "Sedgton: Bring Your Illegals Here"'. Such a xenophobic mindset, which espouses the notion of the Shakespearean text as the ultimate citadel to be protected, is itself ultimately ostracized, with the Sedgton inhabitants revising their attitudes towards transnational mobility when they recognize that Surender has been essential to the success of the production. Within that disturbed field of Englishness, the inner sanctum of the Shakespeare play, it is suggested, can play a public role in an embattled local predicament. A related articulation of prejudice occurs in *Beginner's Luck* in the representation of the preparations of the Vagabond Theatre Company for its production of *The Tempest* in an Edinburgh Indian restaurant. Alex (Sarah Belcher) attempts to seduce one of the waiters with the line, 'What part of India are you from?', only to receive the debunking reply, 'Leicester'. At a moment when the cast are reflecting on the continuing pertinence of Shakespeare's play, the eroticization of a Caliban-like other acts as a salutary warning to white, middle-class complacency. As Gary Jay Williams states, 'in the process of globalization ... the disjunctures between cultures are played out ... [in] theatre and performance'.[23]

A comparable situation of cultural inequity is resolved in *Get Over It* via the symbolic dethronement of the high school favourite – and star Shakespeare performer – Striker (Shane West). Berke's seeming inferiority to Striker is emphasized via shots that reveal him either from behind or otherwise anally characterized.[24] Evolving into Striker's antithesis, Berke is, in his own words, a 'dumb arse' who is homoeroticized when he loses his shorts at a basketball game and humiliated when forced, in a parodic dream sequence, into a pile of horse manure. In contradistinction to the socially disenfranchised Berke, whose abasement brings to mind the humiliations of Bottom in popular representations, Striker is handsome, popular and 'cool', his overweening ego trading on his boy band success and his reputation with the 'ladies'.[25] 'You are my love skud', Striker's hit single runs, the line deploying the image of a US missile to communicate a powerful heterosexuality. In competition with Striker for the sexual attention of the lovely Allison, Berke initially has no chance, until the performative climax dissolves the divide between 'geek' and 'god'. An on-stage explosion – timed to humiliate Berke – backfires, revealing Striker as vain, superficial and effeminate, and leading to his displacement from both the theatrical box and the filmic frame. The binary relationship that obtains between Striker and Berke shifts popularity and desirability to the underdog, as Berke steps in to save the play and the day. In addition, Striker's routing means that the theatrical space can be established as genuinely 'American', which, in the film's symbolic lexicon, is defined as an authentically integrated multiculturalism (the well-known black American rap star Sisqo dances in one of the production's numbers) rather than the fake – white – American value system Striker embodies.

If theatre functions as a corrective, it also works as a prompt for romance. Vividly demonstrated in the films is the extent to which romance emerges from, or at least is affiliated with, the theatrical predilection for the emendation of cultural inequities. Hence, in his attempt to understand Shakespeare, Berke is aided by Kelly (Kirsten Dunst), with whom he eventually falls in love. 'I'm kind of good at that stuff', she states, establishing herself as the mediator of textual mystery. Most often represented in scenes in which she explains the play, Kelly serves as the primary reference point for Berke's Shakespearean and amatory enlightenment. Crucially, Kelly's figuration affords a gendered perspective on the unknowable Shakespeare: women intuit Shakespeare, the argument runs, the implication being that Kelly is able to translate the Bard into a recognizable idiom and that she finds poetry no hindrance to apprehension. A positive relationship with Shakespeare, *Get Over It* contends, authorizes Berke to express his feelings. Thus, when he kisses Kelly during rehearsal, he is transported to an idyllic realm that bears an uncanny resemblance to the film's construction of the world of the play. The implication is that the proper home of the Shakespearean text is a romantic one and that its form will assume the contours of individual longings and aspirations.

18  *Filming Shakespeare in the Global Marketplace*

*Figure 1.*   *Get Over It* (dir. Tommy O' Haver, 2001) culminates in the climactic production of *A Midsummer Night's Rockin' Eve*.

Most importantly, it is through the performance of *A Midsummer Night's Dream* itself that Berke is finally enabled to establish both a heterosexual primacy and a Bottom-like centrality, thereby arriving at an understanding of himself that has previously been lacking. In part this is because the 'opening night' is marked by extemporization at the level of dance, music and verbal delivery – in Philip Auslander's formulation, by 'liveness'.[26] (Figure 1.) 'Performance's only life is in the present', writes Peggy Phelan. Because it 'cannot be saved, recorded [or] documented', the theatrical event 'clogs the smooth machinery of [mass] reproductive representation', 'resists the balanced circulation of capital' and assumes 'a distinctive oppositional edge'.[27] In *Get Over It*, the 'liveness' of the school production is signalled by Berke's impromptu decision to kiss Kelly (who plays Helena) and to reject Allison (who plays Hermia). The spontaneity of the moment allows Berke to act on a newfound knowledge, and that his decision is implicitly 'oppositional' is registered in the departure from the script, the abandonment of Shakespeare's canonical language.[28] At the film's end, both Berke and Kelly are shot walking into this imaginative landscape, suggesting that theatrical participation has finally empowered them to 'dream' not singly but in unison: having 'woken up' to Shakespeare, the film sentimentally insists, they become alive to each other. At a further remove, the corresponding removal of Striker permits 'liveness' to be formulated as the principle to which the now committed and newly self-aware Berke and Kelly subscribe as theatrical practitioners. 'We've got to do this again tomorrow night', states Kelly, to which Berke replies, 'How do you think it's going to end?' Not only does the exchange construct the performance as a mode of 'reality', it simultaneously establishes theatre as an enabler of unpredictable narratives, a site that is privileged precisely because the experiences it makes available are never identical.

The romantic potential attached to the Bard is granted a more concrete embodiment in *Indian Dream* in which the director, Penny (Doon Mackichan), is drawn to Surender not only because of their mutual love of Shakespeare, but significantly because they are passionate theatrical amateurs. Notably, their romance is conducted in a Shakespearean register: Titania-like, Penny is quickly enamoured, responding vitally to Surender's metaphorical equation of tree blossom with clouds. In this scene, as elsewhere in *Indian Dream*, invocations of passages from *Antony and Cleopatra* and *Hamlet* serve to locate the lovers in a poetic zone and to elaborate their courtship as a rarefied performance.[29] More arrestingly, romance is elaborated as one of the salves with which the film's postcolonial rifts are healed. Unfolding on a aeroplane destined for India, the epilogue builds on earlier hints about the need for the multicultural revivification of Shakespeare, and emerges from a scene in which Surender rises from the seeming dead to resume his part, thereby offering a literal and metaphorical meditation on the British–Indian association. Because it takes place in transit, and within an in-between existence, it figures east–west relations as evolving rather than completed, possible as opposed to impracticable. Penny's decision to abandon her profession and join Surender leaves her momentarily placeless – a species of *émigré*. In a dramatization of Puck's plea for the giving of 'hands' (Epilogue, 15), however, the situation is resolved in the representation of Surender taking Penny's hand, a gesture that signals that romantic affiliations might be a means to displace prejudicial divisions.

Erika Fischer-Lichte comments that 'theatre is a communal institution, representing and establishing relationships which fulfil social functions'.[30] Her assessment highlights the ways in which these films point up the development of associations that benefit society as a whole. If 'theatre', in Branagh's somewhat hackneyed formulation, 'is a metaphor for life', it also functions through *In the Bleak Midwinter* as a restorative agent.[31] 'This is my family' (p. 84), Nina's (Julia Sawalha) description of the company, illuminates both the post-show reunion with her own father and the idea that forms of consanguinity are embedded in performance. Clearly, Nina's 'family' is no biological unit; rather, it is an ensemble that, having recognized 'shared ... failings and personal losses', achieves a harmonious kinship.[32] Emerging from that kinship are the positive roles transformed individuals play in their respective communities. *In the Bleak Midwinter*, for instance, equates the unexpected success of the production of *Hamlet* with the rescue of Hope church from property developers. One community is constructed as having been able to revivify another, and, in a punning reminder of *The Winter's Tale*, a 'last play' to which the film indirectly refers, *In the Bleak Midwinter* sees as mutually constitutive the reconciliation of previously fragmented families and the restructuring of a local cultural fabric. *In the Bleak Midwinter* is characterized by a drive to stress co-operative ideals: the inclusivity of the cast's decision to support the production when it founders financially suggests that theatre's distinction, as the film constructs it, resides in its capacity for forging bonds between seemingly disparate individuals.

*Beginner's Luck*, too, closes with a performance that has a socially productive effect. Caren Kaplan writes that 'modes of displacement generate cultural practices' and lead to 'aesthetic gain'.[33] Her assessment helps to contextualize the ways in which the removal of the Vagabond Theatre Company from traditional theatre spaces and a British locale is enabling for a production that is itself concerned with expulsion and exile. Denied a slot at the *Théâtre Obscur*, Mark takes a radically reimagined *Tempest* to the streets of Paris. Only when the vagabond players become truly illegitimate and cease chasing the highbrow theatre epitomized by Andrew Fontaine, it is implied, can they aspire to success; only at the point where the play is envisaged as genuinely inter-cultural (Anya [Julie Delpy], who plays Ariel, is permitted to speak French) are its communicative powers articulated. Central to the enterprise is the transformation of Mark from director to actor, his participation signifying the emergence of a deeper collaboration; in the wake of the company's triumph, a dance ensues and new couples form, testimony to the mood of romantic concord that the performance has engendered. In a turnaround that takes us back to the concerns of *The Tempest*, moreover, the endeavour as a whole receives a blessing. The fact that the production develops around a public fountain suggests baptism, while the reappearance (with money) of Mark's father

(Toby Salaman) points to a Ceres- or Iris-like divine approval. A similarly supportive figure is Jim's wife (Harriet Evans-Lombe), the owner of a house in which the company has been squatting. Her decision not to prosecute establishes her beneficent credentials, but so too does the fact that she resembles the 'woman' for whom Mark has been searching in his 'dreams': the contiguity of the production has allowed the director to meet his muse and helped in the process of his vision being realized. The 'something' with which Mark has been haunted has been identified; the 'island' has been gained.

The postcolonial friction explored in *Indian Dream* prevents it from achieving a comparable sense of *communitas*, although here too the move to integration is a hallmark. As Puck, Rajiv is discovered as seeing a fit between the fairy's epilogue and the antithetical policies of his adopted homeland: Surender is the 'shadow' who has been 'offended', and Sedgton is the community that has been in 'slumber' (Epilogue, 1, 3). Rather than a straightforward essay in metatheatricality, Shakespeare's lines become a plea for accommodation and acceptance. Like the moon, which is glimpsed on several occasions, the English village has been reprehensively changeable. Now, in a meshing of the filmic narrative and the trajectory of its internal production, the only requirement, *Indian Dream* insists, is the exercise of a Shakespearean 'pardon' (Epilogue, 8). By casting Puck's epilogue as *apologia*, the film, it might be argued, slips into unreflective essentialism; however, it is precisely such a sentimentally-inspired interpretation of Shakespeare that allows *Indian Dream* to entertain its closing idealism. As Susanne Greenhalgh and Robert Shaughnessy argue, 'theatrical performance, especially in Shakespeare, is a route to a feeling of truly belonging, a sense of cultural ownership'.[34] The photograph that Surender contemplates on the flight back to India may represent a fantasy of organic inclusivity, but it simultaneously brings to mind the image of a community that has grown in the wake of his departure and that, in view of the doctor's Shakespearean involvement, has been educated in incorporating practices. This 'epilogue proper' speaks, in fact, to issues of national contemporaneousness, reflecting an awareness of global contexts that work for social and cultural inclusion, of networks that unite and converge, and of a theatrical power that travels beyond the limitations of a historically entrenched confinement.

These films not only ratify the importance of community, they also affirm the power of communion: a historically saturated dialectic involving 'the theatre ... the sacred ... religion and ritual' is a frequent sub-text, and nowhere more so than in Branagh's *In the Bleak Midwinter*, which endows the playing of Shakespeare with a redemptive purpose.[35] Contemplating the abandoned church of Hope, Joe describes 'a mission to save this place – to get the developer out and the people back in' (p. 15). Abundantly evident is the notion that Joe, a self-appointed crusader, will subordinate economic exchange as a means of promoting cultural resurrection, trading upon a play (*Hamlet*) that, because concerned with the passing of an older order, might be instrumental in creating a new one. Such an order is made manifest towards the film's conclusion. Thus, Pat Bucker notes that the film's title 'refers to the seasonal lyric "A Christmas Carol" by Christina Rossetti', a version of which is heard over the credits, while Douglas Lanier views *In the Bleak Midwinter* as ultimately discovering 'Shakespearean theatre ... as a secular substitute for the salvific holy family'.[36] Certainly, patterns of resurrection are lent a particular force: the birth of Christ is seen as synonymous with the revitalization of the community; Joe's production reconnects him with his 'origins'; and the director's age ('I was thirty-three years old' [p. 2]) establishes him as a deliverer whose brand of performative sacramentality is responsible for Hope's renewal. Hope is now 'converted' in a process that purposefully merges the social and the spiritual, and is enlivened by the Shakespearean 'word'.

## III

If these films endorse the communal potential of theatre and its unrecognised, less mainstream practitioners, they do so in part by casting a mocking glance at 'professional' stereotypes and the divisiveness of Hollywood. At some level, all the films discussed here ridicule theatre 'professionals', revealing them to be excluded from processes of Shakespearean and self-discovery. In keeping with his aristocratic-sounding name, the school production director, Dr Desmond Forrest-Oates (Martin Short), is represented in *Get Over It* as a camp diva in the Hollywood mould. A gay sexuality is suggested in his rapturous reception of a falsetto rendition of 'Where the bee sucks, there suck I' at the audition, and his points of comparison, in a series of vain fantasy insets, are always to the American cinema industry whose approval he desires.[37] 'Camp', writes Jonathan Dollimore, is the 'expression of ... superficial inauthenticity ... social alienation [and]... inadequate sensibility', and such signifiers are clearly invoked in the ways in which Forrest-Oates displays his inadequate absorption of what the film establishes as genuine Shakespearean values.[38] In addition, because he agitates to establish himself as a songster – his conviction that 'Bill

Shakespeare is a wonderful poet, but Burt Bacharach he ain't' leads him to stage the play as a 'modern musical' entitled *A Midsummer Night's Rockin' Eve* – Forrest-Oates threatens, in the film's uneven imagining of its subject, to impose on Shakespeare a damaging 'superficial inauthenticity'. It is acceptable for Berke to abandon the script for the sake of romantic *rapprochement*, but it is not permissible, *Get Over It* encourages us to believe, for the integrity of Shakespeare to be interfered with in the interests of a self-promoting agenda. Likewise, in *Beginner's Luck*, Andrew Fontaine's arrogance marks him out as a Prospero figure who renders silent and Caliban-like the Vagabond Theatre Company. Usurped from their 'island' dream, they are displaced by a quintessence of Englishness and an embodiment of theatrical colonialism. This emphasis on Fontaine's elitism and superior power only serves to stress his distance from the emotional lessons accruing from an authentic experience of Shakespeare. By the end of *Beginner's Luck*, the theatre practitioner has disappeared, rendered insignificant by the vacuity of his interpretive procedures.

Like *Beginner's Luck*, *In the Bleak Midwinter* would appear to reserve its satire for English theatrical forms and practices rather than American ambitions and careerism. In interview Branagh has described *In the Bleak Midwinter* as concerned at least in part with the 'pointless exercise ... of ... doing ... a definitive production of *Hamlet*', and, certainly, the film offers a comically dispassionate rendering of the seeming impossibility of staging Shakespeare for disinterested audiences and with little financial backing.[39] Yet, as Courtney Lehmann remarks, the final effect of *In the Bleak Midwinter* is more elusive, since the film simultaneously places in a dialogic relationship 'distinctions ... between ... England and America ... true art and mass art'.[40] Hence, while the peculiarly understated English narrative of *In the Bleak Midwinter* is imagined as conforming to a measured theatrical structure (the action is divided into acts), that which is extraneous (the possibility that Joe will 'sell out' to star in a movie called *Galaxy Terminus*) is associated with a Hollywood industry characterized by money and excess: Nancy Crawford (Jennifer Saunders), the American film producer, brags of 'box-office hits' and 'European investors' (p. 82).

On the one hand, these representations underwrite the historical ways in which 'two sets of entertainment, stage and screen, became affiliated with *different* nationalities'.[41] On the other, *In the Bleak Midwinter*'s flirtation with cinematic form steers Hollywood, and its practices, into a ridiculous light. This is clarified when Tom is whisked off to Hollywood to play the science fiction hero 'Smegma', and Fadge

(Celia Imrie), the designer, is selected as his costume assistant. Respectively vain and eccentric, the two, it is implied, will find a ready home in an industry distinguished by these and related characteristics. Even if the 'compensation' (p. 83) Joe receives for Tom and Fadge's departure bankrolls his production and undergirds his future theatrical trajectory, this does not muddy the film's overall identifications. Hollywood may execute raids on English theatre, but the ethos of Shakespeare and his cultural affiliations are untouched. The ultimately recuperative effects of theatre, and the brand of self-fulfilment Shakespeare facilitates, are to be appreciated over and above the immediate rewards of other forms of cultural activity.

Ironically, of course, given the fact that *In the Bleak Midwinter* represents a filmic mediation on the process of staging a play, the opposition is not clear-cut: ensconced in a multiplex, an audience is placed at considerable remove from the theatrical experience. But the Shakespeare that emerges, albeit in shreds and patches, has a commonality that transcends the specifics of place or application.

Central to the Shakespearean 'word' as represented in all four films is its adaptability, flexibility and transferability. The Sedgton production of *A Midsummer Night's Dream* in *Indian Dream* can only go ahead once Surender has pledged himself to it, which suggests both the need for an intra-cultural Shakespeare and an injection of 'new blood' to animate a dying art. The admission of *Indian Dream* is that the kinship of Shakespeare and national singularity is illusory, and that the borders of Englishness demand to be penetrated and rethought. For Shakespeare to continue as a body of cultural wisdom, *Indian Dream* posits, theatrical habits and performative ideologies must look beyond themselves, reject insularity and embrace the multifaceted significations attached to Shakespeare as a postmodern icon, a body of meaning that inhabits a zone of continuing appropriation in the global sphere.

The idea that a fruitful partnership might be shared between the theatrical performance and the appropriation of the Shakespearean text is consistently returned to across the screen productions explored here, forming a pattern of preoccupation that testifies to assumptions about the plays' adaptability and relevance. To cite Susan Bennett, these films 'rely on willing audiences who recognize and are nostalgic for the classical text but who are attracted to the [appropriation] event for its innovation with and renovation of that text'.[42] *Get Over It* illustrates such an innovative manoeuvre in vibrant fashion, since an element of Berke's performative success centres on his ability to rewrite the Shakespearean script after he has abandoned it. 'For, lo, to another belongs this heart' (his rejection speech to Allison) testifies to an adroitness in speaking Shakespearean English and to a talent for making the text his own. John Russell Brown observes that 'improvised performances of Shakespeare [are] ... associated with creative drama classes in schools ... and theatre companies that perform in streets and public places'.[43] In other words, Berke's meditation on Shakespeare allows the film to suggest that the Bard enjoys a demotic, even non-institutional quality as well as possessing a popular and still current educational appeal. 'You can't just change four-hundred-year old literature', Striker angrily protests, but the argument of *Get Over It* is that Shakespeare can and should be altered. Moreover, such reinvention, the film suggests, banishes the charge of elitism and ensures that Shakespeare's work is no longer tainted with a national and therefore inhibiting identification. It is through a species of appropriation that nevertheless respects the tone and feel of the 'original', then, that the notion of Shakespeare as a contemporary is perpetuated.

If the stage production of *A Midsummer Night's Dream* in *Get Over It* is a form of appropriation, so too is the film version of *The Tempest* that *Beginner's Luck* gestures towards. For much of the film, it is Mark who carries the weight of Shakespearean authenticity in his desire to stage an unadulterated *Tempest*. In so doing, he is again represented as the obverse of Andrew Fontaine, whose production of *Stormy Weathers*, it is implied, is a high-concept and big-budget rewriting of Shakespeare's play.[44] Yet, at the end of *Beginner's Luck*, Mark has been transported to the Cannes Film Festival where he plans to mount 'an all-new extravaganza ... [a] movie'. The title of this work – *Escape from Doom Island* – both illuminates a second (cinematic) attempt at *The Tempest* and crystallizes his abandonment of 'pure' Shakespeare in favour of repackaged Hollywood genres. Even in the film's title is encapsulated a dominant tendency of the industry Mark is represented as striving to enter, since an 'escape from' implies an 'arrival at': the director sets to work on the 'sequel' before he has released the 'prequel'. This would appear to suggest that Mark eventually submits to the Fontaine-like attractions he has been cast as resisting, now revelling in a glossy dukedom of his own devising. Yet this would be to downplay the more pragmatic appraisal of Shakespeare's contemporary deployments with which *Beginner's Luck* concludes: the Cannes coda reveals the director to be no less torn than before between theatre and film (the 'Mark Fineman Theatre Company' and 'Mark Fineman Films' both circulate as formulations marking his identity), between competing constructions of himself, and between idealism and the need to tout for custom in the marketplace. It is a qualified 'success story', one that points up the economic demands involved in animating Shakespeare for modernity and the nexus of specific forces that dictate the unpredictable reception of efforts at Bardic reinvention. As part of its final montage, *Beginner's Luck* may mount lush images of islands and sea culled from that other appropriation of Shakespeare, John Madden's *Shakespeare in Love* (1998), a film that managed to rewrite *Romeo and Juliet* in the same moment as it appealed to art-house and commercial audiences, but this is not allowed to detract from the bathetic reality that Mark requires 'fifty million dollars' to launch his initiative. The coda is poised at the intersection between theatre and film, at a beginning point that is also an end point: even if the 'something' here possesses in the film's imagination a more recognizable form, *Beginner's Luck* hesitates to embrace it fully, still harking back to the theatrical narrative that has generated Mark's cultural and geographical displacements, still deliberating over the dangers of altering Shakespeare's inviolable corpus.

## IV

Intervening in, and responding to, a perceived state of crisis, *In the Bleak Midwinter*, *Beginner's Luck*, *Get Over It* and *Indian Dream* unite in operating most forcefully as self-appointed guardians of the manifold virtues of theatre. Dovetailing in a shared hypothesis about the decline of the theatrical institution, these films display a postmodern reliance on the communicative power of film, a medium that is seen as central not only to the continuity of various styles and expressions of performance but also to Shakespearean survival. This is not to suggest that either television or the multiplex is engaged in a preservation mission; rather, the films explored here fragment Shakespeare at the same time as they try to unite the shards of his cultural memory, urgently reflecting on the means whereby theatre, and Shakespeare's relation to it, might still be manageable and meaningful. That is, screen realizations of Shakespeare in his theatrical manifestation endeavour to suggest that the Bard possesses social utility and personal application, even fulfilling therapeutic functions, at the same time as it is recognized that relevancies only emerge in particular conjunctions of circumstance.

Caren Kaplan argues that 'tradition and heritage ... function in opposition to time–space compression and globalization' and, at first sight, the animating rationale of *In the Bleak Midwinter*, *Beginner's Luck*, *Get Over It* and *Indian Dream* would seem to be to place a critical perspective on contemporary trajectories via a concomitant investment in illusions of an anterior cultural practice.[45] The manoeuvre is familiar, for 'a major feature of globalization' is 'wilful nostalgia as a form of cultural politics'.[46] The peculiar species of nostalgia that these films enact is one that understands Shakespeare as a generative agent of *communitas*, of family renewal and of ethical action. The familiarity of the conjunction of these associations and Shakespeare notwithstanding, the films are distinguished by their claim that past beliefs and conventions have a niche in the present landscape. In this sense, the ways in which Shakespeare and theatre are figured in film, and the resonances that cluster around their partnership, stand as testimony to what Fredric Jameson has termed the 'incompleteness of the postmodern process, the survival within it of remnants of the past, which have not yet, as in some unimaginable fully realized postmodernism, been dissolved without a trace'.[47] To imply that the Shakespeare film presents theatre as marked by an unmediated 'pastness' would be a mistake, since *In the Bleak Midwinter, Beginner's Luck, Get Over It* and *Indian Dream* simultaneously register that theatre has not ceased in its evolution as an artform. They acknowledge that, judged inside the realities of its increasing invisibility, theatre will continue to diversify and radicalise, to honour the requirement of recovery, and to respond to the demand for newly relevant icons and institutions. Paul de Man writes that the 'power of memory does not reside in its capacity to resurrect a situation or a feeling that actually existed, but it is a constitutive act of the mind bound to its own present and oriented towards the future of its own elaboration'.[48] By the same token, if the filmic attempt to commemorate the valencies of theatre is retrospective, it is simultaneously energized by the needs of the 'now' and speculation about the future forms, whether performative or otherwise, that 'Shakespeare' may yet inhabit.

# 2
# Sequelizing Shakespeare

Critics have drawn attention to points of contact between Kenneth Branagh's *Much Ado About Nothing* (1993) and Michael Hoffman's *William Shakespeare's 'A Midsummer Night's Dream'* (1999). Typical is the observation of Douglas Lanier, who notes that Hoffman's work, in its 'rural' and 'sensual' orientation, 'unmistakably evokes' Branagh's earlier film.[1] Elaborating such occasional comments, I argue in this chapter that Hoffman's *A Midsummer Night's Dream* can be profitably approached as an ideological reflection on, and a self-conscious elaboration of, *Much Ado About Nothing*'s workings and implications. Engaged in a mutually reinforcing dialectic, *Much Ado About Nothing* and *A Midsummer Night's Dream* consistently speak to and are dependent on each other, appealing to similar sources of cultural reference as part of a bid for cinematic legitimation and authority. *A Midsummer Night's Dream* both mimes the strategies adopted in *Much Ado About Nothing* and replicates that film's imprint for the popularization of Shakespearean comedy, to the extent that Hoffman's connection to the Branagh *oeuvre* is most usefully understood in terms of the sequel phenomenon.

The notion that recent Shakespeare films are sequels and form part of a distinctive and specifically contemporary trend marks a move away from a more conservative notion of the Shakespearean sequel. According to traditional readings, the sequel is commonly seen as being motivated by a writerly anxiety about the importance of the previous text or, more usually, by an authorial will to 'profit', which is itself shaped by 'audience desire', in Paul Budra and Betty A. Schellenberg's formulation.[2] The 'sequel' represents a chronological 'prolongation' of an earlier work 'that in its own time was often considered complete'.[3] The three parts of *Henry VI* (1590–92) and the two parts of *Henry IV* (1596–97) represent sequences answering to the chronological type of sequel in their emphasis on historical continuation. By contrast, a sequel such as Hoffman's *A Midsummer Night's Dream* does not attempt to push further the narrative situation of an already familiar *dramatis personae*. Rather, taking energy from the charisma of its model, the film extends, expands and amplifies in the interests of confronting and providing a Shakespeare that enjoys cross-cultural appeal. In so doing, Hoffman's *A Midsummer Night's Dream* fits with looser and more postmodern definitions of the sequel as a non-chronological development of a pre-existing narrative, one marked by 'extension', 'expansion' and 'amplification' at the thematic and stylistic level.[4] Nostalgic for the form and content of the 'original', sequels gain 'authority' from the 'intertextual traces' of which they are composed, and constitute both 'repetitions' of and 'variations' on the 'root-text', thereby ensuring a species of interpretive pleasure.[5] Derived from *Much Ado About Nothing*, *A Midsummer Night's Dream* is illuminated through its intertextual investment in sequelization; it is a film that makes sense in terms of its participation in an unfinished 'corpus of writing' and encoded references to 'something other than itself'.[6]

In this way, the films can be seen as typical of one intertextual strand of Shakespearean filmmaking at the end of the twentieth century. Hoffman's screen offering recycles what is, in large part thanks to Branagh's *Much Ado About Nothing*, a recognizable repertoire of pseudo-historical devices and gendered perspectives in order to fashion a Shakespeare who is simultaneously postmodern and popular. But intertextuality – or 'hypertextuality', as Gérard Genette more broadly terms it – operates in *A Midsummer Night's Dream* in multiple, inconsistent ways.[7] Arguably because, Branagh's example aside, Shakespeare's comedies have proved less amenable to reinterpretation in the late twentieth and early twenty-first centuries, *A Midsummer Night's Dream* is rarely secure in its imitative enterprise. The film is consistently anxious about the possibilities of successfully progressing from the theatrical medium to the filmic utterance, and, in representations of authority and its screen equivalent, auteurism, betrays the ambitions and agitations of its field of operation. In this chapter, concerns that centre variously on technology, reproduction, reception and the contemporary status of the Shakespearean comedic are pursued into the opening and concluding stages of *Much Ado About Nothing* and *A Midsummer Night's Dream* in order to reflect on sequelization and the perils and the positives of this filmic methodology in the global marketplace.

## I

When Branagh's *Much Ado About Nothing* was released in 1993, it set new standards for the aesthetics of Shakespearean filmic comedy. Simultaneously gesturing towards and surpassing the less ostentatious use of Mediterranean locations subscribed to by Franco Zeffirelli, the film makes the Italian landscape (the Villa Vignamaggio in Tuscany) a central point of interest. Location is prioritized via a maximized use of outdoor settings which involve the majority of the cast to highlight the glory of an Italian summer – burnt umber tones, verdant foliage, relentless sunshine and the dusty industry of a peasant community. Hoffman finds in the Italian environment comparable resonances, deploying his fictional 'Monte Athena' as the tried-and-tested situation that has made Shakespeare's comedies readily comprehensible. Yet, in accordance with the amplificatory aspect of the sequel, Hoffman simultaneously increases the number of locations (Montepulciano, the Palazzo Farneze and the Villa d'Este) to offer a hierarchical social arrangement as a complementary aspect of the same idealized and sumptuous Italian experience. The distribution of locations – Duke Theseus' aristocratic palazzo is perched on a hilltop, while the village over which he presides nestles below – simultaneously draws attention to a less fluid social fabric. While Branagh's emphasis on a utopian community is of a piece with *Much Ado About Nothing*'s prioritizing of an ahistorical Italy taken from 'almost anytime between 1700 and 1900', *A Midsummer Night's Dream* more carefully situates the country and the context: the screenplay makes clear that the 'world of the film is Tuscany' during the 1890s 'at the turn of the last century' to bolster a distinctive, albeit stereotypical, treatment of patriarchal preoccupations and gendered social constrictions.[8] The director's approach means that *A Midsummer Night's Dream* aspires to go beyond *Much Ado About Nothing* even as it reproduces it, reaching more lavishly into modernity while continuing to exploit a topographical register within which the Shakespearean comedic text has become both newly popular and easily identifiable.

Part of that register involves a clichéd – some might say crude – use of classical visuals and imagery. In the case of *A Midsummer Night's Dream*, the film gravitates to the artifacts of Ovidian myth and Virgilian pastoral as a means of piecing out the play: because only the most familiar features are extracted from these traditions, Shakespearean statements are simultaneously simplified (made recognizable) and validated (associated with the cultured past). A typical example suggests itself at the point where Lysander (Dominic West) describes to Hermia (Anna Friel) the escape route afforded by his 'widow aunt, a dowager ... [with] no child'.[9] Here, the camera lingers on a bas-relief in the Villa d'Este of a grave matron and a beautiful youth, the illustrative juxtaposition functioning to inscribe the lovers within a timeless paradigm and pointing up the enduring historical quality of their predicament. Such visual investments, I suggest, trace their inception to Branagh's comparable, but more circumscribed, use of classical motifs. Thus, from the vantagepoint of a fountain dominated by trumpet-blowing Cupids, *Much Ado About Nothing* discovers Benedict (Kenneth Branagh) falling prey to his friends' gulling, the implication being that he is vulnerable to both the dart of love and the gossip trumpeted by conspirators playing the role of amatory messengers. Even if isolated, the scene makes clear that Branagh, like Hoffman, is at pains to apply popular forms of antiquity, enlisting visual rhetoric as the counterpart to verbal business. Where *A Midsummer Night's Dream* departs from *Much Ado About Nothing* is in the extended range of its classical appurtenances, which, from Hoffman's perspective, lends support to the mission to canonize Shakespeare via his partnership with some of the founding stories of western civilization. Hence, at the point where the jealous Helena (Calista Flockhart) encounters the lovers planning their elopement, the three-shot opens to encompass a satyr in a grotto in the Palazzo Farneze gardens. The addition of the figure discovers a distinctive application of the classical field of reference, since it makes visible conflicts between desire and conformity specific to the reinvented narrative. Amplification is similarly at work when mythological creatures and semi-clad personages in the 'mortal' world grow in number in the 'immortal' scenes. At the immediate level, this creates a bridge between various stages of representation in the interests of interpretive accessibility: Oberon (Rupert Everett) is surrounded with fauns (implying latent sexuality) and Titania (Michelle Pfeiffer) placed in the midst of a Medusa and the Furies (suggestive of female rage).[10] Together, these entourages betoken the emotion-laden entanglements and physical urges that inform the film. More generally, they demonstrate the ways in which *A Midsummer Night's Dream* picks up on the hints offered by *Much Ado About Nothing* in order to make synonymous a number of 'high' cultural moments and to assert Shakespeare's privileged niche in a pseudo-historical continuum.

When the illusion of history combines with the impact of visual spectacle a richly communicative filmic occasion is created. Carnival is Branagh's vehicle for effecting this combination, with the importance attached to the festive tradition being indicated, first, in the scene in which Don Pedro (Denzel Washington), on a patio flanked by animal statuary, imparts to Claudio (Robert Sean Leonard) his plan to woo Hero by proxy.[11] Over and above its rehearsal of the fine dividing-line between human and animal passions, the sequence operates to anticipate the prominence of the later animal disguises and their carnival associations. During the revels proper, masks are put to work as charged indicators of typological tendencies. While Beatrice (Emma Thompson) and Claudio don cat and cherub dominoes which respectively indicate their feline wit and innocent impressionability, Benedick is glimpsed sporting a 'Mr Punch' mask, Don John (Keanu Reeves) a red bird visor and Borachio (Gerard Horan) the disguise of a one-eyed giant. If only metaphorically, the schema of the *commedia dell'arte* – a term underscored in early drafts of the film's screenplay – suggests that Don John's dedication to devilish intrigue and Borachio's predilection for incivility and enslavement (he stands as a cipher for the Euripidean and Homeric Cyclops) will be mocked by Benedick who, a type of Ulysses, finds support in the humorous intervention of the 'watch' (III.iii.20).[12] Sapience, percipience and comedy, it is implied, will triumph over evil and barbarity. Carnival in *Much Ado About Nothing*, then, works both as a prefiguring character device and – in common with the film's classical references – as a visual explanation of the verbal. At the same time, in view of the continuing place of celebration in tourist festivals, carnival functions as a constructed mode of behaviour that links the early modern and the contemporary. Via the filmic translation of a long-standing tradition, the enduring legacy of Shakespeare is bolstered. As sequel, *A Midsummer Night's Dream* approaches the formula by way of 'repetition' and 'variation', opening out implicitly to reflect on Shakespeare's viability in the public domain. Festive hints, of course, are already inscribed in the play's references to 'The battle with the centaurs' (V.i.44) and 'The riot of the tipsy bacchanals' (V.i.48), the performances that will grace the marriage celebrations. Hoffman, however, sees such cues for screen treatment as unworkable, granting viewers instead glimpses of more historically renowned 'sports' (V.i.43). In the discovery of a 'holding area' prior to the mechanicals' performance, the film pans past the rehearsals of a *commedia dell'arte* troupe and other carnival practitioners, including fire-eaters, acrobats and jugglers. By returning to the figure of the fire-eater from *Much Ado About Nothing*, *A Midsummer Night's Dream* gives its approval to cinema's carnival signature. Yet the film's movement is complicated by the simultaneous presence in the scene of an Aida, a group of Greek tragedians, and an Othello murdering Desdemona.

Although Sarah Mayo rightly observes that 'Hoffman's film [here] relocates the Shakespearean text in a context of a series of other artistic and cultural discourses', one might add that the juxtaposition signals the nature of a global market in which Shakespeare is sold as a commodity and the filmic entrepreneur competes for funds and attention.[13] And, of course, as the example of Othello makes clear, Shakespeare is also obliged to contend with himself, with proliferating manifestations of his own narratives in a variety of styles and genres. In that the forms represented are more or less spent forces, however, the implication is that the hoped-for cultural supremacy of Shakespeare has already been secured. If only intertextually, Shakespeare is selected as the winning entry, which suggests that the still identifiable cultural importance of the Bard is what this version of carnival aims to celebrate. *Much Ado About Nothing* takes it as a given that Shakespeare is the bedfellow of history; *A Midsummer Night's Dream* proceeds more tangentially, expressing a need to explore that relationship and self-consciously reflecting on the process of cultural elevation in which it is so intimately invested.

In this connection, both films might be said to transmute the meta-textuality of the plays into a meta-theatricality of the screen. A dramatic consciousness about the origins of the play in the poetic imagination becomes, in *Much Ado About Nothing* and *A Midsummer Night's Dream*, a filmic awareness of the institutional precursors of cinema itself. If the plays recall the poet, the films look to the theatre. Thus, while the film of *A Midsummer Night's Dream* clearly identifies itself as a sequel, it simultaneously partakes, in Marian Hobson's words, of no 'tidy seriality'; rather, Hoffman's production is involved a 'complex pattern' of 'recursive' movements that encompasses previous films, plays, cultural practices and authorial processes.[14] Meta-theatricality in *A Midsummer Night's Dream* is initially suggested in references to a range of non-filmic spaces, from the steps of the cathedral where the mechanicals first meet (the humiliation of Bottom by Master Antonio's 'boys' at this point conjures a rival species of theatricality) to the fairy 'grove' (II.i.146), a type of classical amphitheatre.[15] Thematizing theatre is equally underscored in the scene of the King and Queen of Fairies' encounter: Titania is glimpsed parting silk curtains, as if curious about her audience, while Oberon is seen surrounded by his acolytes in a composition that, in replicating Gustave Moreau's 1868 painting 'The Muses Leave Their Father Apollo to Go Out and Light the World', invites us to read him as a dramatic thaumaturge, the narrative's patron saint of poetry and music.[16] Robert P. Kolker writes that the successful 'sequel' depends on the 'viewer's ability to recall, respond to, and favour [previous] films', and, as far as Hoffman's *A Midsummer Night's Dream* is concerned, the favoured recollection is of Branagh's *Much Ado About Nothing*, in which, as befits its status as a 'prior text', a comparable meta-theatricality is evident.[17] The discovery of Hero (Kate Beckinsale) from behind a flimsy veil at the close is typical, but so too is the self-conscious inauguration. As Branagh states in interview, 'in filmic terms, "theatrical" means for me operative boldness ... I'd describe the opening title sequence in *Much Ado About Nothing* – although very filmic, because you could never do what we did on a stage – as a very theatrical moment, and yet it's completely composed of film images that would be utterly impossible to recreate on a stage'.[18] *A Midsummer Night's Dream* and *Much Ado About Nothing* deploy theatrical registers as part and parcel of a commitment to filmic spectacle; they do so, too, in recognition of their medium's contextual underpinnings and artistic antecedents.

Arguably because Shakespeare is inseparable from theatre, an artform that, as chapter 1 has suggested, is increasingly seen in terms of a potential eclipse, *Much Ado About Nothing* and *A Midsummer Night's Dream* undertake a demythologizing mission that strips the dramatist of inhibiting historical baggage. Hence, *A Midsummer Night's Dream* summons and debunks presumed inherited anticipations: to show Puck pissing outside the 'fairy bar', for instance, undercuts the character's stereotypical 'spiritual' ethereality. Lightness is also denied the heavy fairy – hers is a plodding, plaintive 'Over hill [and] over dale' (II.i.2) speech – in a move that underscores effort and bathos even as it plays up a comic response. In this endeavour Branagh is once again Hoffman's point of departure. During the publicity tour for *Much Ado About Nothing*, Branagh remarked that he had wished to remove 'all the clutter ... all the fruity voices being "lovely"': the idea is stated more forcefully when he observed that his film should not be 'seen behind glass ... the work you're engaged in already has an intimidation factor ... you'll do everything you can to get out of the way the notion that "the Brits" do [Shakespeare] best'.[19] Demythologizing is not mentioned, but the point is clear enough: to 'do' Shakespeare in the global marketplace is to participate in a revisionist project. Most obviously, the 'international' cast of the film indicates an avoidance of the British–Shakespearean connection. Less obviously, the DVD of *Much Ado About Nothing* distributed in the US reveals a purposefully tilted axis of reception and appreciation. Prominently featuring interviews with Michael Keaton (Dogberry) and Denzel Washington taken from earlier television features, the accompanying documentary rehearses the actors' previous roles as a means of demonstrating their centrality to the American imaginary. Meanwhile, Branagh approaches Shakespeare by way of 'American film acting', which, the director and co-producer states, he has always 'admired' for its 'emotional recklessness': ahistorical generalization and cultural contradiction here come together as part of a market strategy for denationalizing, streamlining and stretching the Bard's areas of reference. But '"the Brits"' do not disappear from Shakespearean tradition so easily. If sequels involve an imitative commercialism, then Hoffman's *A Midsummer Night's Dream*, at some level, is committed to reviving, to American eyes at least, the golden aura of Branagh's English identity, casting Rupert Everett as Oberon (he is the epitome of Anglophone public school charm), Roger Rees as Peter Quince (the role brings to mind his own Stratford-upon-Avon successes) and Anna Friel as Hermia (her lesbian kiss scene in the English soap opera *Brookside* attracted record viewing figures). By contrast, Sophie Marceau's part as Hippolyta bespeaks a construction of French sophistication. What is 'English' blurs in Hoffman's casting therefore with what is non-'English' to advance a dispersed 'Shakespeare' who is inherently pan-'European'.[20] At the same time, *A Midsummer Night's Dream* places in the forefront American performers. As Helena and Bottom, Calista Flockhart and Kevin Kline set the seal on the film's absorption in television and filmic comedy respectively.[21] Their presence confirms the film's transatlantic aspirations while simultaneously revealing its defining relationship with popular screen icons. Hoffman's Shakespeare is demythologized because his film's players are uniquely poised to counter assumptions about cultural irrelevance and historical circumscription. *A Midsummer Night's Dream* and *Much Ado About Nothing* consort with each other in announcing that neither nations nor history bind the Bard. In elaborating this idealism, however, they acknowledge the possibility that Shakespeare may remain straitjacketed, even if residually. To achieve a culturally denuded Shakespeare is the ambition of both films, even if ideological accretions of Englishness, and American economic realities, complicate that transformative project.

## II

More than simply an effect of globalization or a response to play texts that have become institutionally enshrined, the demythologizing undertaking of *A Midsummer Night's Dream* and *Much Ado About Nothing* is in keeping with a deeper concern about the nature of reproduction and a broader anxiety about the status of Shakespeare in the contemporary moment. For instance, both films elaborate books as key metaphorical utilities: the volumes wielded by Friar Francis (Jimmy Yuill) and the Sexton (Edward Jewesbury) in *Much Ado About Nothing* are indicators of systematized and encoded male voices, while the weighty tome consulted by Theseus (David Strahairn) in *A Midsummer Night's Dream* operates as a visual distillation of the 'law' (I.i.119) and a founding patriarchal text. Yet, in the same moment, these cinematic statements are preoccupied with progressing beyond 'the constraints of bookishness' and the 'burden of the book'.[22] Arguments about the dramatist's accessibility are the inevitable accompaniments to realizing Shakespeare films in postmodernity, but they indicate too the apprehension that engagement and understanding may not be easy or immediate. One finds a pertinent illustration of this in the claim, made in publicity for *Much Ado About Nothing* targeted at secondary education, that 'Shakespeare's poetry' and the '"street slang" of today's raps' are essentially the same.[23] A comparable situation presents itself in Hoffman's relationship to his filmic predecessor. An architect, as Samuel Crowl argues, of a 'Hollywood creation', this director is haunted by the prospect of a historically English Bard who will prove distant and untenable because of the traditions through which he is popularly identified.[24] The 'tyranny of the "Hey Nonny Nonny" Elizabethan cliché' is Hoffman's phrase for the weight of Shakespearean obligation and expectation, a formulation that registers *Much Ado About Nothing*'s successful recasting of that signature tune in the same moment as it balks at stereotypical constructions.[25] *A Midsummer Night's Dream*, in fact, might best be typified as a film that worries about what might be lost in the disappearance of the 'live performance' tradition and what might be gained through the emergence of instruments of mechanical reproduction. Hence, the film juxtaposes music that unfolds in both 'real' and 'recorded' times in such a way as to lament the 'unique existence' (as Walter Benjamin terms it) of the 'original' work of art – 'its presence in time and space'.[26] To adopt Hillel Schwartz's expression, Hoffman's *A Midsummer Night's Dream* looks to Branagh's *Much Ado About Nothing* for 'assurance of continuity, value and authenticity'.[27] In so doing, however, it endorses a mixed attitude towards its cultural lineage, the vitality of Shakespeare and even the filmic idiom itself.

Most obviously, anxieties about Shakespeare and reproduction are played out in *A Midsummer Night's Dream* and *Much Ado About Nothing* in debates about auteurship. Defined by Timothy Corrigan as 'a structuring principle of enunciation, an organizing expression', the auteur in both films works immediately as a substitute for the dramatic author.[28] (In the play *Much Ado About Nothing*, it is Don John, 'author of all' [V.ii.83], who is credited with an albeit perverse will to 'fashion' [II.ii.38] and create; by contrast, in *A Midsummer Night's Dream*, the play, the authorial impulse is more generally encapsulated in references to the power of the 'poet's pen' to give 'airy nothing' a 'name' [V.i.15–17] and the capacity of the 'imagination' to body forth the 'forms of things unknown' [V.i.14–15]). As it is materialized in Branagh and Hoffman's filmic versions, the concept of the auteur simultaneously functions to take further the adjudication between a range of representational options. Crucially, that 'principle' of 'expression' is realized in *Much Ado About Nothing* in the prioritization of a cinematic property – the director's chair – and discovers itself in the ways in which folding canvas seats dominate in the gulling scene and a collapsing deckchair is deployed to underscore Benedick's ineptitude. The idea is recast in *A Midsummer Night's Dream* in the scene in which Oberon summons natural 'brawls' (II.i.87): his seated pose here suggests a directorial as well as a thaumaturgical potency. What Oberon commences as auteur Bottom is figured as completing. A more historically suggestive type of auteurism is at stake when Bottom (regarded by Kevin Kline as an 'artist at heart') casually operates the gramophone that has been stolen by Titania's 'pantomime dwarves', allowing the strains of 'Casta Diva' (from Vincenzo Bellini's opera *Norma*) to waft through the air.[29] In the published screenplay, Bottom's actions are greeted by the fairy refrain, 'Hail, mortal!'[30] The soundtrack, however, which significantly departs from the screenplay both structurally and verbally, has the fairies chorus, 'Hail, immortal!', a shift which implies that, having made music appear 'immortal' through his control of technology, Bottom is accorded a similar status himself. Judged alongside *A Midsummer Night's Dream*'s recreation of the *fin de siècle*, this conjuration of 'immortality' takes us back to the ways in which, at the 'turn of the last century', the gramophone or phonograph, whose name 'not coincidentally derive[s] from writing', struck wonder in listeners because of its capacity to 'store ... time ... as a mixture of audio frequencies in the acoustic realm'.[31] Not surprisingly, at the first public demonstration of the powers of the phonograph, its inventor, Thomas Edison, declared, 'Speech has become, as it were, immortal'.[32] Certainly, Bottom's expertise with music is the passport to his sexual emancipation – he is granted access to Titania in the following scene. Dressed at this point like Oberon, or even like that other 'immortal',

Hercules – he now acts, rather than speaks, in 'erc'les' vein' (I.ii.33) – newly authored, Bottom is welcomed into the private bower. At the same time, given the medium in which Hoffman is working, Bottom's 'immortal' manipulations underscore the fact that the phonograph and the cinematograph enjoyed a simultaneity of cultural emergence: the parallel lends weight to the artist-weaver's auteurial dimensions. As Friedrich Kittler states, commenting on the technical and intellectual connections binding these two forms of artistic reproduction, 'the recording of acoustic data was accomplished with sound tricks, montage and cuts; it is with film tricks, montage and cuts that the recording of optical processes began'.[33] Author and auteur, film and phonograph, find in Bottom a point of negotiation, a forum for comparison and a place affording cinematic connection.

Underlining the relationship between *Much Ado About Nothing* and *A Midsummer Night's Dream* are the ways in which auteurship is specifically gendered. Interestingly, the plays provide the relevant prompt, being preoccupied with the ways in which the articulation of authentic identity for women is invariably compromised. In *Much Ado About Nothing*, for instance, Hero's efforts at independent speech are sidelined (Claudio's epitaph upon 'the tomb' [V.iii.9] reduces her to the status of silenced representation); likewise, in *A Midsummer Night's Dream*, Hermia's verbal opposition is countered by Theseus' assigning her to a barren fate in a convent. Given the gendered dynamic of these constructions, it is not surprising that associated evocations of the printing process are often stamped as masculine: thus, Theseus characterizes Hermia 'as a form in wax / By [your father] imprinted' (I.i.49–50), while Friar Francis proposes to 'publish it that [Hero] be dead indeed' (IV.i.203). Both lines conjure manifestations of a male hegemony, including the subordination of women through the technological instruments of the press. Most obviously, the films figure the constrictions of gender in terms of physical objects of placement and/or displacement. In *A Midsummer Night's Dream*, it is the 'newfangled creation, the bicycle' that mediates the move to female independence and the corresponding inconceivability of mobility.[34] Particularly where Helena is concerned, the bicycle is an encumbrance that illuminates the failures of advancement. For the women of *Much Ado About Nothing*, chairs rather than bicycles thematize failed attempts at directorial authority, nowhere more obviously than when Beatrice, furious at the rejection of Hero, turns over a bench in the chapel. Marked here as a woman frustrated by her inability to perform 'a man's office' (IV.i.265) and denied an effective role in her society's public spaces, Beatrice can only attack, in an enclosed inner sphere, the most suggestive symbol of an overarching auteurism. More generally in the films, the separation of women and auteurs is indicated via writerly metaphors. A scene excised from the film, but present in the shooting script of *A Midsummer Night's Dream*, for instance, shows Hippolyta, having argued with Theseus, at a 'desk covered with the stuff of letter-writing. She sits at the window writing a letter home: she is on the verge of tears'.[35] Writing here noticeably fails to alleviate Hippolyta's despair, the suggestion being that her marriage is enforced and that cultural relocation is a form of imprisonment. By the same token, it is entirely in keeping with *Much Ado About Nothing*'s *mise-en-scène* that Beatrice hides her 'knife's point' (II.iii.224–5) – a sign of the pen – and that Hero wears a blank white mask during the revels, since, as one critic notes, women have historically been 'equated with the white sheet of nature or virginity onto which a male stylus could then inscribe the glory of its authorship'.[36] Women, within a context of the auteur, appear neither to 'enunciate' nor 'organize'.

In this context, too, the opening of *Much Ado About Nothing* is arresting, since it represents a disruption of the narrative of gendered auteurial exclusion. Here, Beatrice/Thompson's disembodied voice beats out the rhythm of the 'Hey Nonny Nonny' refrain. The initial effect is to blur the lines of demarcation between a song and a spoken delivery, a documentary and a motion picture, and a celebrity and an actress. More importantly, however, the opening illuminates the appropriation by women of a standard male text, positing a correlation between a new version of Shakespeare and a peculiarly female act of rewriting. Hélène Cixous and Catherine Clément note that 'it is in writing ... and in accepting the challenge of the discourse controlled by the phallus ... that woman will affirm woman somewhere other than in silence', and their observation is abundantly borne out when the scene of *Much Ado About Nothing* shifts to Beatrice perched in a tree urging on her audience to a joint rendition of Balthazar's verses.[37] (Figure 2.) Not only is Beatrice figuratively empowered through being tied to the auteur or internal director, she is simultaneously placed in the position of musical conductor: in short, a woman orchestrates collaborative revision. (The idea is picked up by Hoffman in the realization of Bottom musically orchestrating his environment.) In addition, at the point where Beatrice descends from the tree, camerawork initiates a multi-layered dialogue between the books she bears and the script delivered by the messenger: there is a conflict between mediated versions of Shakespearean authority, romantic lyric, martial discourse, and

*Figure 2.* Storyboard illustration from *Much Ado About Nothing* (dir. Kenneth Branagh, 1993).

manuscript and print culture. Given these considerations, it is difficult to agree with critics such as Michael J. Collins and H. R. Coursen, who argue respectively that the filmic *Much Ado About Nothing* 'suppresses the play's uneasiness about the roles that gender imposes' and fails to 'mount any subversive challenge to manifest content'.[38] Rather, acting on Kaja Silverman's claim that an 'author "outside" the text [can] speak her subjectivity ... through those forms of identification and textual organization ... which hinge upon a variety of characterological and narrative devices', I would suggest that Beatrice becomes the chief instrument whereby notions of reproduction are tested and discharged. In a radical spirit, the film locates her act of rewriting over and above Leonato's (Richard Briers) work of painting the Tuscan landscape.[39] Equally emphatically, because *Much Ado About Nothing* first 'identifies' Beatrice's voice via the 'devices' of musical overlay, prerecording and computer-generated script – a kind of cinematic karaoke – it is enabled to draw a parallel between a woman's 'author'ity and the powers of technology.

*A Midsummer Night's Dream* is indebted to this opening at several levels. At once, it would appear that the sequel merely amplifies the 'root-text', since Felix Mendelssohn's overture to the play sounds in the place of a solo-voiced Elizabethan jig: orchestral excess is preferable to a single utterance. Yet Hoffman's film is also more directly imitative. A discarded script idea involved a 'voice in the dark', as in *Much Ado About Nothing*, intoning Theseus' the 'lunatic, the lover, and the poet' speech, while in the film proper a directorial eye pans outwards to display, simultaneously, the Tuscan scene and fairy fireflies illuminating the play and film's title.[40] The moment retrospectively reverberates: because these fairy lights are later gendered as female (they are one manifestation of Titania's entourage), the implication is that women have the capacity to rewrite or in this case reanimate the Shakespearean 'original'.[41] Moreover, in view of Hoffman's *fin-de-siècle* setting, 'poised on the verge of a dramatic shift', one is stimulated to contemplate constructions of the 1890s and, in particular, historical developments in the writerly and rewriterly domain.[42] (The fact that the film, playing a 'variation' upon *Much Ado About Nothing*, introduces this information as highlighted script means that we are again subliminally encouraged to reflect on processes of textual production and transmission.) Friedrich Kittler has noted that, at the turn of the nineteenth century, mainly through the aegis of the New York branch of the Young Women's Christian Association and its promotion of the typewriter, a radical coupling of 'sexual innovation' and 'technological innovation' was facilitated.[43] For the first time, the 'handwriting aesthetics of male secretaries' were challenged, with the large-scale employment of women as typists inverting the 'gender of writing', the 'monopoly of script' and even 'the material basis of literature'.[44] A charged historical juncture combines with a gendered iconography to suggest that *A Midsummer Night's Dream* too may be concerned with female 'acting subjects' who assert the 'I' through a 'technique of the self'.[45] As in *Much Ado About Nothing*, although less emphatically, *A Midsummer Night's Dream* rehearses in its opening a filmic intertextuality comprised of writing, reproduction and technology.

## III

It is arguable whether the representation of these gendered considerations, prioritized at the commencements of *Much Ado About Nothing* and *A Midsummer Night's Dream*, is also replicated in the films' closing stages. As Jacqueline Suter writes, commenting on feminine discourse in film, 'isolated interruptions [by women] do not necessarily deconstruct ... narrative discourse in any significant way ... only a systematic rethinking of the entire terms of narrative logic ... may allow the feminine to express itself more forcefully'.[46] Anxious about how Shakespeare might be reinvented and concerned to articulate the category of 'woman' as cinematically relevant, Hoffman utilizes Branagh's example, also subscribing to that director's 'erasure of gender conflicts' which accompany *Much Ado About Nothing*'s nostalgic, if not always straightforward, concluding recuperative gestures.[47] Initially at least, women's agency is affirmed in the communal expression of celebration – culled from Robert Wise's *The Sound of Music* (1965) – with which *Much Ado About Nothing* concludes. The sequence opens in the Villa Vignamaggio's inner courtyards, spaces marked as female. Within this domestic arena, the household's women, ranged on upper balconies and glimpsed from an upward turn of the camera, scatter confetti, suggesting the participation of a *deus ex machina* who blesses, authors and authorizes via the distribution of nuptial tokens. If these women are types of god, moreover, then the confetti they bestow is a species of manna, a final incarnation of the foods and grapes with which the film began. Archetypally, *Much Ado About Nothing*'s ending evokes gendered markers of sustenance and approval. Once the camera progresses beyond these spaces to the outer gardens, however, the point-of-view, and its gendered orientation, change. As the steadicam held by camera-operator Andy Shuttleworth transforms into the final, downward-looking crane-shot, which rises above the trees to display, once again, the Tuscan panorama, one is both reminded of the presence of the male auteur and returned to the masculine world of the earlier 'return from the war' scene.[48] This outer space is implicitly controlled not by women but by men, with Branagh/Benedick and not Beatrice/Thompson stamping the play text interpretation with his imprimatur. In addition, such is the effect of the director-inspired crane-shot that Leonato's pictorial practices and Beatrice's textual orchestrations are alike overturned, incorporated into one overarching, omnipotent gaze. It is entirely apposite, then, that in this assertion of an all-encompassing vision, the solitary word, as in the beginning, should be drowned out by music – invisibly orchestrated and wordlessly choric.

By contrast, *A Midsummer Night's Dream*, while it sequelizes *Much Ado About Nothing* by looking to the film's ending for authority, does not so much repress gender at the close (in Stephen Buhler's words, invest in 'gender inoffensiveness') as contemplate its place in modern media and the global marketplace.[49] Crucially, although he repeats the 'men below look up' and 'women above look down' relation, Hoffman reverses Branagh's inner/outer dynamic, associating the inner space of the apartment with men (Bottom) and the outer space of the night sky with women (Titania and her female entourage). *A Midsummer Night's Dream*'s opening suggestion that women are implicitly partnered with outer, natural spaces is here extended in the illumination of Titania's aerial, 'immortal' perspective. Despite the accompanying insinuation that Bottom, who witnesses her heavenly display, can now author – and commit infidelity – through his imagination, the overwhelming impression is that the weaver-artist is robbed of auteurial aspiration and technological sovereignty, remaining an internal fantasist who contemplates 'virtual, immaterial and unattainable fulfillment' and an isolated mortal.[50] 'Author'ity rests, instead, with the unearthly, with Titania, with the stars. As a superstar of the cinematic institution, Michelle Pfeiffer is, of course, an established and bankable commodity. It may be no accident that the celestial irradiation recollects the respective symbols of Paramount and United Artists, film companies that, through their logos, which represent both 'advertising [opportunities] and brand names', proclaim their 'multinational' credentials.[51] It is also significant that the spiralling lights of the conclusion evoke the non-material form of another fairy – Tinkerbell from *Peter Pan* (1953) – and thus conjure the dominion of 'Disney' as the 'global American ... corporation', in Fredric Jameson's expression.[52] In other words, in this filmic *A Midsummer Night's Dream* at least one closes with the eerie spectacle of Shakespearean magic morphing into American materialism, of text blurring with image, and of ancient Greece being modelled in the guise of global Hollywood. The connection between Shakespeare and Disney may not be as farfetched as it first appears. Certainly, it forms part of a two-way process. The Disney Corporation could be said to authorize Shakespeare (its subsidiary company, Miramax, distributed Kenneth Branagh's *Hamlet* [1997] and John Madden's *Shakespeare in Love* [1998]), just as Shakespeare films themselves turn to Disney for inspiration and filmic resources.[53] If Disney, moreover, mines 'images of the past' to evoke 'nostalgia for' a childhood 'age of innocence', then it is a roughly proximate schema to which *Much Ado About Nothing* subscribes at various stages of its existence.[54] Preliminary plans for the film included privileging the perspective of a Boy (Alex Scott) who, among other outbursts of emotion, would be pictured 'sobbing' at Hero's funeral.[55] These child-centred points of view were, of course, excised, yet evocations of nostalgia survive in the finished *Much Ado About Nothing* in the representation of a Hero who, thought lost and subsequently memorialized, eerily returns. That such a recovery is characteristic of the Disney narrative is confirmed when we consider the finer nuances of *A Midsummer Night's Dream*'s conclusion. As Bottom fondly remembers the romantically transformative but increasingly spectral nature of his history, he is framed toying with a tiny crown – a souvenir of his fairy affair. The scene thus complicates the gendered alignments, since it figures Bottom as a consumer of technologies of representation who has bought into a Disney logic of miniaturization and materialism, and who follows the lead of an industry that packages experience according to a sublimated ideology of patriarchal and imperial conquest.[56] The souvenir, writes Susan Stewart, 'linked to nostalgic versions of childhood and history', offers 'a world [that is] ... frozen ... particularized and generalized in time'.[57] As such, it conjures not only the operations of Disney but also the practices of a 'Shakespeare trade' that commemorates the Bard as timeless through the circulation of mass market products.[58] In fact, Disney and Shakespeare are highly proximate at the close of *A Midsummer Night's Dream*, particularly in terms of the visual pairing of Bottom and Puck, who is glimpsed sweeping a piazza. At once, the juxtaposition encourages a reading that sees both as collectors – one of rubbish, the other of memories. Yet such a collective impulse is itself ideologically freighted, suggesting the performative activities of rubbish collectors in Disney's theme parks and, by extension, the place of the employee in the global workplace.[59] Alluding to an earlier shot of an anonymous gardener with a broom in the Palazzo Farneze grounds, this image of a now 'mechanical' or lower-class Puck is theatrically framed: the action recalls the gathering up of debris after a stage production, and the concentration on a single figure (a ghostly reincarnation of the isolated Don Pedro in *Much Ado About Nothing*) reminds the audience that the metaphorical curtains are about to descend. The final suggestion, it would seem, is that it is not so much the post-technological cinema that illuminates or 'lights up' Shakespeare as the pre-technological playhouse. That is, the mixed nostalgia of this *A Midsummer Night's Dream*'s finale is in accord with its continuing acknowledgement of the theatrical origins of celluloid and its reflection on how much is irrecoverable in the transition to the filmic idiom. Within the 'sequel', writes Michael Zeitlin, 'one experiences narrative as nostalgic', and at one level Hoffman's *A Midsummer Night's Dream* here is nostalgic for, if not in competition with, the theatrical connections of its predecessor and the Royal Shakespeare Company kudos of Branagh himself.[60] As it approaches its end, *A Midsummer Night's Dream* contemplates the past, present and future relationships between Shakespeare as a cultural 'original' and the commercial demands of the Hollywood initiative, an enterprise that, in common with the Disney Corporation, subscribes to sequelization, fantasy, animation and infantilization as the necessary constituents of cinematic postmodernity. This, it seems, is the inevitable accompaniment to producing a Shakespeare that 'belong[s] to the world'.[61]

## IV

Michel Foucault argues that 'the analogous, the similar and the identical never return. Difference recurs'.[62] His thesis reminds us that, crisscrossed as it is with associations and impulses culled from *Much Ado About Nothing*, Hoffman's film can never be a mirror-image. Rather, *A Midsummer Night's Dream*, via expansion, amplification and the kudos of the cast, distorts *Much Ado About Nothing* while simultaneously replicating it, demonstrating Hoffman's ambivalent relation to Branagh – the mixture of antagonism and homage that informs his Shakespearean recreation. In the words of Leonato in Branagh's *Much Ado About Nothing*, Hoffman's *A Midsummer Night's Dream* is 'almost', but not quite, the 'copy'. Recognizing such dimensions to the film points up the extent to which, by working relationally, *A Midsummer Night's Dream* is able to reflect upon the multiple significations attached to Shakespeare – his functions, applications and resonances – at this historical juncture. In this sense, *A Midsummer Night's Dream* reaches outside of itself to contemplate the means whereby Shakespeare is distributed in a sequelized global age. In copying a blueprint and pursuing a prearranged course, the films converse with each other internally rather than externally, creating a system of signification which is largely self-enclosed. Inside such a system, Shakespearean comedy emerges as more disindividuated, and less variegated, than in the early modern period. The Shakespearean template established through the sequelizing procedure is one that places in a delicate equipoise authenticity and fantasy, utopianism and hierarchy, anxiety and cinematic confidence. In the act of striving to progress and remake Shakespeare for the needs and expectations of the global marketplace, *A Midsummer Night's Dream* gravitates back, ironically underscoring the limitations of the comedic form that first granted Hoffman's film its imaginative and material possibility.

# 3
# The Local and the Global

Via reanimation in the cinema, Shakespeare has been confirmed as a cultural property of global proportion. Directors and publicity play on his ubiquitous geographical kudos – Kenneth Branagh, for example, describes his film version of *Much Ado About Nothing* (1993) as 'belonging to the world' and the poster for Baz Luhrmann's *William Shakespeare's 'Romeo + Juliet'* (1996) introduces the 'greatest love story the world has ever known'.[1] The fact that Shakespeare has proved an accommodating friend to the codes and grammars of Hollywood filmmaking has been read as evidence of his universality and timelessness. 'As long as people are being born and having children, and falling in love and getting married, and dying, then Shakespeare is relevant', claims Michelle Pfeiffer (Titania in Michael Hoffman's 1999 production of *William Shakespeare's 'A Midsummer Night's Dream'*).[2] Her observation, typical of those promoting Shakespeare in films of the past decade, reveals a devotion to a fantasy of the dramatist as both transcendent and transnational. His basis in normative sexuality notwithstanding, this is a poet and interpreter who, throughout history and across the globe, delivers the same messages in words that magically retain their communicative efficacy.

Interestingly, the depth and scale of cinematic claims for Shakespeare's universality run counter to the majority of recent critical understandings. Since at least the early 1980s, the trend has been to discredit essentialist notions, such as those pedalled by Shakespeare film purveyors. Instead, attention has been paid to the ways in which individual nations romance Shakespeare, to the importance of different, locally inflected productions, and to the emergence of dissident voices that write the dramatist according to the pressures of discrete environments.[3] In these revisionist approaches, there is no mutually agreed

Shakespeare, only competing 'Shakespeares' that jostle for prominence in the cultural pecking-order. In fact, so dominant is this trend that discussion of universality has mainly ceased, to be replaced by a discourse of endless Shakespearean versatility. Notably underscored is the capacity of the Bard to assume distinctive guises, whether in Belfast, Berlin or Bangkok, and the conviction that there is no agreed sense of his inherited values or ideological applications. Between cinema's universals and criticism's particulars, then, there is something of an impasse, with contemporary culture contemplating a Shakespeare who is free-floating, nationless, constant and homogeneous, and contemporary criticism judging him as contextually tied, heterogeneous, intermittent and nationally specific.

Presented with these apparently polarized positions, Shakespeare film critics have tended to accommodate both in ways that have become predictable. While elaborating the universalizing effect of Shakespeare's film treatments, for example, critics – including Richard Burt, Courtney Lehmann and Sarah Mayo – simultaneously detail such cultural tendencies as necessarily politically retrograde and in thrall to globalizing structures.[4] A complementary critical preoccupation – evidenced in the work of Denise Albanese, Curtis Breight and Linda Charnes – has demonstrated the ways in which the Shakespearean universal is transmuted into, and overtaken by, American culture and its concomitant global identity.[5] For both sets of critics, the Shakespearean local is largely irrelevant; rather, as cinematic myth, it is the Shakespearean universal that requires careful deconstruction.

This chapter sees both cinematic and critical fields of operation as oversimplifying the complex niche occupied by Shakespeare in the global economy. Mediating between current perspectives, it explores film versions of *Hamlet* and *Macbeth* made during the 1990s and beyond as instances of the ways in which a local reading, absence or situation complements and challenges a larger global picture. In so doing, the chapter is situated alongside recent work by such critics as Sonia Massai and Martin Orkin, which seeks to realize that 'if any signifying practice, including Shakespearean appropriation as a mode of (inter)cultural production, is local, then the categories of "local" and "global", which are increasingly invoked to define the current stage in the history of the afterlife of Shakespeare's works, need careful consideration'.[6] The local is not always to be found where one might conventionally expect it. None the less, a comparative assessment of the films' preoccupations reveals the virtues of an approach that emphasizes the meaning of the local inside a mondial arrangement and which discovers the Shakespeare of modernity as a simultaneously local and global phenomenon.

# I

Traditionally, *Macbeth* has been written as one of Shakespeare's most regionally rooted plays. Yet in recent film realizations – Jeremy Freeston's cinematic 1996 version, Michael Bogdanov's 1997 Channel Four production and Gregory Doran's 2001 filmed Royal Shakespeare Company release – it is striking that a gradual evacuation of distinctiveness, or a loss of regional signifiers of 'Scottishness', becomes apparent. The opening of Bogdanov's *Macbeth*, for example, plunges us into an abandoned quarry masquerading as the 'blasted heath' in which dummies, burned-out cars and televisions litter the scene. It is a postapocalyptic – in Susanne Greenhalgh's words, 'devastated' and 'shell-shocked' – moment characterized by ruination, decay and detritus.[7] At the same time, the environment highlights a postmodern condition. Not only do the dummies connote the imitation and the facsimile, so too do the televisions, since their screens reveal both the production's title and the battle action as it happens. In this sense, we are positioned not so much in the expanse of the 'noir western', as Courtney Lehmann has observed of this film, but rather in the territory of Jean Baudrillard, which is 'the third order, no longer the order of the real, but of the hyperreal'.[8] Because a screen is privileged as the prime representational medium in this landscape seemingly recovering from a 'global catastrophe', we confront a further dimension of the postmodern – the extent to which war, in Slavoj Žižek's words, has been 'deprived of its substance' and replaced by 'the spectre of an "immaterial" war where the attack is invisible'.[9] The opening establishes a tone and appearance of mondial homogeneity; indeed, there is little to choose between this 'Scottish' scene and other nuclear wastelands characteristic of recent Hollywood cinematic outings. Despite his film's entertainment of signifiers of Scotland elsewhere, Bogdanov seems more committed to exploring the ways in which a national aesthetic is imperilled at the hands of technology, industrial excess and global conflict.

Bogdanov's prioritizing of homogeneity is a precondition for Gregory Doran's *Macbeth*, which goes further in its anatomization of an increasingly absent Scottish centre. Camerawork in Doran's release is hand-held and giddy, while the editorial technique is impatient, compressed and telegraphic. As a result, one experiences *Macbeth* as a documentary drama in which the Shakespearean play becomes difficult to separate from other generic forms and styles. The production's predilection for lurching tracking-shots and low-resolution green lighting functions to evoke the Gulf Wars and sci-fi television programmes such as

*The X-Files*. Clearly, an investment in introducing contemporary registers has as its objective a reading of *Macbeth* that privileges the unexplained and the arena of international political warfare. An additional by-product, however, is that we come to inhabit a world with no clear dividing-lines or sharp edges: one modality of being fades into, and is synonymous with, the next. Filmed in the stark, brick-lined interior of the Roundhouse Theatre, London, whose only redeeming feature is a metal catwalk, this *Macbeth* gives no clue to its imagined geographical anchorage and favours only the narrative essentials. Lanterns, spotlights and torches focus on leather outfits, silver buttons and military garb, but no attempt is made to suggest factions or affiliations: each major player is, literally, cut from the same cloth. A prevailing greyness means that the constructed mindset of the individual is also the psychology of the collective. Antony Sher, who plays Macbeth, writes that what was aimed for was a sense of a 'modern world but one you can't easily identify. Everything and everyone will be caked in soot, oil, grime, dried blood ... and you can't say which war this is either: Flanders, Vietnam, Balkans?'[10] Global homogeneity, in short, is the production's interpretive template and rationale, and it is applied in such a way as to collapse temporal specificity and flatten national borders. Doran's *Macbeth* situates Scotland at its furthest remove, with the local being hollowed out and vacated.

In this version of *Macbeth* and others, no longer is the dramatist the guarantor of singular or distinctive values: rather, it is anonymity that is stressed and the notion that Shakespeare inhabits an essentially featureless cultural space. Such a suggestion is at work in intriguingly complimentary ways in recent filmic *Hamlet*s, chief among which are Kenneth Branagh's lavish 1997 spectacle and Michael Almereyda's sombre 2000 cinematic outing. Notwithstanding their differences, these films imply that the Shakespearean tragic register becomes comprehensible only inside a disindividuated schema. Design sheets, for instance, make clear that no one European nation is envisaged as the context for Branagh's nineteenth-century *Hamlet*; rather, a vaguely non-English setting is evoked that alludes simultaneously to various countries – France, Italy and Russia – without any being specifically pinpointed. (Figure 3.) To judge from these forms of representation, Russia, in Branagh's *Hamlet*, contrary to the views of many critics, is but one suggested point of reference in a larger and more diffuse territorial whole.[11] Similarly, Almeredya's *Hamlet*, which takes a late twentieth-century millennial moment as its central conceit, seems at first glance to be marked by a comparable lack of particularity. His city

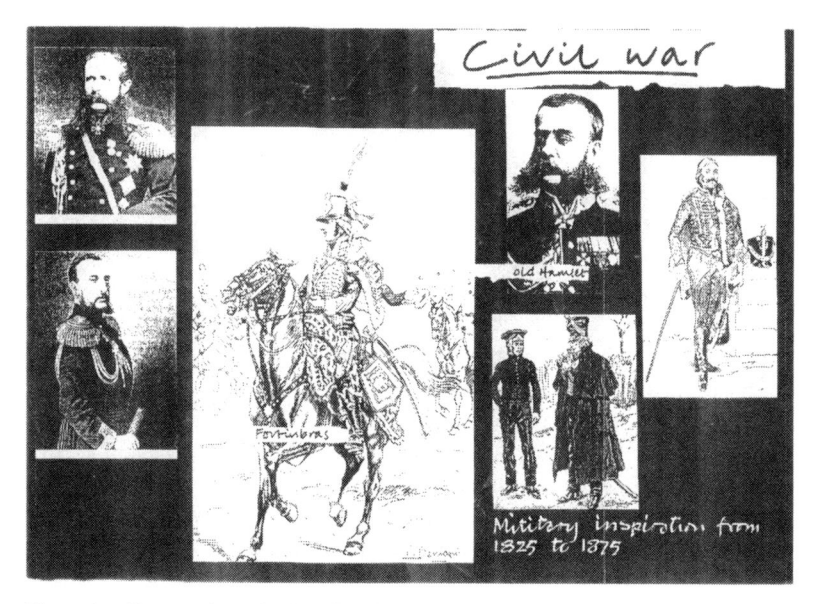

*Figure 3.* Design sheet for *Hamlet* (dir. Kenneth Branagh, 1997).

scene is stamped with signs of corporate facelessness, with a proliferation of brand names and surfaces alerting us to a corresponding diminution of meaningful human interaction. Assemblages of concrete, collocations of rigid glass structures, groupings of physically depthless architecture and 'radiant, ephemeral surfaces' all point up a generic environment recognizable only in its identikit familiarity.[12] For both Branagh's and Almereyda's film of *Hamlet*, these nowhere landscapes are defined, above all, by self-absorption. Elsinore's political isolation is one of the most arresting aspects of the visual vocabulary of Branagh's *Hamlet*. Blinds are shot as drawn; the gates of the castle always feature as closed; a 'watery wintry mist' seals Denmark off; and the mirrors that decorate the state hall stand as testimony to a court that looks inwards rather than outwards.[13] Because Elsinore in Almereyda's *Hamlet* is envisaged as a luxury hotel – the headquarters of the global empire Denmark Incorporated – the action clusters around a self-enclosed world, with the majority of the characters represented as living existences dictated to by the all-consuming insularity of global business. Like the landscape that produces it, the business is never specified – the logo both replaces and negates a finer sense of place.

Crucially, however, in Almereyda's *Hamlet*, the landscape that lacks identity is simultaneously discovered to be New York. This representation is of a piece with films like Greg Lombardo's *Macbeth in Manhattan* (1999), which highlights a rehearsal of *Macbeth* and its connections to the urban condition, and Kenneth Branagh's projected *Macbeth*, which will 'centre on the control of a global media empire ... the murders take place on Wall Street'.[14] In writing New York as a soulless centre, the films avail themselves of one resonant strand of cinematic narrative: Martin Scorcese's *Taxi Driver* (1976), John Carpenter's *Escape from New York* (1981) and Mary Harron's *American Psycho* (2000) establish New York as both a metaphorical gaol and a breeding ground for neuroses and acquisitiveness.

In line with such a trajectory, Almereyda's *Hamlet* and its counterpart *Macbeth*s privilege their unfeeling backdrops as keys to individually damaged psychologies. All three films draw on New York's postmodern connections to melancholia and mental illness, with the realities of 9/11 bringing into tragic focus the sense of psychological affliction with which the city is coloured. Visual designs lend emphasis to inventively introspective investments, such as the scene in Doran's *Macbeth* where Lady Macbeth (Harriet Walter) is filmed upside-down and underwater as her voiceover reflects on her husband's 'human-kindness', or when Hamlet (Ethan Hawke) watches a close-up of himself lamenting the fact that he has 'lost all [his] mirth'.[15] More often in these films, however, characterological particulars are represented as submerged beneath technology: Macbeth looks directly into the camera on accepting the title of Thane of Cawdor, but places his hand over the lens when treacherously speculating on how he will the 'multitudinous seas incarnadine, / Making the green one red'.[16] Here, the filmic discovery of the self is both desired and denied – there is an acknowledgement of the gap between a needful public manifestation and a feared private revelation.

The idea that filmmaking/video-making provides a means of writing a personal script is most fully encoded in Almereyda's *Hamlet*. His camera dwells repeatedly on Hamlet's auteurial eyes, as if alerting us to the ways in which he visualizes a history that is otherwise absent: as Katherine Rowe states, he probes the 'strengths and limitations of different memory technologies'.[17] (Figure 4.) As the film understands it, Hamlet is dislocated in direct relation to the *faux* historical nature of his urban contexts. Imitative Chippendale markers on skyscrapers, the pseudo-real South Street Seaport and ersatz architectural symbols in New York have resulted in a fragmentary landscape in which the

*Figure 4.* The protagonist (Ethan Hawke) as auteur in *Hamlet* (dir. Michael Almereyda, 2000).

inhabitant can only be *angst*-ridden and isolated. The protagonist stands as a cipher for Fredric Jameson's concept of the 'human body' struggling 'to organize its immediate surroundings perceptually, and cognitively to map its position in a mappable external world'.[18] As an experimental filmmaker, Hamlet mobilizes a seemingly unconnected filmic *bricolage*, which involves footage from his own childhood, a greedy cartoon dragon, a skeleton of a dinosaur and a Da Vinci drawing. Within its own logic, the sequence posits a Hamlet who, caught in a 'time' that is 'out of joint' (I.v.189), will look to the evolution or origin of things as a means of creating 'an art of resistance' and contesting late capitalist modalities of consumption.[19]

Constructions of the past appear in different forms throughout Almeredya's film, but they invariably function to evoke counter-cultural practices and possibilities. In contradistinction to the ubiquitous chrome and universal blank modernity of his surroundings, for example, Hamlet's room, with its antique furniture, baroque fabrics and black and white photographs, appears as a dissident cell and also a personal refuge. But most interesting is the film's summoning of Ireland as a multivalent trope betokening release, opportunity and hope. Just as Almereyda detects a withdrawal from the global in the (Gothicized?) cultures of the central protagonists, so does he find in

Ireland a potentially contestatory metaphor. The protagonist's connection with Ireland is initially suggested in the casting of Horatio (Karl Geary). His strong Dublin accent and dominant role work to formulate Ireland – as opposed to New York – as an exceptional landmass where loyalty, support, friendship and integrity are still valued. The corresponding linkage of the University of Wittenberg and the city of Dublin confirms Ireland as the repository of traditions of books, learning and poetry and implies Hamlet's preference for this latter territory. (The film's opening point-of-view shot through the open roof of a limousine can only be that of a prince summoned home against his will.) A map of Ireland hangs on Hamlet's wall, its presence in the *mise-en-scène* continually pointing up a geographical entity that is at one and the same time inspirational and aspirational.

A complementary but older image of Ireland is summoned in Branagh's *Hamlet*. Co-existing with the European anywhere is a vivid sense of an Ireland drawn from eighteenth- and nineteenth-century literary traditions and, particularly, the 'Irish Gothic'. Chiefly a vehicle of representation for the waning control of the Anglo-Irish ascendancy, 'Irish Gothic' tends to privilege a beleaguered, besieged 'Big House', which metaphorically points up, on the one hand, the exhausted and declining state of the landowning class and constitutional politics and, on the other, the potential and threat of revolutionary idealism and mob violence.[20] The genre's domestic elements centre on cells, labyrinths and secret rooms; its familial preoccupations cluster around mad women, usurping uncles and genealogical catastrophe; and its material concerns extend to dispossession, conflagration and exile. Clearly, 'Irish Gothic' and Branagh's *Hamlet* appear as mutually reinforcing: Elsinore (Blenheim Palace) is visualized as a 'Big House' whose interior is a warren of prisons and passageways, while the failure of the Danish royal family to take adequate account of the world beyond is linked to the ease with which Fortinbras and his 'modern mass-political movement' gains power *and* to the rapidity with which the line is extinguished.[21] (Figure 5.) Siobhán Kilfeather has argued that 'Irish Gothic' is mobilized 'more often than not as a response to modernization, a mode of registering loss and of suggesting that new forms of subjectivity are necessary to deal with the new forms of knowledge and power that are conquering past systems and beliefs'.[22] Judged in this light, Branagh's *Hamlet* becomes an instrument of nostalgia, a testament to memory and a paean to politically mythologized heroes of contrasting religious persuasions.

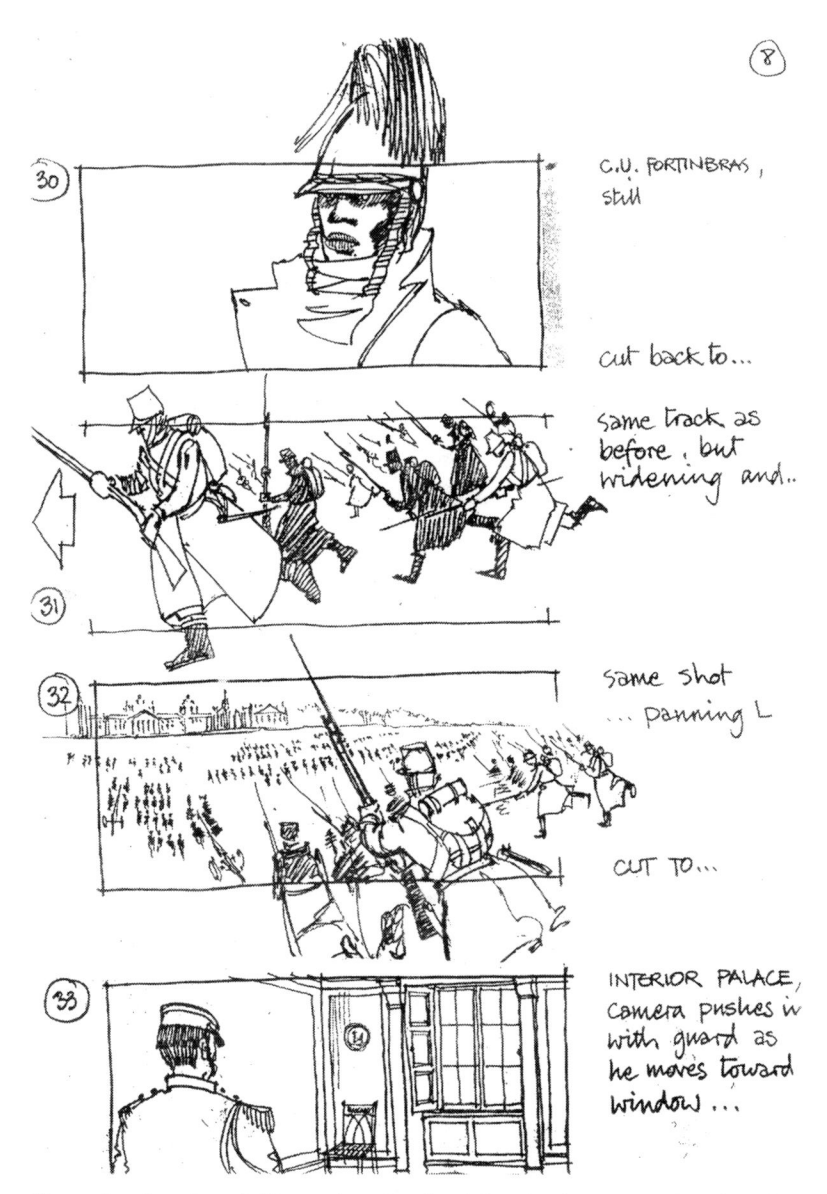

*Figure 5.* Storyboard illustration for Fortinbras' takeover in *Hamlet* (dir. Kenneth Branagh, 1997).

In Almereyda's *Hamlet*, the notion of Ireland as the spiritual home of the Shakespearean hero is at one with Hamlet's more general predilection for revolutionary iconography. Juxtaposed to the map of Ireland are images of Che Guevara and Malcolm X, which suggests a student equation of figures and places historically marked by resistance. But Almeredya's glance towards Ireland is more intimately rooted. A revealing split-screen shot establishes a parallel between the political persecution of the Irish nation and Hamlet's domestic experiences. For the upright, bullying Hamlet *père* replicates the geographical site occupied by England on the map, while a crouching, subordinate Hamlet *fils* imitates the shape and location of a subordinate Ireland. At once, this is a further indication of Hamlet's identification with the Irish subaltern; more broadly, the mediation of Old Hamlet (CEO of a global corporation) via an abusive paternalism links British and American forms of empire. The consequences of the expansionist urge are discernible in the simultaneous shot of a TV monitor broadcasting burning images redolent of Northern Ireland's 'troubles'. Such a damning elision of England and Old Hamlet bolsters Almereyda's unique writing of an aggressive ghost and a dysfunctional father–son relationship. His cartographical configuration notwithstanding, the ultimate location of Ireland is more slippery than that allowed by the film's elaboration of a liberationist ideology. The imagery of Ireland used and the meanings generated deny the material complexities of sectarian conflict, reducing them to a simple colonial paradigm. Similarly, the messy history of partition is elided in the relationship between Horatio and Marcella. An alliance of north and south (Marcella's northern intonation is the counterpart to Horatio's Dublin vowels) suggests Ireland as a seamless ideological unity.[23] (Interestingly, Marcella is the name of the controversial protagonist in Pat O'Connor's ground-breaking *Cal* [1984]. Set in the Belfast of the 1970s, the film is more stridently preoccupied with the perils and possibilities of Protestant/Catholic *rapprochement*.) In fact, what is finally made visible through such a romanticization of Ireland is the nation's commodification in a global economy. Thus, while Hamlet gestures towards Irish models, so too does the evil Claudius (Kyle MacLachlan): ensconced in his limousine, the CEO reaches out to touch a television image of Bill Clinton, a highlight of whose presidency was the brokering of the Northern Irish peace agreement. As a site for social values remote from corporate capitalism, Almereyda's Ireland emerges as a radical ideology and as an imagined idyll spectrally present in spite of current political realities.

The phenomenon of Ireland as spectre is fully and materially realized in Kenneth Branagh's *Hamlet*. Old Hamlet (Brian Blessed) appears as both a species of the local and a particular construction of Ireland. Not least because of his colossal proportions and his association with bogs and quagmires, Old Hamlet evokes the Irish giants of antiquity: among these, Brian Boru, a mythical giant Irish king, was perhaps the most celebrated. Yet, at the same time, in his sallow, pale manner and hollow, preternaturally blue-eyed appearance, Old Hamlet could form a connection with historical Irish giants such as Corney Macgrath, who was exhibited in the eighteenth century and whose ossified remains are still on display in the Anatomy School of Trinity College, Dublin.[24] Like Macgrath, Old Hamlet, in his posthumous manifestation, experiences exhibition, in his case in the form of a statue rather than a skeleton. Moreover, as ghost, Old Hamlet moves across a distinctively 'Irish Gothic' terrain, his presence recalling the place occupied by spirits in the novels of Sheridan Le Fanu and Bram Stoker, works where the undead seek redress for crimes of a specifically national inflection.[25]

Despite their apparently anonymous settings, then, uneasily haunting these filmic versions of *Hamlet* is an Irish spectre, one that assumes different shapes but consistently connotes possibility and registers desire. In their gathering up of stereotypical national associations, both Branagh's and Almereyda's *Hamlet*s chime with the recent filmic *Macbeth*s, which, from a comparable perspective, invest in the past, romance the regional and deploy visuals of place as ciphers of wish-fulfilment.

For instance, despite the claim that Freeston's *Macbeth* 'is set in eleventh-century Scotland', and notwithstanding its diegetic deployment of such regional markers as snow-topped mountains, deer, castles, indigenous accents, heraldic lions and Celtic crosses, this is no historically 'authentic' creation.[26] Rather, the forms enlisted betray a romanticized and stereotypical imperative that accords with Fredric Jameson's description of the 'nostalgia film', a screen narrative that approaches 'the "past" through stylistic connotation, conveying "pastness" by the glossy qualities of the image' and an illusion of medievalism 'by the attributes of fashion'.[27] Bogdanov's *Macbeth* offers a similar case in point. Here, too, a version of Scotland is glimpsed in the tying together of traditional modalities and modes of virtue (Lady Macduff, in a creamy white interior, feeds her children porridge) and in the use of dress (characters appear mainly as twentieth-century street fighters in combat gear with tartan detailing on hats and epaulets). Interestingly, these details survive in the film's fabric only because of their nostalgic potential. The signifiers are periodic, pointing up the occasional quality of 'Scottishness' and the reduction of the 'national particular' to the status of a historical echo.

The notion that a nationless Shakespeare is mediated via a process of localization should not surprise us; as the sociologist Darren O'Byrne states, 'the "global" is itself constructed through local practices'.[28] As synecdoches for the local, Ireland and Scotland become what is not global in the same moment as they constitute themselves as necessary components of the mondial make-up. Out of these filmic re-workings of *Hamlet* and *Macbeth* emerge Irelands and Scotlands that are metaphorical landscapes both local and global ('glocal') in orientation.[29]

The untenability of an unmediated regional frame of reference is encapsulated in the heavily intertextual staging of the closing scene of Freeston's *Macbeth*, which discovers tartan-clad warriors executing bloody charges and falling to their death on rows of sharpened stakes. At this point, the film assembles a composite of edited highlights from Kenneth Branagh's *Henry V* (1989) and Mel Gibson's *Braveheart* (1995), highly successful productions which, backed by the American corporations (the Samuel Goldwyn Company and Paramount respectively), made Shakespeare palatable to non-European audiences and indulged quasi-mythologized delineations of Scotland for American consumption. Both Shakespeare and Scotland can be seen as culturally acceptable only if filtered though global representational requirements.

## II

The Scottish–American connection comes under sustained scrutiny in of one of the more recent *Macbeth*s to be released. *Scotland, PA* (2001), directed by Billy Morrissette, features Scotland in a displaced and disguised incarnation. In the director's cinematic conception, the Gallic region has shifted from Scotland, UK to Scotland, Pennsylvania. Literalizing the movement traced by seventeenth-century Scottish *emigrés* fleeing religious persecution, the film, via its title, underscores the Scottish origins of what, under Morrissette's politicised direction, emerges as a very American tale. The McBeths are white trash restaurant workers of the 1970s with ideas above their station; Norm Duncan is their sleepy, too trusting boss. Matching the more general voyage made by Shakespeare to the US, *Scotland, PA* translates the Renaissance text into modern parlance, with the Shakespearean script remaining at the level of textual allusion, verbal patterning and suggestive imagery.

One of the most consistent of these patterns is a rhetoric of prediction and futurity. Like the play, the dialogue of *Scotland, PA* consistently gestures forwards. Typical here are Norm *Duncan*'s promise that 'Tonight, you two are going to witness history' and Joe *McBeth*'s comment that 'Intercom' is 'the way of the future'. In the terms of the film, that 'history' and 'future' embrace the replacement of the family-run, independent restaurant with large-scale multinational franchises. What is suggested through McBeth's eatery, in fact, is not so much the prominence of 'Enron', as Courtney Lehmann has briefly argued, as the emergence of McDonald's, the incorporated global industry *par excellence*.[30] Confirming this global corporation's inseparability from 'Americanization' is *Scotland, PA*'s representation of McBeth's rise; as he goes from strength to strength, his diner becomes not only more homogenized (with clinical interiors, illuminated menus and regulation uniforms), but crucially more patriotic (the protagonist sports a stars and stripes motif, while an American flag flutters over the corporate sign).[31] In documenting this process, the film charts a movement away from Duncan's benevolent patriarchy and home-cut chips and towards a nutritionally empty landscape of corruption, jingoism and exploitation. In the words of Lauren Schohet, '"Mc" telegraphs how consumer culture replaces the patronymic prefix with a branding prefix'.[32] The range of allusiveness in this film suggests the richness of locality inside constructions of America and the unpredictability of the interaction between Shakespeare and the global marketplace. Even inside what might appear traditional modalities of transference there is scope for both newly localized readings and resistant positions. But *Scotland, PA* is more subversive than even this allows. McDuff (Christopher Walken), who in the play defeats Macbeth and wins freedom for Scotland, is initially figured as a police lieutenant. Over the course of the film, however, and in part because of the time spent in observing the food business during his investigations, McDuff downshifts. The final montage of McDuff chomping on a cigar-like carrot outside his new organic vegetarian restaurant completes his triumph over the McBeths and incarnates a new regime, one that explicitly counters the global threat embodied in both the big 'M' itself and the broader cultural phenomenon that George Ritzer has termed the 'McDonaldization of society'.[33]

*Scotland, PA*, then, not only thematizes McDonald's rise; it simultaneously glances forwards to its decline. In 2002, soon after the film's release, the McDonald's corporation reported its first major loss; share prices slumped; key outlets closed; and health-oriented rivals successfully competed for customers.[34] The closing prominence accorded to McDuff's 'garden burger', as well as signalling the importance of an Almereyda-like counter-culture, encodes a meditation on this more recent trajectory, on the ways in which the global is invariably forced to adapt and co-opt. In this respect, the sequestered Americanism of the film's setting is purposeful, linked as it is to a sense of inwardness and to a historically particular illusion of invulnerability that, at least before 9/11, was actively entertained. *Scotland, PA* addresses but does not endorse fictions of self-sufficiency, the inevitable interpenetration of external influences, the dialogic condition of the global and the ideological work that an applied sense of the local is able to perform.

'At bottom', writes Jacques Derrida, 'the spectre is the future', and the repositioned Scottish ghosts which historically anchor *Scotland, PA* – as well as the choice of the *Macbeth* play – certainly bear this out.[35] Similarly, it is possible to read the ghost of Ireland in Almereyda's *Hamlet* as also enjoying a prophetic role. This is confirmed in the film's penultimate shot of Augustus Saint-Gaudens' sculpture of General William Sherman, which stands in New York's Grand Army Plaza. Accompanying the figure of Sherman is the ethereal Nike, who leads his horse forward with triumphant purpose. It is possible, of course, to read into the statue an allusion to Fortinbras and to detect in Sherman's repression of the 'South' in order to save the 'North' a codified comment on the bipolar structure of Ireland's political organization. Yet Fortinbras seems less forcefully evoked here than Hamlet who, via the statue of Sherman, is situated in a historical idiom: the protagonist eventually resolves his vexed relation with time and with the metropolis. Moreover, because Saint-Gaudens was born in Dublin and, shortly before his death in 1907, was working on a huge figure of Charles Stewart Parnell, the revolutionary Irish leader and spokesperson for agrarian agitation and land reform, the suggestion is that Hamlet, like the sculptor, is being claimed by his national forefathers and guided towards a culturally emancipated spiritual destiny. A passing shot of a plane's jet trail confirms the impression and works as an analogy for a soul-in-progress. Even this reading, however, is compromised by the presence of Nike, not least because this goddess has been hijacked as a logo by the Nike Corporation, a global brand closely associated with third world exploitation.[36] The question of Hamlet's ultimate destination is balanced in the final montage between both local and global scenarios, and any sense of resolution hinges on this uneasy equipoise.

*Figure 6.* Commemorative programme for the European première of *Hamlet* (dir. Kenneth Branagh, 1997).

A material enactment of such cinematic 'glocalism' can be found in the 1997 European première of Branagh's *Hamlet*. Taking place in Belfast at the Waterfront Hall and supporting local charities, the event explicitly figured Branagh as a homegrown talent who was introduced to, and welcomed by, the audience as 'your boy'.[37] (Figure 6.) However, audience expectation was dashed when the local hero appeared in ghostly form via a videotaped message, albeit one put together especially for the occasion. Simultaneously locally rooted (his continuing commitment to his Northern Irish birthplace is well documented) and overtly pledged to a mass market (global) Shakespeare, Branagh signifies above all the perennial artist who finds himself only when he has quit his homeland. Notwithstanding the local sentiments espoused in Branagh's communication, the lure of the mondial stage had proved 'mettle more attractive' (III.ii.99). (Branagh had commenced filming his role as an American detective for Robert Altman's *The Gingerbread Man* [1997].) Intriguingly, one of the main charities to benefit from the première was 'First Run Belfast', an organization founded to enable local thespians to study drama and stage theatrical ventures outside Northern Ireland. Both encouraging a movement away from the local and embracing its worth and particularity, the occasion exemplifies the 'inconsistent and conflicted ... cultural politics' of a creative practitioner who aspires to local participation in the same moment as he is moulded by the global exigencies of the Hollywood movie machine.[38]

An alternative path for the Shakespearean filmmaker presents itself intriguingly in Stephen Cavanagh's *Hamlet* (2005), which is set and filmed in Londonderry, Northern Ireland. To understand his *Hamlet* is to acknowledge the history of Derry and to recognize its origins as a contested English plantation founded by the Corporation of London in 1613, its status, following the famous siege of 1688–9, as the saviour of Protestantism, its narratives of internecine Catholic/Protestant conflict, and its association with the civil rights movement, the 'Bloody Sunday' march of 30 January 1972, and the Saville enquiry.[39] Here, because of the setting, the spectres haunting the *Hamlet*s of Branagh and of Almereyda are granted a more complete embodiment. The use of English in a Northern Irish intonation, for example, allows the dissident accent of Marcella in Almereyda's *Hamlet* to be formulated as a type of universal. Almereyda's linguistic sub-plot now becomes a major narrative, pointing to the telescoping of the director's local gaze. Similarly, the quasi-revolutionary sub-text of Almereyda is pushed to an extreme by Cavanagh; in this respect, Derry is once again richly evocative. During the 1970s, part of the city was declared 'Free Derry', a utopian Catholic enclave inside the 'occupied six counties'. Judged alongside Almereyda's investments, the location signifies a material enactment of the idealized political space Hamlet is represented as striving towards.[40]

Lending Ireland the central role while still managing to accommodate the Shakespearean original, Cavanagh's film opens up new avenues for exploring the relationship between the Shakespearean local and the Shakespearean global. Global gestures are easily discerned: the narrative pace of the film is quick and compressed, and guns and cameras, the insignias of Luhrmannesque filmic readings of Shakespeare, are given pride of place. At the same time, by translating *Hamlet* to Derry, the director explicitly draws on, and makes comprehensive use of, the associations embedded in a locally charged environment. Although overt 'political statements', to quote Cavanagh in interview, are avoided, political images in particular are privileged, with Derry's seventeenth-century walls featuring prominently, as do torch-lit soldiers in combat gear and the Guildhall, seat of a fractured administration.[41] Such visual paraphernalia have a two-fold effect. On the one hand, they lend the film an acute historical suggestiveness, positing the siege of the city (in which the Protestant 'apprentice boys' of Derry famously held the town against the Catholic king, James II) as an event whose mythological overtones are still being replayed. And current political pressures, which have a highly charged importance in Northern Ireland, are felt throughout, as in the alarmed disclosure that Old Hamlet has been seen and Hamlet's own anxiety that his colleagues will 'reveal' (I.v.123) his precious secret. There is, as Cavanagh admits, a 'high security culture under Claudius' and the all too familiar presence of governmental surveillance. On the other hand, the film's visual appeal brings the Shakespearean 'original' to mind, making of Hamlet a type of resistant apprentice and forging a bridge between Derry and Wittenberg, home of Protestant radicalism. Unlike the *Hamlet*s of Branagh and Almereyda, which concentrate respectively on nineteenth- and twentieth-century manifestations, Cavanagh's filmic writing addresses Shakespeare through a longer and more uneven timeframe of Ireland's political fortunes, thereby establishing the inescapable pressures of the past on the present. Thus, while globalization dictates the film's typology and style, Cavanagh's subjects remain locked in a richly determined local distinctiveness. As such, his *Hamlet* offers us a denser reading of the Irish heritage and suggests that the local is at its most communicative only when it has absorbed its historical particularity.

Local distinctiveness can also blur into a confrontational exclusiveness. Whereas Almereyda and Branagh deploy the local to reduce the global, Cavanagh deploys the local to confront Shakespeare and, in particular, his global status as a transnational voice. Offering a verbal counterpoint to Branagh's notion of a cross-cultural Shakespearean tongue and granting the most famous speech its most local purchase, 'To be or not to be' is delivered in Irish. Such an innovative directorial undertaking is explained by Cavanagh as follows: 'Hamlet has the idea that Claudius is listening and he doesn't want to be understood. He doesn't want his intentions to be transparent from what he says.' The use of hand-held camerawork in this scene, as elsewhere, allows for a 'visceral' impression and makes a virtue of the linguistic decision, forcing us to be 'complicit in [Hamlet's] emotional life'. More arrestingly, the notion of an Irish-speaking protagonist brings to mind the ways in which Irish has been used in Derry in opposition to British dominance and helps to formulate Hamlet's bifurcated identity in terms of the unresolved resonances of a disappearing national language. If nothing else, this moment posits the complex necessity of reading local practices alongside the mainstream activities of a multinational film industry.

## III

Understood in relation to the realities of the global Hollywood machine, recent film treatments of *Hamlet* and *Macbeth* exemplify a trajectory that culminates simultaneously in anonymity and in a mediated manifestation of the local. In a period dominated by homogeneity of production values and market forces, the tragedies suggest that the local is never entirely expunged; rather, local concerns are always accommodated by, and in conversation with, global imperatives. Overlapping and multivalent, the local as an operative category is arguably at its most powerful when it discharges critical regional comment. Because of his transnational status, notions of Ireland and Scotland cluster around Shakespeare; moreover, versions of both 'ideoscapes' (to adopt a formulation coined by Arjun Appadurai) return, ghost-like, in such a way as to assert the vibrancy of particularized constituencies and the importance of dissident positions.[42] It is a measure of the scope of the local that, in certain deployments, there is ironization and even interrogation of its global niche. Such a dialogue allows for Shakespearean meanings to be animated and transfigured via 'glocalization', with the dramatist's individual applications continuing to enjoy a salient late twentieth- and early twenty-first-century purchase. Despite current critical constructions, then, no clearly demarcated split between a universal and a particular Shakespeare can easily be maintained, since space for one exists inside the other, each playing a mutually constitutive role.

If Ireland and Scotland are ghosts, so too is Shakespeare, a spectre that comes back from a past that 'never was and can never be lived in the originary or modified form of presence'.[43] It is a symptom of postmodernity that things come back – as parodies, allusions, echoes and fragments – and cinematic representations of Shakespeare betray notably valuable instances of this process. Yet, as this brief catalogue makes clear, the return is intermittently straightforward, consistently different. In this sense, Shakespeare's periodic place in the global marketplace accords with the 'growing disjunctures' and 'increasingly non-isomorphic paths' that some commentators have identified as among globalization's chief features.[44] Saskia Sassen's remark that the mondial system 'generates contradictory spaces characterized by ... internal differentiation' is typical.[45] Certainly, *Macbeth* and *Hamlet* work in the cinema not to suggest that the local substitutes for authenticity but to point out that there is only ever romance and desire. Inside that arrangement, Ireland and Scotland figure, on the one hand, as utopian prospects. With Shakespeare as the facilitative instrument, versions of the Celtic hinterland discover the US recollecting origins and projecting ideas of connection and identification otherwise compromised in the global landscape. The movement, however, is not one-way. A migratory phenomenon moving here and there according to present needs, representational developments and modifications in the geographical ownership of power, Shakespeare demonstrates that, on the other hand, Scotland and Ireland can court America and that film is the means of accessing its values and interpretive registers. Thus, encompassing and complimenting its contestatory capacity, versions of the tragedies on screen point up the fact that the local ultimately performs as a vehicle of fantasy, suggesting through opposition what is unrealizable and self-consciously resurrecting the Shakespearean past to meet contemporary energies and agendas.

# 4
# Racial Identities, Global Economies

More closely than other recent Shakespeare films, Oliver Parker's *Othello* (1995) and Tim Blake Nelson's *'O'* (2001) have become associated with high-profile incidents that were the subject of considerable public controversy and received widespread media attention. Respectively co-incident with these events and distributed in their wake, Parker and Nelson's versions of Shakespeare's *Othello* are indissolubly linked in the popular consciousness to the American football star O. J. Simpson's trial for the murder of his wife, Nicole Simpson, and her friend, Ronald Goldman, and, to the 'massacre' at Columbine High School in Littleton, Colorado, when Eric Harris and Dylan Klebold shot dead twelve students and one teacher, before turning their guns on themselves.[1]

*'O'* updates Shakespeare's play by locating it to 'Palmetto Grove Academy' in Charleston, South Carolina, and casting Odin James or O (Mekhi Phifer), the one black student at the institution and a star basketball player, as the Othello figure. His corruption at the hands of Iago or Hugo (Josh Hartnett) culminates in a murderous rampage in the dormitory, which invites immediate comparison with the Columbine High School shootings, while the corresponding representation of characters who fall from, or are unable to win, popularity could be tied to the ways in which both Harris and Klebold were supposedly 'harassed' as 'outcasts' by their peers.[2] Such a process is glimpsed in *'O'* in the mobilization of the 'loser' motif. Given his exclusion from sports and his corresponding marginalization as a 'fucking loser' and a 'friendless faggot', Roger (Elden Henson) appears the most obvious candidate for the 'loser', yet social ostracization is also seen to threaten all the main players at some point, emphasizing a competitive school ethos where the possibility of violence is omnipresent and where racial conflict is a continual undercurrent.

The opening credits connect Parker's *Othello* in intriguing ways to its later filmic counterpart. A red spot appears inside the 'O' of the 'Othello' scripted in a pseudo-antique style across the screen, thereby drawing attention to the initial of the central protagonist and looking forward to the subsequent incarnation. Briefly, the 'O' functions as an acronym or abbreviation more powerful than the Shakespearean name. Since the red spot suggests a species of eye, a type of camera shutter or a drop of blood, an audience is invited to reflect on themes of spectacle, media attention and physical injury, and hence intersections between sport and identity, all of which formed constituent features of the O. J. Simpson narrative.[3] Points of contact between O's glittering career and his racial status are indicative of a similar contextual dimension to the film of the same name, for, as more than one critic has demonstrated, the titular character also conjures O. J., whose ghost is a haunting presence.[4] Because the film title places quotation marks around O's name, he is figured as a reference to something anterior and as an invocation of a recognized type or practice, quotation being 'the interruption of context'.[5]

Likewise, the engagement in 'O' with forms of recognition that are mediated through physical and athletic accomplishment points up a contemporary equation between sporting success and cultural acceptance. In addition, at the point where O is dismissed as a 'loser – the ghetto just popped out of him', the film suggests the extent to which institutional recognition in the US is invariably conducted along racialized lines. The description of O's loss of grace or power demonstrates that constructions of race can be deployed to underscore achievement, even as they are used to point up antipathetic and historically entrenched stereotypes.

*Othello* and *'O'* have thus attracted critical comment as highly topical mediations intimately rooted in their contexts – as films that, with varying degrees of self-awareness, understand Shakespeare by miming and mining the scandals and tragedies of their time.[6] But the chronological distance between the films, and the commonality of their concerns, suggest an argument that moves beyond topicality and addresses more generally situated interrelationships between race, cultural integration and/or exclusion, processes of self-understanding and the consoling fantasies of meritocracy. Reading the films in juxtaposition, this chapter will suggest that the final effects of *Othello* and *'O'* can be traced to broader considerations that have a longer historical timeframe and are of a piece with some of the major trends of the globalization phenomenon. One of the chief debates in globalization theory is whether a 'global culture', in Mike Featherstone's words, represents a 'homogenizing process' or system of 'codes and practices' that promote 'variety' and 'diversity'.[7] In a sense, both polarities of interpretation are permissible for, as Jonathan Friedman comments, these are not necessarily two 'opposing views of what is happening in the world today, but two constitutive trends of global reality'.[8] Within that conception of the 'world', race and ethnic issues occupy correspondingly extreme positions. On the one hand, it is maintained that homogenizing tendencies, and the structural developments attendant on new economic networks, have resulted in 'forms of racialized disadvantage' and the 'growth of racially defined minorities' – the undergirding and perpetuation of either 'immigration control' or 'racial injustices'.[9] On the other hand, symptomatic of the global economy, it is argued, is the increased emphasis on race, ethnicity and difference: particularism and pluralism are prioritized, a typical instance being the ways in which 'globalization ... introduces possibilities for new ethnic identities' and for rediscovering 'the untainted origins of an ethnic group in history'.[10] 'There is', as Zygmunt Bauman writes, 'a powerful demand for pronounced, though symbolic rather than institutionalised, ethnic distinctiveness'.[11]

Both the homogenizing and the differentiating aspects of the global equation bear witness to the formation and circulation of new forms of identity and identification, to the emergence of contests for, and agreements about, social membership. Because not all racial or ethnic groups fit within nation-state parameters or territorial formations, a subscription to individual or collective identity has become one means of defining the self and selves in a global economy marked by as yet unresolved cultural trends. But global identity is rarely a univocal position. Rather, it belongs with, and is frequently articulated through, categories of hybridity, which are themselves 'generated and reinforced by the real fragmentation occurring within and between nation-states in a global era'.[12] As Jan Aart Scholte puts it, 'the immediacy of the whole world in contemporary conditions of globalization has greatly multiplied and intensified experiences of being several selves at once'.[13]

This chapter argues that *Othello* and '*O*' are most readily understood as reflections on the shifting and uneven processes of the formation of racial identities. In their treatment of Shakespeare's play, both films are attracted to similar – and familiar – critical readings; that is, they understand the blackness of their respective Othello figures as defined within and against white value systems and beliefs. Othello and O are discovered as agitating to become simultaneously like and unlike the white models with which they are surrounded: they are represented, in other words, via a globally recognizable and discursively mediated dialectic involving difference and homogeneity. Above all, the titular characters emerge from their respective narratives marked with hybridity, since they are figured as agitating to combine the roles of black object and white subject, only rarely bringing these extremities of identification together. In short, their respective tragedies are expressed in terms of endeavouring to inhabit 'several selves at once'. Throughout *Othello* and '*O*', these efforts are placed on display, the experience of juggling with more than one form of identity being seen as so many modes of performance. Both films stress forms of surveillance, male bonding and homoerotic allegiance, rely on images of bars, cages and hands, and deploy arresting black and white juxtapositions, suggesting not so much a dialogue as a shared interpretation of the techniques and methods by which hybridity might be translated into a visual idiom. *Othello* and '*O*' are absorbed in their contexts, then, but in ways that are more diffuse and unexpected than topical readings allow, and through means that point up the unpredictability and extremities of a globally racial experience.

# I

At first sight, a common denominator of *Othello* and '*O*' is a subscription to negative racial stereotypes. Nowhere is this seen more obviously than in both films' rendering of the Othello character's racialized sexuality. Barbara Hodgdon is right to suggest that '*O*' entertains the 'white' fantasy that 'black men rape white women', and a more general sense of the titular protagonist's sexual power is expressed via shots of his erectile form reaching for the basketball hoop and of his successful dunking of the ball into the net: proficiency in the game on the court, it is implied, is metaphorically related to prowess in the bedroom.[14] In Parker's film, by contrast, the signature of sexuality wielded is not the ball but the sword: in a scene excised from the distributed film, for instance, Othello (Laurence Fishburne) forces Desdemona (Irène Jacob) to bow down before an altar above which is displayed a 'battle-scarred scimitar', the episode serving to draw a parallel between a phallic worship and a militaristic history.[15] Throughout *Othello*, the protagonist is eroticized as a focus of longing and projection, leading Lisa S. Starks to write that he appears 'not only as the "black stud" but also as the black aggressor'.[16] Certainly, such a figuration is in evidence in the consummation scene, in which an audience is granted direct and energetic access to Othello: the drumming soundtrack functions to summon racially typed expectation, while camerawork operates to privilege Desdemona's simultaneously excited and apprehensive point of view. 'The purchase made, the fruits are to ensue. / That profit's yet to come, 'tween me and you', announces Othello, the transposition of the lines from an external location to the bridal chamber suggesting the physical business still to be completed.[17] Clearly, the objectification of Othello here puts into play ideas about sexuality and blackness, with a white construction of raced masculinity being titillatingly entertained.

In terms of the representation of Othello and O, sexual objectification is frequently linked to a marginal cultural status. Typical in this respect is 'O': not only is the protagonist represented as infantilized and patronized ('he's all alone here ... we're his only family', the otherwise insensitive coach Duke Goulding [Martin Sheen] asserts); he is also directed to move around the basketball court in the same way that he is obliged to conform to particular behaviours by his adoptive institution. At once, this implies that O does not own himself: his value to the school entails his being imagined as its property. In Parker's film, an objectifying process is also at work in scenes which demonstrate the extent to which Othello functions as a minion or servant of the state. The comparable notion that the protagonist is construed as a species of possession is perhaps most fully articulated in an early screenplay draft in which a flashback discovers 'the BOY OTHELLO' struggling in the 'net ... thrown across him' and resisting the 'hot iron [that] brands him': the sequence elaborates a biography of exile and captivity, slavery and ownership, that persists in the film proper.[18] Hence, an echo of the branding idea survives in the representation of the tattoos that decorate Othello's form. Jane Caplan writes that body markings traditionally functioned as 'punitive and stigmatic' signs of 'criminality' or 'property'. By the same token, Othello's tattoos work as an immediate visual registration of colonial forces that have exercised themselves on him and that continue to play themselves out in the operations of Venetian society.[19] It is significant that the film begins with a shot of model ships being pushed around a map by the Duke of Venice (Gabriele Ferzetti): the implication is that Othello will be manipulated and mobilized in just such an imperially motivated fashion.

Such conventionally characterized readings are, however, complicated by a coincident – and opposite – representational strategy. That is, as much as Othello and O are adversely drawn, they are also figured as subjects rather than objects, as dominating rather than dominated, as racially advantaged rather than disabled. The dialogue of the senate scene in Parker's film, for example, is organized so as to corroborate the remark, 'Another of his fathom [we] have none' (I.i.153). This line is given to the First Senator (Philip Locke) rather than to Iago, as it is in the Folio, thereby elaborating a discursive framework within which Othello is given institutional approval and shown to be held in a unique and politically prioritized regard. According to this logic, Othello is the exemplar or representative of Venice rather than a commodity or a dependant within it. '*O*' concentrates no less evocatively on the processes whereby O comes to symbolize and even incarnate state power. The film juxtaposes shots of American flags and O's red, white and blue tracksuit with scenes of his sporting victories, which suggests not only that national values are inculcated through basketball, but also that the hero as athlete is constructed as occupying the vanguard of his institution's official policies and practices. In these representations, then, race is not so much the index of oppression as the means of exercising an important cultural authority.

In fact, in occupying both subject and object positions, the titular protagonists are articulated not only as contradictory but also as hybridized. 'Hybridity', writes Homi Bhabha, involves inhabiting 'the rim of "in-between" reality ... a boundary that is at once inside and outside'.[20] Certainly, in both *Othello* and '*O*', the emphasis is on scenes dedicated to an outsider/insider dialectic. Typical is Parker's *Othello* in which the inset dramatization of Othello's 'round unvarnished tale' (I.iii.90) significantly eschews a visual rehearsal of 'disastrous chances' and 'moving accidents' (I.iii.133–4), concentrating instead on Desdemona's reception and the Venetian setting (a picnic beneath a marquee) in which the revelations are recollected as taking place. The point is clarified in a draft in which Desdemona, in a similar flashback, encounters Othello for the first time: 'she drops a tray of silverware in shock ... fear and fascination in her eyes'.[21] Here, Othello is envisaged as an exotic 'other' who in the same moment is domestically situated: his location is quintessentially that of an '"in-between" reality'.

'*O*' traverses a comparable territory; in this film, however, hybridity is less the defining feature of the individual as it is the symptom of a more general cultural condition. Both black and white characters exploit an archetypally black vernacular (language is hybridized in relation to the polyglot nature of its contexts), and systems of identification cut across ethnic categories, to the extent that racial ideologies interact and cross-fertilize in a two-way process. Thus, Hugo can suggest to O, in a provoking flirtation with racial stereotypes about female sexuality, that 'white chicks' are 'snaky'. Likewise, in the scene in which Dell (Anthony Johnson), the black drug dealer, injects Hugo, he asks, 'Shoot the nigger some tickets'. In a location historically defined by the exploitation of the slave population, it is suggested, the black entrepreneur is enabled to exploit gaps in a mainly white political fabric, Dell deploying racist rhetoric not as a means of confirming abjection but as a route to self-promotion. O, too, is figured in hybridized terms, as when Desi (Julia Stiles) reminds him, jokingly, 'You said I was so fine you'd let me dress you up and play "Black Buck Got Loose in the Big House"'. The statement operates as a forceful illustration of an embracement of, and a resistance to, cultural history, O's professional success legitimating his impersonation of the stereotypes through which the black body was traditionally defined. O, then, shores up an insider's security by acting out the outsider's dangerous alterity. Matching the tendencies of the global scene, Othello and O are characterized by homogenizing and differentiating tendencies, with their racial affiliations sidelined and emphasized at one and the same time. Thus, it is difficult entirely to agree with Pascale Aebischer that Parker's *Othello* 'violently inscribes' a 'racist interpretation'; rather, the film, and '*O*', make available alternating constructions which bear witness to the unstable processes of racial identity formation.[22]

'Individual identity', write Ann Cvetkovich and Douglas Kellner, 'is more and more a question of articulating often conflicting cultural elements into new types of hybridized identity that combine national cultures with global ideas and images', and the often restricted nature of this conception of the self is suggested in an exchange between Dell and O lost on the cutting-room floor.[23] 'I know it's hard being "Mr I'm on my way to the N.B.A."', states Dell, adding, as he concludes his drug deal with O, 'I ... know them alumnis ... offer you all kinds of stuff (cash, cars, jewellery) ... [but] what do you call a million-dollar nigger without a million dollars? Another nigger'. Cynically telescoped, the argument here is that only money differentiates the black man: the sole route to the achievement of wealth, Dell insinuates, is sporting success or organized crime. The 'several selves' that constitute the protagonist are closed down even as they are seemingly expanded. In its fantasy evocation of the rise and fall of a black basketball player, the speech briefly conjures the similar career trajectory of another 'good kid from Carolina', Michael Jordan, who represented a 'global popular', a 'fusion of ... commodity culture and ... Americanized globalization' ultimately undone by an association with gambling, crime and scandal.[24] But, as befits the particular orientation of '*O*', Dell's disquisition is not permitted to function simply at a topical level; instead, it urges reflection on the competing forces and polysemic tendencies that are seen as crucially contributory elements to the black identity process. 'O' continually circles back to the problems and difficulties attendant on racialized selves, and even at the level of its score, with one accompanying rap song featuring the lyrics, 'What is the black star? Is it the cat with the black shades, the black car?' These questions take up where the drug dealer's leave off, not only contemplating the interrelationship between blackness and global pop celebrity but also pinpointing the role of trappings and insignia in self-creation. Such markers of the self are, however, ultimately envisaged as irrelevant to, and preventive of, the expression of an authentic racial integrity. 'There's so much to life when you just stay black', the song continues, 'Who ... else is a black star? ... Me'. In the song at least, O's identity is implicitly placed through a dedication to an unadulterated black value system, but this is only arrived at through a pluralizing, and hence potentially disruptive, negotiation with related, hybridized selves that inhabit the racial imaginary.

## II

Eric C. Brown notes that 'O' shapes and forms in the film of the same name bring to mind the 'wooden O' of Shakespeare's Globe.[25] In this sense, the signal letter provides a self-conscious basis for the film's playful manipulation of the motif of the ball of the basketball court and for the narrative emphasis on the performance of basketball itself. 'Terms of cultural engagement', writes Homi Bhabha, 'whether antagonistic or affiliative, are produced performatively'.[26] In the case of both O and Othello, theatrical actions and racialized modalities of playing constitute some of the ways in which the protagonists address their respective environments. During a slam dunk contest, O destroys and subsequently parades the broken frame of the hoop: the point is not simply that he is represented as advertising the symbolic shorthand of his name but that he enacts or dramatizes, with props, his dominant role in a game that is already inscribed with theatrical power. (Figure 7.) Given the fact, moreover, that basketball is performed in and through a number of transnational contexts ('the game', David L. Andrews suggests, is particularly suited for television because of its 'fast-paced telegenic quality'), the episode recalls to an audience that global media are no less powerful theatrical spaces for identity dissemination.[27] A performance before one audience is shaped by the presence

*Figure 7.* O (Mekhi Phifer) parades the broken basketball hoop in '*O*' (dir. Tim Blake Nelson, 2001).

of another mode of spectator, the interchangeability of the venues stressing the mediated nature of O's theatrical self-presentations.

If '*O*' culminates in a climactic display of performative power, *Othello*, by contrast, commences with a moment of theatrical subterfuge. The opening night-time montage shows a gondola crossing the Rialto canal in which a black man, dressed in black, lifts up to his face the white mask of classical tragedy. Several critics have seized on the resonances of the scene's racial impersonation, arguing that it suggests that 'in marrying a white woman, Othello is playing at being white himself'.[28] In terms of its overall effects, however, the scene has a more complex function. Its oppositional tonal scheme, for instance, anticipates Othello's contest with various articulations of himself, the *mise-en-scène* returning repeatedly to images of black and white that are blurred and conjoined. Contrary to audience expectation, Othello does not enact the gesture, which implies a difficulty of arriving at surety of knowledge. The anonymous black man is both like and unlike Othello, is similar to and different from the film's titular *alter ego*. The scene is also complicated by the simultaneous presence of Desdemona who, in a white nightgown, is discovered in a gondola moving in the opposite direction. If Othello plays at being white, Desdemona, according to the filmic logic, plays at being black, the purpose of her deceitful mission being marriage to the black protagonist. Associations of blackness and dissimulation circulating in the opening transfer themselves to Desdemona and to her rebellious flight from white, patrician society. What is performative about the scene, then, is revealed via a 'process of splitting on both sides of the [racial] division ... doubling[s] ... play across the structures of otherness'.[29] That is, the theatre staged in *Othello* reveals the extent to which racial identities can be traded even as they are self-consciously chosen: rather than pointing up the arbitrariness of race, this illustrates the ways in which selves move back and forth inside a dynamic continuum of representation, and are not always dictated to by a binary arrangement.

Identities that strive for similarity in the same moment as they aspire to difference are constructed in the films via spectacle and gaze of various kinds – a visual grammar of inspection and judgement. Not only does *Othello* reify for spectatorly involvement the bodies of the main protagonists; it simultaneously steers them into positions of public visibility: Othello is frequently pointed out and pointed at, while the lovers' reunion on Cyprus is accompanied by a lingering kiss that receives an embarrassed response from the assembled onlookers. More often than not examined from the outside rather than capable of effectively scrutinizing himself from within, it is implied, Othello and his sense of self are in jeopardy because of an imperfect connection (which is itself shaped by his racial liminality) to the visual systems of his world. In filmic realizations of the play's emphasis on sight, and matching its involvement in types of ocular proof, eyes in *Othello* become the devices of interpretation and authority. These 'looking relations', to cite Barbara Hodgdon, are abundant in one of the film's opening episodes, which shows Roderigo (Michael Maloney) watching Othello and Desdemona's marriage ceremony through a grille.[30] Because a rounded red blur briefly covers Desdemona's form in a shot that approximates Roderigo's point of view, his voyeurism functions as a cultural urge to efface white–black sexual relations. At the same time, what is glimpsed by Roderigo recalls, in order to re-enact, the play with colour, stains and spots inaugurated in the title sequence. In that composition, ideas of vision and evidence were lent a racialized cast, to the extent that Roderigo's surveillance serves to underscore the animating anxieties of his rival's identity and its unfolding narrative contours. Principally, however, it is through Iago (Kenneth Branagh) that *Othello*'s dialogue between the operations of the gaze and the trajectories of the self is conducted. Sarah Hatchuel notes that Iago 'makes the spectators participate in his plot, calling them to witness'.[31] Yet one might also add that, because he continually speaks intimately to camera and commands the filmic frame, his elaborations of identity are allowed to hold sway, his designations are granted priority and his perspective becomes a dominant. Iago excels in manipulating the audience's gaze in a series of set-pieces or vignettes. In the first, he explores the uneven reflection of Cassio (Nathaniel Parker) and Desdemona in the blade of his knife. The implication is that, just as he peels the skin from his fruit in order to eat it, so will he make naked and vulnerable the couple as part of a mission to persuade Othello to a fantastic consumption. Central to his plan is a drive to have Othello accept – in Frantz Fanon's term, 'epidermalize' – at the level of his 'skin' colour his racial 'inferiority'.[32] The knife thus acts as a deforming screen, a distorting device, which prepares the path for the equally disproportioned incarnations of the protagonist's projections. Once again, Othello's distance from a personally determined scopic regime forecasts the plotline of his tragedy, calling into question the stabilities of a potentially fragile selfhood.

Initially at least, the gaze in 'O' is less the property of a particular onlooker as it is the precondition for the hero's pre-eminence. Achievement on the basketball court is subject to continual inspection; here, key to the maintenance of a coherent identity is the visibility of O's sporting prowess. Yet, as the film develops, O is increasingly figured as inverting the ocular dynamic that constructs his performances as the focus of attention. It is through a library window that he first notices Desi and Michael (Andrew Keegan) together, while the climactic scene with the handkerchief takes place in a mirrored reflection. At these and others moments, glass functions not only as the medium of voyeurism but also as the barrier that frustrates the move to white membership and cultural integration. Thus, when O destroys the basketball hoop at the slam dunk contest, he simultaneously shatters the glass backboard, his action functioning, at least at one level, as an attempt to regain visual clarity and dismantle illusion. More urgently, his behaviour symbolically plays out a collision with, and destruction of, the forms through which infidelity has been confirmed, suggesting that, as O's fantasy constructs her, Desi too has been a reflective surface, a type of glass that must now be broken. Because the filmic narrative shows the slam dunk contest being televised on a local channel, O's glass-shattering comes to enact a separation of the self from the instruments of its media reproduction. As the protagonist's identity falters, it is suggested, so it becomes incompatible with the technologically mediated representations of successful sport spectacle.

If *Othello* and 'O' discover the flux of identity via visual registers, they also continually make racial their respective representational strategies, indigenizing motifs and images as part of the elaboration of conflicting selves. In particular, the films deploy and disrupt black and white not simply as an effect of the splitting of binary arrangements, but also as a function of the multiple claims of projection and desire, as an index to longings and avoidances that constitute psychic configurations excited by and absorbed in alterity. One of *Othello*'s vignettes is richly suggestive in this connection, since it reveals Iago picking up a log from a fire, blackening his hands and reaching forwards to cover the camera lens. On the one hand, of course, this betokens concealment: Iago obscures the process of his machinations. Thus, it is not so much that the 'soot [Iago] spreads over the "eye" of the camera ... suggests ... that the characters are overly blind', as Patricia Dorval writes; rather, to adopt Judith Buchanan's discussion of the film, Iago's gesture hints at an 'identification' with Othello that is both ongoing and inconclusive.[33] Crucially, Iago's blackening is racially charged, suggesting that, as Othello strives to whiteness, so his lieutenant agitates for blackness. Within the fiction established by this moment of filmic self-consciousness, Iago darkens the image that the camera sees, thereby playing at being black himself. As so often in *Othello*, identity is seen to slip across and between stretched racial classifications. In fact, in view of the mimicry at work in the scene, Iago's conduct evokes the minstrelsy tradition, which, as Linda Williams has argued, 'takes the form of a desire to become (at least temporarily) the primitive "Other" depicted in the caricature'.[34] The idea receives a more strident articulation in an early version of the screenplay. Here, Iago follows through the blacking-up process hinted at in the film: he 'draws his fingers down his face, smearing it black ... RODERIGO squints quizzically at the charcoal on IAGO'S face. They both look tired and faintly ridiculous: one with a face smudged with black, the other bruised and in tatters'.[35] The scene plays a variation on Venetian society's curious or 'quizzical' relationship with the hybrid, a type neither black nor white but somewhere at the 'rim of "in-between" reality'. Characteristic of other reversals and doublings is Roderigo's taking on of the mantle of a fascinated Iago, and Iago's assumption of the part of an Othello only partially successful in imposture. Together, these comprise actions that, in privileging imitation and reception contexts, draw attention to the uses of race and the extent to which it might be rethought in order to be reinvented.

'Globalization', writes Reinhart Kössler, 'is ... about the ... reorganization [and] rearrangement of difference'.[36] Certainly, the notion of difference reorganized squares with *Othello*'s racial disruptions, helping to illuminate the entertainment in '*O*' of an imagistic framework marked by discontinuity. Barbara Hodgdon observes that the bird images in '*O*' are linked to several characters at once, yet neglects to explore the ways in which these emblems are expressive of the film's alternating racial positions.[37] Unfolding in a dovecote, the opening montage overlays shots of birds with Hugo's voiceover: the effect is to suggest that he is akin to a dark hawk, while O resembles a white dove. Yet these identifications are upset as voice, narrative and music combine to muddy easy analogies: the game in progress reveals that the hawk is the mascot of the Palmetto Grove Academy basketball team and that O is the bird's synecdochal counterpart. Clearly, associations between the peaceful and the predatory are merged, but so too are conventional signifiers of race: the film undoes conventional racial attributions and reinscribes them, with O implicitly departing from and moving back to type. Complicating the scene's identifications still further are the claims for the hawk's emancipatory powers. Contrary to Hugo's view that the bird is able to 'take flight, to soar over everything and everyone', the accompanying image discovers a hawk that, in jesses, is trapped, controlled, servile. A fantasy of freedom via a raced athleticism is seen to be misplaced. This is reinforced in the film's periodic return to images of doves awash in blue: the use of a filter here points to both romanticization and misapprehension. Once again, race is troubled in order to be reinforced, the implication being that the black athlete is both a free agent and a captive object. Ideas of emancipation and captivity extend, too, to the attention '*O*' devotes to hands and cages. Frequently, the film returns to scenes that take an erotic impetus from the physical juxtaposition of the lovers' bodies. Early on, these show Desi's hand draped over O's form in a symbolic manifestation of the operations of white hegemony upon black subjectivity: Desi's father is Dean Brable (John Heard), the source of O's school sponsorship programme and thus the genealogical endpoint of racialized institutional privileges. Later, the power relation is seen to shift, and it is significant that the moment of Desi's death is accompanied by a shot of O's hand resting on her shoulder: a system-shaped nexus involving patronage and desire, protectorship and oppression, is graphically unhinged, with the reversal of the motif of the hands enacting a corresponding reversion in the protagonist's fortunes. The particular imaging of the film's climax again pushes to the fore the question of the 'free' O. It is not accidental that, bolstering Hugo's misreading, the net of the basketball hoop recalls the bars of a cage, suggesting that the protagonist is enabled and imprisoned in his calling, opened up and closed down through sport, liberated from and returned to his contexts by practices of which he is the chief representative.

Although the reorganization of difference has a place in *Othello* too, this film revolves more insistently around the phenomenon of a fated protagonist hemmed in by, and in thrall to, the symbolic and material accoutrements of his white environment. Hence, images of black and white hands indicate the trajectory of Othello's exclusion and confinement. The fact that the hands are clasped points to a form of captivity, while a succeeding inset of a white on white handclasp suggests that Othello is exiled in his scopic fantasies and increasingly set at a racial remove. Such suggestions of imprisonment are repeatedly glimpsed – the black jacket decorated with webs that Othello wears is typical – to the extent that species of cage assume a visual ubiquity. When Iago reflects on the 'web' in which he will 'ensnare ... a fly' (II.i.169), his remark makes a logistical sense, realizations of the metaphor having been allowed tellingly to circulate. Stephen M. Buhler writes that chains in *Othello* function to indicate 'the racist categories Iago has led [the protagonist] to internalize'; certainly, in the film's deployment of chess images, an attention to racial contexts, and racialized history, is implicit.[38] The black and white colour configuration of chess embeds a spectrum of colonial narratives; thus, when Iago is represented as appropriating the pieces, he effectively assumes a position of political dominance or, at least, imperial power. This is made manifest in a draft screenplay in which Iago takes over the chess game that the Duke has commenced, casting its figures on the floor and breaking in two the 'piece of the queen, [snapping it] at the neck'.[39] These moments inscribe Iago as acting out by proxy a ducal role, one which allows him to rewrite Venetian policy according to, and using the symbols of, a predetermined racial scheme. Miniaturizing and strategizing in emulation of the practices of the political elite, Iago foists onto Othello an Ottoman alterity, at each stage indoctrinating viewers in the skewed rules of his deadly racial game.

## III

The play in *Othello* and '*O*' with racial impulses that move back and forth among white and black markers of identity expresses itself intriguingly in the constructions of same-sex desire. Here, a desire for the 'other' can be seen to highlight the anxieties attendant on the disturbance of categories organized around a differential framework. Homi Bhabha writes that 'desire for the Other ... emerges *in-between* disavowal and designation', and such a movement inside a spectrum of psychological contrarieties is particularly in evidence in '*O*' and its most stridently realized homoerotic moment.[40] 'I'm going to take care of you ... brother', announces Hugo, as he cradles O in his arms, but the choreography of the scene suggests the complexities of the encounter, since the embrace is accompanied by the dealing out of cocaine to a now dependent protagonist: the conflicted amalgam of impulses sketched at this point, and the implied sublimation of desire, are the preconditions for a sexual longing that can never explicitly articulate its name. In '*O*', the narrative impetus is directed towards the growing desolation of O's form, the dependencies visited on him functioning to enable the prospect of homoeroticism. Arguably, *Othello* presses further at its same-sex subtexts, making it difficult to agree with Kenneth Rothwell's assertion that the film 'pays no attention to the fashionable vogue for ... homoerotic attraction'.[41] For the film in fact privileges the richly apparent combination of loathing and possessiveness that characterizes Iago's visual contemplation of Othello; that this constitutes a homoerotic relation is clarified during the episode of the ancient's brutal lovemaking with Emilia (Anna Patrick), in which the suggestion of sodomy bespeaks a barely suppressed imaginary of male-on-male consummation. Typically, *Othello* deploys a freeze-frame of black and white hands joined to communicate its homoerotic agenda, only here the motif indicates the loss of an old union and the rise of a new, same-sex confederacy. Thus, at the moment where, in a parody of the earlier marriage ceremony, Othello and Iago pledge themselves to each other, their alliance is registered in an act of bloodletting which is also an expression of racial mixing. As the pair's bloody hands co-mingle, the scene opens out briefly to contemplate the spectre of miscegenation, or at least the paradoxically reproductive implications of a queerly raced coupling. Of course, Iago and Othello are not figured as straightforwardly generative; rather, the sequence illuminates a discursive syntax of fear and horror, and a narrative emphasis on pollution and defilement.

It is with the extended scenes of Iago/Hugo's seduction/corruption of O/Othello that articulations of homoeroticism, and conjurations of race, receive their most sustained statement. The carefully gradated orchestration of Iago's manipulation of Othello in Parker's film opens with a militaristic stave-fight training exercise, modulates to a scene of communal washing and concludes in a conversational climax. Yet these practices, which suggest an equality of status and a racially levelled zone, are undercut by the action. Hence, Othello's aggressively sexual packing of a pistol barrel with explosives in the arsenal anticipates the explosion of his own black and white identities. At least in part, the dialogue is animated by its homoerotic undercurrents, as when Iago is figured whispering into Othello's ear: the two-shot not only figures language as the explosive force which will upset the protagonist's delicately balanced equipoise, but also establishes an idea of aural intercourse. In fact, Othello is less the comrade-in-arms here as the racialized effect of military process, the criss-cross of the gun holders evoking imprisonment and anticipating the terminus for the playing out of Iago's plot – the castle dungeons. Here, Othello walks past prisoners and is directed to his own solitary cell. The sexually-loaded trajectory of his enslavement to Iago, and the latter's implied predilection for forms of bondage, have come full circle. Crucially, the movements traced by Othello also betray the experience of his cultural abjection. A focus on instruments of torture, for instance, reinforces a sense of an empire that makes captive, tortures and 'others' enemies because of their perceived ethnic status. That Othello's imprisonment is racially determined is confirmed in a working draft of the screenplay in which the protagonist is forced to share a cell with a 'deranged' Turk, who closely 'studies' the new occupant and 'joins in' with Iago and Cassio's laughter.[42] The prisoner's curious scrutiny, it is suggested, as well as his mad fellowship, echo the theme of Othello as an object of erotic attraction while simultaneously inverting the binary that sees black as superior to Ottoman by virtue of the former's Venetian connections. In addition, the scene's ironic logic – Othello is reduced by the ideological praxis he ostensibly upholds – serves only to emphasize the fluid movements of his racial self, as his hybridity – and identity – are forced to confront unexpected combinations and proximities.

*Othello* invests in unravelling the implications and consequences of Iago's seduction; by contrast, '*O*' attends to the network of circumstances that brings it into being. Thus, while '*O*' invokes *Othello* in its representation of the protagonist's succumbing to sexual suggestion (the arsenal is replaced by a gym, with all its associations of male bonding and homoeroticism), the film is more interested in the formative process of Hugo's alienation. Within that schema, a rhetoric, and increasingly an acting out, of racial differences is paramount. During the opening basketball game, for example, the coach informs his team that 'they [the opposition] are not going to foul ... Hugo and Todd are decoys'. At once, the coach's presentation of strategy serves a narrative point: himself the exponent-to-be of strategy, Hugo will cause O to be 'fouled', or 'decoyed', by falling prey to the suggestion that Desi is 'foul' or sexually impure. Even wordplay of a less obvious kind functions retrospectively to underline the inception of Hugo's intrigue.[43] Kim Hall has argued that Shakespeare's 'language of fairness', because of its participation in a culture that distinguished between types of 'skin colour', was a 'key factor in the ... development of racial distinctions' in the early modern period.[44] Her thesis throws further light on 'O', since, by implication, what is 'fair' is antithetical to and constitutive of what is racially 'foul'. Indeed, that which is 'foul' is, according to some dictionary definitions, that which is 'foreign'.[45] Emerging from the opening is not only the gathering storm of the plotline but the raced complexion it goes on to assume. Doubled meanings, hints of a racially jealous Hugo and shots of him looking fondly and enviously at the triumphant O point up the culturally illicit desire that, at least in part, informs his developing intrigue. In William Ian Miller's words, 'what lies behind ... disgust is not foul at all but fair ... the disgusting ... has the power to allure'.[46]

Quite why Hugo is attracted to and by O is never fully addressed, although the film periodically hints at the motivating force of paternal neglect. More usually, 'O' establishes an intricate absorption in a racialized power dynamic as a context for Hugo's conduct. Discovered to be a drug-user, Hugo is penetrated by needles by the black dealer Dell: a white body made vulnerable by black power becomes the prompt for the displaced unfolding of a physically exploitative scheme. If Dell is imagined as one inspiration for the inception of strategy, so too is the English teacher who, analysing in class Lady Macbeth's persuasions to her husband, offers inadvertent encouragement to Hugo's misogynist reflections. Discussing the 'How tender 'tis to love the babe that milks me' speech, the teacher remarks, 'Lady Macbeth purposefully uses this maternal imagery to get [Macbeth] into doing [her] dirty work'.[47] Obviously, the gloss panders to constructions of female scheming, but implicit too is the idea of sexual excess: O, instructed by Hugo's fantasies, must eliminate the woman exposed as his 'dirty Desi'. To be 'dirty', however, is also to be 'foul' or 'black', and in this sense the teacher's explanation introduces the notion of a Desi who is unacceptable because she is racially 'other'. Invoking the play's elaboration of a Desdemona who, as Othello remarks, has become as 'begrimed and black / As mine own face' (III.iii.392–3), the episode establishes Desi, at least in terms of the impressionable O, as marked by a sexuality that is all the more unsettling for its departure from white normative standards or, in Elizabeth A. Deitchman's words, a concept of 'whiteness' that depends for its continuing existence on an affirmation of 'purity'.[48] The colour co-ordinates circulating in the scene, moreover (the quotation from *Macbeth* appears in white chalk written on a blackboard), means that the whole scene is infused with racial potential. Consequently, and thanks to the canonizing mediation of Shakespeare, a destructive design takes shape: Hugo will 'milk' O and parasitically nurture himself as his host – and victim – declines.

The trajectory of decline in Parker's *Othello* is momentarily halted by the film's prioritization of a belatedly articulate protagonist. 'Nay, stare not, masters. It is true indeed' (V.ii.195), Othello instructs the assembly, pointing to the bed where Desdemona's body lies and gaining a measure of autonomy in that he at last assumes for himself visual control. This does not, however, amount to healing the film's subject/object impasse. Othello's suicide by means of a chain round his neck returns us to the film's construction of a racial 'other' whose barbarity positions him as the prisoner of larger cultural forces. (Crucially, the act of Othello's self-strangulation recalls photographic images of lynchings of blacks in the American Deep South, suggesting that the significance of Laurence Fishburne as the first African-American to play Othello in a mainstream release extends well beyond his immediately filmic role.) Qualifications to the protagonist's declarations of self continue into the film's closing sequence, which shows the swaddled bodies of Othello and Desdemona being ceremoniously tipped into the sea. Imaged as separate, joined and white, the bandaged forms, it is implied, have been physically 'made good', salvaged, repatriated and given an identical racial designation. Yet that affirmation is in turn interrogated by an earlier image of the bandaged effigy of a Turk being unceremoniously dumped on a Cyprian bonfire. In that composition, the effigy worked not only as a reminder of Othello's liminal situation, but also as a predictive instrument of his later psychological conflagration. We are presented not so much with a romanticized denial of race at the end as with a reassertion of the field of operation of its differences. It is a theme that, in an excised version of the film's close, is granted a particular urgency. Lost in the editing process were two scenes: in one, the dying Iago 'presses his bloody lips and teeth to OTHELLO'S scarred shoulder-blade (where he was branded as a slave)'; in the other, the ancient's 'eyes' contemplate the 'instruments of torture clamped to his limbs. His face remains impassive'.[49] Once again, the detail of the mutual shedding of blood carries significant ideological freight. If, as Bryan S. Turner argues, 'tattoos' and 'body marks ... indicate social membership', the first scene betrays the culmination to Iago's homoerotic projections and a vampiric resolution to belong with Othello's physical and cultural space.[50] The second scene, in a meting out of narrative justice, begins to shunt onto Iago the racial identifications he had excelled in manipulating. Implicitly the 'Turk'/black body/'other' here, Iago is represented as being punished – even sexually violated – by the very symbols and mechanisms of the state system he had made his own. But, as the detail of his 'impassive' countenance implies, his captive condition is accompanied neither by the thrill of orgiastic satisfaction nor by the release of the racialized mysteries of his inner workings.

At his decline's nadir, O also recovers to deliver an impassioned peroration. 'You make sure you tell them the truth', he states, 'I ain't no different than none of you all. My mom ain't no crackhead. I wasn't no gangbanger. It wasn't some hood rat drug dealer that tripped me up. It was this white, prep school mother-fucker standing right here'. Arrestingly, O here distances himself from what bell hooks describes as the cultural construction of 'black males ... socialized to be rage-oholics'.[51] In so doing, he attempts a denial of stereotyping tendencies and prioritizes the importance of 'decent', bourgeois credentials. Drawing on the charge of accumulated negatives, O is discovered as endeavouring to redeem himself of the accusation – or expectation – that his career has been no more than a demonstration of already proven negative racial traits. The notion of redemption is extended in the accompanying soundtrack to the speech. Because the 'Ave Maria, piena di grazia' ('Hail Mary, full of grace') aria from Verdi's *Otello* is heard, it might be suggested that at its end '*O*' aspires to a recuperatively transcendent moment. Barbara Hodgdon writes that the passage functions 'deliberately [to] refer to the story's antecedents'; a fuller reading, however, comes into view if we consider its contextual anchorage.[52] Sung by Desdemona in act 4, the 'Ave Maria', as it is appropriated in '*O*', allows Desi's previously silenced perspective to enter the film's concluding polyphony and to offset its dissonances. Verdi's Desdemona, of course, is patently unlike the 'dirty Desi' of '*O*': her prayer for compassion overshadows the gendered slanders that the film and Hugo have put into circulation. As such, the operatic Desdemona is central to the re-establishment of affirmative notions of maternity. There are no invitations to maternal 'dirty work' here; instead, the aria offers a paean to the 'maternal womb' and its 'blessed fruit'. An even more general plea for redemption is also implicit, since the libretto requests mercy to be visited upon 'the sinner ... the innocent ... the weak ... the oppressed ... [and] him who bows beneath injustice': it is not difficult to see the applicability of this reflection on the marginalized to the questions of racial status and representation raised by 'O'. Yet Verdi's *Otello* is simultaneously an ambiguous and culturally riven document. The one opera in the repertory where it is still practice to perform in blackface, *Otello* has caused considerable controversy in recent years because of the continuing tradition of allowing white tenors to play the lead.[53] To bring into play *Otello*, then, is to raise issues of impersonation and hybridity, to contemplate considerations of educational training and opportunity, to gesture towards race-flecked traditions of exclusion and elitism, and even to question the limited number of professional cultural niches available to historically disadvantaged black communities. Further compromising the ending's recuperative gestures is the discovery of the fictional transmission of the film's elaboration of its racial rehearsals. The *montage* of conversations with a film crew, and the self-conscious crane-shot that shows the body-bagged participants being loaded into an ambulance, remind us of other forces that determine and divide identity, technologies of media reproduction that are typically interested in sound-bite, scandal, selective representations and the broadest picture. In the final instance, the tragedy of O is replicated only inside a demand for streamlined subjectivity and in accordance with the structural rhythms of globally dictated time slots and regimes.

## IV

Ann Cvetkovich and Douglas Kellner have argued that, 'as a response to homogenizing global forces', the late twentieth and early twenty-first centuries have witnessed an increased 'emphasis on ... individual identity'.[54] In their responses to homogeneity, filmic versions of Shakespeare's *Othello* read identity in terms of race, probing the values and applications of that conceptual and cultural category. That is, *Othello* and 'O' form a potent alliance in positing the importance of difference, both as an alternative to homogeneity and as a contributory element to it. Neither film offers a settled construction of racial identity in the global economy: racialized possibilities and limitations are entertained, negative stereotypes are erected and dismantled. The identity that is centred on race is, according to these films, insecure, vacillating and various: it is, on occasions, consciously selected as a crucial component of strategies of individual agency. This helps to explain why both films are self-conscious about names (O, 'O', Othello), not because of an anxiety about the canonical name Shakespeare, but because of the stresses and strains placed on identity in the creation of any racialized self. Very rarely in these representations do *Othello* and '*O*' make narrowly contextual their concerns; indeed, what is topical is invariably incidental, and topical parallels are suggested only to have their inapplicability exposed.

'*O*' and *Othello* trouble the multiple positions their protagonists occupy, with white and black characters imagined as projecting onto each other in ways and via movements that are fractured and plural. Such instabilities within the racialized systems of *Othello* and '*O*' permit and produce both uncertain sexual selfhoods and non-normative sexual desires. Certainly, O and Othello, according to their individual representations, circulate around several unspecified points of reference. Their in-between status suggests a process of psychological splitting and recalls Julia Kristeva's observation that 'the absence, or the failure ... to establish a unitary bent between subject and object produces [a] strange ... encompassment that is ... "empty" [and] "null" ... "powerless" outside, "impossible" inside'.[55] At one level, the films' concentration on homoeroticism is simply a displaced manifestation of what Andrew L. Barlow describes as 'a new type of conflict', generated by 'globalization', over 'membership in society'.[56] In this sense, the homoerotic subtexts of these films point up questions about how and where the self – and its variants – might be located and defined.

Even the films' elaboration of hybridity is unpredictable: it is not a constant; it does not accommodate all scenarios; it is only one identity possibility. Hybridity, in fact, is all too often the characteristic of the culture rather than of the individual. It is seen in the films to extend across, even as it determines, several players and their various cultural placements. And, if its operations are wide-ranging, they are also preeminently theatrical. The performance of the racial self in '*O*' and *Othello* goes hand-in-hand with the films' reflections upon modern media and the effects and implications of powers of reproduction. Iago's absorption in the camera in *Othello*, and O's relation to the technological programmes of global sponsorship in '*O*', remind us of the shifting and changing forms culture deploys to construct racial taxonomies and of the ways in which those taxonomies are made and unmade by the means of their dissemination.

# 5
# Remembrance, Holocaust, Globalization

Itself a commemoration of the applicability of literary representations, Michael Radford's *William Shakespeare's 'The Merchant of Venice'*, released nationwide on 3 December 2004, entered the end of its run as the 'Day of Remembrance' – the sixty-year anniversary of the liberation of Auschwitz – unfolded.[1] The film works inside historically sensitive representations of Judaism, salient indications of which are inscribed in the ways in which the Holocaust has been skirted around in *The Merchant of Venice*'s critical reception. Either the legacy inherent in the film has been cursorily introduced or it has been summoned only to be rejected.[2] In interview, the director touched on the issue in a curiously noncommittal fashion, stating, '[the play] is about anti-Semitism ... in a particular period of history'. 'When we've been through the Nazi holocausts', he continues, 'when we've been through the Russian pogroms of the nineteenth century, and all the rest of it, at the moment you don't really want to bring all this stuff up again'.[3] Even as Radford conjures the informing insistence of the Holocaust, so he endeavours to deny the significance of its role in an argument that edges towards playing down the Nazi atrocity. The contradictory logic takes refuge in a construction of 'history' that does not repeat itself in the same moment as it conflates and homogenizes very different expressions of ethnic persecution.

Even as Radford faced the press came a forceful reminder of the associations embedded in Shylock's name. A Labour Party election campaign poster depicting Jewish Tory Party leader Michael Howard, 'clad in black, one hand outstretched and the other clutching a gold watch', was arraigned in the media for suggesting 'characterizations of Shylock' and was deemed particularly offensive in view of the coincident honouring of victims of genocide.[4] Another Labour poster distributed that week caused concern because it superimposed Howard's face on a pig in flight.[5] Both images were criticized for their ideologically loaded content; and both were questioned for mortgaging Shylock and anti-Semitism in ways that the history of the twentieth century has made morally reprehensible. The controversy confirmed that any invocation of Shakespeare's play enters into an anxiously written over and ideologically fraught global field.

In the charged proximity of its period of release, and in the peculiarity of its conception of Shylock, *The Merchant of Venice* betrays what amounts to a marked sensitivity towards – combined with a paradoxical reluctance fully to acknowledge – the framing conditions of its imaginative scheme. The director's circumlocutions notwithstanding, *The Merchant of Venice*, sometimes openly, sometimes in spite of itself, is dialectically determined by evocations of and returns to the Holocaust. In its rendition of the relations between Christian and Jew, and its invention of fundamentalist cultures which, enabled by the involvement of the dominant class, promote persecution, the film deploys a grammar of Holocaust memory, while at the same time enlisting stereotypical images of an idealized early modern Venice as a means of distancing itself from too close a contemporary engagement. That is, *The Merchant of Venice* mobilizes two opposing strategies: it seeks (either through visual appeals or textual contraction) to install itself inside a recognizable rubric of ostracization and suffering even as it aims at forestalling the summoning of modern analogies on the part of its audience. The aestheticization of Venice is, in fact, a form of anaesthetization, a means of offsetting what is unpalatable about the film's subject and its content. The procedure constitutes a double movement – what Jacques Derrida has labelled in another context 'a double gesture' – which amounts to 'a general displacement of the system'.[6]

In this sense, *The Merchant of Venice* is rarely consistent in its operational methods. A common strategy is for it to traverse and bring together, even as it separates and distinguishes between, two constructions of the Jew in global culture. On the one hand, particularly in its representation of Shylock, *The Merchant of Venice* bears witness to David Carroll's argument that 'aggressive "self-defence" at all costs must be the political principle of the post-Shoah era'.[7] On the other hand, it plays out the ways in which 'the image of the Jew as absolute victim emerges from a re-reading of history in the light of ... genocide in a period in which victims as such occupy a privileged place'.[8] Consequently, *The Merchant of Venice* as a film is less anti-Semitic as it is about anti-Semitism, a cinematic work that is distinctive for attempting to pursue – and withdraw from – the implications of its field of ideological production. As such, the film is keen to elaborate, but never to become wholly reliant on, instances of cultural bias through the use of the documentary mode, the privileging of set-pieces, structural reorganization and the deployment of visual motifs. Typical here is the way in which, in the build-up to the trial scene and during its aftermath, *The Merchant of Venice* either conjures, in order to mediate, landmark Hollywood productions about the Holocaust or interpolates reminders of Shylock's fate. Unlike the play, in which Shylock disappears from act 4 onwards, the film fills the absence his departure creates: it is unable to exorcize the Jew. In this connection, the prioritizing of Jessica, and nowhere more obviously than in the film's final montage, makes sense as a means of addressing the culturally resonant – and contemporaneously inflected – question of Shylock's alienation from his community. Bearing the responsibility for testifying to and articulating *The Merchant of Venice*'s traumatically (un)spoken subtexts, Jessica carries the narrative beyond the generic resolution of act 5 into the generative epilogue required by the twenty-first century's global marketplace.

I

In the opening moments of *The Merchant of Venice*, a quick-fire montage shows, variously, a Franciscan friar (Jules Werner) in a boat engaged in an anti-Semitic harangue, a riot taking place on the Rialto Bridge in which a Jewish usurer is tipped into the Grand Canal, and the movements and activities of the central players. The interpolated sequence serves a variety of purposes: at once, it introduces us to the film's forms and manifestations of religious hatred, establishing a milieu of fanaticism in which Shylock (Al Pacino) is a potential object of attack and in which Antonio (Jeremy Irons) is complicit in the violence directed at the Jewish population. (Figure 8.) This is implied both in a cross-cut shot that links Antonio with the ejection of the usurer from the bridge and in an accompanying episode that reveals the merchant receiving the sacraments at the waterside. Because the officiating priest was seen earlier as the xenophobic friar, and because both he and Antonio are visually connected via crucifix motifs, the film suggests that church sanctions facilitate and legitimate persecution on an individual and group basis. John W. Mahon has remarked that the Latin chant sounding here includes the refrain 'Adjutorium nostrum in nomine domini' ('Our help is in the name of the Lord'), but neglects to consider that such diegesis reinforces a sense of the way in which a

*Figure 8.* Shylock (Al Pacino) and Tubal (Allan Corduner) contemplate their inimical environment in *William Shakespeare's 'The Merchant of Venice'* (dir. Michael Radford, 2004).

phobic practice may be institutionalized.[9] The presence in the waterside scene of Salerio (John Sessions) and Solanio (Gregor Fisher) clarifies the point: although the narrative impression is that they seek a blessing for their forthcoming voyages, the contrary idea – that they are thanked for their parts in the riot – is allowed simultaneously to circulate. Together, these sequences are crucial in initiating a powerful interplay between Christian hypocrisy and Jewish exclusion. Images of visored Venetians and bare-breasted prostitutes preparing for a nighttime assignation point up the ways in which Christian sexuality and moral dissimulation are inextricably allied. In addition, the fact that masks are represented as being worn as a fashion statement rather than as carnival accessories suggests that, in the film's vision of dank repression and seedy extremism, there is forever something to hide. From such a world Shylock is visibly distanced. An audience is granted several shots of Bassanio (Joseph Fiennes), Graziano (Kris Marshall) and Lorenzo (Charlie Cox) having doors unbolted for them – the Christian majority controls entrance into and egress from the ghetto – but *The Merchant of Venice* offers no corresponding image of mobility from Shylock's perspective. Both in terms of civic freedom and urban bias,

Shylock is constructed as marginal even before his first appearance, and this is confirmed when, during the Rialto Bridge sequence, he is spat upon by Antonio: the expulsion of the fluid, it is suggested, mimes Venice's exiling of the Jews, with the Christian body displacing onto the Jewish 'other' that which it does not wish to incorporate. Enacting in cinematic language Shylock's observation that Antonio expectorates 'upon my Jewish gabardine', *The Merchant of Venice* gives graphic illustration to a culture of intimidation and rejection.[10] At the same time, because it contains a number of spitting scenes, the film works to establish antithetical treatments of 'others' as belonging to a perniciously pervasive condition. Shylock, in fact, to adopt Slavoj Žižek's term, is seen as an 'external intruder into [the Christian] social body': if not the 'cause of the antagonisms which threaten the harmony of this body', he is certainly one of its symptoms, as the 'antagonism' that envelops his appearance is both played out on him and directed at the economic practices of which he is a chief representative.[11]

Characteristic of Radford's filmic procedure is a prioritization of visuals and institutions that, in terms of modern memory, are forcefully communicative. The detailing of the ghetto is one such instance, but so too is the attention to the red hat Shylock wears outside its confines.[12] This resonates less with an audience's awareness of sixteenth-century practice as with a knowledge of the insignia thrust on Jews during the Third Reich, for, as early as 1939, all 'Jews and Jewesses' were ordered to wear a white arm band and a blue Jewish star as distinguishing markers of difference.[13] At every stage of the film's opening, such layerings of representation are in evidence. Hence, the friar's harangue – 'if [a man] has exacted usury and taken increase ... he shall not live ... he shall surely die' – closely echoes the Book of Ezekiel, and, in view of the Old Testament book's fiery conception of law and rightfulness, judgment and truth, this seems a peculiarly pertinent text to instance in the context of a filmic representation of religious conflict.[14] There is more than a connection implied between the angry millenarian dream of destruction in Ezekiel and the genocidal realities of modernity. As Doris L. Bergen notes, Nazi propaganda was distinctive for deploying allusions from the Old Testament negatively to identify perceived Jewish practice and to license and rationalize anti-Semitic programmes.[15] Similarly, if glimpses of torches setting alight the Talmud and the Torah cohere with the narrative stress on Christian antipathy to Jewish culture, they bring to mind in more strident fashion the propaganda spectacles of Hitler's Germany: in May 1933, Goebbels organized a book-burning ceremony in Berlin, claiming that 'the era of an exaggerated Jewish intellectualism is forever over'.[16] *The Merchant of Venice* is both selective and self-aware in its elaboration of a world in which Jew and Christian uneasily coexist: it aims at precision in its realization of sixteenth-century Venice while simultaneously allowing the identifying features and political forms of modern mass persecution movements to surface.

At the start of the introductory sequence, an explanatory text scrolls across the screen: receiving particular emphasis is the establishment of a place and a time – 'Venice 1596'. Several reviewers have commented on the 'documentary' feel of this attempt at verisimilitude; more striking, however, is the fact that the documentary mode, either as it emerged in such features as Leni Riefenstahl's *Triumph of the Will* (1934) or as it has been taken up in more recent television programming devoted to the rise and fall of Hitler, has evolved into a charged site for assessing and interrogating anti-Semitism in particular and the minoritization of ethnic peoples in general.[17] Equally important is the documentary's possession, as one critic writes, of 'an indexical bond, a referent, to the historical real', and nowhere is that association with authenticity more obvious than in representations of the aftermath of the Holocaust, with location footage of concentration camps bringing the critical import of the documentary into the public forefront.[18] In such a way, Radford's decision to favour a realist mode for at least part of *The Merchant of Venice* might be seen as ideologically freighted: his concept of the early modern is invariably mediated, filtered through the twentieth century's most seared images and associations. The film understands Renaissance history as part of a trajectory that culminates in the Holocaust. Its salient moments are invariably retrospective: they stand in for the particularity of history as well as its sweep and development, always functioning to signify in relation to a modernity that is as purposefully instanced as it is unwittingly conjured.

Such is the force of the inaugural sequence that its reverberations continue to be felt into the film proper. Central here is the mode enlisted for the realization of the 'Hath not a Jew eyes?' protest, which, alongside the opening, constitutes the episode most concerned with the political processes of anti-Semitism. 'We put the camera on the shoulder', states Radford, reflecting on the filming of Shylock's denunciation of his Christian detractors, 'It was as if we were doing a documentary'.[19] Shaky visuals and unsteady POVs are forcefully indicative of the genre, but so too are the washed-out hues and pale-blue filters that throw into relief the richly saturated palette of the rest of the film. In a work that is otherwise wholly realist, this is the closest *The Merchant of Venice* comes to black and white, a tonal decision that is made all the more arresting in the light of the one colour – Shylock's red hat and gabardine – that the scene makes obvious. The meanings summoned by black and white, of course, are dependent on the context-specific nature of its deployments. 'That is how we recall the Holocaust', states Steven Speilberg, justifying his use of black and white in his film *Schindler's List* (1993), and arguably lending credence to his reading is the landmark documentary, Alain Resnais' *Nuit et Brouillard* (1955).[20] Here, a 'searing indictment' of the Nazi genocide appears inside the 'frequent shifts between black-and-white archive footage of the extermination camps, and sequences in warm colour filmed in the verdant surroundings of a former camp'.[21] The interplay between past and present, harrowing activity and present-day abandonment, human desolation and natural fecundity, are integral to the documentary's polemical project. Radford's referencing system enables *The Merchant of Venice* implicitly to ponder representation and aesthetics, with his film not so much invoking the Holocaust itself as the media through which its horrors have been transmitted.

Lending a particular urgency to the allusive rendering of 'Hath not a Jew eyes?' is *The Merchant of Venice*'s mobilization of what is arguably *Schindler's List*'s key motif. Standing out from the prevailing black and white is the image of a red-coated little girl separated from her parents during the deportation from the ghetto to the concentration camps. Later glimpsed as a corpse tossed on a cart, her anonymity stands in synecdochal relation to the extermination of nameless masses at the same time as her colour-specific particularity constructs her as a point of individual emotional reference. Identified through the use of the same primary colour, the girl and Shylock are allied, suggesting that the latter's situation is paradigmatic of a history of suffering, both early modern and modern, and that his volubility speaks to the trials and fates of the Holocaust's lost generations. For if, as Richard Burt argues, Shakespeare's 'sublime status ... available only through memory, is the means by which the Holocaust may indirectly be given a sense of tragic grandeur', then the Holocaust is also enshrined in Shakespeare, and particularly in films which cite the Bard as part of their engagement with the inexplicable horrors of twentieth-century forms of persecution.[22] In a fraught moment of Roman Polanski's *The Pianist* (2002), for instance, Henryk Szpilman (Ed Stoppard) reads out the 'Hath not a Jew eyes?' speech, to which his brother, Wladyslaw Szpilman (Adrian Brody), responds, 'Very appropriate'. In this reworking of the play's most canonical passage, there is seen to be a mutually enabling relation between the physical deprivations of the Jews and

Shylock's demand for an acknowledgement of sensory and bodily universality. In a reversal of this dynamic in *Schindler's List*, Amon Goeth (Ralph Fiennes) quotes the same lines to Helen Hirsch (Embeth Davidtz) as part of his attempt to sexually intimidate his Jewish domestic. Here, it is the Christian rather than the Jew who summons a theory of sameness, ultimately, however, to reject the notion that the two may appear alike. Whatever position these films assume, they still discover Shylock's eloquence as symptomatic of a recurring scenario of the playing out of anti-Semitic prejudice. Even before *The Merchant of Venice* offers its particular reading of Shylock, his most impassioned moment has been transformed. To adopt a formulation of Žižek, his 'always-already symbolized' speech is 'constituted' and 'structured' by the filmic understandings of the Holocaust that precede it.[23] Over and above its ostensible point, 'Hath not a Jew eyes?', by virtue of intertextuality, takes on both the ideologies and the execution of the Holocaust as its underlying premise.

## II

If the mediation of 'Hath not a Jew eyes?' testifies to the emphasis the film places on it, so too do the actions that preface, accompany and follow its delivery. In and of itself, the play's set-piece is also a heightened filmic moment: passers-by are represented as pausing to listen to Shylock's self-defence (it is envisaged as a civic spectacle), while reaction shots of prostitutes suggest that this is a justified outburst that is received sympathetically. Furthermore, because the speech is filmed in its entirety, the narrative rhythm is obliged to slow, with attention being directed to utterances that are underscored as interpretively important. These foregrounding strategies are complemented by a rhetorical and structural scheme that, in prioritizing praxes of exploitation, once again conjures Holocaust spectres, albeit at several removes. Before the exchange with Solanio and Salerio, for instance, Shylock is figured approaching a brothel from whose upper window come prostitutes' interpolated taunts, 'Take some pleasure with us! Taste my Christian flesh!' The communal mockery, and the metaphorical approximation of meat, flesh, eating, consumption and sexual/financial exchange, grant a new visual focus to Shylock's separateness as well as providing a narrative backdrop for his subsequent imaginings. For, as this moment functions to reveal Shylock's own subjugation and continuing exemption from Christian practice, so does it generate the fantasy projection in which Jessica is seen kissing a woman, trading her ring for a monkey and watching a dice game. The brothel is the connecting key: Jessica, as she appears in the flash-cut accompanying Tubal's (Allan Corduner) delivery of 'news' (III.i.88) from Genoa, has transformed herself through money into a type of prostitute – or, at least, has cheapened in the wake of profligacy and the renunciation of her Jewish identity. After 'Hath not a Jew eyes?', then, as the book-ended exploitation sequence concludes, reflections on loss and faithlessness, which are mediated through a reminder of the intersections between bodies and economics, make Shylock's condition the point of interest. Jessica's elopement positions the filmic gaze on the social and cultural abandonment of Shylock, with the pointing up of the 'daughter' and the playing down of the 'ducats' being used to invite empathetic engagement.

Interiors and interpolations are instrumental in *The Merchant of Venice* in privileging Shylock's outsider role. The interior of his house, for instance, is imagined as small, cramped and nervously patrolled and protected, a sharp contrast to the sumptuous garishness of the Christian residences: deputized by Shylock, Jessica (Zuleikha Robinson) is entrusted both with the keys and the responsibility for closing the curtains and shutters, suggesting a fortress-like living space and a domestic environment marked by its inaccessibility. The sepia tones enlisted, and the corresponding idea of a 'blackout', function to establish an impression of wartime frugality and anxiety. The designer Benoit Delhomme wanted the 'look' of these scenes to be 'murky ... sombre [and] ... dark'.[24] Certainly the film produces such an atmospheric effect; more powerfully, however, it is a mediated construction of the modern ghetto, here merged with a quasi-photographic discovery of the experience of the London blitz, that makes for a sense of Jewish dispossession and besiegement. Notable is the distinctive treatment accorded Shylock's discovery of Jessica's flight. In Q1, his reactions are a matter of report; the film, however, intercuts between dramatizations of the return from the feast, the departure of Bassanio, the opening of the house and the aftermath of Jessica's elopement. Consequently, because an audience sees Shylock and hears his responses – 'Jessica!' and 'No!' are inserted exclamations – access to an illusion of a fraught subjectivity is granted and a construction of agony is made directly accessible, one which anguished sobs make all the more emphatic. What is entirely mediated in the play is only partially mediated in the film: Solanio's report is half-realized and, on delivery, is adversely affected by the encounter with Shylock that has been previously emotionally engineered in the *mise-en-scène*. Coloured adversely by the temporal sequence into which it is inserted, Solanio's report, despite its inclusion of Shylock's 'O, my ducats! O, my daughter!' (II.viii.15), is angrily jaundiced, particularly in view of the 'dog Jew' (II.viii.14) ascription which takes a tonally dominant role. All is cinematically subdued to the prevailing image of Shylock in the rain and to an experience of isolation that, because set alongside the representation of the festively communal enterprise of Bassanio's departure, is granted ideological priority.

Typically, the film pares down the text, but it does so significantly to shift the play's orientations and premises. Hence, cuts minimize the markers of Shylock's stereotypical Jewishness, as is testified to by the removal of his economic rivalry with Antonio (I.iii.37–47), his 'interest' speech (I.iii.72–86) and the lamentations (II.viii.16–22, III.i.73–4) relating to his monetary losses. The effect is to downplay the elaboration of Shylock's own prejudices, to bypass suggestions of miserliness and fiscal probity, and to spotlight hatreds whose unsettling circulation resides in their apparent causelessness.[25] As several reviewers have noted, referring to the fact that, as Thomas A. Pendleton remarks, this 'is in effect the first post-holocaust film of the play', emerging from such amputations is a forcefully realized sense of Shylock's victimhood.[26] The notion informs Pacino's method-acting approach, as when he observes that 'Shylock ... was alone, his wife died recently [and] he was the victim of an abusive ... restricted life'.[27] The prior narrative of love and exile developed here is channelled through a construction of oppression and ill-treatment. Victimhood is also signposted in the film proper, as when the stealing of Shylock's jewels is graphically demonstrated (the effect is to suggest that his home is looted or ransacked) and lines that editorial tradition has consigned to asides (such as 'I have a daughter' [IV.i.290]) are delivered as public utterances. Consequently, a tension in imaginative response is generated, with the courtroom crowd rebuffing a Shylock who, because less inward and more expressive, becomes a focus for the film audience's identification.

'Much as the flesh' in the play 'becomes impossible to define in clearly delimited terms', writes Lisa Freinkel, so do 'Janus-like ambivalences render the difference between Jew and Christian undecidable'.[28] Under Radford's direction, such a lack of distinction is expressed via visual motifs that analogize the interrelations with which film wrestles. Taking the place of text, these function to privilege ideas about persecution and identification, cultural tension and physical violence, and the contemporary resonances of these conceptual categories. When Shylock, contemplating the bond, requests that a goat's throat be cut, the film is provided with its most abundantly articulate visual motif.

At once, of course, the goat stands in a metonymic relation to Antonio: both man and animal, in a montage that embraces this moment of bloodletting and the trial scene, are subjected to knives and scales, and both are deployed to imply species of 'innocence'. The fur collar that Antonio wears reinforces the parallel, operating as it does to elide human and non-human distinctions. Inserting itself into the film's verbal scheme, the motif also works figuratively to render the desire for a 'pound' of 'flesh' (I.iii.145–6): the purchase of the goat as a commodity prefaces and inflects the financial bartering that will take place in and around Antonio's body. Yet if the 'scapegoat' phenomenon, described by René Girard as 'the very basis of cultural unification, the source of all rituals and religion', is enacted and directed in an animal's death-throes, it is no less forcefully broadened in its field of identification.[29] Shylock's actions suggest that he too is a scapegoat – of Christian policy and attitude – and the substituted body required for anti-Semitic activity. As Theodor W. Adorno and Max Horkheimer acknowledge, writing 'when the end of the Nazi terror was within sight', 'Jews' are 'the scapegoats ... for individual [and] ... broader ... manoeuvres and machinations'.[30] Their argument helps to illuminate the ways in which *The Merchant of Venice* divides and brings together Christian and Jewish notions of 'flesh', finally electing, through what is at a narrative level the sale of kosher meat, to identify Shylock as the type and individual selected by the dominant culture for the purposes of its 'unification' programme. Through its analogical application, and the symbolic signals its visual deployment generates, the goat is constitutive of a fractious connection between Jew and Christian and a shared endeavour to remain distinct. More specifically, by working in two directions, the motif summons in order to question the kinds of adversarial mindset that, in terms of the formation of Fascist ideology, played a crucial historical role.

At its first and last physical appearance, the goat is linked to the film's second visual motif, which reveals itself in a series of shots of blood or blood-related images. First impressions suggest a Christian frame of reference for the schema. For instance, in a transitional visual interlude, we see the bond being sealed with blood-red wax that, because heart-shaped, reinforces a sense of the vulnerability of Antonio's anatomy and hints at the 'part of [his] body' (II.i.147) that Shylock will later target. (At a subsidiary level it is an unrequited 'heart' – or a repressed homoeroticism – that leads Antonio to come to Bassanio's financial rescue and fatefully to contract himself.) Yet blood is also instrumental in guiding responses to Shylock during the trial scene, in keeping the implications of 'Hath not a Jew eyes?' at the imaginative forefront and in expanding upon the representation of a cultural system inimical to Jewish participation. A characteristic of *The Merchant of Venice* is its diegetic dovetailing, and the sizzling sound made by the wax in the sealing of the bond extends into an aural register the persecutory ramifications of the book-burning scene, while the insignia of a cross on Antonio's ring recalls the film's juxtaposition of Christian and fundamentalist registers and the organizational aspects of anti-alien feelings. Interestingly, although Antonio is figured as sealing the bond with his ring, he does not touch the paper: his hand is gloved, suggesting that he strives to avoid contact with Shylock, to remain apart from the physical processes of their unwelcome fraternization. To adopt Adorno and Horkheimer's discussion of 'false projection', there is a strategy of 'morbid' and 'hostile' avoidance about this 'intimate experience', and this is continued in the transitional composition, which shows Portia, dressed in red and wearing a red-jewelled tiara and necklace, greeting Morocco.[31] Such colour-specific details, combined with the accompanying image of black and white hands conjoined, underscore Portia's unwilling involvement in a world in which her body is mortgaged to a cross-racial encounter: her line about Morocco's 'complexion' (II.vii.79) may be cut, but her association with blood and her entry into the film's symbolic economy work to position her too as a qualified repository of prejudice. Commenting on the play's metaphorical clusters, Eric S. Mallin states that however 'we take "blood" ... Shylock's exclusion from [it] absolutely figures his position on the social and spiritual margins'.[32] By contrast, in the film, Shylock and blood share an inclusive relation, perhaps nowhere more obviously than in the feast celebrating Bassanio's departure for Belmont. Shylock is represented with a full glass of red wine in front of him which he studiously avoids drinking, while Antonio is seen digging into the flesh of a piece of fruit with his knife. The ideas of bodily penetration and blood loss at work here apply not so much to Antonio as to Shylock, the implication being that it is the latter rather than the former who will be harmed, injured and violated. That suggestion is taken up in the trial scene when, lifting up the wax-encrusted bond to public scrutiny, Portia declares that 'no drop of blood' (IV.i.301) must be shed: given that her announcement coincides with Shylock's defeat, an audience is stimulated to contemplate the points of contact running between the operations of state institutions and the treatment accorded minority constituencies. Or, to put this deployment of the blood motif in terms of a Holocaust imaginary, the visual organization of the trial continues the circulation of the associations embedded in Shylock's questions, 'Hath not a Jew eyes? ... If you prick us do we not bleed?' (III.i. 49–50, 54). Crucially, the tracing through of red into the film's most succinct statement of rejection and expulsion means that *Schindler's List* is once again visually recalled, with Shylock's proximity to blood becoming synonymous with the red-coated little girl. As a result, the process of Shylock's formation as a cultural outsider is granted an unsettling prominence, and the forces that contribute to his segregation are critically illuminated.

It is during the trial scene that the film pushes to the furthest point its victim-aware exposition of Shylock and displays to the full its post-Holocaust representational manoeuvres. 'I [tried] ... to design it as a bear pit', states Radford, commenting on the trial in a formulation that reveals a historically divided interpretation of the treatment to which Shylock is subjected.[33] On the one hand, the invocation of the sixteenth-century sport of bear-baiting points to a stress on cinematic realism and the recovery of a historically authenticated locale.[34] On the other, the associated echoes of 'Jew-baiting' in the observation – and the submerged allusion to the beatings, boycotts, lootings and disturbances that preceded and in part justified the institution of the ghettos – mean that Radford installs Shylock inside, and understands his construction according to, a modern idiom: Nazi Germany's attempted eradication of the Jewish people.[35] Typically, this is a 'double gesture', one that encourages an analogy only to 'displace' its field of reference. That these modes of exploitation have an ethnic or racial bias is confirmed when Shylock, noting that the 'purchased slave' is 'use[d] in abject ... parts' (IV.i.89, 91), gestures to a black servant fanning his master. The textual point – that Antonio is owned in the same way as the slave – is upstaged by the film's general absorption in forms of ethnic persecution and the trial scene's particular reading of Shylock, who, encircled, embattled and spat upon, appears an unlikely prospect for the execution of a citizen's rights. Not so much the Venetian master as the raced servant, he is, via the film's positioning of his physical form, unfavourably judged from the sequence's inception, and not even the stichomythic banter (V.i) between Lorenzo and Jessica can alleviate the impression of an unsympathetically predetermined legal system. In the film's organization of events, the exchange appears *before* the climactic juridical encounter and is therefore robbed of its remedial and recuperative functions. Yet the trial scene also works to privilege competing versions of Shylock – he is martyr and revenger; his anger is justified and excessive – and mediates this via moving between Tubal's appalled and empathetic reaction shots. Across Tubal's face is written a crucial understanding of Shylock's motivation, but not his means for righting wrongs, of the legitimacy of his rage, but not the mode of execution. In this connection, it is significant that such an alternating picture is patently not a feature of the inarticulate Shylock who receives the court's final judgment. Because his choked response to the pronouncement that he must give up his goods and convert to Christianity recalls his anguish at the loss of Jessica, a romantic or at least familial modality is again momentarily entertained. The nodding, bobbing motions that Shylock is glimpsed as performing here, moreover, hark back to the opening scene in the synagogue and emphasize the cultural dislocation involved in the narrative reversal of fortune – it is as if his prayers have gone unanswered. Consistent with the film's visual strategy, a focus on an image carries the weight of the broken Shylock, as he exits with luggage that has been wrenched into a signifier of his homelessness and defeat.

## III

Playing on the suggestion of rejection and loss is the film's deployment, in a specially composed musical adaptation, of the final lines of *Paradise Lost*, in which Adam and Eve are described as leaving paradise: 'The world was all before them, where to choose / Their place of rest, and providence their guide: / They hand in hand with wandering steps and slow, / Through Eden took their solitary way'.[36] The score overlays both an image of a pensive Jessica by the Belmont seashore and an inset of Shylock being barred from the synagogue: this establishes a further connection between them, with the film suggesting that, either through choice or force, father and daughter have both lost their prelapsarian existence. Moreover, it is the removal of the father's world that has jeopardized the happiness of Jessica's new state. Countering the play's unsatisfactory withdrawal from the main plot, the film inset of the significantly hatless Shylock keeps his situation active: his rejection by his community introduces another form of ghettoization, while the spectacle of his displacement is akin to a deportation. If, as Siniša Malešević argues, ethnicity 'is a social relation in which social actors perceive themselves ... as being culturally distinct collectivities', Shylock here is robbed of those performances of belonging and thus of the defining terms of his identity.[37] As Arthur Isak Applbaum remarks in a discussion of the 'dread' of globalization, 'losing one's culture is one of the gravest injuries ... because it damages personhood itself'.[38]

Certainly, the representation of Shylock's eviction strikes a chord in the context of the geographical displacements and cultural disorientations that have been generated in part by the global process. *The Merchant of Venice* cannot allow Shylock's narrative extermination, of course, but it is ready to contemplate – and prioritize – his exile and diaspora. In terms of the discourses of subsequent histories of the Holocaust, 'trauma', as Cathy Caruth writes, 'can make possible survival', but this in turn is dependent on the knowledge that 'there has been a death', the 'death encounter [being] central to [the survivor's] psychological experience'.[39] By extension, what is memorialized in Jessica is the cultural 'death' of Shylock, and her 'experience' of what amounts to his 'death encounter' becomes in the film and in terms of a narrative beyond one of the conditions of her recovery.

The ending of *Paradise Lost*, sandwiched, as it is, between the tragedy that was and the better world that might be, thus seems an apposite moment to invoke for a film preoccupied with the traumatized relationship between the past, the present and the future. For, at the same time as the diegesis allows *The Merchant of Venice* to look forwards, so it facilitates a backward glance. Immediately before the inset of Shylock an audience is granted a glimpse of Antonio gazing out of Portia's palazzo. The implication is clear: Antonio too has forfeited his paradise, with the commencement of the Miltonic musical theme at this point reinforcing the sense of loss. Because of the momentary alignment of Shylock and Antonio, answers to questions about definition and identification are clearly enunciated. At once, an emphasis on Antonio's solitary status, and the nostalgic modality in which he is wedged, definitively establish the character's inseparability from ideas of surrogate victimhood and personal sacrifice. To be denied paradise, moreover, is to be symbolically castrated. The fact that the *Paradise Lost* lines are sung by the counter-tenor Andreas Scholl illustrates the point, for the counter-tenor voice is the closest modern approximation to the early modern castrato, suggesting that a combination of filmic retrospection and musical accompaniment functions to fix Antonio in the role of a 'tainted wether of the flock' (IV.i.113).[40] In another sense, *The Merchant of Venice* aspires to figure all of its central players as in some ways robbed of potency: by positioning in quick succession Antonio, then Shylock and finally Jessica, it points to a common praxis, or shared heritage, of renunciation and involvement – exile is general, the 'fall' is a universal.

It is, of course, Shylock's departure from the narrative after the trial scene that necessitates Jessica's increasing visual and aural prominence.

Emerging from the expansion of her role is a form of guilt into which the film reads a culturally restorative component. Whereas the play centres on a Jessica who is 'much ashamed of [her] exchange' (II.vii.35) into a boy, the film represents a woman who is tortured by the knowledge of the abandonment of her father and 'tribe' (I.iii.52). Her anxiety and suffering are consistently returned to, not least through a lingering concentration on her pained countenance, on adverse weather conditions and on wistfully traditional Israeli music. Such a reading takes further what Lisa Lampert has identified as an ambiguity at the heart of the play; as she states, there is always the possibility that Jessica's 'beautiful exterior may belie an intractable Jewish essence'.[41] Certainly, Jessica is discovered ill-at-ease in her Christian surroundings. She finds little pleasure in the banter with Lorenzo, not least because the exchange is denuded of its comic buoyancy (V.i.1–24). Contrary to her lover's protestations, there is no 'sweetness' or 'harmony'. And, at the announcement towards the close that she and her husband are to inherit her father's possessions, Jessica can appear only faintly horrified. It is significant, then, that *The Merchant of Venice* elects to show Jessica choosing not to retire with Lorenzo: the implication is that she refuses to 'lie' (V.i.153), verbally or sexually. Instead, she is figured running down to the shoreline, looking longingly back towards Venice and fingering a ring on her finger. This is the 'turquoise' (III.i.101) that Shylock feared his daughter had sold, and the contrasting precious retention of the familial ring points up a misplaced construction of Jessica's behaviour. Samuel Crowl writes that this episode illuminates Jessica's 'divided loyalties', yet the *mise-en-scène* works more incisively, I would argue, to underscore a continued devotion to familial relations and histories.[42] It is at Portia's promise to 'answer ... faithfully' (V.i.298) that Jessica elects to leave, implying that, in many ways, she comes to embody this virtue. In sharp contrast to Portia's ring, which, as Karen Newman states, 'in its multiple metonymic travels ... accumulates ... associations of cuckoldry ... female unruliness [and] ... women's changeable nature and ... deceptiveness', Jessica's ring signifies steadfastness, constancy and obedience.[43] Crucially, the faith that Jessica incarnates is religious rather than romantic, a distinction that the design of her ring is instrumental in establishing. Incorporating a miniature ark of the covenant, the repository of the Ten Commandments, the ring enshrines an allegiance to Old Testament 'law' as opposed to New Testament 'mercy'. In so doing, it both directs attention to the unsettling clash of convictions on display in the trial scene, arguably inviting further identification with Shylock's construction of justice, and hints at Jessica's disavowal of her conversion. Via the introduction of a ring that the play barely mentions, *The Merchant of Venice* institutes another layering of betrayals and allegiances, pressing at the presence of Jessica in order to assert a reaffirmation of her Jewish attachments. And, because Jessica is represented holding her hands together as if in prayer, the suggestion is that she venerates, rather than simply remembers, the symbols of the religion that has been left behind.

To this cinematic composition several implications are attached. Jessica's crossed palms may also signify pregnancy: her continuing connection with her faith accords with the observance that Jewishness and matrilineage are co-dependent. The idea has already been broached in the film, for, in the midst of the 'Hath not a Jew eyes?' (III.i.49–50) peroration, the phrase 'her mother' is added to the reference to 'Leah' (III.i.101). At once this gestures towards a previous life characterized by intimacy, child-rearing and heterosexual domestic conformity, but it also moves beyond exposition to elaborate the role of mother and the system whereby Judaism is both transmitted and perpetuated. It is through an invocation of the maternal that *The Merchant of Venice* underscores Jessica's key role as survivor and its absorption in a post-Holocaust historical moment. That is, Jessica's faith, set inside the context of the mass exterminations of the twentieth century, represents another response to persecution and the future of her religion: hers is the pain of nations and peoples, and her testimony, the film makes clear, will not be ignored. As in films and television features such as *Playing for Time* (dir. Daniel Mann, 1980), *Sophie's Choice* (dir. Alan J. Pakula, 1982), *Escape from Sobibor* (dir. Jack Gold, 1987) and *Life is Beautiful* (dir. Roberto Benigni, 1997), one means of addressing the incomprehensibility of the Holocaust is to stress escape and the 'survival myth' so as to eschew total annihilation.[44] But this is not to argue that what Jessica is constructed as testifying to is easily accessed. The closing image is of a woman who does not speak and, in this sense, Jessica's situation is not unlike that of traumatized survivors of the Holocaust who, as Shoshana Felman and Dori Laub write, tend to 'prefer silence ... as a sanctuary and as a place of bondage. Silence is for them a fated exile, yet also a home, a destination and a binding oath'. As a result, the 'listener has to feel the victim's ... silences, know them from within, so that they can assume the form of testimony'.[45] *The Merchant of Venice*'s audience are such listeners: the work undertaken by Radford's screen statement enables testimony, and this is generated from an experience of interpretation and engagement.

Notwithstanding Jessica's distance from verbal communication, the film functions to restore her imagined language and give voice to a past that is unspeakable.

The continuing resonances of the Holocaust are also felt in the scene that Jessica witnesses, which shows a group of long-boat fishermen spearing their prey. In a comprehensive account of the 'Jew' in cinema, Omer Bartov has pinpointed the significance of films that 'subliminally' bestow on the 'Jewish victim' the 'status of ... Christian saint', while, in his discussion of the 'American soul', Andrew R. Heinze writes that, for 'liberal Christians', the 'innocent suffering [of] ... Jews who were killed not as dissenters or combatants but simply for who they were' strongly evokes the 'crucifixion' narrative.[46] Something approximating this merging of usually polarized symbolic systems is held in play in the closing sequence of *The Merchant of Venice*. On the one hand, the composition refracts an iconographical tradition of representations of Saint Sebastian, the Roman officer who, because of his protection of Christians, was martyred by being tied to a tree, pierced with arrows and left for dead. On the other hand, the persecutory associations at work in this tradition shift the montage out of a Christian register and towards a history of Jewish oppression. The 'theme of the "epilogue"', then, is not so much 'love's power to destroy', as Carol J. Carlisle surmises, as it is Shylock's martyrdom and its impact on Jessica's heightened consciousness.[47]

If *The Merchant of Venice* unravels Jessica's testimony through what is witnessed, then, building on earlier diegetic decisions, it also grants her a voice via that which is heard. In the place of speech, the film substitutes a score which verbalizes the various components that the ending brings together. 'I am never merry when I hear sweet music' (V.i.68), she announces, her confession forming a bridge between her melancholy and the soundtrack which accompanies the closing credit sequence. Important here is composer Jocelyn Pook's musical adaptation, sung by Hayley Westenra, of Edgar Allen Poe's poem 'Bridal Ballad'. Imagining the plight of a woman who, mistaken in her belief about the loyalty of her first love, contracts an undesirable marriage, the poem concludes, 'Would God I could awaken! / For I dream I know not how, / And my soul is sorely shaken / Lest an evil step be taken, / Lest the dead who is forsaken / May not be happy now'.[48] Clearly, the lines are expressive of the film's discovery of Jessica: the ventriloquized voice of the bride reflects the difficulties of arriving at an unmediated female statement; a crisis afflicts the speaker's spiritual state; the poetic persona is racked by haunting reminders of the past; and the whole is suffused with despairing embitterment. From the vantage-point of *The Merchant of Venice*, the 'dead' and 'forsaken' is Shylock: as Dori Laub observes, a characteristic preoccupation of the speaker who manages to overcome 'broken promises' and testify to trauma is the guilty knowledge of having survived.[49] Mediated subliminally through song, these concerns find a conduit in Jessica, to the extent that guilt that is, paradoxically, not openly articulated assumes a redemptive moral centrality. Importing one of Shakespeare's most interpretively recalcitrant plays into the global marketplace of film, Radford aims at a modern historical particularity in the same moment as he assumes a Bard of culturally transcendent importance.[50]

## IV

After the horrors of the twentieth century, there can be no imaginative realization of Shakespeare's play that is not shaped by the Holocaust. Like the commemorations dedicated to the liberation of Auschwitz, *The Merchant of Venice* functions as a memorial: its construction of a Shakespearean past is tunnelled through a more immediate legacy, with the inevitable result that its pre-images are also after-images: early modern antecedents and modern developments are interweaved, and the religious fundamentalisms of the sixteenth century are represented in ways that are both constitutive of, and recognizable to, contemporary sensibilities. This is not necessarily to argue, as Samuel Crowl does, that 'the film ... is ... as much about our age as Shakespeare's', but it is to suggest that adaptation is a means of addressing the changing forms of prejudice, of acknowledging the lessons of the past and of attempting to locate aesthetic opportunity in the midst of the traumatic loss of innocence that the Holocaust engendered.[51] In this sense, although the distancing strategies of the film bring back the Holocaust – or a version of it – *The Merchant of Venice* does not endorse Adorno's argument that 'to write poetry after Auschwitz is barbaric'.[52] Nor can the film be said to be compatible with the observation that 'our metaphysical faculty is paralyzed because actual events have shattered the basis on which speculative metaphysical thought could be reconciled with experience'.[53] This is because *The Merchant of Venice*, mainly through the aegis of Jessica's endeavour to remember and reconcile, contains within it a 'political pessimism' that harbours a 'frail utopian impulse'.[54] It builds towards a gesture that is as much culturally protective as it is historically recuperative. It would be a mistake to see this simply as a return to the liberal, sentimental tradition that would try to rehabilitate

Shylock. Rather, the film, eschewing the view that history has been vitiated, operates to restore to the aesthetic a crucial historical component, transforming Jessica's paralysis in speaking into a promise to survive.

In this way, *The Merchant of Venice* progresses beyond Adorno's contention that 'history ... has dehydrated the power of consciousness to think history, the power of remembrance'.[55] For, in its self-conscious mobilization of a variety of aesthetic registers, extraction of potential from acknowledged modalities of representation, and dovetailing of conventional and newer technologies of description – above all, in its attention to human continuity – *The Merchant of Venice* might be said to pay tribute to values of belonging, the possibilities of restoration, the power of recollection. In particular, *The Merchant of Venice* shares common ground with Shoshana Felman's proposal that 'if art is to survive the holocaust – to survive death as a master – it will have to break, in art, this mastery, which insidiously pervades the whole of culture and the whole of the aesthetic project'.[56] Part of the film's responsiveness to the questioning of such mastery is revealed in its mediatory techniques, its capacity for filtering and aesthetic differentiation. More specifically, *The Merchant of Venice* confronts the presence of 'death' in 'art' by deploying remembrances and remembering to facilitate a movement between political and ethical territories. As in Alain Resnais' *Nuit et Brouillard*, in which the 'voice-over adopts the attributes of human memory and reminiscence, speaking ... as a generalized voice of conscience', *The Merchant of Venice* asks for a moral response, demanding from an audience that the Holocaust is never forgotten, that its material manifestation is never replayed.[57] Such an emphasis enables *The Merchant of Venice* subliminally to contemplate the images and ideologies that have determined its direction, while the film's methodology allows a work that is implicitly concerned with Holocaust testimony to become a testimony to the Holocaust in its own right. Thus, if the idealism of *The Merchant of Venice* is taken as exemplary, there is the potential to apply models capable of properly articulating the circumstances of the Nazi genocide, techniques for resacralizing conditions of representation and meanings at the heart of interpretive systems. The 'new subjectivity' that is attendant on Jessica's 'catastrophe' belongs with that imperative.[58] This is not to suggest that *The Merchant of Venice* boldly shackles itself to what has been termed elsewhere the 'Holocaust industry'; instead, it is to contend that the film elects to aspire towards a future in which the terrors and traumas of the past can begin to find a healed relation with present requirements and realities.[59]

# 6
# Spirituality/Meaning/Shakespeare

During a typically *angst*-filled episode in Michael Almereyda's *Hamlet* (2000), the protagonist (Ethan Hawke) watches a video of a Buddhist monk expounding a philosophy of interrelatedness:

> We have this word to be. But what I propose is ... a word to interbe ... Because it is not possible to be alone. You need other beings in order to be. Not only do you need father, mother, but also uncle, brother, sister, society ... sunshine, river, air, trees, birds, elephants, and ... it is impossible to be by yourself, alone. You have to interbe with everyone and everything else. And, therefore, to be means to interbe.

As at other moments in Almereyda's film, the sequence points to a Hamlet who suffers from a familiarly contemporary affliction – in Peter Donaldson's words, a 'sense of missed contact with sources of spiritual fulfilment or wisdom'.[1] The clip originates in a documentary entitled *Peace is Every Step: Meditation in Action* (1998), while the bestowed-at-ordination name of this Vietnamese guru, Thich Nhat Hanh, translates as 'one action'.[2] Such an emphasis on thoughtful 'action' obviously chimes with Hamlet's dilemma (he fears that his great 'enterprise' might 'lose the name of action'), both illuminating the film's particularized construction of the protagonist and pointing up the 'new age' resonances of Shakespeare's oft-repeated utterance. Passed directly to Almereyda by Hawke himself, and playing on 'to be or not to be', the video clip operates as 'the perfect ramp leading up to Hamlet's most famous soliloquy' and replaces reflections on a deathly disconnection with the contemplation of a harmonious vitality.[3] More specifically, it functions intertextually to rob Hamlet of the monopoly of the Bard's celebrated intellectual deliberation, for the speech, in this multinational universe, has been ethnically pluralized and philosophically transformed by an alternative brand of spirituality and its concomitant manifestations. Also suggested is a correlation between Hamlet's difficulties and his isolated state: despite an attempt to 'interbe' with Ophelia, whose image he is studying on his pixel monitor, he is discovered as linguistically dispossessed and notably removed from any sense of communal interaction.

Compounding Hamlet's psychological affliction is the fact of his being in thrall to, if not adversely shaped by, the inimical realities of his urban contexts and the global corporate business empire to which he is unwillingly attached. Immediately after the citation of the Thich Nhat Hanh documentary, for instance, Hamlet is glimpsed in a diner writing to 'the celestial, and my soul's idol, the most beautified Ophelia', only to find that he cannot productively put pen to paper: the implication, assisted by the subsequent shot of the protagonist walking past a storefront emblazoned with discounted prices, is that there is an inadequate communion with the divine, even with its sublimations, and that the idols of the soul are jeopardized by the economies of the market.[4] The idea is taken up in a different key in a scene involving Ophelia. Immediately before the documentary inset, she appears cradling a diorama 'featuring ... a view of a gravel road disappearing into a dim forest glade' in a composition that points up a yearning for a world beyond, another modality of existence.[5] The accompanying image of pigeons soaring above a church cupola overlays Ophelia's desire for flight, and cultivation of constructions of nature, with a religious dimension, suggesting the 'naturalness' of her urges and imperatives. For both Hamlet and Ophelia, versions of the spiritual are agitated for, yet not without the characters' longings being compromised, through globalized systems of commodification and representation, in the very moment of their articulation.

In this respect, it seems peculiarly ironic that Hamlet should be tempted by the tenets of an eastern philosophy that has itself been transmuted into a global phenomenon by the operations of the late capitalist marketplace.[6] An 'exchange of influences' between east and west, states Christopher Partridge, is 'a result of globalization'; or, to put the point more critically, as does Slavoj Žižek, the 'pop-cultural' species of western Buddhism with which Hamlet identifies, by insisting on an aloofness from 'the frantic pace of ... competition', paradoxically becomes both 'the most efficient way for us to participate in ... late capitalism' and its ideal ideological supplement.[7] The pronouncements of Thich Nhat Hanh, and in particular his 'interbe' proposal, have been distributed through a variety of world-wide media, including books and television, to the extent that he has been described by at least one of his hagiographic biographers as a 'global hero'.[8] For Thich Nhat Hanh is no distant eastern mystic: he resides in Plum Village, a 'community centre' in southwest France, to which, according to his disciples, parties from 'many different religious traditions and backgrounds', both 'European and North American', gravitate for 'summer family retreats'.[9] At some level, then, Hamlet's entertainment of repackaged Buddhism is distinctive for its involvement in precisely the same circuits of exchange that he ostensibly strives to resist and escape.

What the *Peace is Every Step: Meditation in Action* inset demonstrates is Hamlet's vexed relation, in Richard King's words, to a '"spirituality"' that has emerged in the late twentieth and early twenty-first centuries as a signifier of 'the indescribable nature of intense and private experiences rather than ... the transcendental majesty of God or the ultimate reality'.[10] In what have become recognized as classic accounts, of course, the contention is that organized religion and spiritual realms have fared badly under the global process. 'Modern globalizing conditions', writes Peter Beyer, produce 'disadvantages' for 'the religious modality', adding, 'we have witnessed the greater or lesser depriveleging of traditionally religious concerns, symbols and professionals'.[11] Illustrative are the parallels that have been drawn between the destabilization of faith and conventional values, the withering of transcendentalist sources of meaning and the rise of secular materiality. At the heart of these trajectories, it is argued, lies a crisis in the belief process itself. Eric Higgs, for example, states that the 'globalization of imagery ... creates confusion over what to believe', and he is joined by David F. Ford, who asserts that 'global expansion ... helps generate disorientation ... that has ... strained practices of wisdom and hope'.[12] Yet such views need to be counterbalanced by another perspective which suggests that spirituality and globalization are not necessarily incompatible. Thus, Judith Fox's argument that 'increasing globalization ... has led to an increased access to knowledge about religions, the net result being an increase in religious choice' has found considerable support.[13] Commentators now tend to argue that the global marketplace has fostered a revitalization of religion in some incarnations, the acceleration of more imaginative encounters with a plurality of 'spiritualities' and a raising of the profile of 'religions' on the world stage.

Interestingly, this shift accords with one recent development in, and qualification of, theories of deconstruction and postmodernism. For even if the tenets of postmodernism would seem to figure the world in terms of indifferentiation, a simulated second-handedness and the tenuous 'credibility' of the 'grand narrative', this has not prevented attention being devoted to its spiritual and religious implications and reverberations.[14] Fully cognizant of the intellectual lessons of the late twentieth and early twenty-first centuries, yet also persuaded that, in Kevin J. Vanhoozer's formulation, 'the postmodern condition is ... constitutionally open to the coming of the other', some critics are arguing for the virtues of 'negative theology'.[15] Paradoxically, according to one strand of theoretical reflection, an established 'nihilistic tradition of thought' harbours 'a new ... spiritual dimension', with a variety of cultural practices and tendencies being seen as affirmative recurrences of religious fundamentals.[16] It is possible, according to Bill Brown, to detect a 'religious unconscious at work in [a] decidedly secular understanding': from the 'secular vision', an innate 'religiosity' invariably comes to 'light'.[17] A more urgently impassioned variation on the same idea reveals itself in some readings of deconstruction, as when John D. Caputo equates its critical orientation with 'a deep desire for a Messiah who is never to show and whom we accordingly desire all the more'.[18] Constant here is the renewed conviction of a spiritual otherness, a glimpse of ineffable possibility.

Given the Bard's apparently 'universal' credentials, it is perhaps not surprising that a reawakened interest in the spiritual is being developed around, and applied to, the body of Shakespeare. In keeping with a revised approach to theoretical dicta, that Shakespearean manifestation of spirituality is neither closed nor final, but rather, as Ewan Fernie writes, 'a questionable and open structure of being and experience', which 'involves competition between ... absolutes, and resistance to the absolute as well'.[19] Two recent Shakespeare films, Greg Lombardo's *Macbeth in Manhattan* (1999), an award-winning American production initially screened at the Long Island Film Festival, and Kristian Levring's *The King is Alive* (2000), a creation of the Dogme-95 movement, the Danish collective committed to a rigorous aesthetic, testify in discrete and shared ways to a filmic engagement with renewed spiritual considerations.[20] In both, the Shakespearean text is key to new spiritual understandings, and particularly so in its interactions with alternative landscapes such as the wastes of the desert and the interstices of the city. The sacrality associated with Shakespeare in these situations is neither easily identifiable nor straightforwardly recoverable. It is 'present' as a qualification or an expectation, and as such lends weight to John D. Caputo's observation that 'we no longer live by the simple distinction between presence and absence. Our lives are suffused and haunted by shades and spectres, quasi and virtual realities'.[21] *The King is Alive*, in particular, displays a responsiveness to the ghostly by eschewing artificial lighting, imported sound and special effects, thereby presenting itself as a work allied to the earliest era of filmmaking, when spectral forces were imagined as inhabiting the cinematic machine.[22] More generally in the films, the ghosts of Shakespearean pasts and traditions are conjured as part of a discussion about the Bard's perceived spiritual utility. Both *Macbeth* and *King Lear*, the plays that *Macbeth in Manhattan* and *The King is Alive* recast, come back from history, sometimes uncontrollably, to question and correct gaps and transgressions in an experience that is essentially spiritual in complexion.

In terms of the spiritual force of a variety of ghosts and of the Bard's association with supernatural justice, the plays beyond the films are figured as sources of origin and sustaining connection, with Shakespeare at some level filling the place of the '"missing" transcendental' in the global marketplace.[23] In this sense, despite (or perhaps because of) the globalized exposure of some aspects of western Buddhism, *Macbeth in Manhattan* and *The King is Alive* deploy Shakespeare as the point of 'interbeing' with, or even the 'other' for, a spirituality that modernity has mythologized. Moreover, as the plays and the filmic characters begin to collapse into each other, facilitating in some instances the onset of a spiritual sensibility, it is clear that the resultant ethical implications have a political as well as a psychological purchase. Here, the films' titles play an important role. *The King is Alive* and *Macbeth in Manhattan* assert the primacy of the contemporary: if these are works that express themselves as dramas of spiritual 'presence', then their significances are resolutely of the present. Ewan Fernie writes that the present 'matters ... much more than history' because 'we may still intervene and alter it': there is in the 'here and now' an opportunity for political action, a 'pretext for immediate real change'.[24] In the case of *Macbeth in Manhattan*, the implication is that Macbeth is alive and well in late twentieth-century New York, while with *The King is Alive* an associated idea, which ironizes the US-based commodification of a still living Elvis, is that Shakespeare has been reborn. At one and the same time, however, these titles are purposefully ambivalent, since they alternate between the character and the play, the author and the protagonist. (*The King is Alive*, for instance, encodes a meditation upon the after-lives of Lear as well Shakespeare's posthumous vitality). In so doing, *The King is Alive* and *Macbeth in Manhattan* suggest that a multiplicity of Shakespeares serves spiritual functions in a present that, by conversing with the past, offers scope for a corrected, transfigured future.

I

*The King is Alive* and *Macbeth in Manhattan* take as their initial premise the absence of Shakespeare from his assumed locations. Neither directly tied to theatre nor mediated through film, Shakespeare is imagined as outside institutions and beyond the parameters of elite culture: instead, his presence emerges in memory, in expressions of quotidian practice and urban alterity, even in encounters with desolation and death. *The King is Alive*, for example, concerns a group of tourists who, marooned *en route* to Namibia's airport, take refuge in the German mining 'ghost town' of Kolmanskop (Figure 9). The opening scenes on the bus quickly establish human requirements, such as drinking and evacuating, as integral to, and communicative of, a dispossessed situation, an exilic predicament. Utilizing the conceit of an aimless or off-

*Figure 9.* Ray (Bruce Davison) reflects upon an abandoned landscape in *The King is Alive* (dir. Kristian Levring, 2000).

course journey, which is primarily captured in off-centre and shaky camerawork, the film describes the characters as displaced, wandering and lost, as in *King Lear*, which is similarly preoccupied with the vagrant movements of human derelicts. Inside this scenario, the desert operates less as a metaphor for godlessness or the global depletion of natural resources, although these meanings may be implicit, and more as an index to spiritual possibility. Crucially, it is the experience of the desert that summons Shakespeare into being. Hence, Henry (David Bradley), a former London-based theatre producer, proposes to stage *King Lear* as 'a communally distracting game'.[25] *The King is Alive* goes on to alternate between scenes of Charles (David Calder) – 'surely some tribal chief', he states, 'will see [our fire], God willing' – and Henry: 'Just imagine', he ponders, 'if you could put on *King Lear* out here, in this god-forsaken place, with all these lost souls'. Both implicitly subscribe to the idea of a divinity, yet for Henry the godhead is manifested in Shakespeare, with *King Lear* offering a means of clawing back that which has been 'lost'. In the process of staging the play, Henry's speculation suggests, what has been lacking and what is still missing might be restored: the 'soul' will be found via a text whose resurrection reveals its immanence. The implication is that Shakespeare is to be found away from western assurances, in environments of disorientation and displacement. As Mark C. Taylor writes, deserts, because lacking in 'depth ... lights [and] ... light', make available 'delivery to a certain *re-pas* that is beyond ... where the absence of shadow is the shadow of spirit'.[26] In this sense, to adopt a formulation of Carolyn Jess, the desert in *The King is Alive* becomes 'both a Bardic text and ... a representative of the Shakespearean body': Shakespeare's meanings merge with the associations of his newfound location, forming an inextricably organized and mutually constitutive interpretive nexus.[27]

Although very different in style and execution, *Macbeth in Manhattan* is characterized by a similar undertaking: the title suggests that Shakespeare's domicile is New York, yet there is a question mark over the actual address. Thus, while the narrative mainly unfolds in the Cherry Lane Theatre, Shakespeare is explicitly apprehended elsewhere. Conspicuous for not accommodating Shakespeare, even if it is precisely in this institution where actors, audiences and the media seek him, the theatre is continually debunked in *Macbeth in Manhattan*, being satirically tied to neurosis and indulgence, petulance and moral myopia. Typical is the response of William/Macbeth (Nick Gregory), the leading man, to his costume: 'I'm not wearing this ... I'm the hero', he exclaims, his judgement crystallizing a filmic preoccupation with theatrical vacuities of ego, appearance and self-importance. The satirical orientation of *Macbeth in Manhattan*, in fact, is developed so as to shift Shakespeare's presumed position entirely. The first hint that Shakespeare is to be experienced somewhere other than the theatre comes when the director, Richard (John Glover), explains that 'New York is a place where evil and violence are very easy to find. Turn a corner and there it is. Macbeth is right at home'. The easy habitation sketched here has as its precondition the prior installation of evil and violence: the Shakespearean 'presence' is one mediated via psychic disruption and cultural transposition. A sinister undercurrent is made all the more generally applicable by the refusal of the dialogue to clarify if this is the character or the play. Intrinsic to the woof and the warp of the metropolitan condition, Shakespeare's protagonist is also connected to the witches in such a way as to point to a literal recasting of Macbeth as a ghostly city force. When Wendy (Tertia Lynch), who plays a witch in the play-within-a-film production of Shakespeare's drama, is glimpsed off-Broadway exclaiming, 'A drum, a drum – Macbeth doth come', her extra-theatrical situation implies that Macbeth currently pounds the pavements as part of a pre-existing arrangement.[28] The suggestion is reinforced by a series of low-angle shots of a kilted figure: because we never see the face, the quasi-demonic idea is of a threateningly anonymous type whose strength and influence go undetected.

The point is developed in the director's disquisition on 'power' and 'ambition': these are elaborated to suggest that Shakespearean universals map effortlessly onto New York's historical reputation as a place associated pre-eminently with narratives of mobility and self-advancement. Accelerated and unsettlingly angled sequences of cars traversing the city testify to the idea: they occur at precisely the moments where the film elects to privilege the play's construction of Macbeth's bloody rise to dominion. On the one hand, given the fact that *Macbeth in Manhattan* makes much of an urban locale that is associated in the popular consciousness with postmodernism and late capitalism, one could argue that such montage shots, to adopt a discussion by sociologist David Leiwei Li, betray a 'speed-up of social life on a global scale ... [a] shrinkage of physical space through technology and the reduction of time to a perpetual and schizophrenic present'.[29] On the other hand, links between artificially engineered movements and a time–space contraction underscore the ubiquity of an urge to get ahead, to move forward quickly and competitively in the system: the cars are of a piece with a filmic approach that emphasizes both the overlapping status of Shakespeare and New York and the transmigration of his essence to open, public and plural spaces. *Macbeth in Manhattan*'s frequent deployment of drums on the soundtrack and in scenes featuring pavement musicians is indicative of this representational procedure. Crucially, drums are only ever heard and seen outside the theatre, which again suggests that Shakespeare is not culturally constricted. Rather, in anticipation of the Shakespeare/desert equation in *The King is Alive*, he emerges from inside an 'underground' urban register – a reservoir of spiritual energy – comprised of street sounds and actions. The beat of the drums rephrases the iambic pentameter of the play, pointing up a ubiquitous residency for Shakespeare that is consistently and insistently conjured. For both *Macbeth in Manhattan* and *The King is Alive*, then, Shakespeare resembles a spirit, an entity that exists in relation to primeval and unorthodox environs.

If Shakespeare has moved, he is still represented as carrying with him a baggage of theatrical tradition, which, in both films, is understood as indivisible from, and spectrally related to, the text and its meanings. The process whereby *King Lear* is recovered in *The King is Alive*, for example, mimes an aspect of early modern playhouse practice, suggesting that part of the drama's value inheres in its potential for rousing ghosts from their slumbers. 'A long time ago, when things were written by hand', states Henry, 'in order to avoid having to write out the play several times, each player was given his own roll'; punning on the term role/roll, the self-appointed director delivers his pronouncement as an explanation to Catherine (Romane Bohringer) of the individually designed paper rolls, sutured with sticking plaster, that function as the cast's scripts. Paisley Livingstone insightfully observes that 'the roles Henry has written out from memory are not ... [accurate] reproductions of ... *Lear*', yet neglects to make the arguably more arresting point that such misremembering is of a piece with the ways in which plays could culturally circulate in the early modern period.[30] Although the Q1 (1608), Q2 (1619) and F (1623) texts of *King Lear* are now understood to represent stages of revision, they have traditionally been thought of as embodying 'corrupt' forms of an 'original', and thereby 'perfect', play 'memorially reconstructed' by a touring acting company.[31]

*The King is Alive* honours its mythology of the play's origins by revealing characters that conflate, extemporize and omit: it thereby establishes *King Lear* not only as a Shakespearean text that can be adapted but as a body of work for which there is a legitimate precedent for ghostly reinvention. Part of the authority of *King Lear*, according to the film, emanates from the fact that its identity is defined by the histories of adaptation in which it participates. By implication, Henry substitutes for the touring actors, misremembering their parts, as well as Shakespeare, remodelling the play in relation to present needs. *King Lear* is *par excellence* the play that lends itself to desert(ed) appropriation because the authority with which it is associated is transferable, because the text has already been incarnated and reincarnated in spectral versions of itself. This works to justify scenes that discover characters misremembering the play in such a way as to prioritize only their own circumstances. In forceful realizations of the process of reconstruction, narcissistic interpretations that bring *Macbeth in Manhattan* to mind are allowed to circulate, as in the representation of a pair of summaries of *King Lear* that betrays underlying frustrations and expectations. When Liz (Janet McTeer), who is married to Ray (Bruce Davison), for instance, simplifies the story for his benefit, she states that 'it's about a king who has two daughters – or maybe it's three ... Nobody has to fall in love', and when Catherine explains the play in French to Gina (Jennifer Jason Leigh), a young American, she stresses themes of sexuality and cross-generational attraction. In the former case, the emphasis on children reflects back on a childless and, the film insinuates, unfaithful marriage; in the latter, an attention to age and youth testifies to Catherine's misplaced conviction in her own desirability. Both Liz and Catherine narrate so as to draw attention to individually apprehended experiences and requirements; their methods are symptomatic of the ways in which *The King is Alive* avails itself of theatrical history to produce an amorphous but always personally significant Shakespearean charge.

*Macbeth in Manhattan* invests in a similarly sustained use of theatre mythology. Just as *The King is Alive* is haunted by theories of reconstruction, so is *Macbeth in Manhattan* (anticipating the theme of the second series of the television drama, *Slings and Arrows*) fuelled by the damnable reputation of the so-called 'Scottish play'. Throughout the film, *Macbeth*'s feared status is a matter of feverish fascination. Ousted as the star of the show and given the much less desirable part of Macduff, Max (David Lansbury), for instance, is informed that 'the play's ... cursed ... an actor [was] playing Macbeth on stage and a sandbag inexplicably fell ... and [killed] him'. To the cast's reluctance to name the work specifically can be added Max's gift to Claudia/Lady Macbeth (Gloria Reuben) of a book that explains, if not demystifies, the 'history' of *Macbeth*: at moments such as these, the suggestion is of a ghost that returns from the past to preoccupy the present, of a textual spirit, or a spirituality of text, that 'begins by coming back'.[32] Such is the preoccupation with the play, and the implications of its being staged, that the in-film production attracts an intense media attention. Thus, the television reporter's question to the director – 'Now Shakespeare wrote [*Macbeth*] in the seventeenth century, so how is it, in the waning years of the twentieth century, we're still enthralled?' – is precipitated not so much by historical distance as by the recent, seemingly accidental death of William: because the production is *Macbeth*, a keen sense of the play's ghostly capabilities is forwarded. Interestingly, the overweening William, who is a soap star, had been drafted in to boost audience ratings: the implication is that the play revenges itself on an act of generic transgression and that arrogant, Macbeth-like behaviour will receive a punitive comeuppance. This is a reading that prioritizes Shakespeare's immanent capacities, with William's removal illustrating Jacques Derrida's argument that spectres are distinctive for their identification of 'guilty' bodies and their exercise of 'expiation'.[33]

## II

Tied simultaneously to Duncan, Macbeth and finally Banquo, William moves between three identifications. The process is typical of the ways in which *Macbeth in Manhattan* and *The King is Alive* represent characters as haunted by their Shakespearean equivalents in a variety of contrasting ways. In *The King is Alive*, a series of interlinked dilemmas and crises suggests a dovetailing of the play's characters and the film's personalities – Ray and Liz argue vociferously, while Paul (Chris Walker) and Amanda (Lia Williams), husband and wife, disagree over the former's ill-fated attempt properly to 'get to know' his father – which in turn underscores the brutal realities of relationships that have faltered, used themselves up or died. In this connection, the 'sterility' that is endemic in *King Lear* becomes the constitutive element of interactions that, in John J. Joughin's words, evoke a powerful impression of 'depletion and exhausted resource'.[34] More particularly, Charles' comments operate to establish him as Lear-like, his fallibility susceptibility to praise: 'I've always been ready for love ... I'm flattered', he states, exulting in the sexual bargain he has engineered with Gina (he will join the play in exchange for her favours). 'These white hairs', Gina's misquotation from Cordelia (IV.vii.30), reinforces the connection, although the remainder of the 'original' speech moves from mere identification to the articulation of sympathy. Remodelling and censoring one incarnation of *King Lear*, Gina imagines herself as an abused daughter, an innocent who pinpoints in the play a language coincident with her victimization. If they are extensive, the identifications that *The King is Alive* mobilizes are also inconsistent; as Amy Scott-Douglass states, 'the correlation between the tourist and the Shakespeare character is not a matter of simple substitution'.[35] Ashley (Brion James) is cast as Lear but resembles the king only briefly (on seeing him dancing foolishly, Henry is reminded of Shakespeare, musing, '"Is man no more than this?" ... It's good old *Lear* again – perfect'); there are two Cordelias (Gina and Catherine); and, while Charles brings Shakespeare's protagonist to mind, he is simultaneously, in his abuse of women and moral blindness, a type of Gloucester.[36] *The King is Alive* invites and frustrates efforts to fit and classify according to a Shakespearean paradigm, with its construction of several sites of reference both miming the textual slipperiness of the play and opening out *King Lear* to unexpected spiritual relevancies.

Central to both films are the ways in which the elaboration of parallels is seen to have a keen psychic effect. Frequently, *Macbeth in Manhattan* discovers its key players indulging in imaginative sequences in which their dramatic set-pieces receive a heightened, hyperbolic treatment, as when Claudia/Lady Macbeth is pictured in a red dress urging on the hesitating William/Macbeth to his 'bloody business' (II.i.48). These carefully layered narratives show rehearsal scenes merging inexorably with, and becoming inextricable from, grandiose fantasy projections in which the characters inhabit inflated versions of their Shakespearean *alter egos*. Here, Claudia becomes one with a seductive and all-powerful Lady Macbeth whose rhetorical hold leaves William weak with desire. On the one hand, such insets function as articulations of delusion, revealing the ways in which the play provokes, or even ratifies, a yearning for power, romance and spectacular clothing. Particular sequences ensue in response to a cast member's distinctive preoccupations, the suggestion being that *Macbeth* is always read in terms of an egocentric need or lack. On the other hand, because an additional emphasis is placed on the capability of the Shakespearean work supernaturally to exert itself, one could argue that *Macbeth* is viewed as possessing an independent purchase: over and above personal sublimation, it enters and infiltrates, exerting an influence beyond the actions of its human manipulators.

In a discussion of *The King is Alive*, Carolyn Jess writes that performance enables the group to 'excavate ... repressed emotional issues that are ... derived from ... "infantile" scenarios'.[37] Certainly, Gina's experience means that she is empowered to leave behind a child-like dependency, rejecting Charles and confessing to having faked her sexual enjoyment: 'I don't want anything from you', she states, 'you're an old lech ... a mean fucking son of a bitch'. From the 'dumb American blonde' that she initially appears, Gina is elaborated as moving into eloquence, thereby rewriting the fundamental lack of *King Lear* – the woman's capacity to disclaim and disinherit. However, given the similarity between Gina's development and the psychic journey of other women in the film, it is possible to suggest that it is actually the ghostly conjunction of the *King Lear* text and the desert that facilitates a strong and assertive self-image. Hence, Amanda, having internalized her part of the Fool, takes Paul to task for a history of domestic violence: the scene both rephrases the previous encounter between Gina and Charles and pushes ideas of female protest into a new register. 'I never knew you were a pig', Amanda states, concluding, 'For once I'm absolutely clear-headed'. Here, the film both conjures a straightforward parallel (in the same way that the Fool is authorized to criticize Lear, so Amanda is emboldened to berate her husband) and expands on it (Amanda does not mysteriously disappear, like the Fool, but persists into an unambiguous visibility).

The notion that the Shakespearean work possesses an independent – and unpredictable – life is also evident in scenes devoted to psychic reconstruction. 'Connected to trauma', and 'perceived as a way of coming to terms with terrible events', recollection, writes Pam Cook, 'has a therapeutic value, and can be seen as a form of exorcism, in which the past is laid to rest in order that the person remembering can move on'.[38] That constellation of memory, trauma and attempted recovery appears most obviously in *The King is Alive* at the point where Henry's re-creation of *King Lear* is tied to his endeavour to build a bridge to his estranged daughter: 'You got lost ... I couldn't find you', his tape-recorded confession runs, 'These past days I've been thinking of you more and more ... the mistakes'. At once, of course, the disclosure helps to fashion Henry as another of the film's Lears (and his daughter, by implication, as a third Cordelia); at the same time, through an emphasis on geographical disorientation, it establishes, in Bill Brown's words, the 'specular' importance of 'cognitive mapping' as a route to 'salvation'.[39] Tracing his way back to his daughter via shards of memory and *King Lear*, Henry, it is implied, will be spiritually regenerated and cleared of the crime of paternal abandonment. This is clarified in a subsequent scene in which he speaks feelingly the rejection of Cordelia speech (I.i.120–6). For Henry, *King Lear* is not simply 'a means for attaining a better understanding', but rather a vehicle for the expression of repentance, becoming, in revival, a ritual of absolution.[40] If 'fragments', as David Tracy argues, constitute in the global era 'our spiritual situation', then Henry, in a manner akin to the reflections of Kanana (Peter Khubeke), the indigenous commentator, on the group's experience, will deploy the remembered pieces of his daughter and Shakespeare's play as indexes of a 'genuine hope in some redemption, however undefined'.[41] Through that process, *The King is Alive* argues, Henry will be cleansed – purged of the dereliction of his familial duties – and healed in the journey of seeking to make amends.

*Macbeth in Manhattan* develops a related process in which guilt, punishment and a sense of consequence are the constituent parts of a narrative that consistently looks forwards to the unhappy results of current actions. Nowhere is this better illustrated than when Claudia, awaiting her lover William, drenches herself in perfume, the episode anticipating Lady Macbeth's lament that 'the perfumes of Arabia' (V.i.42–3) will wash away neither her bloody 'spot' (V.i.27) nor the memory of her crime. This dramatic set-piece the film later manifests twice, suggesting a particular concentration on the long-term effects of individualistic wrongdoing. In line with this orientation is a shower scene that both hints at Claudia's appalled acknowledgement of her infidelity and illuminates an attempt, as with her Shakespearean counterpart, to cleanse herself of sin. Blood and its spiritual complexions receive a more strident emphasis at the film's conclusion. Taking the 'history' of *Macbeth* to heart, Max elects to take revenge on his rival, William, by staging the very same death-dealing theatrical 'accident' which was earlier related to him. The idea is that the play will be Max's alibi: he will rise above suspicion because there are terrible precedents for *Macbeth*'s demonstration of its cursed status. However, in a spectacular recasting of the banquet scene, Max finds that, when he steps on stage having secured the part he covets, the bloody ghost of William stares at him from the audience, pointing up his guilt with an accusatory finger: displaced as Macbeth, the soap star posthumously gravitates to inhabit the role of vengeful spirit. Here, Shakespeare's essence moves from its urban environs to the theatre, crucially remaining with the spectators rather than ascending onto the hallowed space of the stage. In fact, Shakespeare's return – or re-entrance – is discovered as a coup, a movement from below that ensures the production's closure on its first night.

Via this climactic sequence the film literalizes, in particularly ghoulish fashion, the ways in which the film has established the Shakespearean text as a vital force circulating independently of human affairs. The final scene visualizes the text 'coming to life': as in *Macbeth*, reincarnation is horrifically plausible. As befits this process, the closing stages bring to a head the film's intersecting strands and subject them to a distinctive temporal twist. The ending refers back (Max asks William for a private 'rehearsal', imitating the latter's method for seducing Claudia), combines several constructions of the present (insets of 'Birnam Wood' approaching are spliced with the would-be Macbeth's gathering resentment) and hints at a horrible futurity. That 'other', and the future it incarnates, may even be possessed of a socially and politically corrective function, for, as John D. Caputo asserts, 'democracy ... a porous, permeable, open-ended affirmation of the other ... is the best name we have for what is to come'.[42] Neither Macbeth, it is implied, has understood the repercussions of his self-absorbed practice or the particular power of the play: as the ghost of William identifies the culprit, it is clear that Max, in the film's construction of the play's predilection for repeating itself, must now live with his conduct's shocking consequences. Beyond the fictions of the film (and *Macbeth in Manhattan* purposefully dissolves even these parameters), Max and the *alter ego* to whom he has pledged allegiance will be obliged to take stock of a larger world. They cannot simply 'be'; there are others, if not an 'other', against which individual action is judged. The film might not explicitly articulate a desire for global inclusiveness and obligation, but that ideological prospect is expectantly anticipated.

If death in *Macbeth in Manhattan* evokes presence, or at least the promise of a spiritual futurity, then *The King is Alive* extends the notion in its conclusion, the communal lament. Here, personal and transnational differences recede in the wake of a movement from silent self-preservation (Kanana's original perception of the company is that 'they did not talk') to communication and co-dependency. Around a campfire, the characters are figured as recalling their respective earlier lives and speaking the play meaningfully to themselves and each other: it is a subdued but epiphanic moment, one informed by a sense of mutual commitment and individual awareness. 'This cold night will turn us all to fools and madmen' (III.iv.75), for instance, Amanda's fragmented gesture to the Fool, demonstrates her sensitivity to the forces impinging upon the group as a whole, while 'Thou are not vanquished, / But cozened and beguiled' (V.iii.152–3), Liz's rendition of Goneril's speech to Gloucester, suggests an awakening to her own deceptions. A common learning experience has shaped a variety of educations, with *King Lear* receiving its longest rehearsal at the point where its messages touch on the members of the beleaguered party most keenly. If, according to Richard Halpern, 'responsibility, the ethical covenant, arises within the visual field of a spectre whose regard contains us without being seen', then it is the ghost of Shakespeare, and beyond it the promptings of the desert, that have generated the emergence of a new form of spiritual accountability.[43] The individual-collective orientation of the campfire scene is crystallized at the point where Henry cradles the dead Gina in his arms, adding to the chorus of other excerpts from the play Lear's 'O, you are men of stones' (V.iii.256) mourning speech. As the group recollects Gina, so does Henry, now having assumed his rightful place as Lear, recall his daughter. In addition, because isolated segments of the play are finally working in concert, the solitary vigil over the substitute Cordelia becomes a shared exercise. Michael Bishop writes that the 'global' process of 'redivinization' facilitates 'the most improbable of equivalences, the ... creation of equations, contacts [and] relationships in circumstances seemingly powered by a principle of division, of non-reversal'.[44] Despite the intractability of its circumstances, *The King is Alive* finally suggests, the abandoned tourist party is still pushed to develop connections that bespeak the importance of a sacral interrelatedness, the rediscovery of a spiritual agenda.

Crucial to the meanings of the campfire lament, then, is the elaboration of a cycle that leads from death to delivery. It is here that the film's concern with the intersecting filaments of retextualization, ghostliness and spirituality comes into its own. Perhaps the most obvious departure from any of the texts of *King Lear* in *The King is Alive* can be seen in the particular casting of the rejection of Cordelia speech, in which Henry is represented as substituting the 'barbarous Scythian' (I.i.116), with which the enraged Lear identifies, for the 'barbarous Chronos'. In Greek mythology, Chronos is instructed by his parents, Gaia and Uranus, that he will be deposed by his son just as he had deposed his own father. By swallowing his offspring at birth, he attempts to reverse the prophecy. His strategy is unsuccessful, however, for, yielding to his son, Zeus, Chronos disgorges the previously consumed children in an act that culminates in his eventual disenthronement.[45] Linked to time and memory, the 'convoluted and inverted architecture' of Chronos is more powerfully associated, as Michel Foucault argues, with 'becoming ... new beginnings [and] ... a solid thread [that] allows us to retrace our steps and to rediscover the ... light of day'.[46] Via the troping of Chronos, it is implied, Henry will be enabled to evacuate or give birth anew to the daughter he once rejected, thereby discovering that affirmation and value may still be gleaned from his past. A species of psychological ingestion permits Henry/Chronos to deploy a version of *King Lear*, his own, in a process that results in the child's return to consciousness, the parent's coming into the 'light'. Contrary to expectation, the deployment of such symbolic and aspirational forms (the physical resurrection of Gina is only ever hinted at) does not mean that *The King is Alive* compromises its construction of Shakespeare's spiritual efficacity. Instead, adumbrated in the introduction of Chronos is a 'condition of ... impossibility' that is nevertheless informed by what is 'possible' or, to cite Jacques Derrida, an 'experience of the impossible' that has not yet cancelled out a concomitant 'affirmation'.[47] Not appearing does not draw a line under another coming; deferral can be the harbinger of redemption; the present is the precondition for the (im)possibility of a better future.

## III

If *Macbeth in Manhattan* traces a movement from theatre to city, the chorus, played by Harold Perrineau, is the agency that distinguishes between, and brings into conversation, the two locations. The chorus' functions are intertextually assisted by Perrineau's previous Shakespeare incarnations: Mercutio in Baz Lurhmann's *William Shakespeare's 'Romeo + Juliet'* (1996) and Ariel in Jack Bender's *The Tempest* (1998), a made-for-television reworking of the play set in the Mississippi bayous during the American Civil War. Both roles, of course, invested heavily in what Denise Albanese has termed the 'raced body' of the performer: as Barbara Hodgdon writes, Perrineau's Mercutio is marked by a 'flagrant racial "exoticism"' that nevertheless 'acknowledges the contributions' of 'African-American experience' to 'both popular- and high-culture art forms', while his Ariel is deeply inserted into ongoing debates about slavery and alterity in the early modern and postmodern eras.[48] Perrineau's role in *Macbeth in Manhattan* unfolds in and out of the theatre, operates among multiple circumstances, and crosses demarcations of culture and gender (some lines are granted a purposefully 'camp' delivery), all of which assist in the process of remapping Shakespeare's spiritual situations and applications. Throughout, his black actor status is crucial to the direct-to-camera mediations for which the chorus is responsible, a particular effect of which is to focus attention on the introspection of the player-characters and the erring of the institution with which they are identified. This suggests both a unique understanding of the drama and a form of communication/

communion that supersedes traditional performance practice. It explains the chorus' initial function, which is to dissolve the artificiality of theatre and demystify its language: to this end, an idiomatic vernacular is highly instrumental, as when Macbeth is described as 'the guy everyone wants to know: numero uno' or Lady Macbeth is seen as 'nobody's fool: she knows what a man wants and how to give it to him'. Not only is the chorus defined by the use of African-American slang (Macbeth, for instance, is described as a 'dude'); he is simultaneously represented as pointing up the interpretive failings of a white cast, which suggests a further, and yet more radical, realignment of Shakespeare's traditional cultural affiliations. A theatrical chorus, Martin Puchner writes, superimposes 'onto the mimetic space of the stage layers of description whose purpose is not to replicate the stage ... but to adapt, transform and interrupt it'.[49] This is literalized in the chorus' interruptions in *Macbeth in Manhattan*, with Shakespeare being removed from environs of spiritual vacuity, stripped of his hegemonic history and granted an alternative ethnic habitus. In this sense, what is distinctive about the chorus is not so much a commentary that, through summary, appropriates and intervenes in the play as a mediating exercise that brings into visibility deeper spiritual realities. And, as this process unfolds, divisions and discrepancies, which instruct an audience in spiritual truths, are discovered.

Given the films' shared interest in mediation, the chorus in *Macbeth in Manhattan* throws into stark relief the more searching linguistic implications of the part of Kanana, the indigenously-speaking choric figure in *The King is Alive*. Homi Bhabha writes that any discourse of the nation is always a 'double writing or dissemi-*nation*' which finds, in the 'chronotope of the local', 'oppositional' modes of 'cultural signification' that are often 'performative' in nature.[50] The chorus' interventions are similarly 'performative': the English sub-titles accompanying Kanana's words indicate a responsiveness to the language of a global audience, while the narrative authority he embodies is revealed in commentaries essentially meta-theatrical in nature. For instance, the reflection, prompted by the experience of watching one of the rehearsals of *King Lear*, that 'the desert crept into [the group's] hearts at night', represents a unique recognition of incipient spiritual connection. Like the chorus in *Macbeth in Manhattan*, Kanana, through periodic observation, is constructed as piecing together the disparate elements he witnesses, recuperating and in some senses acting out another alternative version of *King Lear* and thus a further incarnation of the Shakespearean text. The workers and soldiers who arrive at the film's end are as much Kanana's audience as they are the abandoned party's, and he, it is suggested, is the spiritual conduit through which western modes of interpretation are retransmitted and localized. The film's close departs from the voiceover in representing Kanana, as in *Macbeth in Manhattan*, speaking directly to camera, emphasizing the dominant role that has always been his implicitly. Moreover, because Kanana's address here combines in the film with his machine-mediated voice, an appropriation or manipulation of a mechanical means of reproduction that historically defined the implementation of white colonial power is implied. Constituting a 'double writing or dissemination', Kanana's chorus offers an account that, by supplementing the experience of a white majority, detracts from its importance even as it hints at the prospects of spiritual reformation. Occupying intermediary positions, and acting as interlocutors as well as interpreters, the choric voices of *Macbeth in Manhattan* and *The King is Alive* keep active the spiritual dimensions of Shakespeare. In reaching beyond their respective filmic frames, they come to be characterized by a spiritual imprimatur and to speak to if not for a sacral agenda. The 'process of global reflexivization', writes Slavoj Žižek, 'generates not only its own immediacy, but also its own ghosts, its own spectrality'.[51] In self-consciously disappearing and coming back, and in inhabiting more than one world, the choruses of *The King is Alive* and *Macbeth in Manhattan* function in just such a ghostly capacity.

In part personal, in part social, the ending of *The King is Alive* is complicated by a gesture to national, if not global, considerations. The spiritual state of the company is placed in dialogue with the setting's historical contexts, while the pasts of Namibia are invested with a spiritual presence, bringing to a head a revisionary conception of the connections binding globality, governance, ethics and the political sphere. Such relations are initially glimpsed in the figure of Jack (Miles Anderson), the Dutch-accented, safari-suited and quintessentially colonial type who advises the company on survival tactics before setting off for help. If he seems to qualify as a type of saviour, however, Jack is simultaneously stripped of his symbolic prowess: his communion with nature ('I'm the only one who stands a chance out there', he states) turns out to be illusory; he fails to 'get help' from the neighbouring 'village'; and his engulfment by the desert, which leads to his death, hints at a misplaced confidence in his own abilities. The blindfold he wears on the bus suggests that, contrary to his declared knowledge, he has inadequately 'seen' both the perils of his environment and the coach passengers' predicament.[52]

More importantly, Jack's presence and removal bring the history of Namibia to mind. As Thomas Cartelli and Katherine Rowe have noted, the status of the film's set represents a 'physical testament to the barren legacy of the European scramble for Africa'.[53] Annexed to Germany during the late nineteenth century, Namibia, between 1884 and 1914, was officially a 'Protectorate'.[54] Yet this designation appeared ironically inappropriate in the light of the simultaneous mass persecution of the indigenous Herero and Nama peoples, who rose in 1904 to challenge land seizures and exploitation by the German occupants. The rebellion was savagely put down, concentration camps were set up as a punitive measure, genocide may have been systematically practised, and the deaths of three-quarters of the population of some 80,000 provoked world-wide protest.[55] German rule ceased in 1915 when the local army surrendered to the allies in the guise of a South African expeditionary force; subsequently, South Africa controlled Namibia, divided up available land among white farmers, founded 'reserves' to confine black workers and foster an apartheid policy, and instituted a systematic application of forced labour. The latter, in particular, was the impetus for the development of a national consciousness during the 1950s and the rise of a mass demonstration culture, with independence from South Africa finally being granted in 1990 after decades of internal conflict. Part of Namibia's value in colonial eyes were the rich diamond deposits discovered in 1908: Kolmanskop where, we will recall, *The King is Alive* is set, subsequently became a thriving German mining community, employing 800 Ovambo workers in appalling conditions. (The town was abandoned in 1956 following the exhaustion of the seam and a slump in the world diamond trade.)

*The King is Alive* is richly responsive to the meanings of its filmic context: like his European settler predecessors, Jack is defeated by his environment, and like his political counterparts, he is unequal to the task of 'protectorship'. His excision in a film that agitates for redemptive possibilities, moreover, leaves open the saviour function he seemingly embodied. It is here that the film's closing stages are particularly pertinent: with multiple lorries rather than a single coach as a mode of transport, a party of indigenous workers and soldiers arrives, the implication being that this 'second coming' into the desert is a means of rescue. Immediately, of course, the suggestion that the black saves the white reverses the peculiar colonial history of Namibia: the past has been turned on its head in a new dispensation of salvation. At the same time, however, the inversion of a traditional power dynamic recalls a similar, earlier situation in which Moses (Vusi Kunene), the driver, refuses to have sex with Liz so that she can humiliate her husband: the 'black man' rejects a stereotypical designation that equates sexuality and enslavement. Such interruptions of an indigenous perspective shift the point of view and recover, so as to place under critical scrutiny, a narrative of racial inequity. Thus, it is difficult to agree with Jennifer J. Bottinelli in her criticism that 'the representation of ... Africans' in *The King is Alive* 'denies their individuality ... [they] are a ... contrived group [lacking in] any distinct' identity.[56] Rather, the arrival in the film of the local embodies, in Jacques Derrida's words, 'a structural messianism ... an idea of justice'.[57] There is an apocalyptic scenario of freedom and enlightenment sketched here, even if it is one that may never be fully realized. For example, the workers and soldiers constitute salient reminders both of the native labour required to support the diamond mines and the political vicissitudes that prepared the way for Namibian independence: in this sense, we are urged to recognize in the contemporary postcolonial moment the consequences that a prior 'division of the kingdoms' had generated. Amputated reflections on *King Lear* in *The King is Alive* evoke multiple memories and histories, summoning through Shakespearean revival the spirits of the place of the plays' unfolding in an uncomfortable rewriting of constructions of power, nation and deliverance. A reification of spiritual awakenings that generate political resistances lies at the heart of the new theoretical paradigm. For Ewan Fernie, 'spirituality holds out the hope of a more positive leap into a revolutionary alternative', while, for Slavoj Žižek, 'the brief apparition of a future utopian Otherness' will attach itself to 'every authentic revolutionary stance'.[58] Ghosts and spirits, spirits and ghosts, combine to argue for a spirituality that will make a difference in the wider world, which can precipitate reforms and reformation on a global basis.

## IV

If Shakespeare has displaced himself in *The King is Alive* and *Macbeth in Manhattan*, and if his spokespersons and representatives have altered, he has lost nothing in transit, for his spiritual meanings are manifested in hauntings, his wisdom is accommodated in secular places and his work is allowed to speak on behalf of urgent 'present' concerns. Writing on the status of Shakespeare's present spiritual applications, Richard Kearney argues for the need to develop 'a way of being and acting and suffering in the world so that the inwardly subjective and reflective is never sacrificed to the ... impersonal imperatives of the global techno-capitalist network'.[59] What *Macbeth in Manhattan* and *The King is Alive* demonstrate, by contrast, is something altogether less oppositional, and more intricately involved, a situation in which globalization is the spur to spirituality, in which, to adopt a formulation of David Tracy, 'a new global sense of polycentrism' permits and produces a renewed spiritual dimension.[60] Such a state of play is revealed in the ways in which characters in the films inhabit Shakespeare in a process that allows for an access to spirituality, or are led to spiritual points of contact through private experience. At different moments of the life and death trajectory, it is implied, Shakespeare is the prompt for the reactivation of a far-reaching spiritual instrumentality. What this is not is a return to essentialism; rather, engaging with a modality of 'negative theology', and identifying sacrality even in the void, *The King is Alive* and *Macbeth in Manhattan* suggest that notions of 'interbeing' can be constructively striven towards, whether that connective concept is imagined in relation to a remote godhead or the traffic of human intercourse.[61] Hope is attached to interrelatedness, there is a faith inside language, and globalization and spirituality consort in a necessary partnership – these are among the arguments that audiences within the films and beyond are urged to contemplate.

# 7
# Post-Millennial Parody

*Shakespeare's Happy Endings*, a spoof documentary produced as part of BBC's 2005 'Shakespea(Re)-Told' season, concludes with a scene outside Holy Trinity Church, Stratford-upon-Avon.[1] Here, the erstwhile presenter, Professor Simon Starkman (Patrick Barlow), greets William Shakespeare (Kevin Eldon), welcoming him as the 'man' of the 'millennium' and announcing a birthday celebration in his honour. But the church is closed: the vicar has forgotten about the party, no one has bothered to turn up and, in a sublime rendition of bardic demythologizing, Shakespeare is reduced to kicking the locked doors and battering at a window in an attempt to gain entrance. The dramatist's inability to make a connection with his renowned place of birth is part of a comic collision between what Shakespeare has come to signify (the commodified rhetoric of the industry) and the 'reality' of an early modern writer revealed as an embarrassing and confused unsophisticate. Certainly, many at the end of the twentieth century would lend their voices to this debunking. Writing in 1999, Gary Taylor contended that 'Shakespeare's reputation ... has passed its peak of expansion, and begun to decline', resulting in a diminution of the Bard's 'cultural authority'.[2] Richard Burt, surveying the field in 2000, goes one step further, arguing for 'the end of the Shakespearean' or what he terms 'the Shakespeare apocalypse'.[3]

In their dismissively irreverent emphases, these critics typify a recent swing in interpretation that highlights the 'exhaustion' or 'senescence' of the Shakespearean canon, the sense that, in reworkings of the Bard on film, 'no particular meaning [or] ... source of value' remains.[4] Yet a more affirmative prognosis emerges if we consider the creative valences embodied in a series of post-millennial acts of appropriation and re-invention. The post-2000 period has been characterized by an extensive range of screen realizations loosely based on Shakespeare's plays, from teen thrillers and television modernizations to independent satires and thirty-something comedies – all of which rely on a particularized form of parody as both generic category and interpretive mechanism. In its earliest incarnation, as Gérard Genette writes, a mocking 'counter-song' or a 'literary reprise', parody is now widely seen to embrace a more nuanced set of operations, centred on imitative transactions that involve 'loving reconstruction as well as political outrage' and the conversion of 'repositories of wisdom' into 'places of contestation'.[5] Linda Hutcheon, the foremost commentator on parody, elaborates this notion in her thesis that the 'parodic' engagement with the 'past' is not 'nostalgic; it is always critical', and argues that parody challenges 'humanist assumptions about artistic originality and uniqueness and ... capitalist notions of ownership and property', working finally to 'foreground the *politics* of representation'.[6] Her argument is grounded in recent thinking which has seen postmodernism working as a logical supplement to globalization.[7] Such work suggests that, despite Fredric Jameson's famous injunction, parody takes on a renewed contemporary urgency as one of globalization's most salient cultural expressions or analogues.[8] For, in the same way that globalization is characterized by the circulation and transformation of goods and capital, so too does parody put into play in order to change products and 'originals'. Mobility, movement, repackaging and translation, all constitutive elements of globalization, are integral to parody's field of operation, with technological developments having advanced global initiatives and parodic constructions of Shakespeare in the same moment. But parody is most recognizable, I think, as a variation on the 'global flows' identified by commentators such as Arjun Appadurai.[9] Like parody in its post-millennial applications, 'global flows' dictate and shape new species of communication and migration, the transmission of information and the acceleration of trade across boundaries, time and space. Shakespeare, according to this paradigm, becomes a test-case for the effects of the new economy, a prompt for cultural production and a 'space of flows' in which exchange, negotiation and transmutation are granted an individual parodic licence.[10]

This chapter concentrates on three post-millennial films, James Gavin Bedford's *The Street King* (2002), Roysten Abel's *In Othello* (2003) and David Lachapelle's *Romeo & Juliet* (2005), and argues that they parodically traverse individual Shakespearean works in a variety of ways. At once these films parody the status of Shakespeare via a purposeful summoning of titles, invoking echoes of, or extensions to, the 'originary' play names. *Romeo & Juliet*, for instance, a six-minute film that constitutes a loose rehearsal of Shakespeare's play, appeared in late 2005 as part of an advertising campaign developed by the H&M fashion empire. Airing in cinemas and as a playable clip on the H&M website, Shakespeare is kept at a remove from the film's stylish evocation of an urban, American environment.[11] Instead, *Romeo & Juliet* announces itself in its subtitle as *By David Lachapelle*, the specification of this music video producer and *Vanity Fair* contract photographer as auteur indicating the discrete modality of its field of reference. Because its subtitle is *A Film Where Shakespeare Invades Real Life*, *In Othello* would seem to take its inspiration from those 'play-within-a-film' productions, such as *A Double Life* (dir. George Cukor, 1947), in which the experience of performing a Shakespeare play precipitates a series of extra-theatrical crises. An adaptation of *Othello: A Play in Black and White*, a stage production which over the course of 1999 enjoyed a highly successful run in Delhi and won the Fringe First Award at the Edinburgh Festival, *In Othello* represents a more intriguing variation on the 'play-within-a-film' formula. Remodelling his play for film, Roysten Abel mobilizes the concept of a Shakespearean interiority to contemplate ideas of essence, the appropriation of the Bard in particular circumstances of reproduction and dissemination and, above all, the notion of dwelling in an alternative psychological space. Film parodies thrive on narratives of impersonation and alternative identity – *Being John Malkovich* (dir. Spike Jonze, 1999) is perhaps the most obvious instance – and *In Othello* extrapolates the theme, trading on other modes of habitation, the revelation of inner existences, and a phenomenon of an 'inside' that bears a parodic relation to its 'outside' sphere of influence. In this manner, Shakespeare recedes in importance and is replaced by a sense of the histories of the plays' adaptations: at the same time as they recast Shakespearean language, the films reveal their distance from notions of source and origin. As Judith Butler writes, 'the parodic repetition of "the original" ... reveals the original to be nothing other than a parody of the *idea* of ... the original'.[12]

*The Street King* appears as the exception to the rule of a title betraying a parodic Shakespearean reading, for this production is so named as to direct immediate attention to its subject, the drug trade warfare conducted by rival Latino groups in East Los Angeles, a 'contested terrain where ... social classes', as Victor M. Valle and Rodolfo D. Torres write, 'vie for strategic advantages'.[13] In this sense, *The Street King* would seem to owe its lineage and identity not so much to Shakespeare as to the 'hood' and 'barrio' films of the 1990s, such as *American Me* (dir. Edward

132  *Filming Shakespeare in the Global Marketplace*

James Olmos, 1992) and *Bound by Honour* (dir. Taylor Hackford, 1993), works similarly preoccupied with Chicano ghetto gangs and their feuds and mores.[14] Hence, in *The Street King*, the intimate rapport shared by drug culture and East LA is signalled, at an immediate level, in the opening montage, which features flashing lights and glimpses of nodding toy dogs: there is disorientation and disturbance here as well as a suggestion of dementia, all of which are underscored by the soundtrack. Tellingly renamed 'La Marihuana', a traditional carnival song overlays the sequence with new lyrics that, in specifying a dry mouth and bloodshot eyes, testify to the effects of drug use. Yet titles are not entirely neglected, and nowhere more obviously than in a fleeting introductory credit which establishes that the film is 'based on' the 'Tragedy of Richard III' by 'William Shakespeare'. Although all that remains of the Shakespearean stimulus is the film's allusion to royalty, a kinship with *Richard III* is still implicit, and particularly in *The Street King*'s original release title, *King Rikki*. (The film was renamed for video and DVD distribution.) *The Street King* signals through its title a systemic equation between (to adopt a formulation of Manuel Castells) 'global ... restructuring', the 'criminal economy' and 'the growing dereliction of the ghetto'.[15] At the same time, it rehearses its generative point of departure, recalling to an audience the remains of a Shakespearean monarchy that now exists only in a parodically rephrased and culturally displaced guise.

This chapter argues that, over the course of conjuring a presence that is and is not Shakespeare, *In Othello*, *Romeo & Juliet* and *The Street King* display a range of methods for executing their parodic procedure. Either they demonstrate an alliance with Shakespeare via his proverbial association with books and texts, or they look to his current location as a multicultural icon in global context. This is a 'double-coded' operation, one that mediates a presumed past in order to judge the nature of present processes.[16] Such representational procedures are 'critical' in that they both pass pejorative comment on the functions of power and subject to scrutiny the workings of transnational and postcolonial ideologies. Notwithstanding very different national and cultural genealogies, each of the films contemplates the difficulties of language and subjectivity, identity and mobility, inside informing global structures. The parodic translation of Shakespeare becomes a means of pointing up inequities in a global system that has exacerbated already entrenched divisions and discrepancies. Equally distinctive is the way in which *In Othello*, *Romeo & Juliet* and *The Street King* agitate to accommodate the inequities they have identified: Shakespeare here is less a suturing agent as an occasion for continuing to highlight the irresolvable ills that globalization perpetuates. All three films culminate in circulations of conflicted values and acknowledgements of fractured and still evolving points of reference, giving voice to a shared context of 'flow' and fluidity. What this illuminates is a post-millennial purchase for Shakespeare that is at once more suggestive and less easily identifiable than *Shakespeare's Happy Endings* communicates. Parody, as deployed in these films, assists in promoting reflections on the means of production, and the forms of representation, that distinguish the post-millennial Shakespeare, thereby revealing the extent to which particularized rewritings of the Bard are energized by multiple contextual locations. As Linda Hutcheon observes, 'the parodic appropriation of the past reaches out beyond textual introversion and aesthetic narcissism to address the "text's situation in the world"'.[17]

# I

Beyond titular play, *The Street King*, *Romeo & Juliet* and *In Othello* pursue their parodic agendas by periodically invoking the narrative contours of the plays from which they derive and by alerting audiences to the traditionally textual manifestation of the Shakespearean utterance. Of *The Street King* Thomas Cartelli writes that the tendency is to 'gesture, [rather] than defer, to the plot-line', but, in fact, the film is more deeply committed to *Richard III* than this allows.[18] Throughout, Rikki Ortega (Jon Seda) is modelled on Shakespearean Ricardian lines: his discoloured eye and facial scar are the equivalents of Richard III's twisted frame; his impersonation of a doctor in order to murder his brother, Eduardo (Timothy Paul Perrez), accords with the would-be king's pose as a 'holy and devout' prince; and his failure to outwit rival drug gangs in the shoot-out at the close is indebted to Shakespeare's representation of the ways in which the protagonist is outmanoeuvred at the Battle of Bosworth.[19] Via these and other translations, director James Gavin Bedford finds a modern vocabulary for the 'original'; in particular, he rewrites a version of 'monstrosity' as an effect of culture rather than a biological aberration, and installs loyalties of *familia* as the ties that ideally bind political allegiance. In this sense, by favouring a subculture already established with its own motifs and conventions as his subject, Bedford avails himself of a conceit that permits him simultaneously to honour the design of *Richard III* and to meet the requirements of the early twenty-first-century cinema consumer. Crucially, the film's conversionary scenes 'de-doxify' Shakespearean assumptions: that is, they cater to constructions of the early modern while elaborating out of them a logic and a set of accoutrements that have a firmly contemporary relevance.[20] Shakespeare is the prompt for reinvention but not the absolute point of reference, a presence that is both confirmed and subverted through being conjured. Moreover, in a world in which monarchical conflicts are the internecine warfare of rival gangs, *Richard III* finds an easy niche, with reference to the play pointing up the ways in which the subordination of women is politically motivated, a culture of local violence replaces institutional opposition, and particularized workings of class substitute for the operations of inherited status. This is a parodic reading of *Richard III* that has a material as well as an ideological plausibility.

The shadow that *Richard III* casts over *The Street King* alerts us to the fact that, in post-millennial filmic representation, Shakespeare is purposefully overwritten and written over in reflections on the 'original' and invocations of appropriation. The activity is inherently parodic, for, as Linda Hutcheon argues, commenting on the etymological roots of the term, the prefix 'para' can connote 'rewriting' or 'transposition' and does not point to a 'counter-song' alone.[21] It is significant, then, that *The Street King* consistently favours narratives of 'writing' and/or 'lettering' that are culturally resonant. Hence, a shot of Rikki spray-painting his signature on a rock functions to suggest that the articulation of his identity is managed by acts of defiling and defamation: the protagonist marks himself by 'monsterizing' his environment in much the same way that he has been disfigured by the barrio experience. The reverberations set up here extend into the scene where Rikki, now firmly installed as the head of the *familia*, exchanges his cross for a necklace bearing an 'R'. Possibly this serves to recall the importance accorded the 'letter G' (I.i.55) in *Richard III*, but, more likely, the substitution works to indicate that the protagonist can now openly sign himself in terms of a newly acquired street regality. Both 'writing' and 'letters' are metaphorically tied in the film's opening pan of an image (culled from the Droeshout engraving) of Shakespeare's face: as the familiar countenance is shown to be covered in graffiti, features are added – a bandana, an earring and shades. The composition as a whole is signed 'LCN'. Demotically hinted at is a perception that culture circulates in unbounded registers, that rewriting and appropriation are interconnected, that the visual is parodically entangled with the textual in postmodernity, and that Shakespeare can be deployed as a marker of social protest and communal identity: 'LCN' is the acronym for the 'brotherhood' to which three of the film's characters once belonged. Such expressions of gangland fraternity are exclusively male.

Women, for example, are glimpsed having tattooed onto their bodies the names of their lovers in revealing representations of the ways in which barrio culture invests in a violent and repressive masculinity. As the reproduction of Shakespeare's image has proverbially been associated with the workings of patriarchy and hegemony, so too are women in *The Street King* written on and written out in a process that discovers the female form being inscribed with and controlled by the male's imprimatur.

In these operations a parodic force is powerfully at work. When Anita (Tonantzin Carmelo), for example, requests that the phrase 'Siempre Rikki' ('Rikki Forever') be inked indelibly on her midriff, a connection is afforded with the perennially timeless reputation of Shakespeare: he is 'always' there, it is suggested, 'siempre' suggesting the unchanging nature of Bardic inheritance. Yet Shakespeare is not invulnerable to transformation, *The Street King* simultaneously asserts, and not least because his iconic image is defaced and distorted in a visual trajectory that characterizes the moral fortunes of the film's unscrupulous protagonist. Here, the text that accompanies the image comes into its own. The word 'plata' ('silver') is placed high over Shakespeare's face and the word 'plomo' ('lead') is placed low: at once the terms play on stereotypical gangland practices ('plata' is slang for 'bribes' and 'plomo' for 'bullets') that, as Carolyn Jess-Cooke observes, were epitomized in the Shakespearean-like cultural and economic ascendancy of Pablo Emilio Escobar Gaviria, the 'Colombian drug lord who became the seventh richest man in the world'.[22] Given the positioning of the vernacular terms and the general parodic flavour, however, it might also be argued that the montage functions to indicate the bifurcated status of Shakespeare himself. 'Shakespeare' is pulled in antithetical directions in the post-millennial moment, *The Street King* suggests, and the textual additions that move upwards and downwards across his countenance discover opposing claims on his importance. Already overwritten, Shakespeare is subsequently overdrawn or overpainted in an assembly of alterations that wrests control of the process of the Bard's reproduction and mimes the film's central conceit, a social and cultural journey that has as its objective Rikki's eventual abandonment of the 'the street'. A modestly budgeted, edge-of-Hollywood work, *The Street King* is here, ironically, at its most academic, replicating the purposeful re-jigging of Shakespeare's appearance on the covers of countless recent monographs and essay collections.[23] The rewriting of *Richard III* is advertised as akin to the writing of the Shakespeare industry as a whole, with the film honouring its source in a specifically angled parodic procedure.

The writing of Shakespeare is further hinted at in Rikki's periodic addresses to camera since, Richard-like, he is figured as taking the off-screen audience into his confidences: 'I'm Rikki, this is my story', he states. 'Mano', the term he deploys to endear himself to spectators, represents an ethnic variant on the demotic English 'man'; as the Spanish word for 'hand', however, the term simultaneously alerts us to the part of the body familiarly linked to writing and, by extension, to acts of inscription and authorship. There are even grounds for suggesting that Rikki's association, through his predilection for graffiti, with the process of rewriting Shakespeare establishes him as a species of Shakespearean dramaturge. Commenting on the barrio film *Zoot Suit* (dir. Luis Valdez, 1981), Mark Pizzato writes that El Pachuco (Edward James Olmos), the narrator, 'controls the sequencing and editing of scenes as they appear by snapping his fingers and thus becomes, like Shakespeare's Prospero, a figure of the playwright'.[24] Not only do the self-conscious autobiographical excursions of Rikki bring El Pachuco to mind; the cultural vandalism which *The Street King* prioritizes means that the central protagonist emerges as a paradoxically creative force, a rival to if not a replacement for Shakespeare, a type for whom the craft of the drug trade is indissoluble from the art of the director-dramatist.

If *The Street King* parodically conjures Shakespeare via an overlaying of a famous engraving, *Romeo & Juliet* invokes his presence by rehearsing a broader history of Shakespearean encryptions and reinventions. At an immediate level, as in *The Street King*, a construction of Shakespearean textual authority offers a means for mediating and situating the millennial romance of the attractive and fetchingly attired leads, Juliet (Tamyra Gray) and Romeo (Gus Carr): thus, a glimpse of the graffiti-sprayed name of 'Paris' both indexes the 'original' and interprets the Bard according to a logic that combines citation with fragmentation and amputation. Such signifying details go hand-in-hand with visual prompts (the image of Juliet on a fire escape substituting for the balcony) and cinematic allusions (the reflection in a window of a billboard announcing a film entitled *The Lady Doth Protest*), which unsettle a unitary conception of the Shakespearean in the same moment as they affirm the authenticating rationale for the film, the culture of conjuration and parody within which *Romeo & Juliet* exercises its particular appeal.[25] And, as the urban environment of the film reveals itself as New York, a further summoning of the Shakespearean comes into view, with *West Side Story* (dir. Robert Wise and Jerome Robbins, 1961), itself a revisiting of *Romeo and Juliet*, being instanced as another inner city parable that takes the play into modernity. This *Romeo and Juliet* is acutely responsive to, and self-conscious about, the 'sources' of its own existence and the practices of revision that intercede in, and give shape to, its imaginative possibility: to adopt the discussion of one commentator on parody, it re-reads 'the past' in such a way as to make 'us aware' of 'the limits and powers' of a prior history of 'representation'.[26] Both the ghostly background of *West Side Story* and the titular presence of the fictional Shakespeare film, *The Lady Doth Protest*, then, suggest that in *Romeo & Juliet* the screen pasts of Shakespeare are a function of his current comprehensibility; that is, the ways in which the Bard has been packaged and transmuted through film are the precondition for the works' accessibility and applications, however displaced they might be from their early modern contexts and associations. What transpires in the wake of the authorial, material Shakespeare becomes the conceptual template whereby the play is made familiar.

Hence, it is peculiarly apposite that the film should make a point of consistently invoking other Shakespeare and Shakespeare-related screen outings. The emphasis on fashion – in this case, jeans – is of a piece with the film's reminder of the lineage of Shakespeare's popular culture visibility. The opening menu, for instance, discovers Romeo and Juliet standing against a graffiti-sprayed image of a flaming rose. At once, the composition harks back to the panoply of interrelated flaming hearts and logos deployed in Baz Luhrmann's *William Shakespeare's 'Romeo + Juliet'* (1996), thereby elaborating a context in which it is the icon rather than the word that is prioritized. The Luhrmann film is instanced again in the sequence showing the heroine as a descending angel (an allusion to the appearance of Claire Danes as a Botticelli-inspired angel during the party-masque), while Michael Almereyda's *Hamlet* (2000) lurks behind the fleeting capture of a photo montage adorning the walls of Juliet's bedroom. Films already inscribed with the market stamp of youth culture and urban *angst* lend their reputations to Lachapelle's advertising utterance, pointing up a modality of articulation and reception in which Shakespeare is 'hip' and in which an affiliation with the Bard is as cool and current as the acquisition of the latest designer label.

Writerly defacements and previous filmic incarnations constitute the texts through which *Romeo & Juliet* and *The Street King* insert themselves into a parodic register. By contrast, *In Othello* takes the Shakespearean book itself as its point of departure, thereby taking a particularly forceful approach to the question of Shakespearean canonicity and demonstrating a developed awareness of its ideological foundations. This is despite the fact that *In Othello* initially appears essentially disinterested in the role that the text – or any form of text – might play in the process of parodically animating Shakespeare after the millennium. For, from the evidence of the opening, the emphasis of the film would seem to fall on the multicultural features of the fictional Indian Shakespeare Company's production of *Othello*. Hence, the cast is glimpsed preparing for rehearsal by adopting traditionally yogic positions and engaging in western limbering-up exercises. Classical violins combine with sitar music, which suggests that Shakespeare is defined not so much by his textual affiliations as his in-between cultural status. Both *Kathakali* acting conventions (which the company imitates) and European theatrical methods are invoked by *In Othello*, and in such a way as to locate the Bard at a point of cross-fertilizing intersection and to define him according to a practice of performative fusion. As *In Othello* constructs it, a huge potential is attached to seeing Shakespeare in such terms: for instance, when Vivek (Vivek Mansukhani), one of the actors, announces that 'this Indian-style *Othello* ... is going to be really funky', the expectation is of a desacralized approach that will find an energizing legitimation in a multiplicity of informing interpretive trajectories. Yet, later in the film, Vivek articulates a less upbeat reflection: 'all this business of multilingual theatre', he states angrily, 'so convenient, such a lot of bullshit'. Part of the problem, at least according to diehard theatre practitioners such as Vivek, is Adil (Adil Hussain), the 'outsider' from 'rural India' who, in the words of the production's director, Roy (Roysten Abel), has been chosen to play Othello 'in an urban milieu'. Ill-at-ease in English, deferential and alienated, Adil does not fit easily with a production template that trades on intercourse between east and west and on a coming together of apparently unconnected cultural elements. In addition, because he is represented as having been transplanted to Delhi, the 'rural' Adil is immediately set apart from a city that, according to commentators such as Madhu Jain, has recently evolved into a 'corporate', metropolitanized and 'magnet' urban conglomerate.[27] Such differences are underscored in scenes that discover the various cast members pursuing leisure activities: thus, while Dilip (Dilip Shankar), who plays Cassio, works out at the gym and Sheeba (Sheeba Chaddha), who plays Desdemona, shops for clothes, Adil eats at a dingy, roadside café, a potent image of his divorce from the bourgeois sophistication of Delhi and a forceful indication of a life that, in some senses, is still in transit.

Even 'fifty years after independence', writes Gopal Guru, 'structures of hierarchy and segmentation, and the accompanying cultural and behavioural codes, still persist in India', and these are gestured towards in the film in the comments and actions of Barry (Barry John), the only white member of the cast: his view is that Adil's failure to integrate can be explained in terms of his 'class'.[28] 'Class' is certainly conjured in the film's exploration of Adil's exclusion, but, as *In Othello* unfolds, it is clear that regionalism and elitism enjoy a greater prominence in the narrative of his disaffection. In the opening rehearsal scene, the general expectation is that Barry, the most experienced in terms of the performance of Shakespeare, will play Othello, suggesting a construction of the Bard that equates the views of white authority with English or British theatrical values. Inside this process, the centre of identification is not so much India as the former 'mother country' and an idealized memory of the cultural accoutrements of imperial power. It is inconceivable that Adil will be allowed to disrupt this tradition (he is indeed confused for the '*Kathakali* trainer'), to the extent that a palpable shock is registered when Barry is passed over for the coveted Othello role. The director's presumed liberalism, it turns out, only serves to precipitate a more extreme form of hegemonic entrenchment.

It is here that *In Othello*, following in the footsteps of *The Street King* and *Romeo & Juliet*, comes into its own as a film that mediates an idea of parody in terms of an emphasis upon texts and textuality. For Barry, the presence and promotion of Adil threaten to parody a crucial lineage of transmission and interpretation. Thus, it is revealing that, in the rehearsal scenes, Adil is glimpsed without a play edition in his hands whereas Barry is seen desperately clutching his paperback *Othello*. Like the other films explored in this chapter, *In Othello* stages an abandonment of 'text', yet differs from them in the ways in which such a departure becomes indissoluble from expressions of colonially inflected exasperation and hostility. Typical is Barry's soliloquy to camera: '"Fair is foul and foul is fair"', he states, continuing, 'I'm quoting abundantly ... I have both knowledge and experience of the texts. It's a pity these young upstarts don't read their texts ... what about the willow that has weathered a thousand winters? ... These robes are very dear to us ... and ... will not be handed over ... easily.' Strikingly, Barry's reflections occur at precisely the point where the cast, seen for the first time in full *Kathakali* make-up and costume, is preparing for the opening night: the guardianship of the 'text', then, is prompted by a fear of its being superseded by a form of performative multiculturalism. In addition, a generational dimension is highlighted in Barry's denunciation of 'young upstarts': by associating himself with the 'willow', the actor is figured as articulating both a belief in his own venerability and (because the tree in Shakespeare functions as an 'emblem of bitterness and sorrow' and is linked to death and mortality) an anxiety that he may soon be made redundant.[29] 'Text' for Barry, therefore, encompasses not only Shakespeare but also a validating record of theatrical dissemination. And that record, Barry's words implicitly suggest, extends to the uses to which Shakespeare has been put in an Indian context. According to the Indian Education Act of 1835, a privileged class of Indians would be trained, in Thomas Babington Macaulay's phrase, to be 'English in taste, in opinions, in morals, and in intellect', thereby, as Paromita Chakravarti states, forming an 'anglicized' constituency that 'would help to perpetuate British rule'.[30] Within that system, the cultivation and mastery of Shakespeare operated to inculcate doctrines of humanism and civilization, with the Bard subsequently coming to enjoy a quasi-mythological importance. *In Othello*, a film which thematizes the parodic process as a central premise, is itself a parodic statement: it investigates claims on Shakespeare, complicates assumptions about his cultural niche, extends if not inverts a local practice of his ideological applications. And if the 'text' of *Othello* is subordinated in this process, *In Othello* insists, this is an inevitable by-product of the globalization of Shakespeare as the Bard is repackaged and remade according to 'flows' comprised of increasingly interpenetrating and interdependent cultural influences. Emerging from the emphasis on 'text' in *Romeo & Juliet*, *In Othello* and *The Street King* is an exposure of the hierarchies of power and ideology within global systems that are understood on a discrete and individual basis. The films' different reflections upon comparable issues bear out Arjun Appadurai's thesis that the 'contests' embodied in and thrown up by 'global flows' are 'infinitely varied' in appearance and complexion.[31]

## II

Despite its multicultural emphasis, *In Othello* chooses not to acknowledge the rich tradition of Indian adaptations of Shakespeare, which, as Poonam Trivedi observes, were characterized by 'indigenizing' and 'democratizing' elements.[32] Nor is the film consistent in its subtitling procedures: well-known Shakespearean speeches, even in their non-English manifestations, are generally left untranslated, with translation being reserved for Adil's subjective reflections in his own language. It is an obvious instance of 'subtitles', in Atom Egoyan and Ian Balfour's expression, working to promote 'pressing matters of difference [and] otherness'.[33] Yet, as Ania Loomba writes, commenting on the drama on which the film is based, the director rarely 'play[s] into a simple Indian/Western opposition'.[34] As part of its parodic debunking of regionalism and elitism, the film continually shows up the shortcomings of the institutions to which the in-film production of *Othello* is affiliated. For example, although Vivek appears a cosmopolitan, boasting of his career as a 'model' and a 'DJ', this does not prevent him from harbouring inflexible attitudes towards newer forms of Shakespearean interpretation. In a film marked by a variety of tongues for the registration of Shakespeare, Vivek is implicitly criticized for his embarrassment at Adil's impassioned Assamese language delivery of Othello's speeches. In his subsequent ostracization of Adil, Vivek rephrases a history of British colonial policy for, from 1826 onwards, Assamese, sometimes considered inferior or corrupt, was obliged to cede place to an imposed Bengali and also Hindi, the official language of state government. Rustom Bharucha notes that 'there are new hierarchies among Indian languages through the incursions of the global media and the market', and, in a realization of these developments, *In Othello* interrogatively associates the emergence of a worldly consciousness in India with the growing dereliction and interiority of Adil as the central Shakespearean protagonist.[35] The global markings of multiculturalism are abundantly testified to by *In Othello*, but not to the exclusion of an unsettling diagnosis of the local consequences of the practice.

Crucially, that local dimension is suggested in the ways in which Adil is represented as alternating between polarized positions in the interests of arriving at an authentic Shakespearean understanding. In the production itself, for instance, he is fully realized as a *Kathakali* performer; earlier in the film, however, at Barry's party, Adil appears in blackface in a parodic rendition of the white impersonations of blackness of theatrical tradition. What this points up is not so much a psychic disturbance on Adil's part as a broader critique of the hidebound forms through which Shakespeare has been disseminated. Even in the languages that Adil inhabits, including English and Hindi, a dissatisfaction with the treatment accorded him is conjured, thereby demonstrating the continuing application of the film's parodic technique. During a staircase conversation, Sheeba asks Adil how he would like to 'take' his 'lines'; the scene immediately shifts to a sequence in which both characters ride across a river on the back of an elephant. (Figure 10.) Immediately revealed here is the film's construction of Adil's internalization of his role: the episode represents a 'fantastical' (II.i.219) narrative, an Othello-like 'story' (I.iii.157) of fabulous proportions. But this is

*Figure 10.* A typical fantasy sequence from *In Othello* (dir. Roysten Abel, 2003).

not to suggest that Adil is merely the passive recipient of inscrutable, omnipotent forces, for a resistance to Shakespearean hegemony is equally asserted. Significantly, the locale is rural rather than urban, suggesting that, for Adil, it is in such an environment that Shakespeare belongs: this is where the 'lines' must be 'taken'. It is a singularly parodic gesture, an act of re-colonization and re-appropriation. The idea that Shakespeare can be taken 'home' to Assam – or at least to a different sort of 'home' from that of the Delhi hinterland – is reinforced in the accompanying voiceover, an Assamese language version of Othello's 'It gives me wonder great as my content' (II.i.180) address. Because this is the speech that signals the protagonist's triumphant return from routing the Turkish fleet, the implication is that Adil too is staging a kind of victory, one that involves the redirection of Shakespearean identifications. The poetic highlighting of the line, 'If it were now to die / 'Twere now to be most happy' (II.i.186–7), moreover, underscores the fact that this is a sexual victory as well as a declaration of regional connection. In keeping with the pun upon the word 'die', the screen briefly goes blank: such is the 'Bollywood' convention for sexual consummation, and the idea is bolstered in the scantily dressed appearance of the couple and the swaying movement of their means of transport. If only at the level of metaphor, Adil wins out over the rest of the cast, securing the woman who is the object of a general longing: the sequence here shifts away from the 'fantastical' in order to suggest that, in translation, Shakespeare operates as a refuge as well as a force for cultural realignment.

In *Othello*'s particular contribution to the parodic remodelling of Shakespeare is to underscore the historically specific character of a struggle for rights of possession. The film shows up how the Bard is either gravitated to or fought over in different parts of the same nation-state; in doing so, it demonstrates the ways in which Shakespeare is reiterated and remoulded according to demands and pasts that move beyond immediate national perimeters. In this sense, *In Othello* forms an unlikely partnership with *The Street King*, which also debates notions of ownership, bringing into the spotlight concerns of cultural subordination and the functions of representation via a distinctive but complementary parodic movement. *Richard III* is parodically mimed and mined in *The Street King* in meditations on cultural and geographical boundaries that either restrict physical movement or prompt a desire for transgression and escape. Part of Rikki's testimony, for instance, involves his familiarizing the audience with borders inside California that, running between Bakersfield and Fresno, define and police the drug cartels' respective areas of control. Because it is Rikki's voice that dominates, one is forcefully reminded of the extent to which, as Claudia M. Milian Arias writes, 'border culture' is central to the 'struggle' of 'Chicanas and Chicanos' to 'transform oppressive social and cultural conditions in the theory and practice of their subjectivities'.[36] But borders are no less powerfully insisted on in the film's realization of the landscape of LA itself, peppered as it is with barbed wire, canals and arteries, material features that stand as symbolic ciphers of institutional policies of segregation and division. Rosa Linda Fregoso writes that the border paradigm illuminates 'asymmetrical power relations ... created by uneven global and hemispheric developments and political instabilities', and certainly *The Street King*'s panoply of images of ghettoization are indicative of a history of exclusion and of the larger global processes that have contributed to migration.[37] For Rikki is no naturalized indigene: the film makes clear that he has been uprooted from Mexico to California and that his predilection for establishing territories is intimately related to a 'notion of origin'.[38] As a result, Rikki is represented as reproducing the realities of the US–Mexico confrontation in the geographies of his own drug-dealing: the complexion of his identity is linked to his originary *frontera* experience, and, in the wake of crossing into California, he replays the conditions of the emergence of his selfhood.

The immediate historical contexts for the border narratives of *The Street King* are global reorganizations of labour and capital and accelerated developments in migration prompted by directives associated with, variously, the Immigration Reform and Control Act, the International Monetary Fund and the North American Free Trade Agreement.[39] In terms of the film itself, the point of reference for Rikki's gangland career is his abandonment by his mother at the US–Mexico border: this *The Street King* elaborates as a traumatic childhood event, to the extent that the agitation to be 'king' is seen as a compensatory means of redressing if not transcending the poverty that gave rise to a primal moment of rejection. Contrary to the sentiments expressed in one of Rikki's voiceovers, his family is scarred by a history of not having 'taken care'. The episode serves as a salient illustration of Smadar Lavie and Ted Swedenburg's thesis that 'borders are zones of loss ... pain [and even] death', for, in his subsequent conduct, Rikki mobilizes, in his own words, a 'complex' of maternal neglect that finds its most potent articulation in a culture of misogyny.[40] On Rikki's shoulder is tattooed the face of a boy, suggesting that his past continually returns to haunt him, while, on a street pavement, is glimpsed the graffiti-sprayed declaration, 'Viva Mexico: me vale madre'. Literally, the phrase translates as 'Long live Mexico: my true mother', but, read metaphorically, it articulates a less affirmative message – 'Long live Mexico: I don't fucking care'. The equation of maternity and cynicism held in play here points up both Rikki's evolving misogyny and a vexed relation to his national lineage. What is distinctive about *The Street King* is the extent to which the film associates misogyny with imitative forms of economic initiative, as if the decision to embrace the US as a substitute mother precipitates the adoption of some of its most stereotypical cultural pursuits and practices. Hence, Rikki is represented as collecting women in ways that evoke less the sexual ethics of the barrio as a late capitalist ethos of consumption and accumulation. Once Anita is seduced, therefore, Lupe (Isabella Donato), the girlfriend of Jorge Ortega (Manny Perez), is won over and subdued. With both women, moreover, the exercise of Rikki's masculinity is defined by how much he might add and subtract – even his own body is described as a commodity to be portioned out as he sees fit. 'I figure there's enough of me to go around', he confides on seducing Lupe, his punning comment ('figure' and 'enough') functioning to underscore both the idea that sexuality is a property to be bestowed and the suggestion that, through his successes in the boudoir, Rikki participates in self-aggrandizing circuits ('around') of exchange. For Rikki, the self-determined reproduction of his prowess is what legitimates his enterprise. There is, of course, an intertextual pleasure to be gained from recognizing overlaps between the exploits of Rikki/Richard; at the same time, however, a uniquely parodic energy is generated from the discovery of a misogyny that has its roots in a specific and ongoing historical predicament.

If the assertion of Rikki's aggressive brand of masculinity is inseparable from vulgarized American values, then this accords with some of the uses to which Shakespeare has been put in an American context and the applications that his work has been seen to have in the process of the nation-state's development. For Michael Bristol, the 'history of Shakespeare's reception in America presupposes an identification ... with ... cultural advancement', while, for Lawrence W. Levine, productions there of *Richard III* over the course of the nineteenth century unmistakably evoked 'American sensibilities concerning the centrality of the individual'.[41] Richard III, in particular, it seems, operated as a precursor to the Horatio Alger type, or what has been termed the 'self-made man', a figure who finds profit in disadvantage and who fashions himself according to principles of promotion and self-improvement. At once in *The Street King* it is Juan Vallejo, the police officer with a 'transfer from the [wealthier] West Side' to patrol his indigenous East

LA neighbourhood, who appears the most likely candidate for the self-made man's post-millennial descendant. Committed to an ideology espoused by an America comprised, in Michael Kimmel's words, not of 'hereditary titles' but of 'democratic ideals' and 'immigrants', Juan, the film's version of a Latino Richmond, is consistently realized according to a template of upward social mobility.[42] As Mario López, the actor who takes Juan's part, states in the film's DVD commentary for the American market, *The Street King* is 'not all about living in the hood ... You can get out of there and make something of your life'. Enshrined in this exhortatory rhetoric is the suggestion that an unmediated identification with the 'hood' is ultimately incompatible with, or antithetical to, the successful execution of the 'American Dream'.

In this connection, it is revealing that Rikki, who rarely moves beyond the barrio, is increasingly figured as a parodic expression of American individualism. Because of his association with national flags, and in the light of his boast that 'I can do anything', Rikki could be seen as a filmic exemplification of the recent thesis that 'Mexican-Americans [are] more patriotic than Anglos ... [they act] to prove their loyalty to the nation so as to overcome their minority status and end the discrimination that they continue to experience'.[43] Yet, as *The Street King* progresses, it is clear that Rikki's professions of allegiance are no more than means to an end. 'We're all looking to move up in life, right? That's the American way', he states, but his construction of a legitimate national agenda serves only to mask a self-interested, illegitimate enterprise. On a later occasion, when challenged to defend the wisdom of doing 'business' with his 'enemy' Ortega cousins, Rikki announces: 'There's a US deal with Russia: you've got to think global for the twenty-first century'. A logic of free market exchange is summoned to prop up once again a self-oriented economic practice, and an additional irony is that a hypothesis about the porosity of borders is deployed to reinforce discrete connections and influences. Inside these operations, even the *familia* becomes a utilitarian concept that can be taken up and discarded at will, with all being mortgaged to Rikki's parodic acquisition of a personal rule.

A further parody of individualism comes into view in the representation of Rikki's failure to achieve psychic wholeness. His divorce from *familia* in Mexico, the film suggests, does not lead to a corresponding creation of community or solidarity in California; indeed, Rikki is akin in his displacement to the diasporic subject defined by Seán McLoughlin as continually ravaged by a sense of 'doubt, crisis and alienation'.[44] 'By myself: just me', states Rikki, describing an increasing experience of insularity in a formulation that echoes Richard III's 'Myself? ... I am I' (V.v.136–7) acknowledgement even as it evokes the cultural losses migration precipitates. Crucially, Rikki is constructed as unable to settle upon any one cultural affiliation, traversing two linguistic registers (English and Spanish) and frequently translating Spanish terms into their English equivalents. Such code-switching might be seen as a legitimate part of Rikki's education of (presumably untutored) cinematic spectators and listeners, but it also communicates a split, an identity in mutation and, in the words of Roger Rouse, a species of 'cultural bifocality' which makes everywhere 'a border zone'.[45] In this sense, Rikki is bifurcated in a similar fashion to the Shakespearean image to which he is originally linked. Directed in his actions towards 'the way of the future', Rikki is returned only to his past: stretched between different places, he stands ultimately as an emblem of crushed individualism and uncertain assimilation, no more than an insignificant 'flow' on the broader map of mondial movement.

*In Othello* and *The Street King* self-consciously deploy parody to point up divisions and inequities; by contrast, in *Romeo & Juliet*, investment in a parodic method has the effect of illuminating the film's unwitting participation in, and shaping contribution to, a repressive and ongoing postcolonial and/or global state of affairs. Earlier versions of *Romeo and Juliet*, such as *West Side Story* and *William Shakespeare's 'Romeo + Juliet'*, prepare the way for *The Street King* in privileging ideas of division and in presenting urban life as an ethnic war zone involving, respectively, Puerto Rican and Polish-American youth, and Anglo and Latino rival groupings. *Romeo & Juliet* is distinctive for not following the lead of these films, approving instead a vaguely and ambiguously racialized constituency that belies any straightforward identification. Described on the H&M website as a 'true icon' who 'appeals to a wide range of ages and ethnicities', Gus Carr (Romeo) might be characterized as Asian or Latino or a combination of the two; similarly, although black, Tamyra Gray (Juliet) inhabits the aesthetically whitened extreme of the Afro-American experience. Ethnic specificity is not the point; instead, it is the notion of a free-floating, cross-cultural and transatlantic ethnicity that *Romeo & Juliet* asks its audience to countenance. In this connection, the film brings to mind what Mary C. Beltrán has described as the 'new Hollywood racelessness': in action movies such as *Romeo Must Die* (dir. Andrzej Bartkowiak, 2000) and *The Fast and the Furious* (dir. Rob Cohen, 2001), she argues, 'mixed-race individuals' who nevertheless subscribe to a 'white ethos' embrace 'identities that are achieved through the ... sharing of music, fashion and cultural forms ... rather than by [an acceptance of] former ethnic ... allegiances and in-group prejudices'.[46] Such a vision of 'cultural *métissage*', to adopt a formulation of Ronald Niezen, is, as Beltrán suggests, a reflection of 'contemporary shifts in US demographics' as well as 'concerns regarding ... the nation's burgeoning ... creolization'.[47] *Romeo & Juliet* models itself along the lines of these 'raceless' narratives: devotion to a product is seen to be preferable to absorption in a community, and expectations about conflict are resolved in the spectacle of an ethnically diluted, and accessory-driven, homogeneity.

On the one hand, such a 'raceless' *Romeo & Juliet* would seem to lend credence to notions about Shakespearean universality as it is mediated through the mechanisms and accompaniments that characterize film in its post-millennial manifestations. Thus, the Lachapelle film features a soundtrack of two songs, one of which, 'When I First Saw You', is performed by Mary J. Blige. This 'confessional singer', the website informs us, is possessed of 'an inner strength' and 'raw honesty [that are] used to tackle ... personal pain, [so that her] uncompromising recordings reveal the universality of [her] heartaches and demonstrate the healing power of music'. Arresting here is the implied juxtaposition of the singer and the heroine, to the extent that this *Romeo & Juliet* becomes, in some sense, Juliet's story or, at least, her attempt at the articulation of suffering and psychological reparation. But more striking is the idea that the confessional form, because it rests upon a Shakespearean 'original', is listened to over and above the confines of the film's New York locations. Emerging from the construction of a narrative free of clearly demarcated ethnic markings is the representation of a personal journey that achieves a transcendently communicative efficacity. The song relies for its presumed effect on Shakespeare, and Shakespeare is the guarantor of its 'soulful' appeal.

On the other hand, to argue for a 'universal' version of Shakespeare's play is to ignore the details of any film's political and ideological underpinnings. *Romeo & Juliet* is no exception for, as much as the film gestures towards a whitened value system that traverses the restrictions of place and history, so does it betray both the structures of thought that lend its conceptions shape and the larger contemporary contexts that inform its mindset. Originally a clothing outlet founded in Stockholm in 1947, H&M has subsequently grown into a world-wide consortium, with stores in over twenty countries across North America and Europe. New York's flagship H&M store opened in 2005 with a timeliness that, given the Lachapelle film, cannot have been unintended. For all of its Swedish antecedents, then, H&M is a fashion empire distinguished by a global frame of reference and, as we will see, by particularly American representational methods and interpretive tendencies. For example, Tamyra Gray, who plays Juliet and performs the other song on the soundtrack, 'And I Am Telling You I'm Not Going', is a former runner-up of *American Idol*, the syndicated pop contestant show. Part of a global export network, *American Idol* testifies to the competitive cult of manufactured celebrity that characterizes the US in the twenty-first century even as it expresses an illusion of traditions of meritocracy that contributed to the nation's ideological orientation.

Perhaps the most revealing moment of 'And I Am Telling You I'm Not Going' comes when, in a seemingly innocuous diegetic detail, the lyrics interact with the filmic image. Previously, Romeo's killer is identified as a gunman who, from a passing car, unaccountably aims a fatal shot at the hapless lover. Because the killer is hooded and the audience is granted only a brief glimpse of his eyes, a parallel is afforded with the infamous Carl Juste photograph 'Mask' (1994), which shows an anonymous hooded Haitian migrant detained at the US military base at Guantánamo Bay, Cuba.[48] The reminder of 'Mask' encourages further identifications, not least with constructions of Muslim and/or Islamic extremists: the stereotype of the lone, crazed assassin has in the US, in particular, acquired a fearful currency. The point is that this does not connote the ethnic gang disputes of the ghetto or, indeed, of previous film versions of *Romeo and Juliet*; rather, the hero's death is symptomatic of the attitudes informing American foreign policy and participates in what Ken Booth and Tim Dunne term 'a global war against terrorism'.[49] Crucially, the gunman appears as a black 'other': his is the film's most conventionally ethnicized appearance. Yet, towards the end, another view of the now police-escorted killer is granted. The hood is pulled back and the countenance is repentant as the lines from the Tamyra Gray song sound: 'We're part of the same place, / We're part of the same time, / We will share the same love, / We both share the same mind'. Ostensibly, the 'we' are the star-crossed lovers themselves; however, judged alongside such fundamentalist rhetoric of identicalness, 'we' simultaneously signals the born-again spirit of American patriotism. The moral conversion of Romeo's murderer makes sense in this framework, the assumption being that the American people, regardless of ethnic affiliation, share a goal and must band together against the outsider. At a deeper remove, the assassin's repentance, and the suggestion that he has already been punished, justifies the aggressive military tactics of the Bush administration. In the post 9/11 moment, there can be no differences, only unity: racial alterity is absorbed or incorporated, and 'racelessness' comes to serve a politically expedient purpose. The quotation from *The Merchant of Venice* – 'I will buy with you, sell with you, talk with you' (I.iii.29–30) – that adorns a shop awning is in keeping with this tendency, suggesting as it does fraternization rather than rejection, intercourse rather than ostracization. But, in a telling instance of ironic counterpoint, the Shylock citation also works against itself, alluding to earlier US relations with Iraq, a history of trade in armaments, and a complicity in the engendering and perpetuation of authoritarian regimes. *Romeo & Juliet* styles itself to rehearse the concerns of a world in which American attitudes and actions are often dominant at the same time as it dispassionately withdraws from the informing determinants that are among the conditions of its own production.

Ultimately, of course, both the evident presence of Shakespeare and the more muted reminder of US foreign policy must give way in the film to its primary directive, which is to sell the product. Here, Shakespeare comes into his post-millennial own, being mortgaged to, and deployed in promoting, the narrative's commercial requirements. *The Merchant of Venice* quotation is a subliminal part of this imperative; so too is the shop awning reference to *The Two Gentlemen of Verona* – 'Win her with gifts' (III.i.89) – and the general equation of romance, youth and the designer lifestyle. Contrary to the hood, which obscures the identity of the gunman, the jeans worn by Romeo and Juliet have an individuating effect. That, at least, is the claim of the film's website, which states: 'Each &denim pair are different ... created ... for the fashion of today and the one we will honour tomorrow'. As this parodic recasting of the language of the marriage service suggests, the '&denim' range of jeans is conceived of internally rather than externally, as the carrier of a sublime virtue rather than the demonstration of a must-have materiality. Jeans with the H&M label, therefore, are 'true ... companions in long and honest relationships': they are purveyors not so much of momentary needs as timeless realities. There is a purposeful blurring here with one cultural construction of Shakespeare: like the Bard, whose works live on in the popular imaginary, '&denim' jeans will survive vicissitude. Or, to put it another way, the wearer/consumer enjoys a personal and permanent connection with his/her clothes, filling out the vacant space preceding the '&' and responding affirmatively to the invitation to buy the item and complete the romantic circuit.[50] Canonically entrenched ideas about the ageless applications of Shakespeare recur in the part of the menu devoted to the jeans themselves. Different styles are represented variously as 'loyal', 'classic' and 'original': the descriptors deployed suggest that, by acquiring a particular garment, the consumer partakes of, and comes to inhabit, precisely that Shakespearean attribute. To enjoy '&denim', it is implied, is to become acculturated, to claim a past that has a present purchase and an assured future. Inside this semiotic structure, all is geared towards facilitating the interested party and bolstering an impression of his/her buying power. Such a process is hinted at in the on-screen message at the close, 'With Love From H&M', which equates the experience of watching the film with the receipt of a gift. Yet, within this economy, to be so honoured is simultaneously to enter a system of debt and exchange whereby the primary act of giving must be responded to and repaid. *Romeo & Juliet* endows consumers with 'values' that span more than one cultural category, that privilege and implicate in the interests of broadcasting the '& denim' range's multivalent irresistibility.

## III

The rewriting procedures of *The Street King*, *Romeo & Juliet* and *In Othello* gesture towards resolution at the same time as they continue to highlight the unsettling realities of the post-millennial global moment. Suggested in the endings of these films are the ways in which parody moves in contrary directions depending on discrete requirements and contexts, comprising a 'flow' that generates new constructions of Shakespeare in the act of discarding and/or endorsing the old.

*Romeo & Juliet* represents a particularly apposite instance of a work that, from its parodic beginnings, allows for a cross-section of points of reference, a 'flow' of identification options. Given the interplay between recollection and fantasy that makes up the film, it is unclear which of *Romeo & Juliet*'s endings is granted priority. The penultimate sequence discovers Juliet seizing Romeo's mobile 'phone in order to shoot his assassin, yet the final composition displays the lovers reclining on a bed, barely moving as they gaze adoringly at each other. Vengeance is entertained, but so too are ideas about resurrection, survival, a shared approach to death and the embrace of an alternative reality. The confusion is, in fact, integral to the broader workings of the film: via the selection of jeans the consumer is encouraged to make particular narrative choices. Viewers are placed in the position of mixing and matching various readings of Shakespeare's play as part of the process whereby the desirability of the product is reified. Thus, it is not so much the case that, as the website informs us, 'the importance of fashion yields to the forces of true love'; rather, the ending(s) of the film reveal how a conservative construction of Shakespearean 'love' is the instrument through which 'fashion' is affirmed: the consumer is empowered at the level of narrative in order to be targeted in the extra-filmic economy. Because of these narrative layerings, *Romeo & Juliet* emerges as no straightforward filmic statement. It represents a collocation of texts to be decoded as much as it appears as a cross-media tie-in for the latest initiative of global garment industry. A work in which Shakespeare is himself a brand or an implied icon, this *Romeo and Juliet* is part-homage, part-imitation, part-trailer, part-promotion, part-PC experience. To adapt one definition of parody, the film reveals itself as both 'playfully ludic' and 'seriously respectful', a paean to consumerism in the same moment as it is an offering to the activity of Shakespearean recreation.[51]

If *Romeo & Juliet* draws attention in its mode of operation to the parodic play of modern media, *The Street King* emphasizes how media function in the enforcement of political borders and subjects. Contrary to expectation, Rikki's departure from the narrative is not heralded by the corresponding elevation of Juan/Richmond; rather, it is the roving anchorwoman, Margarita Salcido (Danielle Camastra), and her fictional news bulletin insets, that assume prominence. A mastery of the media rather than a domination of the drug trade of East LA is what permits Margarita to move in and out of the ghetto at will. In this respect, she represents the postmodern replacement for the self-made man: masculinity yields to the anchorwoman's manifestation of female power; her appeals to camera repress Rikki's *testimonio* (she makes herself by representing his self-made 'story'); and she comes to inhabit the public sphere that the Ortega *jefe* had agitated to name as his own. Her increased prioritization throws into relief Rikki's failed individualism as a global subject, for, as the film understands it, 'anything' is not possible, despite the protagonist's conviction of his own abilities. Pinned down by his dagger blade in the shoot-out, symbolically castrated and, in Saskia Kossak's phrase, now 'truly handicapped', Rikki is finally seen as the victim of a dream of *el norte* and a statistic of downward migratory mobility: the closing shot is of Los Angeles at night, glittering but available, a city of desires and aspirations only inadequately realized.[52] As Mike Davis remarks, 'Los Angeles ... has come to play the double role of utopia and dystopia in advanced capitalism'.[53] Assuming the position vacated by Rikki, Margarita, in part because a close-up of her face and eyes dominates in the *dénouement*, takes narrative centrality and occupies the place of Shakespeare, the ultimate, mobile and transcendent storyteller.

More than simply rewritings of one of the mythologies that undergirds *The Street King*, these manoeuvres bear a further, uniquely Shakespearean imprint, since Margarita, in her relationship with Juan/Richmond, stands in for Elizabeth in *Richard III*. 'She's from the barrio [and] she's made something of herself, [so] it's important that our characters get together because they can procreate', states actor Mario López on the film's DVD commentary, registering both a sense of the reproductive aspirations of the last act of Shakespeare's play and the prospect of a 'good mother' who will 'care for' her *familia*. Yet, speaking for plurality ('our community' is a repeated formulation) rather than for Rikki's brand of singularity, the anchorwoman in fact has only a tenuous relation to the ghetto. Hers is a pragmatic approach (she enters the barrio merely to report on its difficulties), and her distance from 'origin' is signalled in the polished, unadulterated English she speaks. The nodes of connection she cultivates are official, and the programming she represents is typically hegemonic; as Clara E. Rodríguez states, commenting on mainstream American broadcasting, 'news coverage tends to present Latinos as "problem people" ... to Anglo society'.[54] Via Margarita's interventions, *The Street King* becomes complicit in the demonization of Rikki: the film imagines cultural advancement taking place only in terms of a disavowal of the place of departure and is hence unable to conceive of positive change inside the barrio perimeter. Migratory success is strictly bourgeois in orientation, with parody in *The Street King* moving in a constant 'flow' that precludes a fundamental questioning of the concluding ideological premises of the play on which it is based.

There are two endings in *The Street King*, Margarita's and Rikki's. By the same token, *In Othello* culminates in a pairing of conclusions, although in this film the more trenchant dimensions of a parodic criticism are allowed to circulate. The first ending engages with the question of the extent to which Adil has been inhabited by his part. Climaxing in the production of *Othello*, *In Othello* discovers the strangled Desdemona opening her mouth to reveal a red rose. (Figure 11.) Embedded in the bloody appearance of the flower is the suggestion that Adil, having succumbed to the colonial pressures of the text, dispatches Sheeba in drama as well as 'real life': the rose, at least in Shakespearean terms, is associated with what has come to be seen as Laurence Olivier's racist interpretation of Othello in the 1965 film of the same name. Over the course of rehearsals, Adil is taught English by

*Figure 11.* Sheeba/Desdemona (Sheeba Chaddha) produces a rose during the concluding moments of *In Othello* (dir. Roysten Abel, 2003).

Sheeba, with the implication being that, in a post-millennial revisitation of Othello or even Caliban, the actor from 'rural' India finally reverts to type, thus legitimating the anxieties that bedevil Delhi's theatrical establishment.

This in-play ending, however, is ambiguated by the filmic conclusion, which challenges the power of a colonially bound or even multiculturally revivifed Shakespeare in such a way as to continue the idea of a local Indian reclamation. Admittedly, all forms of cultural practice in India may be aesthetically and ideologically compromised when mediated through western representational methods. Ania Loomba writes that '*Kathakali* ... has become an increasingly touristy form both within the country and abroad ... vulnerable to being read as an easy symbol of an authentic India ... [and] a potent commodity for the new global market', while Rustom Bharucha takes a more forceful approach to the question, protesting against the 'cosmetic' and '"cosmopolitan vernacular"' constructions of '"eternal India"' affiliated with local 'cultural resources'.[55] Yet, as Poonam Trivedi argues, 'mimetic theatres like *Kathakali* have the resources to articulate the unspoken, to embody and concretize the subtext and thereby lift the performance into another realm of imaginative involvement'.[56] It is such a capacity, I suggest, that is hinted at in the final wordless scene of a Shivite who, before a mirror, takes off the make-up and accoutrements of his religious order. Previously in the film, the same Shivite (a penitential follower of Shiva who dresses in the garb of the deity) is seen soliciting 100 'bucks' or rupees from Barry, acting out the alms-taking practices of his discipline, but also turning the economic tables on this representative of Shakespearean conservatism. What is 'unspoken' about the film's closing image, then, is not so much a Shakespearean idea of the character acknowledging the performer, or vice versa, as an authenticated incorporation into India of Shakespearean traditions and conventions. Because Adil and the Shivite resemble each other, and because the divestiture occurs in front of a miniature theatre, a connection is afforded between the various versions of theatricality testified to in the film. Moreover, in the act of the removal of surface appearances is implied a stripping away of Shakespearean accretions, a return to 'naturalness', even a regional or a folk-oriented adaptation of the Bardic body that the film itself has overlooked. In the moment of self-inspection in the mirror there is, of course, a continuing concern with the workings of interiority, yet an associated idea, which draws attention to the operations of refraction and parody, is made no less powerfully manifest. This 'subtext', and the 'imaginative' potential of the episode, become clearer in the light of the forces to which Shiva is tied in Indian mythology. On one level a destroyer of old habits and a harbinger of death, Shiva is simultaneously endowed with vital and creative capabilities; in this sense, destruction is seen as a positive in that it works as the condition for change and renewal.[57] Parody, too, is creative – it can both 'preserve' and produce – and there is more than a hint of this function in Shiva's generative energies.[58] The trident with which Shiva is armed (he routs evil-doers with the weapon) is the most expressive image of the god's power, since it signals both his threefold charge (creation, sustenance and destruction) and the authority wielded over past, present and future. If the Shivite whom *In Othello* prioritizes is a Shakespearean cipher, then the formation of new Shakespeares from old is purposefully anticipated via a 'flow' that puts paid to the otiose and the irrelevant so as to bring forward the vibrant, the indigenous, the pertinent and the possible.

## IV

Any translation, writes Walter Benjamin, contains 'the life of the originals', and parodic filmic versions of Shakespeare after the millennium certainly invite acknowledgement of their textual/theatrical beginnings, if only at the level of the Bard operating as a prompt rather than a model, a corpus of suggestions rather than a script to be replicated.[59] Yet, despite the fact that film parody, as Dan Harries writes, involves 'reiteration' (the 'evocation or quotation of particular elements from the targeted text'), Shakespeare in *The Street King*, *Romeo & Juliet* and *In Othello* is not always easy to detect, sometimes appearing as no more than a sign, an echo or a tendency.[60] The emphasis falls less on the linguistic intricacies of Shakespeare as on the ways in which he – and his authority – are shored up and distributed, the means whereby the Bard has been judged and continues to be appreciated. A film such as *In Othello*, for instance, finds in parody a convenient vehicle for assessing the locations of the Bard in India, the cultural considerations that cut across the continent, and the class- and region-inflected process of Shakespearean reproduction. One could argue that such filmic negotiations result in an affirmation of Shakespeare as a central component of the literary tradition. The 'parodic', one commentator notes, has recently 'become so marketable ... that its status has mutated into the very thing it has long assailed: a canon'.[61] But the global face of modernity allows for neither permanent fixtures nor historical stability, with the lexical and syntactic inversions and manoeuvres of Shakespearean filmic parody working more persuasively as a transforming and transformative contact zone. Parody, a 'dialogue' that, according to Linda Hutcheon, is distinctive because it 'recirculates' is, as these films amply demonstrate, a 'flow' that makes and remakes Shakespeare in a continually shifting variety of images, icons and modalities.[62]

Put another way, what *In Othello*, *Romeo & Juliet* and *The Street King* endeavour to discover is the extent to which Shakespeare is bolstered and undone, refreshed and relegated, in complementary processes that, more often that not, take place simultaneously and side-by-side. Opening out to embrace the forms in which the Shakespearean utterance can circulate, the films draw cultural attention to 'the *politics* of representation' and are thereby enabled to acknowledge that each parodic act, every marker of continuity and difference, entail an ideological consequence. Such is the field of reference within which the films function most significantly in returns to, and movements away from, plays that are seen as speaking with a particular urgency to some of the conflicted concerns of the contemporary era – belonging, loyalty, identification and citizenship. The works are elaborated as notably receptive to discussions of the new urban condition, with the physical and political motifs that parody detects in Shakespeare's texts being remodelled to match current interest in, among other features of globalization, the movement of capital, deterritorialization, cultural homogeneity and the impact of technology. Michael Cronin writes that 'translation is ideally placed to understand both the transnational movement that is globalization and the transnational movement that is anti-globalization' in a formulation that can equally well be applied to parody and its double-coded interpretive and critical dimensions.[63] For *In Othello*, *Romeo & Juliet* and *The Street King* do not mark a straightforward trajectory of attitudes towards Shakespeare, at least not in and of themselves; nor is their ultimate effect to bring contemplation back to the 'essence' of the author or of the play. Instead, the films 'de-doxify' the drama and its multiple constructions, displaying collectively a discrete moment of parodic intervention and analysis. Slipping in and out of radical and conservative tendencies, these films are archetypically postmodern in recycling what has been so as to pass particular comment upon what is and might be. They demonstrate the continuing value of Shakespeare, not so much an ending but another chapter, a fresh beginning. They suggest that new Shakespeares can be produced, that authority continues, even if its presence is differently mediated, and that scope exists for further inscriptions, whether on film or elsewhere. Despite the forgetfulness of Stratford-upon-Avon's fictional vicar, there is still much to celebrate.

# Epilogue

Complementing its on-screen investment in a 'dream of Japan', *As You Like It* (dir. Kenneth Branagh, 2006) is energized by an impulse grounded in the material realities of the contemporary western world. As the director and filmmaker explains, his film offers a conceptual equivalent for 'an escape from the rat race and a desire for the simple life'.[1] 'Buy the papers ... and look at the travel sections', he enjoins in interview, continuing, 'You'll see ... a competition to find the ... most away-from-it-all and isolated place ... there's an ache ... to find peace ... and contemplative time, even in ... [the popular television show] *I'm a Celebrity Get Me Out of Here*, to which I have to confess a minor addiction'. Implicitly acknowledged here is a dynamic relationship between media attention and interior locales, the ways in which 'dreams' of an alternative modality bear traces of the global mechanisms that bring them into being. It is revealing that, at the start of the twenty-first century, *As You Like It* should avail itself of a construction of an eastern existence at a time when the mondial economy in general and Hollywood in particular have brought China, Japan and their neighbours forcefully into the cultural register.

'[My] film developed organically, however one might explain the thinking', observes Branagh, keen to disassociate himself from the recent commodification of the Orient in such productions as *Crouching Tiger, Hidden Dragon* (dir. Ang Lee, 2000) and *House of Flying Daggers* (dir. Yimou Zhang, 2004), yet, in terms of its glossy appearance and stereotypical markers alone, this Shakespearean initiative caters to preconceived fantasies that bespeak the west more eloquently than the east. Hence, Tim Harvey's design continually plays up Kabuki-inspired images, combining glimpses of the lantern-lit palace hall with visual details of prayer flags, fans and geisha girls in order to reinforce the familiar contours of occidental assumptions. Diegetically, in its meshing of the sounds of frogs and crickets with Patrick Doyle's eastern-inspired musical refrains, *As You Like It* executes a similar function, while the prioritizing of physical activities, such as gravel raking and tai chi, is also directed towards the promotion of what is, in Branagh's words, not so much 'Japan' as an 'impression' or 'version' of how it is constituted in the popular imaginary. Interestingly, the England-based location for *As You Like It* mimes the process of the film's projections. Dating back to the Elizabethan period, Wakehurst Place, in West Sussex, which was used for the exteriors, features several ornamental lakes and an 'Asian' garden boasting such 'rarities' as 'Japanese' maples, dwarf rhododendrons and Himalayan blue poppies and lilies. The estate was bequeathed to the National Trust in 1963 and, from 1965 onwards, has been leased to the Royal Botanic Gardens. In its history of the collection and acquisition of non-native species, Wakehurst Place illuminates a broader trajectory, a colonially determined aspiration to situate on indigenous soil the flora and fauna of the world. The environs of Wakehurst Place make visible a range of narratives of empire, which encompass a trade in exotica, the miniaturization of foreign spaces and the possession on a single site of natural global variety. The estate and its gardens, it might be argued, are as much a global participant as the film to which they lend an illusion of cultural and geographical anchorage.

According to Branagh, his film is simultaneously driven by an urge to realize a specific moment when Japan, too, was beginning to respond to incipient global requirements. 'I found myself ... fixed on this period in the second half of the nineteenth century', he remarks, going on to note:

> Japan did indeed open up for trade with the west. The Americans went there ... [The Japanese] wanted to turn themselves from an agricultural society to an industrial one, so not only did they invite people in, they sent tens of thousands of their people across the world to gather commercial experience and knowledge of the industrial age, and there are many accounts of westerners and English folk who went there and, because they were not ... given licence by the people who traded in silk and rice and other commodities, ended up living around treaty ports, like Osaka, where trade was done ... The dukes and brothers, I felt, had a natural home amongst those merchant adventurers, many of whom had transplanted themselves ... for a while, and under extraordinary circumstances of

excitement and opportunity, a vast portion of the world got to this strange and mysterious [place] ... that had been closed in for centuries.

Of interest in Branagh's reading is the way in which a concept of 'English men abroad', in his words, is mapped onto a template that brings to mind some of the more recent features of late global capitalism. The hegemony of the US is hinted at, as is the idea of Japan as a superpower that has a mastery of technology as a prime directive. In its vision of cross-national *métissage*, the account accords with the polymorphous and constantly evolving nature of some modern global identities, and there is more than a hint of the last throes of imperial power in the detailing of an 'opportunity' for the expansion of cultural horizons. 'Transplantation' too, as this book has sought to indicate, is a constituent part of globalization as an economic phenomenon and a force that dictates both the shaping and movement of migratory populations. *As You Like It* offers a historical window on Japan at the same time as it imagines itself as inhabiting the forms and the rhetoric of the global marketplace.

Its global currency notwithstanding, *As You Like It* was protracted in gestation. 'If I absolutely nail it down', remarks Branagh, 'this [film] was a development and refinement of sitting in a stone garden [in Kyoto] for a couple of hours mostly on my own one spring day in 1990. It seemed as if my whole life was changing by sitting there.' It was not until 2000, however, that Branagh signed with Intermedia to direct and produce *As You Like It* (and also *Macbeth* and *Love's Labour's Lost*) in an agreement that enabled the director and filmmaker to promote 'Shakespeare [as] a natural for the cinema'. 'He is', publicity at the time exhorted, 'the ultimate popular entertainer ... If Shakespeare were alive today, he'd have a development deal at every studio.'[2] Unfortunately, as the subsequent reception of *Love's Labour's Lost* (2000) demonstrated, neither Shakespeare's 'popular' cachet, nor the 'development deal' enjoyed by his most erstwhile 'cinema' enthusiast, was sufficient seamlessly to continue the Bard's resurgence within the filmic medium. For not only did *Love's Labour's Lost*, as Ramona Wray writes, confuse and disorient punters with its 'generic mismatch', it was also an economic disappointment: the budget of $13,000,000 was not recouped by box office returns of £143,649 and $284,291, in Britain and the US, respectively.[3] Branagh elaborates:

> The companies involved ... [only] got their money back ... [and] the option on the agreement that I had with [Intermedia] expired. They

were all honourable men and, had one wanted to raise the money for [another] film and make it within that period, I'm sure there might have been a chance. But I didn't feel that it was the right time for me. Also, it was a disappointment to me that the critical reception of *Love's Labour's Lost* was as negative as it was: I confess to being perplexed and disappointed by that ... So I wasn't keen to jump into another Shakespeare film until I had thought that through a good deal.

Abundantly evident in the passage is a sense of the unpredictability of film as a global idiom. As Arthur De Vany writes, the movie 'industry is never in equilibrium and is constantly renewing itself'.[4] Partly as a result of *Love's Labour's Lost*'s performance, *Macbeth*, at one time slated as being the next film in Branagh's trilogy, was put on hold, although one might also suggest that the concept of a 'Scottish play' set in the corridors of a 'media empire' on 'Wall Street' had already been sapped and superseded by Michael Almereyda's deployment of a similarly global locale and idea in *Hamlet* (2000).[5] (Figure 12.) Even *As You Like It* appeared in trouble until the intervention of an unexpected supporter, as Branagh relates:

> I was [in the US] shooting and had mentioned [*As You Like It*] to HBO, and this coincided with a point in the development of [the cable and telecommunications company] where they essentially wanted to create a low-budget, independent feature film division that was absolutely aimed at the theatrical market and not just television. There was a sort of general conversation or trade-off: 'Keep this slightly bizarre or unfamiliar idea – Shakespeare, *As You Like It*, Japan – and see if you can find a way to shoot it that makes sense' ... Initially, though, there was a certain incomprehension about why the film should be done [in Japan] ... 'We can see to some extent how there may be a neat idea in here', [HBO] said, 'and you can have a sumo match for the wrestling, and perhaps a few other things that are superficially enticing, but isn't it just tricksy and novel for its own sake?' ... [So I simply tried to] disarm people, saying, 'I'm being as free with this as Shakespeare was with the original source material. This needs to be the case for us to justify this classic expressing its classic status, for its being available and [sufficiently] elastic for every generation to approach.'

Illustrated in this example is the way in which film is, as Diana E. Henderson reminds us, invariably a 'collaborative' endeavour involving

162  *Filming Shakespeare in the Global Marketplace*

*Figure 12.* An announcement for Kenneth Branagh's projected film of *Macbeth*.

'labour, agency and craft'; certainly, in Branagh's encounters with executives at HBO, a back-and-forth movement that privileges negotiation, reflection and contest is a crucial contributory element.[6] Making Shakespeare films emerges from the episode as inherently arbitrary and utterly contingent, dependent on adjustments and alterations, commissions and conduct, even on the force of personality and Gallic charm. Inside that process, intersecting attitudes towards Shakespeare become apparent. One, which might be associated with HBO's position, resists a resituating of Shakespeare; the other, to which Branagh might be allied, argues for a loosening of Shakespeare from the straitjacket of previous interpretations. Earlier disappointments aside, Branagh returns to the rhetoric of the earlier millennial celebration of Shakespeare and, if he seems to speak against a corporate reification of the Bard, simultaneously speaks for his ongoing applicability. As Emma French states, in the 'marketing of Shakespeare', a 'complex hybrid of veneration and irreverence' must achieve a 'balance' in order to guarantee a film's 'commercial success'.[7]

Such difficulty in securing patronage and profit is of a piece with how other films have fared in market-driven global environs. In this sense, the fortunes of Branagh's Shakespeare films are indicative of the twists and turns of the industry as a whole. Even a critically acclaimed production such as his *Hamlet* (1997), despite a budget of $18,000,000, grossed only $4,414,535 during its opening American run, and similar examples can easily be cited. In contradistinction, the resounding triumph of *Much Ado About Nothing* (1993) – the film generated a gross of $22,551,000 in the US and £4,139,294 in the UK from a original budget of $8,000,000 – can be set alongside the similar success stories of *William Shakespeare's 'Romeo + Juliet'* (dir. Baz Luhrmann, 1996) and *Shakespeare in Love* (dir. John Madden, 1998). The former, from an initial outlay of $14,500,000, earned $46,338,728 and £3,422,173 respectively, while the latter, building on an investment of $25,000,000, made $100,241,322 and £20,080,703 in box office revenues. Yet even these instances of the Bard's drawing power need to be juxtaposed with the impact of other types of film ('setting aside really "high concept" and "summer blockbuster" films', writes Russell Jackson, 'a popular comedy might reach nine figures on its first release') and with the commercial failures of a gamut of related Shakespeare on screen undertakings.[8] The Shakespeare film occupies a discrete niche in the market sector; in addition, it is expected to answer to the demands of a range of consumers, from broadcasters and distributors to preview audiences and exhibitors. Such is the finely tuned and delicately devised business of selling Shakespeare in which, as Peter Holland states, the product must be 'marketable to studio and backers, to stars and directors ... to chat-show hosts and film reviewers before it is ever sold to the cinema-going public'.[9] Above all, film is dictated to by corporations – media organizations that may embody in their workings a galaxy of smaller enterprises. Many of the independent film companies that have produced Shakespeare films, as Mario Falsetto writes, 'are, in fact, owned by the majors', including Castle Rock (owned by Warner Brothers, a division of Time Warner), Miramax (part of the Disney empire) and Twentieth-Century Fox (part of the News Corporation consortium).[10] In part as a result of the control of globally funded conglomerates, the Shakespeare film can claim a tenuous position at best. This book has already drawn attention to processes of revision and to the vicissitudes of a film such as 'O' (dir. Tim Blake Nelson, 2001), and there is more than an intimate relation shared between the abandoned idea or project and the intervention of the executive. Crucially, global forms of reproduction and dissemination also determine the afterlives of films. Works such as *Macbeth in Manhattan* (dir. Greg Lombardo, 1999), *In Othello* (dir. Roysten Abel, 2003), *Indian Dream* (dir. Roger Goldby, 2003) and *Hamlet* (dir. Stephen Cavanagh, 2005) have yet to appear on commercial video and/or DVD; other Shakespeare screen outings, including *Makibefo* (dir. Alexander Abela, 1999), a version of *Macbeth* performed by Madagascar fishermen, and *Henry V* (dir. Peter Babakitis, 2004), a painterly rendition of Shakespeare's play that makes extensive use of digital technology, appear consigned to a comparable fate. Specific relations of production, which are tied to time and place, suggest the Shakespeare canon. What defines a 'Shakespeare film' is very often its availability, a process in which corporate influence and market criteria are all important. The canon of films on which the critic might work can be a narrowly defined grouping, the visibility of which is decided by the vagaries of globalization's multiple incarnations. In turn, such constructions of both 'Shakespeare' and 'film' inevitably filter through into pedagogical practice and into a strictly demarcated conception of the ways in which the Bard's screen presence is understood.

In this connection, the production history and public exposure of the Derry Film Initiative's *Hamlet* points up complicating connections between the Shakespeare film and the global marketplace. It was one of my graduate students who, flicking through a newspaper in 2001, told me that parts of a new *Hamlet*, made in Northern Ireland by a recently formed group of Londonderry-based practitioners, were to be screened at the Derry Film Festival. Travelling to Derry to watch these segments, I met Stephen Cavanagh, this other Irish director of Shakespeare, and, because already working on this book and impressed by the local vibrancy and innovativeness of his *Hamlet*, suggested we communicate with the Shakespeare Association of America with a view to a screening at one of the organization's annual conferences. Yet, supported more by goodwill than external funding, and bedevilled with production problems, the project seemed destined to falter. 'Look', Stephen confided during later telephone conversations, 'people are difficult to get hold of, I'm doing other things, there's no money and, as far as the film's concerned, we haven't really done any more work on it'. Thus, it was particularly gratifying when, at the 2005 meeting of the SAA, the 'world première' of the Derry Film Initiative *Hamlet* was announced.

I was to introduce the occasion but, as the Friday night approached, I was afflicted with doubts. Had the film been completed? Would the director and members of the cast, as advertised, be present for the question-and-answer session? I needn't have worried. The film unfolded smoothly in the auditorium, the audience were more than appreciative and Stephen and his associates – Richard Hughes (Producer) and Colin Stewart (Rosencrantz) – responded to enquiries with a mixture of gifted articulacy and diverting self-deprecation. Amidst a lively and enriching discussion of filmic choices and design ideas, some of the more rarefied questions were met with a healthy dose of material pragmatism. Q: 'What is the symbolic significance of Yorick's red skull?' A: 'Well, I'm not sure if it has any: I was in a production recently and just found it kicking around at the back of the theatre'. Q: 'Which of the three texts of *Hamlet* – Q1, Q2 and F – did you choose for interpretation and why?' A: 'To tell you the truth, I simply downloaded the first one I came across on the internet'. Q: 'Are you a regular reader of *Hamlet Studies*?' A: 'I've not come across that one!' The knowing laughter produced by these dialogues seemed only to affirm the success of the film in the audience's mind; certainly, there were murmurs of general assent at the point where an unidentified woman loomed from the back of the auditorium to deliver an impassioned encomium in Russian then rendered as 'I salute your humanity!' by her translator. When she was later revealed as Veronika A. Kosenkova of the Moscow International Theatre Laboratory, it seemed as if the Derry Film Initiative had received a benediction and come of age. The notable differences of scale and ambition between this *Hamlet* and a Shakespeare film such as *As You Like It* notwithstanding, the occasion bolstered the occasional small part the scholarly community has to play in the global film phenomenon. In the wake of a mutually starstruck première, the Initiative was made a domestic distribution offer, the director was invited to screen *Hamlet* at a number of American universities and colleges, and the film went on to a series of showings in England and Ireland that garnered considerable praise.[11] What role, if any, the première event played in this process is difficult to gauge. But it is certainly the case that the location of the conference – Bermuda – lent the film a gravitas and exoticism in its subsequent career and that the support of an American organization functioned to legitimate and complement the local sources of funding (the Heritage Lottery Fund, The Honourable The Irish Society and the Northern Ireland Film and Television Commission) that the film secured in its final production stages. Does Shakespeare sponsor the possibility of film or does the process work in the opposite direction? To what extent is the conference itself a species of global corporation or a market in which Bardic wares are authorized and internationalized? Cavanagh and Branagh may appear miles apart, yet, at another level, both are equally active players in the business that is Shakespeare on film and the market mentality that globalizes and localizes in the interests of securing the Bard's cinematic legacy.

# Notes

## Preface

1 Julie Taymor, *'The Tempest': Adapted from the Play by William Shakespeare* (New York: Abrams, 2010), p. 14.
2 Taymor, *'The Tempest'*, p. 15.
3 See Cath Clarke, 'Full-metal Shakespeare', *The Guardian*, 7 May (2010), p. 5.
4 See 'About the Production', available at http://weinsteinco.com/sites/coriolanus.
5 See http://tempest-themovie.com.
6 Kenneth Branagh, *'Much Ado About Nothing' by William Shakespeare: Screenplay, Introduction and Notes* (New York and London: W. W. Norton, 1993), p. x.
7 Lúcia Nagib, 'Towards a Positive Definition of World Cinema', in Stephanie Dennison and Song Hwee Lim, eds, *Remapping World Cinema: Identity, Culture and Politics in Film* (London and New York: Wallflower, 2006), p. 35. See also Mark Thornton Burnett, 'Screen Shakespeares: Knowledge and Practice', *Critical Quarterly*, 52.4 (2010), pp. 48–9.
8 A commercial DVD of *Makibefo* came out nine years after the film's first release.
9 *'Makibefo': An Alexander Abela Film based on William Shakespeare's 'Macbeth'*, press booklet (London: Blue Eye Films, 2000), p. 4. For a longer discussion of the auteur, see Mark Thornton Burnett, 'Madagascan Will: Cinematic Exchanges/Transnational Exchanges', *Shakespeare Survey*, 61 (2008), pp. 239–55.
10 See Mark Thornton Burnett, 'Shakespeare and Contemporary Latin American Cinema', *Shakespeare Quarterly*, 62.3 (2011), pp. 396–419.
11 See 'Asian Shakespeares on Screen: Two Films in Perspective', a special issue edited by Alexander C. Y. Huang of *Borrowers and Lenders: The Journal of Shakespeare and Appropriation*, 4.2 (2009), available at http://www.borrowers.uga.edu.
12 Fredric Jameson, *Postmodernism, or, the Cultural Logic of Late Capitalism* (London and New York: Verso, 1991), p. 19.
13 For Shakespeare and the online environment, see Christy Desmet, 'Paying Attention in Shakespeare Parody: From Tom Stoppard to YouTube', *Shakespeare Survey*, 61 (2008), pp. 227–38; Lauren Shohet, 'YouTube, Use, and the Idea of the Archive', *Shakespeare Studies*, 38 (2010), pp. 68–76. A general overview is provided in 'Shakespeare and New Media', a special issue edited by Katherine Rowe of *Shakespeare Quarterly*, 61.3 (2010).
14 Ramona Wray, 'Shakespeare on Film in the New Millennium', *Shakespeare*, 3.2 (2007), pp. 277–80.

## Introduction

1 Richard Langhorne, *The Coming of Globalization: Its Evolution and Contemporary Consequences* (Basingstoke: Palgrave, 2001), p. 2; Tony Schirato and Jen Webb, *Understanding Globalization* (London: Sage, 2003), p. 10.

168  *Notes*

2. Philip B. Zarrilli, Bruce McConachie, Gary Jay Williams and Carol Fisher Sorgenfrei, *Theatre Histories: An Introduction* (London and New York: Routledge, 2006), p. 415.
3. Fantu Cheru, 'New Social Movements: Democratic Struggles and Human Rights in Africa', in James H. Mittelman, ed., *Globalization: Critical Reflections* (Boulder, CO and London: Lynne Rienner, 1997), p. 145; David Held and Anthony McGrew, 'The Great Globalization Debate', in David Held and Anthony McGrew, eds, *The Global Transformations Reader: An Introduction to the Globalization Debate* (Cambridge: Polity, 2000), p. 3.
4. Jan Aart Scholte, *Globalization: A Critical Introduction* (Basingstoke: Macmillan, 2000), p. 23.
5. Rob Wilson and Wimal Dissanayake, 'Introduction: Tracking the Global/Local', in Rob Wilson and Wimal Dissanayake, eds, *Global/Local: Cultural Production and the Transnational Imaginary* (Durham, NC and London: Duke University Press, 1996), p. 1.
6. Ulrich Beck, *What is Globalization?* (Cambridge: Polity, 2000), p. 75.
7. Held and McGrew, 'Globalization Debate', p. 4; Arie de Ruijter, 'Globalization: A Challenge to the Social Sciences', in Frans J. Schuurman, ed., *Globalization and Development Studies: Challenges for the 21st Century* (London: Sage, 2001), p. 32.
8. Beck, *What is Globalization?*, p. 26; Langhorne, *Coming*, p. 17.
9. Michael Walsh, 'Jameson and "Global Aesthetics"', in David Bordwell and Noël Carroll, eds, *Post-Theory: Reconstructing Film Studies* (Madison: University of Wisconsin Press, 1996), p. 487; Langhorne, *Coming*, pp. 19–20.
10. Aida Hozic, *Hollyworld: Space, Power, and Fantasy in the American Economy* (Ithaca, NY and London: Cornell University Press, 2001).
11. Fredric Jameson, 'Notes on Globalization as a Philosophical Issue', in Fredric Jameson and Masao Miyoshi, eds, *The Cultures of Globalization* (Durham, NC and London: Duke University Press, 1998), p. 58.
12. See Tino Balio, '"A major presence in all of the world's most important markets": The Globalization of Hollywood in the 1990s', in Steve Neale and Murray Smith, eds, *Contemporary Hollywood Cinema* (London and New York: Routledge, 1998), p. 58; Toby Miller, Nitin Govil, John McMurria and Richard Maxwell, *Global Hollywood* (London: BFI, 2001), p. 146.
13. Hozic, *Hollyworld*, p. xiv; Miller et al, *Global*, p. 3.
14. Peter Donaldson, '"All which it inherit": Shakespeare, Globes and Global Media', *Shakespeare Survey*, 52 (1999), p. 185.
15. Zarrilli et al., *Theatre Histories*, pp. 444, 445.
16. Carolyn Jess-Cooke, 'Screening the McShakespeare in Post-Millennial Shakespeare Cinema', in Mark Thornton Burnett and Ramona Wray, eds, *Screening Shakespeare in the Twenty-First Century* (Edinburgh: Edinburgh University Press, 2006), pp. 163, 165.

## Chapter 1  Screening the Stage

1. Samuel Crowl, *Shakespeare at the Cineplex: The Kenneth Branagh Era* (Athens, OH: Ohio University Press, 2003), p. 1.

## Notes 169

2  Andreas Huyssen, 'Present Pasts: Media, Politics, Amnesia', *Public Culture*, 12.1 (2000), p. 37.
3  Caridad Svich, 'Theatre in Crisis? Living Memory in an Unstable Time', in Maria M. Delgado and Caridad Svich, eds, *Theatre in Crisis? Performance Manifestoes for a New Century* (Manchester: Manchester University Press, 2002), p. 18.
4  Baz Kershaw, *The Radical in Performance: Between Brecht and Baudrillard* (London and New York: Routledge, 1999), p. 5.
5  Susan Bennett, *Theatre Audiences: A Theory of Production and Reception*, 2nd edn. (London and New York: Routledge, 1997), p. 116; Kershaw, *Radical*, pp. 5, 32.
6  Caridad Svich, 'The Dynamics of Fractals: Legacies for a New Tomorrow', in Caridad Svich, ed., *Trans-global Readings: Crossing Theatrical Boundaries* (Manchester: Manchester University Press, 2003), p. 2.
7  Susan Bennett remarks that 'the two most common "advertising" techniques' are 'word of mouth and a habit of attending a particular theatre' (*Theatre Audiences*, p. 123). Mark's company is portrayed as having been unable to master either method.
8  Robert Shaughnessy, *The Shakespeare Effect: A History of Twentieth-Century Performance* (Basingstoke: Palgrave, 2002), p. 9.
9  Philip Auslander, *Liveness: Performance in a Mediatized Culture* (London and New York: Routledge, 1999), p. 36. Hence, the English group Forced Entertainment staged a *Five Day Lear* which constituted a video-based 'mapping of the play, rather than a reading of it'; the German dramaturge Karen Beier presented a version of *A Midsummer Night's Dream* involving 'fourteen actors from nine countries ... speak[ing] in their own languages'; and the Brazilian collective Grupo Galpão adapted *Romeo and Juliet* for a world tour, combining in the production such 'multivocality' as 'comic swordplay, puppetry ... physical buffoonery ... and ... a Volvo'. See Anthony B. Dawson, 'International Shakespeare', in Stanley Wells and Sarah Stanton, eds, *The Cambridge Companion to Shakespeare on Stage* (Cambridge: Cambridge University Press, 2002), p. 182; Shaughnessy, *Shakespeare Effect*, p. 188; W. B. Worthen, *Shakespeare and the Force of Modern Performance* (Cambridge: Cambridge University Press, 2003), p. 157
10  In the US, Laurie Anderson, John Jesurum, Robert Wilson and the Wooster Group are among the foremost practitioners of these and other tendencies.
11  Kathy M. Howlett, *Framing Shakespeare on Film* (Athens, OH: Ohio University Press, 2000), p. 190.
12  Russell Jackson, 'Actor-Managers and the Spectacular', in Jonathan Bate and Russell Jackson, eds, *Shakespeare: An Illustrated Stage History* (Oxford: Oxford University Press, 1996), p. 124.
13  Worthen, *Modern Performance*, p. 29.
14  Kenneth Branagh, *In the Bleak Midwinter* (London: Nick Hern, 1995), p. 5. All further references appear in the text.
15  See Auslander, *Liveness*, pp. 1, 2, 6.
16  See Peggy Phelan, *Unmarked: The Politics of Performance* (London and New York: Routledge, 1993), pp. 146–9.
17  Dennis Kennedy, 'Shakespeare and the Global Spectator', *Shakespeare Jahrbuch*, 131 (1995), p. 50.

170  *Notes*

18  Courtney Lehmann, 'Shakespeare the Saviour or Phantom Menace? Kenneth Branagh's *A Midwinter's Tale* and the Critique of Cynical Reason', *Colby Quarterly*, 37.1 (2001), p. 65.
19  Steve Blandford, Barry Keith Grant and Jim Hillier, *The Film Studies Dictionary* (London: Arnold, 2001), p. 73.
20  Wolfgang Iser, *The Act of Reading: A Theory of Aesthetic Response* (London and Henley: Routledge & Kegan Paul, 1978), p. 111.
21  *A Midsummer Night's Dream*, in *The Norton Shakespeare*, ed. Stephen Greenblatt, Walter Cohen, Jean E. Howard and Katharine Eisaman Maus (New York and London: W. W. Norton, 1997), IV.i.144. Unless otherwise stated, all further references to the plays appear in the text.
22  Homi K. Bhabha, 'DissemiNation: Time, Narrative, and the Margins of the Modern Nation', in Homi K. Bhabha, ed., *Nation and Narration* (London and New York: Routledge, 1990), p. 318.
23  Philip Zarrilli, Bruce McConachie, Gary Jay Williams and Carol Fisher Sorgenfrei, *Theatre Histories: An Introduction* (London and New York: Routledge, 2006), p. 411.
24  *Get Over It* offers a sexually nuanced variation on the idea of a performance that facilitates self-discovery by playing out the thesis that *A Midsummer Night's Dream*, as Bruce Thomas Boehrer puts it, 'is patently about' bestiality and buggery. See Bruce Thomas Boehrer, 'Bestial Buggery in *A Midsummer Night's Dream*', in David Lee Miller, Sharon O' Dair and Harold Weber, eds, *The Production of English Renaissance Culture* (Ithaca, NY and London: Cornell University Press, 1994), p. 123.
25  In draft screenplays for Michael Hoffman's film version of *William Shakespeare's 'A Midsummer Night's Dream'* (1999), for instance, Bottom is punished for his performative excesses in a public square by two 'errant boys' who scoop 'donkey shit' into a bag, tipping its 'contents out' upon him and scoring 'a direct hit'. See Michael Hoffman, *William Shakespeare's 'A Midsummer Night's Dream'* (New York: HarperCollins, 1999), pp. 14, 16; Twentieth-Century Fox Film Archive, Los Angeles, '*A Midsummer Night's Dream*' by William Shakespeare, 1st draft (1997), pp. 15–16.
26  Auslander, *Liveness*, passim.
27  Phelan, *Unmarked*, pp. 146, 148.
28  At the close of *In the Bleak Midwinter*, one could also argue that the spontaneous performance of Hamlet – suitably advertised as '*Hamlet*: Live Here: Now' – accords with the notion that theatre is never repeatable and, in the light of the company's continuing competition for custom with a Hollywood film unit, that it is invested with an important critical energy.
29  *Antony and Cleopatra*, in *The Norton Shakespeare*, IV.xv.2–7; *Hamlet*, in *The Norton Shakespeare*, III.ii.345–51.
30  Erika Fischer-Lichte, *The Show and the Gaze of Theatre: A European Perspective* (Iowa City: University of Iowa Press, 1997), p. 25.
31  Kenneth Branagh Archive [hereafter KBA], Interview between Kenneth Branagh and Pierre Berthomieu, 14 and 15 August (1997).
32  Douglas Lanier, '"Art thou base, common, and popular?" The Cultural Politics of Kenneth Branagh's *Hamlet*', in Courtney Lehmann and Lisa S. Starks, eds, *Spectacular Shakespeare: Critical Theory and Popular Cinema* (Madison and Teaneck, WI: Fairleigh Dickinson University Press, 2002), p. 155.
33  Caren Kaplan, *Questions of Travel: Postmodern Discourses of Displacement* (Durham, NC and London: Duke University Press, 1996), pp. 40–1.

34 Susanne Greenhalgh and Robert Shaughnessy, 'Our Shakespeares: British Television and the Strains of Multiculturalism', in Mark Thornton Burnett and Ramona Wray, eds, *Screening Shakespeare in the Twenty-First Century* (Edinburgh: Edinburgh University Press, 2006), p. 107.
35 Mark Fortier, *Theory/Theatre: An Introduction*, 2nd edn. (London and New York: Routledge, 2002), p. 56.
36 Pat Bucker, 'The "Hope" *Hamlet*: Kenneth Branagh's Comic Use of Shakespeare's Tragedy in *A Midwinter's Tale*', *Shakespeare Yearbook*, 8 (1997), p. 290; Lanier, '"Art thou base, common and popular?"', p. 155.
37 The song derives from *The Tempest*, in *The Norton Shakespeare*, V.i.88, rather than *A Midsummer Night's Dream*.
38 Jonathan Dollimore, *Sexual Dissidence: Augustine to Wilde, Freud to Foucault* (Oxford: Clarendon Press, 1991), pp. 56, 310.
39 KBA, Interview between Kenneth Branagh and Jamie Payne, ABC Cinema, London, 7 June (1997).
40 Lehmann, 'Shakespeare the Saviour', p. 73.
41 Michael T. Gilmore, *Differences in the Dark: American Movies and English Theatre* (New York: Columbia University Press, 1998), p. 8.
42 Bennett, *Performing Nostalgia*, p. 20.
43 John Russell Brown, *Shakespeare and the Theatrical Event* (Basingstoke: Palgrave, 2002), p. 151.
44 Here, *Beginner's Luck* may be self-consciously recalling the ironic placing of the song, 'Stormy Weather', as performed by 'veteran black singer Elisabeth Welch', in Derek Jarman's 1979 art-house film meditation on *The Tempest*. For a trenchant discussion of the implications of this moment, see Kate Chedgzoy, *Shakespeare's Queer Children: Sexual Politics and Contemporary Culture* (Manchester and New York: Manchester University Press, 1995), pp. 204–5.
45 Kaplan, *Questions*, p. 151.
46 Roland Robertson, *Globalization, Social Theory and Global Culture* (London: Sage, 1992), p. 155.
47 Fredric Jameson, *Signatures of the Visible* (New York and London: Routledge, 1992), p. 229.
48 Paul de Man, *Blindness and Insight: Essays in the Rhetoric of Contemporary Criticism*, 2nd edn. (Minneapolis, MN: University of Minnesota Press, 1983), p. 92.

## Chapter 2   Sequelizing Shakespeare

1 Douglas Lanier, 'Nostalgia and Theatricality: The Fate of the Shakespearean Stage in the *Midsummer Night's Dream*s of Hoffman, Noble and Edzard', in Richard Burt and Lynda Boose, eds, *Shakespeare, the Movie, II: Popularizing the Plays on Film, TV, Video, and DVD* (London and New York: Routledge, 2003), p. 155. Comparable remarks may be found in Stephen M. Buhler, *Shakespeare in the Cinema: Ocular Proof* (New York: State University of New York Press, 2002), p. 183; Samuel Crowl, *Shakespeare at the Cineplex: The Kenneth Branagh Era* (Athens, OH: Ohio University Press, 2003), pp. 172, 180; Jay L. Halio, *Shakespeare in Performance: 'A Midsummer Night's Dream'*, 2nd edn. (Manchester: Manchester University Press, 2003), p. 152; MacDonald P. Jackson, '"A Wood Near Monte Athena": Michael Hoffman's *A Midsummer Night's Dream*', *The Shakespeare Newsletter*, 49.2 (1999), p. 37.

## 172 Notes

2  Harold Bloom, *The Anxiety of Influence: A Theory of Poetry* (New York: Oxford University Press, 1973), passim; Paul Budra and Betty A. Schellenberg, 'Introduction', in Paul Budra and Betty A. Schellenberg, eds, *Part Two: Reflections upon the Sequel* (Toronto, Buffalo and London: University of Toronto Press, 1998), p. 6; Gérard Genette, *Palimpsests: Literature in the Second Degree*, trans. Channa Newman and Claude Doubinsky (Lincoln, NB and London: University of Nebraska Press, 1997), p. 395.
3  Genette, *Palimpsests*, p. 162.
4  Genette, *Palimpsests*, pp. 260, 262.
5  Budra and Schellenberg, 'Introduction', p. 17; Thomas Carmichael, '"After the Fact": Marx, the Sequel, Postmodernism, and John Barth's *LETTERS*', in Budra and Schellenberg, eds, *Part Two*, p. 174; Genette, *Palimpsests*, p. 44; Robert P. Kolker, 'Algebraic Figures: Recalculating the Hitchcock Formula', in Andrew Horton and Stuart Y. McDougal, eds, *Play it Again, Sam: Retakes on Remakes* (Berkeley, Los Angeles and London: University of California Press, 1998), p. 36; June Sturrock, 'Sequels, Series and Sensation Novels: Charlotte Yonge and the Popular-Fiction Market of the 1850s and 1860s', in Budra and Schellenberg, eds, *Part Two*, p. 102.
6  Jacques Derrida, *A Derrida Reader: Between the Blinds*, ed. Peggy Kamuf (New York and London: Harvester Wheatsheaf, 1991), p. 256.
7  Genette, *Palimpsests*, passim.
8  Kenneth Branagh, *'Much Ado About Nothing' by William Shakespeare: Screenplay, Introduction and Notes* (New York and London: W. W. Norton, 1993), p. xiv; Michael Hoffman, *William Shakespeare's 'A Midsummer Night's Dream'* (New York: HarperCollins, 1999), p. vi.
9  *A Midsummer Night's Dream*, in *The Norton Shakespeare*, ed. Stephen Greenblatt, Walter Cohen, Jean E. Howard and Katharine Eisaman Maus (New York and London: W. W. Norton, 1997), I.i.157–8. Unless otherwise stated, all further references to the plays are taken from this edition and appear in the text.
10  Courtney Lehmann helpfully identifies Helena (Ally McBeal) rather than Titania (Michelle Pfeiffer) as the 'bitch ... whose key behavioural attribute is [a] commitment to raging' ('Crouching Tiger, Hidden Agenda: How Shakespeare and the Renaissance are Taking the Rage out of Feminism', *Shakespeare Quarterly*, 53.2 [2002], p. 266).
11  One of the first drafts of the screenplay for this scene makes a point of referring to the animal 'statues' on the Villa Terrace. See Kenneth Branagh Archive [hereafter KBA], *'Much Ado About Nothing' by William Shakespeare: Adapted for the Screen by Kenneth Branagh*, 1st draft (1992), p. 23.
12  KBA, *'Much Ado About Nothing' by William Shakespeare: Adapted for the Screen by Kenneth Branagh*, 1st draft (1992), p. 31.
13  Sarah Mayo, '"A Shakespeare for the People?": Negotiating the Popular in *Shakespeare in Love* and Michael Hoffman's *A Midsummer Night's Dream*', *Textual Practice*, 17.2 (2003), p. 304.
14  Marian Hobson, 'History Traces', in Derek Attridge, Geoff Bennington and Robert Young, eds, *Post-structuralism and the Question of History* (Cambridge: Cambridge University Press, 1987), p. 101.
15  Interviews suggest that introducing a theatrical dimension into *A Midsummer Night's Dream* was a conscious strategy on Hoffman's part. For

instance, he has remarked that 'I chose to make the forest an artificial place ... You get these theatrical effects while people are behaving in [sets] ... in a relatively naturalistic way' (Michael LoMonico, '"Is all our company here?": An Interview with Michael Hoffman', *Shakespeare*, 3.2 [1999], p. 12).
16 On Apollo's patronage, see Pierre Grimal, *The Dictionary of Classical Mythology*, trans. A. R. Maxwell-Hyslop (Oxford: Blackwell, 1986), p. 50. Even the DVD version of Hoffman's film rehearses these elements, since the opening frame is designed as a red-curtained stage.
17 Kolker, 'Algebraic Figures', p. 36.
18 KBA, Interview between Kenneth Branagh and Pierre Berthomieu, 14 and 15 August (1997). As has been frequently noted, the opening self-consciously parodies the numerous horse-mounted group shots animating John Sturges' *The Magnificent Seven* (1960). But it is also important to register *Much Ado About Nothing*'s in-built parody of its own inauguration: one can mention here the fictional horses ridden by Dogberry (Michael Keaton) and Verges (Ben Elton), and the scene in which Don John, exulting in the success of his conspiracy in a subterranean corridor, punches the air. Both moments recall the united gesture on the part of the galloping horsemen of the start and point to new, if misguided, masculine alliances.
19 KBA, *David Letterman: 'Much Ado About Nothing'*, 15 May (1993); KBA, *Charlie Rose Interview: 'Much Ado About Nothing'*, 23 May (1993).
20 Such casting elements are arguably designed to heighten an illusion of Shakespearean authenticity; or, as H. R. Coursen states, 'His [Hoffman's] script seems to be made up of words that will prove that "this is Shakespeare!"' (*Shakespeare in Space: Recent Shakespeare Productions on Screen* [New York: Peter Lang, 2002], p. 78). One also thinks here, of course, of the implications of the use of Shakespeare's name in the film's title.
21 Calista Flockhart is, as Courtney Lehmann observes, a 'pop-cultural icon of ... love' known for her role as Ally McBeal in the television show of the same name ('Crouching Tiger, Hidden Agenda', p. 267); Kevin Kline is a major player in Hollywood comedy.
22 Douglas Lanier, 'Drowning the Book: *Prospero's Books* and the Textual Shakespeare', in James C. Bulman, ed., *Shakespeare, Theory, and Performance* (London and New York: Routledge, 1996), pp. 191–2.
23 KBA, *'Much Ado About Nothing': Suggested Classroom Activities* (1993), p. 2.
24 Crowl, *Shakespeare at the Cineplex*, p. 186.
25 The formulation appears on the notes to the 'Original Motion Picture Soundtrack' CD of the film published by Decca in 1999.
26 Walter Benjamin, *Illuminations*, trans. Harry Zohn (London: Fontana/Collins, 1982), p. 222. See also Lanier, 'Nostalgia and Theatricality', p. 170; Peggy Phelan, *Unmarked: The Politics of Performance* (London and New York: Routledge, 1993), pp. 146–9.
27 Hillel Schwartz, *The Culture of the Copy: Striking Likenesses, Unreasonable Facsimiles* (New York: Zone, 1996), p. 212.
28 Timothy Corrigan, 'The Commerce of Auteurism', in Virginia Wright Wexman, ed., *Film and Authorship* (New Jersey and London: Rutgers University Press, 2003), p. 97.
29 Hoffman, *William Shakespeare's 'A Midsummer Night's Dream'*, p. 13.

30 Hoffman, *William Shakespeare's 'A Midsummer Night's Dream'*, p. 58.
31 Friedrich Kittler, *Gramophone, Film, Typewriter*, trans. Geoffrey Winthrop-Young and Michael Wutz (Stanford, CA: Stanford University Press, 1999), p. 3.
32 Oliver Read and Walter L. Welch, *From Tin Foil to Stereo: Evolution of the Phonograph* (Bloomington and Indianapolis: Indiana University Press, 1959), p. 12.
33 Kittler, *Gramophone, Film, Typewriter*, p. 115.
34 Hoffman, *William Shakespeare's 'A Midsummer Night's Dream'*, p. vi.
35 Shakespeare Institute, Stratford-upon-Avon [hereafter SI], *'A Midsummer Night's Dream' by William Shakespeare: Shooting Script*, 3 March (1998), p. 4.
36 Kittler, *Gramophone, Film, Typewriter*, p. 186.
37 Hélène Cixous and Catherine Clément, *The Newly Born Woman* (Minneapolis, MN and London: University of Minnesota Press, 1986), p. 93. In early drafts of the screenplay, the idea of an individual woman rewriting was extended into the suggestion of a like-minded female community. 'The last line' of the refrain, it is stated, 'is accompanied by at least three other female voices at raucous and merry full volume' (KBA, *'Much Ado About Nothing' by William Shakespeare: Adapted for the Screen by Kenneth Branagh*, 1st draft [1992], p. 2).
38 Michael J. Collins, 'Sleepless in Messina: Kenneth Branagh's *Much Ado About Nothing*', *Shakespeare Bulletin*, 15.2 (1997), p. 39; H. R. Coursen, *Shakespeare in Production: Whose History?* (Athens, OH: Ohio University Press, 1996), p. 115. My position is closest to that of Celestino Deleyto, who writes that the song 'is turned by the film's contemporary discourse into a song of celebration of a female space' ('Men in Leather: Kenneth Branagh's *Much Ado About Nothing* and Romantic Comedy', *Cinema Journal*, 36.3 [1997], p. 96).
39 Kaja Silverman, *The Acoustic Mirror: The Female Voice in Psychoanalysis and Cinema* (Bloomington and Indianapolis: Indiana University Press, 1988), p. 207.
40 S. I., *'A Midsummer Night's Dream' by William Shakespeare: Shooting Script*, 3 March (1998), p. 2.
41 Hoffman's film here follows in the footsteps of five other films that figure the fairies in *A Midsummer Night's Dream* as lights or fireflies. See *Sen Noci Svatojánské* (dir. Jiří Trnka, 1959), *A Midsummer Night's Dream* (dir. Peter Hall, 1969), *A Midsummer Night's Sex Comedy* (dir. Woody Allen, 1982), *Bottom's Dream* (dir. John Canemaker, 1983), *Dead Poets Society* (dir. Peter Weir, 1989).
42 Hoffman, *William Shakespeare's 'A Midsummer Night's Dream'*, p. viii.
43 Kittler, *Gramophone, Film, Typewriter*, p. 193.
44 Kittler, *Gramophone, Film, Typewriter*, pp. 183, 194.
45 Janet Staiger, 'Authorship Approaches', in David A. Gerstner and Janet Staiger, eds, *Authorship and Film* (London and New York: Routledge, 2003), p. 50.
46 Jacqueline Suter, 'Feminine Discourse in *Christopher Strong*', *Camera Obscura*, 3–4 (1979), pp. 147–8.
47 Eveyln Gajowski, '"Sigh no more, ladies, sigh no more": Genesis Deconstructed in Kenneth Branagh's *Much Ado About Nothing*', *Journal of Theatre and Drama*, 5–6 (1999/2000), p. 121.
48 Preliminary drafts for this scene suggest an even greater stress upon stereotypical masculine features, with planned close-up shots of the 'anatomy' of

horsemen 'naked to the waist'. See KBA, '*Much Ado About Nothing*' *by William Shakespeare: Adapted for the Screen by Kenneth Branagh*, 1st draft (1992), p. 11; KBA, '*Much Ado About Nothing*': *Day Breakdown* (1993), scene 15.
49 Stephen Buhler, 'Textual and Sexual Anxieties in Michael Hoffman's Film of *A Midsummer Night's Dream*', *Shakespeare Bulletin*, 22.3 (2004), p. 52.
50 Nicholas Jones, 'Bottom's Wife: Gender and Voice in Hoffman's *Dream*', *Literature/Film Quarterly*, 32.2 (2004), p. 132; Megan M. Matchinske sharply notes that Bottom's wedding ring is missing from his finger at this point ('Putting Bottom on Top: Gender and the Married Man in Michael Hoffman's *Dream*', *Shakespeare Bulletin*, 21.4 [2003], p. 52).
51 Fredric Jameson, *Postmodernism, or, the Cultural Logic of Late Capitalism* (London and New York: Verso, 1991), pp. 85–6.
52 The Tinkerbell connection is made by Jackson, '"A Wood Near Monte Athena"', p. 37; Fredric Jameson, *The Seeds of Time* (New York: Columbia University Press, 1994), p. 205.
53 See Stephen M. Buhler, 'Shakespeare and Company: *The Lion King* and the Disneyfication of *Hamlet*', in Brenda Ayres, ed., *The Emperor's Old Groove: Decolonizing Disney's Magic Kingdom* (New York: Lang, 2003), pp. 117–29; Richard Finkelstein, 'Disney Cites Shakespeare: The Limits of Appropriation', in Christy Desmet and Robert Sawyer, eds, *Shakespeare and Appropriation* (London and New York: Routledge, 1999), pp. 179–96. The Disney film that is based upon a Shakespeare play represents a complicating component of this process.
54 Alan Bryman, *The Disneyization of Society* (London: Sage, 2004), p. 18; Frank A. and Virginia A. Salamone, 'Images of Main Street: Disney World and the American Adventure', *Journal of American Culture*, 22.1 (1999), p. 85.
55 KBA, '*Much Ado About Nothing*' *by William Shakespeare: Adapted for the Screen by Kenneth Branagh*, 1st draft (1992), p. 120; KBA, '*Much Ado About Nothing*': *Day-Out-of-Days Schedule* (1993), single sheet.
56 For a discussion of these features of the Disney experience, see Julianne Burton-Carvajal, '"Surprise Package": Looking Southward with Disney', in Eric Smoodin, ed., *Disney Discourse: Producing the Magic Kingdom* (New York and London: Routledge, 1994), p. 132; Ramona Fernandez, 'Pachuco Mickey', in Elizabeth Bell, Lynda Haas and Laura Sells, eds, *From Mouse to Mermaid: The Politics of Film, Gender, and Culture* (Bloomington and Indianapolis: Indiana University Press, 1995), p. 239; Eric Michael Mazur and Tara K. Koda, 'The Happiest Place on Earth: Disney's America and the Commodification of Religion', in Eric Michael Mazur and Kate McCarthy, eds, *God in Details: American Religion in Popular Culture* (New York and London: Routledge, 2001), p. 313.
57 Susan Stewart, *On Longing: Narratives of the Miniature, the Gigantic, the Souvenir, the Collection* (Durham, NC and London: Duke University Press, 1993), pp. 48, 69.
58 See Barbara Hodgdon, *The Shakespeare Trade: Performances and Appropriations* (Philadelphia: University of Pennsylvania Press, 1998), pp. 191–240.
59 On performative rubbish collectors at Disney's theme parks, see Bryman, *Disneyization*, pp. 103, 126; Salamone and Salamone, 'Images', p. 86.
60 Michael Zeitlin, 'Donald Barthelme and the Postmodern Sequel', in Budra and Schellenberg, eds, *Part Two*, p. 160.

61 Branagh, *'Much Ado About Nothing' by William Shakespeare*, p. x.
62 Michel Foucault, *Language, Counter-Memory, Practice: Selected Essays and Interviews*, ed. Donald F. Bouchard (Oxford: Blackwell, 1977), p. 194.

## Chapter 3   The Local and the Global

1 Kenneth Branagh, *'Much Ado About Nothing' by William Shakespeare* (New York and London: Norton, 1993), p. x.
2 Michael Hoffman, *William Shakespeare's 'A Midsummer Night's Dream'* (New York: HarperCollins, 1999), p. 45.
3 Representative studies include Pascale Aebischer, Edward J. Esche and Nigel Wheale, eds, *Remaking Shakespeare: Performance Across Media, Genres and Cultures* (Basingstoke: Palgrave, 2003); Michael D. Bristol, *Shakespeare's America/America's Shakespeare* (London and New York: Routledge, 1990); John Russell Brown, *New Sites for Shakespeare: Theatre, the Audience and Asia* (London and New York: Routledge, 1999); Mark Thornton Burnett and Ramona Wray, eds, *Shakespeare and Ireland: History, Politics, Culture* (Basingstoke: Macmillan, 1997); Thomas Cartelli, *Repositioning Shakespeare: National Cultures, Postcolonial Appropriations* (London and New York: Routledge, 1999); Michael Hattaway, Boika Sokolova and Derek Roper, eds, *Shakespeare in the New Europe* (Sheffield: Sheffield Academic Press, 1994); David Johnson, *Shakespeare and South Africa* (Oxford: Clarendon, 1996); Dennis Kennedy, ed., *Foreign Shakespeare: Contemporary Performance* (Cambridge: Cambridge University Press, 1993); Francesca T. Royster, *Becoming Cleopatra: The Shifting Image of an Icon* (New York: Palgrave, 2003); Xiao Yang Zhang, *Shakespeare in China: A Comparative Study of Two Traditions and Cultures* (Newark, DE: University of Delaware Press, 1996).
4 Richard Burt, 'Shakespeare, "Glo-cali-zation," Race, and the Small Screens of Post-Popular Culture', in Richard Burt and Lynda E. Boose, eds, *Shakespeare, the Movie, II: Popularizing the Plays on Film, TV, Video, and DVD* (London and New York: Routledge, 2003), pp. 14–36; Courtney Lehmann, *Shakespeare Remains: Theater to Film, Early Modern to Postmodern* (Ithaca, NY and London: Cornell University Press, 2002), passim; Sarah Mayo, '"A Shakespeare for the People?": Negotiating the Popular in *Shakespeare in Love* and Michael Hoffman's *A Midsummer Night's Dream*', *Textual Practice*, 17.2 (2003), pp. 295–316.
5 Denise Albanese, 'The Shakespeare Film and the Americanization of Culture', in Jean E. Howard and Scott Cutler Shershow, eds, *Marxist Shakespeares* (London and New York: Routledge, 2001), pp. 206–26; Curtis Breight, 'Elizabethan World Pictures', in John J. Joughin, ed., *Shakespeare and National Culture* (Manchester: Manchester University Press, 1997), pp. 295–325; Linda Charnes, *Notorious Identity: Materializing the Subject in Shakespeare* (Cambridge, MA: Harvard University Press, 1993), pp. 148–53.
6 Sonia Massai, 'Defining Local Shakespeares', in Sonia Massai, ed., *World-Wide Shakespeares: Local Appropriations in Film and Performance* (London and New York: Routledge, 2005), p. 3; Martin Orkin, *Local Shakespeares: Proximations and Power* (London and New York: Routledge, 2005), pp. 1, 2, 4.

7 Susanne Greenhalgh, '"Alas poor country!": Documenting the Politics of Performance in Two British Television *Macbeths* since the 1980s', in Aebischer, Esche and Wheale, eds, *Remaking Shakespeare*, pp. 96, 105.
8 Courtney Lehmann, 'Out Damned Scot: Dislocating *Macbeth* in Transnational Film and Media Culture', in Burt and Boose, eds, *Shakespeare, the Movie, II*, p. 236; Jean Baudrillard, *Selected Writings*, ed. Mark Poster (Cambridge: Polity, 1988), p. 121.
9 Slavoj Žižek, *Welcome to the Desert of the Real* (London and New York: Verso, 2002), pp. 17, 37.
10 Antony Sher, *Beside Myself* (London: Hutchinson, 2001), p. 341.
11 For views which see an evocation Russia and its revolutionary era as central to Branagh's film, see Samuel Crowl, *Shakespeare at the Cineplex: The Kenneth Branagh Era* (Athens, OH: Ohio University Press, 2003), p. 142; Douglas Lanier, '"Art thou base, common, and popular?": The Cultural Politics of Kenneth Branagh's *Hamlet*', in Courtney Lehmann and Lisa S. Starks, eds, *Spectacular Shakespeare: Critical Theory and Popular Cinema* (Madison and Teaneck, WI: Fairleigh Dickinson University Press, 2002), p. 158; Nina da Vinci Nichols, 'Branagh's *Hamlet* Redux', *Shakespeare Bulletin*, 15.3 (1997), p. 38; Kenneth S. Rothwell, *A History of Shakespeare on Screen: A Century of Film and Television*, 2nd edn. (Cambridge: Cambridge University Press, 2004), pp. 244, 246; Carol Chillington Rutter, *Enter the Body: Women and Representation on Shakespeare's Stage* (London and New York: Routledge, 2001), p. 52; Julie Sanders, 'The End of History and the Last Man: Kenneth Branagh's *Hamlet*', in Mark Thornton Burnett and Ramona Wray, eds, *Shakespeare, Film, Fin de Siècle* (Basingstoke: Macmillan, 2000), pp. 154–6.
12 Barbara Hodgdon, 'Re-incarnations', in Aebischer, Esche and Wheale, eds, *Remaking Shakespeare*, p. 200.
13 Kenneth Branagh Archive [hereafter KBA], '*Hamlet*' by William Shakespeare: Adapted for the Screen by Kenneth Branagh, 1st draft, September (1995), p. 33.
14 KBA, *Kenneth Branagh's The Shakespeare Film Company* (London: Intermedia, [2000]), unpaginated insert.
15 Michael Almereyda, *William Shakespeare's 'Hamlet': A Screenplay Adaptation by Michael Almereyda* (London: Faber, 2000), p. 55.
16 *Macbeth*, in *The Norton Shakespeare*, ed. Stephen Greenblatt, Walter Cohen, Jean E. Howard and Katharine Eisaman Maus (New York and London: W. W. Norton, 1997), II.ii.60–1. Unless otherwise stated, all further references to the plays are taken from this edition and appear in the text.
17 Katherine Rowe, '"Remember Me": Technologies of Memory in Michael Almereyda's *Hamlet*', in Burt and Boose, eds, *Shakespeare, the Movie, II*, p. 43.
18 Fredric Jameson, *Postmodernism, or, the Cultural Logic of Late Capitalism* (London and New York: Verso, 1991), p. 44.
19 Douglas M. Lanier, 'Shakescorp *Noir*', *Shakespeare Quarterly*, 53.2 (2002), p. 172.
20 For useful discussions, see Seamus Deane, *Strange Country: Modernity and Nationhood in Irish Writing since 1790* (Oxford: Clarendon, 1997), pp. 21, 87–8, 91, 117–18, 166, 196; Vera Kreilkamp, *The Anglo-Irish Novel and the Big House* (New York: Syracuse University Press, 1998), pp. 9–10, 21–3, 73, 96–7, 106–9, 119–20, 249–52; W. J. McCormack, *Dissolute Characters: Irish Literary*

*History through Balzac, Sheridan Le Fanu, Yeats and Bowen* (Manchester: Manchester University Press, 1993), p. 101; W. J. McCormack, 'Irish Gothic and After', in Seamus Deane, ed., *The Field Day Anthology of Irish Writing*, 5 vols (Derry: Field Day Publications, 1991–2002), II, pp. 831–54. Philippa Sheppard's otherwise very useful study ('The Castle of Elsinore: Gothic Aspects of Kenneth Branagh's *Hamlet*', *Shakespeare Bulletin*, 19.3 [2001], pp. 36–9) neglects to mention that the 'Gothic' is invariably nationally and locally differentiated.

That Ireland is remote from Branagh's own conception of shifting national borders in the nineteenth century is indicated in his remarks on the film's evocation of historical context: the 'emerald isle' does not feature in the field of reference. See KBA, *Commemorative Programme: William Shakespeare's 'Hamlet' directed by Kenneth Branagh* (Belfast: Graham and Heslip, 1997), p. 4; KBA, '*Hamlet*': *Production Information* (1996), pp. 4, 10; Crowl, *Shakespeare at the Cineplex*, p. 151; Ramona Wray and Mark Thornton Burnett, 'From the Horse's Mouth: Branagh on the Bard', in Burnett and Wray, eds, *Shakespeare, Film, Fin de Siècle*, pp. 170–1.

While Branagh has argued in interview that his film eschews the 'Gothic' (KBA, *Pamela Wallin: Live* [19 December 1996] and KBA, *Voices from the Smithsonian Associates: Kenneth Branagh* [21 December 1996]), it seems that what he mainly sought to avoid was a sense of prevailing cinematic gloom. Moreover, from another perspective, it is clear that, in the original conception of the film, there was to have been a greater reliance upon another strand of the 'Gothic', as indicated in the first screenplay's references to skulls, death-heads, maggots, falling trees and mutilated anatomies. See KBA, '*Hamlet' by William Shakespeare: Adapted for the Screen by Kenneth Branagh*, 1st draft, September (1995), pp. 44, 52, 86, 135, 187, 188.

21 See Lanier, '"Art thou base, common and popular?"', in Lehmann and Starks, eds, *Spectacular Shakespeare*, p. 162.
22 Siobhán Kilfeather, 'The Gothic Novel', in John Wilson Foster, ed., *The Cambridge Companion to the Irish Novel* (Cambridge: Cambridge University Press, 2006), p. 83.
23 Almereyda is himself an active participant in the stereotypical construction of Ireland, remarking in interview that 'the entire cast is American except for a couple of Irish people thrown in for good luck'. See Ross Anthony, 'Interviews with Actor Ethan Hawke and Director Michael Almereyda of *Hamlet*' (www.rossanthony.com/interviews/hawke.shtml).
24 Peter Somerville-Large, *Irish Eccentrics* (London: Hamish Hamilton, 1975), pp. 46–50.
25 See Victor Sage, 'Irish Gothic: C. R. Maturin and J. S. Le Fanu', in David Punter, ed., *A Companion to the Gothic* (Oxford: Blackwell, 2000), pp. 81–93.
26 The quotation is taken from the film's video jacket.
27 Jameson, *Postmodernism*, p. 19.
28 Darren O'Byrne, 'Working-Class Culture: Local Community and Global Conditions', in John Earle, ed., *Living the Global City: Globalization as Local Process* (London and New York: Routledge, 1997), p. 73.
29 Roland Robertson, 'Glocalization; Time–Space and Homogeneity–Heterogeneity', in Mike Featherstone, Scott Lash and Roland Robertson, eds, *Global Modernities* (London: Sage, 1995), pp. 23–44.

30 Lehmann, 'Out Damned Scot', in Burt and Boose, eds, *Shakespeare, the Movie, II*, p. 247.
31 Anthony Giddens, *Runaway World: How Globalization is Reshaping Our Lives* (London: Profile, 2002), p. xxi.
32 Lauren Schohet, 'The Banquet of Scotland (PA)', *Shakespeare Survey*, 57 (2004), p. 192.
33 George Ritzer, *The McDonaldization of Society* (London: Sage, 2000).
34 See *Big Mac under Attack*, BBC2 (15 July 2003); John Arlidge, 'The Healthy Option from Mr McHamburglar', *The Sunday Times: Business*, 28 March (2004), p. 10.
35 Jacques Derrida, *Spectres of Marx: The State of the Debt, the Work of Mourning, and the New International*, trans. Peggy Kamuf (New York and London: Routledge, 1994), p. 39.
36 See Robert Goldman and Stephen Papson, *Nike Culture: The Sign of the Swoosh* (London: Sage, 1998), passim. As a 'global power' company, Nike has itself been seen as a revealing symptom of the 'McDonaldization' process. See Steven Miles, 'McDonaldization and the Global Sports Store: Constructing Consumer Meanings in a Rationalized Society', in Mark Alfino, John S. Caputo and Robin Wynyard, eds, *McDonaldization Revisited: Critical Essays on Consumer Culture* (Westport, CT: Praeger, 1998), p. 63.
37 For Julie Christie's description, see Mark Thornton Burnett, 'The "very cunning of the scene": Kenneth Branagh's *Hamlet*', *Literature/Film Quarterly*, 25 (1997), p. 82.
38 Douglas Lanier, '"Art thou base, common and popular?"', in Lehmann and Starks, eds, *Spectacular Shakespeare*, p. 166.
39 See Jonathan Bardon, *A History of Ulster* (Belfast: Blackstaff, 1992), pp. 128-30, 152-8, 687.
40 Bardon, *Ulster*, p. 662.
41 Interview between Stephen Cavanagh and Mark Thornton Burnett, 4 April (2003). All further Cavanagh quotations are taken from this interview and appear in the text.
42 Arjun Appadurai, *Modernity at Large: Cultural Dimensions of Globalization* (Minneapolis, MN and London: University of Minnesota Press, 1996), p. 35.
43 Jacques Derrida, *A Derrida Reader: Between the Blinds*, ed. Peggy Kamuf (New York and London: Harvester Wheatsheaf, 1991), p. 42.
44 Appadurai, *Modernity*, p. 37.
45 Saskia Sassen, *Globalization and Its Discontents* (New York: The New Press, 1998), p. xxxiv.

## Chapter 4   Racial Identities, Global Economies

1 For typical readings, see Ariane M. Balizet, 'Teen Scenes: Recognizing Shakespeare in Teen Film', in James R. Keller and Leslie Stratyner, eds, *Almost Shakespeare: Reinventing his Works for Cinema and Television* (Jefferson, NC and London: McFarland, 2004), p. 133; Judith Buchanan, 'Virgin and Ape, Venetian and Infidel: Labellings of Otherness in Oliver Parker's *Othello*', in Mark Thornton Burnett and Ramona Wray, eds, *Shakespeare, Film, Fin de Siècle* (Basingstoke: Macmillan, 2000), pp. 193-4; Barbara Hodgdon, *The Shakespeare Trade: Performances and Appropriations* (Philadelphia: University

180  *Notes*

of Pennsylvania Press, 1998), pp. 59–73; Hodgdon, 'Race-ing *Othello*: Re-engendering White-Out, II', in Richard Burt and Lynda E. Boose, eds, *Shakespeare, the Movie, II: Popularizing the Plays on Film, TV, Video, and DVD* (London and New York: Routledge, 2003), p. 100.

2. Brooks Brown and Rob Merritt, *No Easy Answers: The Truth Behind the Death at Columbine* (New York: Lantern, 2002), pp. 20, 46.
3. Among other contours connecting *Othello* and *O. J.*, one might mention, 'accusations of the wife's adultery and the husband's uncontrollable jealousy [and] ... stories of the husband's efforts to collect "ocular proof" by stalking and spying on his wife'. See Jeffrey Martinek, '"An Ebullition of Fancy": *Othello*, Orenthal James Simpson, and the Play of the "Race Card"', *Studies in the Humanities*, 25.1–2 (1998), p. 67.
4. Eric C. Brown, 'Cinema in the Round: Self-Reflexivity in Tim Blake Nelson's "*O*"', in Keller and Stratyner, eds, *Almost Shakespeare*, pp. 74–5; Hodgdon, 'Race-ing *Othello*', p. 100.
5. Marjorie Garber, *Quotation Marks* (New York and London: Routledge, 2003), p. 2.
6. The withholding from distribution for almost two years of '*O*' in the wake of the Columbine High School shootings is discussed in Tim Blake Nelson, 'There's a Price You Pay for Getting Too Real: Delay', *The New York Times*, 26 August 2001, pp. B8, B15.
7. Mike Featherstone, 'Global Culture: An Introduction', in Mike Featherstone, ed., *Global Culture: Nationalism, Globalization and Modernity* (London: Sage, 1990), p. 2.
8. Jonathan Friedman, 'Being in the World: Globalization and Localization', in Featherstone, ed., *Global Culture*, p. 311.
9. Caroline Knowles, *Race and Social Analysis* (London: Sage, 2003), p. 116; Jan Aart Scholte, *Globalization: A Critical Introduction* (Basingstoke: Macmillan, 2000), p. 30.
10. Malcolm Waters, *Globalization*, 2nd edn. (London and New York: Routledge, 2001), pp. 192–3.
11. Zygmunt Bauman, 'Modernity and Ambivalence', in Featherstone, ed., *Global Culture*, p. 167.
12. Stephen May, 'Multiculturalism', in David Theo Goldberg and John Solomos, eds, *A Companion to Racial and Ethnic Studies* (Oxford: Blackwell, 2002), p. 133.
13. Scholte, *Globalization*, p. 180.
14. Hodgdon, 'Race-ing *Othello*', p. 102.
15. Kenneth Branagh Archive [hereafter KBA], '*Othello*': *A Screenplay by Oliver Parker Based on the Play by William Shakespeare*, 3rd draft, February (1995), p. 75.
16. Lisa S. Starks, 'The Veiled (Hot)Bed of Race and Desire: Parker's *Othello* and the Stereotypes of Screen Fetish', *Post Script*, 17.1 (1997), p. 72.
17. *Othello*, in *The Norton Shakespeare*, ed. Stephen Greenblatt, Walter Cohen, Jean E. Howard and Katharine Eisaman Maus (New York and London: W. W. Norton, 1997), II.iii.9–10. All further references appear in the text.
18. KBA, '*Othello*': *A Screenplay*, p. 12.
19. Jane Caplan, 'Introduction', in Jane Caplan, ed., *Written on the Body: The Tattoo in European and American History* (London: Reaktion, 2000), pp. xi, xiv.

20 Homi Bhabha, *The Location of Culture* (London and New York: Routledge, 1994), pp. 13, 14.
21 KBA, *'Othello': A Screenplay*, p. 11.
22 Pascale Aebischer, *Shakespeare's Violated Bodies: Stage and Screen Performance* (Cambridge: Cambridge University Press, 2004), p. 147.
23 Ann Cvetkovich and Douglas Kellner, 'Introduction: Thinking Global and Local', in Ann Cvetkovich and Douglas Kellner, eds, *Articulating the Global and the Local* (Boulder, CO: Westview Press, 1997), p. 10. The deleted scene is featured on the American DVD version of the film.
24 Douglas Kellner, *Media Spectacle* (London and New York: Routledge, 2003), pp. 69, 84.
25 Brown, 'Cinema in the Round', p. 74.
26 Bhabha, *Location*, p. 2.
27 David L. Andrews, 'The (Trans)National Basketball Association: American Commodity-Sign Culture and Global–Local Conjuncturalism', in Cvetkovich and Kellner, eds, *Articulating*, p. 75.
28 Deborah Cartmell, *Interpreting Shakespeare on Screen* (Basingstoke: Macmillan, 2000), p. 76; Hodgdon, *The Shakespeare Trade*, p. 66.
29 Stuart Hall, 'New Ethnicities', in Linda Martín Alcoff and Eduardo Mendieta, eds, *Race, Class, Gender, and Nationality* (Oxford: Blackwell, 2003), p. 92.
30 Hodgdon, *The Shakespeare Trade*, p. 66.
31 Sarah Hatchuel, *Shakespeare, from Stage to Screen* (Cambridge: Cambridge University Press, 2004), p. 105
32 Frantz Fanon, *Black Skin, White Masks*, trans. Charles Lam Markmann (London and Sydney: Pluto, 1986), p. 13.
33 Patricia Dorval, 'Shakespeare on Screen: Threshold Aesthetics in Oliver Parker's *Othello*', *Early Modern Literary Studies*, 6.1 (2000), p. 8; Buchanan, 'Virgin and Ape', p. 191.
34 Linda Williams, *Playing the Race Card: Melodramas of Black and White from Uncle Tom to O. J. Simpson* (Princeton, NJ: Princeton University Press, 2001), p. 138.
35 KBA, *'Othello': A Screenplay*, pp. 39–40.
36 Reinhart Kössler, 'Globalization and Human Rights: Some Developmental Reflections', in Frans J. Schuurman, ed., *Globalization and Development Studies: Challenges for the Twenty-First Century* (London: Sage, 2001), p. 85.
37 Hodgdon, 'Race-ing *Othello*', pp. 101, 103.
38 Stephen M. Buhler, *Shakespeare in the Cinema: Ocular Proof* (New York: State University of New York Press, 2002), p. 27.
39 KBA, *'Othello': A Screenplay*, pp. 8, 20, 86.
40 Bhabha, *Location*, p. 50.
41 Kenneth Rothwell, *A History of Shakespeare on Screen: A Century of Film and Television*, 2nd edn. (Cambridge: Cambridge University Press, 2004), p. 226.
42 KBA, *'Othello': A Screenplay*, pp. 65, 66.
43 A 'fowler' is glossed as 'one who hunts', and 'fowling' represents a kind of 'snaring'. See *The Compact Edition of the Oxford English Dictionary*, 2 vols (London: Book Club Associates, 1979), I, p. 1070.
44 Kim Hall, *Things of Darkness: Economies of Race and Gender in Early Modern England* (Ithaca, NY and London: Cornell University Press, 1995), pp. 177, 264.
45 *The Compact Edition of the Oxford English Dictionary*, I, p. 1067.

46 William Ian Miller, *The Anatomy of Disgust* (Cambridge, MA.: Harvard University Press, 1997), p. 111
47 *Macbeth*, in *Norton Shakespeare*, I.vii.55.
48 Elizabeth A. Deitchman, 'Shakespeare Stiles Style: Shakespeare, Julia Stiles, and American Girl Culture', in Barbara Hodgdon and W. B. Worthen, eds, *A Companion to Shakespeare and Performance* (Oxford: Blackwell, 2005), p. 490.
49 KBA, *'Othello': A Screenplay*, pp. 105, 107.
50 Bryan S. Turner, 'The Possibility of Primitiveness: Towards a Sociology of Body Marks in Cool Societies', in Mike Featherstone, ed., *Body Modification* (London: Sage, 2000), p. 40.
51 bell hooks, *We Real Cool: Black Men and Masculinity* (London and New York: Routledge, 2004), p. 63.
52 Hodgon, 'Race-ing *Othello*', p. 101.
53 Stephen Moss, 'Blacked up and Proud', *Guardian*, 28 July 2005 (www.guardian.co.uk/arts/features/story/0153798300.html).
54 Cvetkovich and Kellner, 'Introduction', p. 9.
55 Julia Kristeva, *Powers of Horror: An Essay on Abjection*, trans. Leon S. Roudiez (New York: Columbia University Press, 1982), p. 49.
56 Andrew L. Barlow, *Between Fear and Hope: Globalization and Race in the United States* (Lanham, MD: Rowman and Littlefield, 2003), p. 104.

## Chapter 5   Remembrance, Holocaust, Globalization

1 For accounts of the 'Day of Remembrance', see Chris McGreal, 'We Must Rely on Ourselves, says Sharon', *Guardian*, 27 January (2005), p. 17; Ian Traynor, 'The World Remembers', *Guardian*, 28 January (2005), p. 1.
2 See, for instance, Thomas A. Pendleton, 'The Editors go to the Movies: Michael Radford's *The Merchant of Venice*', *The Shakespeare Newsletter*, 54.2–3 (2004), p. 69.
3 Rebecca Murray, 'Interview with *The Merchant of Venice* director, Michael Radford' (www.romanticmovies.about.com/od/merchantofvenice/a/merchntmr122304.htm). In a related interview, Radford alludes to his Jewish heritage, saying, 'My mother is an Austrian-Jewish refugee whose father decided to get his family as far away from the Nazis as he possibly could, and so he got a job as a doctor in Bombay' (Mario Falsetto, *Personal Visions: Conversations with Independent Filmmakers* [London: Constable, 1999], p. 278).
4 Benedict Brogan, 'Is Labour Sinking towards Anti-Semitism as it Tries to Derail the Tory Challenge?', *Daily Mail*, 29 January (2005), p. 9.
5 Brogan, 'Is Labour Sinking towards Anti-Semitism?', p. 9.
6 Jacques Derrida, *A Derrida Reader: Between the Blinds*, ed. Peggy Kamuf (New York and London: Harvester Wheatsheaf, 1991), p. 108.
7 David Carroll, 'Foreword: The Memory of Devastation and the Responsibilities of Thought', in Jean-François Lyotard, *Heidegger and 'The Jews'*, trans. Andreas Michel and Mark S. Roberts (Minneapolis, MN and London: University of Minnesota Press, 1990), p. ix.
8 Esther Benbassa and Jean-Christophe Attias, *The Jew and the Other*, trans. G. M. Goshgarian (Ithaca, NY and London: Cornell University Press, 2004), p. 136.

## Notes    183

9  John W. Mahon, 'The Editors go to the Movies: Michael Radford's *The Merchant of Venice*', *The Shakespeare Newsletter*, 54.2–3 (2004), p. 69.
10 *The Merchant of Venice*, in *The Norton Shakespeare*, ed. Stephen Greenblatt, Walter Cohen, Jean E. Howard and Katharine Eisaman Maus (New York and London: W. W. Norton, 1997), I.iii.108. All further references appear in the text.
11 Slavoj Žižek, *Welcome to the Desert of the Real* (London and New York: Verso, 2002), p. 154.
12 Robert Bernasconi, 'The Ghetto and Race', in David Theo Goldberg and John Solomos, eds, *A Companion to Racial and Ethnic Studies* (Oxford: Blackwell, 2002), p. 341.
13 Raul Hilberg, 'Ghetto Formation', in Simon Gigliotti and Berel Lang, eds, *The Holocaust: A Reader* (Oxford: Blackwell, 2005), p. 124.
14 'He that hath ... given forth upon usury, and hath taken increase ... shall not live ... he shall surely die' (*The Bible: Authorized King James Version with Apocrypha*, ed. Robert Carroll and Stephen Prickett [Oxford: Oxford University Press, 1997], Ezekiel, 18/13).
15 Doris L. Bergen, 'Old Testament, New Hatreds: The Hebrew Bible and Anti-Semitism in Nazi Germany', in Leonard J. Greenspoon and Bryan F. LeBeau, eds, *Sacred Text, Secular Times: The Hebrew Bible in the Modern World* (Omaha: Creighton University Press, 2000), pp. 35–46.
16 Robert S. Wistrich, 'From Weimar to Hitler', in Gigliotti and Lang, eds, *Holocaust*, p. 56.
17 Andy Dickson, rev. of *William Shakespeare's 'The Merchant of Venice'*, *Sight and Sound*, February (2005), p. 80; Conrad Gellner, rev. of *The Merchant of Venice*, *Cineaste*, 30.2 (2005), p. 49.
18 Steve Blandford, Barry Keith Grant and Jim Hillier, *The Film Studies Dictionary* (London: Arnold, 2001), p. 74; Erik Barnouw, *Documentary: A History of the Non-Fiction Film*, 2nd edn. (New York and Oxford: Oxford University Press, 1993), p. 180.
19 The observation forms part of the 'Director's Commentary' section on the American DVD version of the film.
20 Stella Bruzzi, *New Documentary: A Critical Introduction* (London and New York: Routledge, 2000), p. 105.
21 Barnouw, *Documentary*, p. 180. It should be noted that *Schindler's List* also shifts to a colour palette in its closing, modern-day sequence.
22 Richard Burt, 'Shakespeare and the Holocaust: Julie Taymor's *Titus* Is Beautiful, or Shakesploi Meets (the) Camp', *Colby Quarterly*, 37.1 (2001), p. 81.
23 Slavoj Žižek, *The Žižek Reader*, ed. Elizabeth Wright and Edmond Wright (Oxford: Blackwell, 1999), p. 73.
24 The quotation is taken from the press pack for the film available at www.sonypictures.com/classics/merchantofvenice/flash.html.
25 Admittedly, cuts work in several directions, and the film simultaneously removes expressions of prejudice (as at II.vii.79, III.ii.217 and III.v.31–3) from the sub-plot to bring it into alignment with the cinematic codes of romantic acceptability.
26 Pendleton, 'The Editors go to the Movies', p. 69. See also Gellner, rev. of *The Merchant of Venice*, p. 49; Mahon, 'The Editors go to the Movies', p. 69.

184 *Notes*

27 Stephen Applebaum, 'Al Pacino: *The Merchant of Venice*' (www.bbc.co.uk/films/2004/11/30/al_pacino_the_merchant_of_venice_interview.shtml).
28 Lisa Freinkel, '*The Merchant of Venice*: "Modern" Anti-Semitism and the Veil of Allegory', in Hugh Grady, ed., *Shakespeare and Modernity: Early Modern to Millennium* (London and New York: Routledge, 2000), p. 140.
29 René Girard, *Violence and the Sacred*, trans. Patrick Gregory (Baltimore, MD and London: Johns Hopkins University Press, 1977), p. 302.
30 Theodor W. Adorno and Max Horkheimer, *Dialectic of Enlightenment*, trans. John Cumming (London: Allen Lane, 1973), pp. ix, 174.
31 Adorno and Horkheimer, *Dialectic*, p. 187.
32 Eric S. Mallin, 'Jewish Invader and the Soul of the State: *The Merchant of Venice* and Science Fiction Movies', in Grady, ed., *Shakespeare and Modernity*, p. 162.
33 A 'Director's Commentary' remark.
34 See Christina Hole, *English Sports and Pastimes* (London: Batsford, 1949), pp. 103–4.
35 Ian Kershaw, *Hitler 1889–1936: Hubris* (London: Allen Lane, 1998), pp. 472–4, 482, 562.
36 John Milton, *John Milton*, ed. Stephen Orgel and Jonathan Goldberg (Oxford and New York: Oxford University Press, 1990), p. 618.
37 Siniša Malešević, *The Sociology of Ethnicity* (London: Sage, 2004), p. 4.
38 Arthur Isak Applbaum, 'Culture, Identity and Legitimacy', in Joseph S. Nye and John D. Donahue, eds, *Governance in a Globalizing World* (Washington, DC: Brookings Institution Press, 2000), p. 319.
39 Cathy Caruth, 'Trauma and Experience: Introduction', in Cathy Caruth, ed., *Trauma: Explorations in Memory* (Baltimore, MD and London: Johns Hopkins University Press, 1995), p. 10; Robert Jay Lifton, 'An Interview', in Caruth, ed., *Trauma*, p. 128.
40 Despite the excision of the line from the film, aural and visual business is instrumental both in associating Antonio with castration and in raising questions about the precise physical execution of the bond. As James Shapiro remarks, 'an occluded threat of circumcision informs Shylock's desire to cut a pound of Antonio's flesh' (*Shakespeare and the Jews* [New York: Columbia University Press, 1996], p. 114).
41 Lisa Lampert, *Gender and Jewish Difference from Paul to Shakespeare* (Philadelphia: University of Pennsylvania Press, 2004), p. 143.
42 Samuel Crowl, 'Looking for Shylock: Stephen Greenblatt, Michael Radford and Al Pacino', in Mark Thornton Burnett and Ramona Wray, eds, *Screening Shakespeare in the Twenty-First Century* (Edinburgh: Edinburgh University Press, 2006), p. 121.
43 Karen Newman, 'Portia's Ring: Unruly Women and Structures of Exchange in *The Merchant of Venice*', *Shakespeare Quarterly*, 38.1 (1987), p. 31.
44 Bruzzi, *New Documentary*, p. 114.
45 Shoshana Felman and Dori Laub, *Testimony: Crises of Witnessing in Literature, Psychoanalysis and History* (New York and London: Routledge, 1992), p. 58.
46 Omer Bartov, *The 'Jew' in Cinema: From 'The Golem' to 'Don't Touch My Holocaust'* (Bloomington and Indianapolis: Indiana University Press, 2005), p. 157; Andrew R. Heinze, *Jews and the American Soul: Human Nature in the*

*Twentieth Century* (Princeton, NJ and Oxford: Princeton University Press, 2004), p. 322.
47 Carol J. Carlisle, 'Letter to the Editors', *The Shakespeare Newsletter*, 54.4 (2004/5), p. 100.
48 Edgar Allen Poe, *The Poems*, ed. Killis Campbell (New York: Russell & Russell, 1962), p. 101.
49 Dori Laub, 'Truth and Testimony: The Process and the Struggle', in Caruth, ed., *Trauma*, pp. 73–4.
50 'What I feel about this play is that it's about all humanity', states Radford in interview, continuing, 'There are so many universal themes in it' (Murray, 'Interview').
51 Crowl, 'Looking for Shylock', p. 116.
52 Theodor W. Adorno, *The Adorno Reader*, ed. Brian O' Connor (Oxford: Blackwell, 2000), p. 210.
53 Adorno, *Reader*, p. 86.
54 The phrase is taken from Terry Eagleton, *The Ideology of the Aesthetic* (Oxford: Blackwell, 1990), p. 358.
55 Adorno, *Reader*, p. 326.
56 Shoshana Felman, 'Education and Crisis, or the Vicissitudes of Teaching', in Caruth, ed., *Trauma*, p. 39.
57 Bill Nichols, *Representing Reality: Issues and Concepts in Documentary* (Bloomington and Indianapolis: Indiana University Press, 1991), p. 120.
58 E. Ann Kaplan, *Trauma Culture: The Politics of Terror and Loss in Media and Literature* (New Brunswick and London: Rutgers University Press, 2005), p. 20.
59 Norman Finkelstein, *The Holocaust Industry: Reflections on the Exploitation of Jewish Suffering* (London and New York: Verso, 2000), p. 3.

## Chapter 6   Spirituality/Meaning/Shakespeare

1 Peter Donaldson, 'Hamlet among the Pixelvisionaries: Video Art, Authenticity and "Wisdom" in Almereyda's *Hamlet*', in Diana E. Henderson, ed., *A Concise Companion to Shakespeare on Screen* (Oxford: Blackwell, 2006), p. 225.
2 Richard Burt, 'Shakespeare and Asia in Postdiasporic Cinemas: Spin-offs and Citations of the Plays from Bollywood to Hollywood', in Richard Burt and Lynda E. Boose, eds, *Shakespeare, the Movie, II: Popularizing the Plays on Film, TV, Video, and DVD* (London and New York: Routledge, 2003), p. 292; Sister Annabel Laity, 'Introduction', in *Thich Nhat Hanh: Essential Writings*, ed. Robert Ellsberg (New York: Orbis, 2001), p. 1; Michael Almereyda, *William Shakespeare's 'Hamlet'* (London: Faber, 2000), p. 52.
3 Almereyda, *William Shakespeare's 'Hamlet'*, p. ix.
4 Almereyda, *William Shakespeare's 'Hamlet'*, p. 38.
5 Almereyda, *William Shakespeare's 'Hamlet'*, p. 36.
6 Towards the end of Almereyda's *Hamlet*, forced onto a transatlantic flight to meet his destiny in England, the protagonist is represented reflecting on a postcard of a defaced Buddha. Glancing back to the earlier video inset, the sequence immediately anticipates a contemporary act of iconoclasm, the destruction in March 2001, on the orders of Mulla Mohammed Omar, of the

Buddhas of Bamiyan in central Afghanistan: here, it is prescient of the film that it juxtaposes a symbol of eastern religion and a fictional embodiment of American late capitalist imperialism. For, as he contemplates the savaged mystic figure, Hamlet also watches an in-flight entertainment shopping channel which combines clips of Fortinbras – a multinational CEO – and a Hollywood action movie. These are 'powers' (Almereyda, *William Shakespeare's 'Hamlet'*, p. 92) that, in response to Hamlet's question to the captain, incarnate a peculiarly American brand of violence and consumerism, market ethics and corporate militarism. Emerging from the sequence, then, are similar questions about the ownership and framing of religion, the movement of global politics and the flow of spiritual commodities. Moreover, an additional manifestation of US hegemony quickly comes into view. As in late capitalism, the postcard makes a souvenir of, and establishes as valuable material property, the image of the Buddha, in such a way that Hamlet's problematic reification of a repackaged religion is once more illuminated.

7  Christopher Partridge, *The Re-Enchantment of the West: Alternative Spiritualities, Sacralization, Popular Culture, and Occulture* (London and New York: Continuum, 2004), p. 109; Slavoj Žižek, *The Puppet and the Dwarf: The Perverse Core of Christianity* (Cambridge, MA: MIT Press, 2003), p. 26.
8  Robert H. King, *Thomas Merton and Thich Nhat Hanh: Engaged Spirituality in an Age of Globalization* (New York and London: Continuum, 2001), p. 167; Nhat Hanh, *Essential Writings*, p. 56.
9  King, *Thomas Merton*, p. 171; Laity, 'Introduction', p. 13.
10  Richard King, 'Mysticism and Spirituality', in John R. Hinnells, ed., *The Routledge Companion to the Study of Religion* (London and New York: Routledge, 2005), p. 320.
11  Peter Beyer, *Religion and Globalization* (London: Sage, 1994), pp. 94, 97.
12  Eric Higgs, 'Nature by Design', in Eric Higgs, Andrew Light and David Strong, eds, *Technology and the Good Life?* (Chicago and London: University of Chicago Press, 2000), p. 202; David F. Ford, 'Holy Spirit and Christian Spirituality', in Kevin J. Vanhoozer, ed., *The Cambridge Companion to Postmodern Theology* (Cambridge: Cambridge University Press, 2003), p. 285.
13  Judith Fox, 'New Religious Movements', in Hinnells, ed., *Routledge Companion*, p. 331.
14  Jean-François Lyotard, *The Postmodern Condition: A Report on Knowledge*, trans. Geoff Bennington and Brian Massumi (Manchester: Manchester University Press, 1984), p. 37.
15  Kevin J. Vanhoozer, 'Theology and the Condition of Postmodernity: A Report on the Knowledge of God', in Vanhoozer, ed., *Cambridge Companion*, p. 18.
16  Philippa Berry, 'Introduction', in Philippa Berry and Andrew Wernick, eds, *Shadow of Spirit: Postmodernism and Religion* (London and New York: Routledge, 1992), p. 4.
17  Bill Brown, 'The Dark Wood of Postmodernity (Space, Faith, Allegory)', *PMLA*, 120.3 (2005), pp. 735, 748.
18  John D. Caputo, 'Apostles of the Impossible: On God and the Gift in Derrida and Marion', in John D. Caputo and Michael J. Scanlon, eds, *God, the Gift, and Postmodernism* (Bloomington and London: Indiana University Press, 1999), p. 186.

19 Ewan Fernie, 'Introduction: Shakespeare, Spirituality and Contemporary Criticism', in Ewan Fernie, ed., *Spiritual Shakespeares* (London and New York: Routledge, 2005), p. 7.
20 The manifesto and 'vow of chastity' of the collective are available at www.dogme95.dk.
21 John D. Caputo, 'Foreword: Of hyper-reality', in Fernie, ed., *Spiritual Shakespeares*, p. xviii.
22 See Jeffrey Sconce, *Haunted Media: Electronic Presence from Telegraphy to Television* (Durham, NC and London: Duke University Press, 2000), pp. 7–12.
23 Andrew Wernick, 'Post-Marx: Theological Themes in Baudrillard's *America*', in Berry and Wernick, eds, *Shadow of Spirit*, p. 69.
24 Ewan Fernie, 'Shakespeare and the Prospect of Presentism', *Shakespeare Survey*, 58 (2005), p. 178.
25 Judith Buchanan, *Shakespeare on Film* (Harlow: Longman, 2005), p. 221.
26 Mark C. Taylor, 'Reframing postmodernisms', in Berry and Wernick, eds, *Shadow of Spirit*, p. 11.
27 Carolyn Jess, '"The Barbarous Chronos": (Post)Colonialism, Sequelization, and Regenerative Authority in Kristian Levring's *The King is Alive*', *Shakespeare Studies in South Africa*, 15 (2003), p. 11.
28 *Macbeth*, in *The Norton Shakespeare*, ed. Stephen Greenblatt, Walter Cohen, Jean E. Howard and Katharine Eisaman Maus (New York and London: W. W. Norton, 1997), I.iii.28–9. All further references appear in the text.
29 David Leiwei Li, 'Introduction: Globalization and the Humanities', *Comparative Literature*, 53.4 (2001), p. 275.
30 Paisley Livingstone, 'Artistic Self-Reflexivity in *The King is Alive* and *Strass*', in Mette Hjort and Scott MacKenzie, eds, *Purity and Provocation: Dogma 95* (London: BFI, 2003), p. 110.
31 Laurie Maguire, *Shakespearean Suspect Texts: The 'Bad' Quartos and Their Contexts* (Cambridge: Cambridge University Press, 1996), pp. 269–70.
32 Jacques Derrida, *Spectres of Marx: The State of the Debt, the Work of Mourning, and the New International*, trans. Peggy Kamuf (New York and London: Routledge, 1994), p. 11.
33 Derrida, *Spectres*, p. 136.
34 *King Lear* (Conflated Text), in *The Norton Shakespeare*, I.iv.255 (unless otherwise stated, all further references appear in the text); John J. Joughin, 'Lear's Afterlife', *Shakespeare Survey*, 55 (2002), p. 74.
35 Amy Scott-Douglass, 'Dogme Shakespeare 95: European Cinema, anti-Hollywood sentiment, and the Bard', in Burt and Boose, eds, *Shakespeare, the Movie, II*, p. 259.
36 *King Lear* (Conflated Text), in *The Norton Shakespeare*, III.iv.95–6.
37 Carolyn Jess, 'Newness, Sequelization, and Dogme Logic in Kristian Levring's *The King is Alive*', *New Cinemas: Journal of Contemporary Film*, 3.1 (2005), p. 10.
38 Pam Cook, *Screening the Past: Memory and Nostalgia Cinema* (London and New York: Routledge, 2005), p. 98.
39 Brown, 'The Dark Wood of Postmodernity', p. 745.
40 Scott-Douglass, 'Dogme Shakespeare 95', p. 262.
41 David Tracy, 'Fragments: The Spiritual Situation of Our Times', in Caputo and Scanlon, eds, *God, the Gift, and Postmodernism*, p. 173.

42 John D. Caputo, *Deconstruction in a Nutshell: A Conversation with Jacques Derrida* (New York: Fordham University Press, 1997), p. 122.
43 Richard Halpern, 'An Impure History of Ghosts: Derrida, Marx, Shakespeare', in Jean E. Howard and Scott Cutler Shershow, eds, *Marxist Shakespeares* (London and New York: Routledge, 2001), p. 41.
44 Michael Bishop, 'Tournier, Simon, Hyvrard and Cixous', in David Bevan, ed., *Literature and Spirituality* (Amsterdam and Atlanta: Rodopi, 1992), p. 121.
45 Pierre Grimal, *The Dictionary of Classical Mythology*, trans. A. R. Maxwell-Hyslop (Oxford: Blackwell, 1986), pp. 115–16.
46 Michel Foucault, *Language, Counter-Memory, Practice: Selected Essays and Interviews*, ed. Donald F. Bouchard (Oxford: Blackwell, 1977), p. 193.
47 John D. Caputo and Michael J. Scanlon, 'Introduction: Apology for the Impossible: Religion and Postmodernism', in Caputo and Scanlon, eds, *God, the Gift, and Postmodernism*, p. 8; Derrida, *Spectres*, p. 35.
48 Denise Albanese, 'The Shakespeare Film and the Americanization of Culture', in Howard and Shershow, eds, *Marxist Shakespeares*, p. 216; Barbara Hodgdon, '*William Shakespeare's "Romeo and Juliet"*: Everything's Nice in America?', *Shakespeare Survey*, 52 (1999), p. 95.
49 Martin Puchner, *Stage Fright: Modernism, Anti-Theatricality, and Drama* (Baltimore, MD and London: Johns Hopkins University Press, 2002), p. 27.
50 Homi K. Bhabha, 'DissemiNation: Time, Narrative, and the Margins of the Modern Nation', in Homi K. Bhabha, ed., *Nation and Narration* (London and New York: Routledge, 1990), pp. 295, 299.
51 Slavoj Žižek, *The Fragile Absolute: Or, Why is the Christian Legacy Worth Fighting For?* (London and New York: Verso, 2000), p. 11.
52 The detail of the blindfold also constructs a kinship with Gloucester, whose failure to 'see' is his signal characteristic, while Jack's disappearance from the narrative provides another variant on the fate of the Fool.
53 Thomas Cartelli and Katherine Rowe, 'Surviving Shakespeare: Kristian Levring's *The King is Alive*', *Borrowers and Lenders*, 1.2 (2005), p. 11.
54 Peter Fraenkel and Roger Murray, *The Namibians*, The Minority Rights Group Report No. 19 (London: The Minority Rights Group, 1985), pp. 6, 8; Duncan Innes, 'South African Capital and Namibia', in Reginald H. Green, Kimmo Kiljunen and Marja-Liisa Kiljunen, eds, *Namibia: The Last Colony* (Harlow: Longman, 1981), pp. 61, 64, 68; Kimmo Kiljunen, 'National Resistance and Liberation Struggle', in Green, Kiljunen and Kiljunen, eds, *Namibia: The Last Colony*, pp. 145–6; Colin Leys and John S. Saul, *Namibia's Liberation Struggle: The Two-Edged Sword* (Athens, OH: Ohio University Press, 1995), pp. 1, 9; Caroline Moorehead, *Namibia: Apartheid's Forgotten Children* (Oxford: Oxfam, 1989), p. 5.
55 *Genocide and the Second Reich*, BBC2 (15 August 2005).
56 Jennifer J. Bottinelli, 'Watching Lear: Resituating the Gaze at the Intersection of Film and Drama in Kristian Levring's *The King is Alive*', *Literature/Film Quarterly*, 33.2 (2005), p. 108.
57 Derrida, *Spectres*, p. 59.
58 Fernie, 'Introduction', p. 10; Žižek, *The Fragile Absolute*, p. 160.
59 Richard Kearney, 'Spectres of *Hamlet*', in Fernie, ed., *Spiritual Shakespeares*, p. 179.

60 Tracy, 'Fragments', p. 170.
61 If the traditional Buddha's 'gaze ... simply lets things be' (Žižek, *Puppet and the Dwarf*, p. 20), then it is striking that this also characterizes the look that the post-England protagonist in Almereyda's *Hamlet* bestows upon his spiritual surroundings. 'Let be' (Almereyda, *William Shakespeare's 'Hamlet'*, p. 118), his subsequent instruction to Horatio (Karl Geary) and, in this film version, the ghost of his father (Sam Shepard), indicates that this is a Hamlet who can locate his own spirituality and who is advancing towards a sense of peace with himself and the world. There is no need for the dilemma of 'to be' at this moment of discovery of an 'interbe', since Hamlet is seen as having properly internalized and taken heed, as having recuperated a confidence of action and purpose. In this sense, Hamlet and Thich Nhat Hanh merge into the same entity, a fused action in a diversified world, traces of the one remaking the image of the other.

## Chapter 7    Post-Millennial Parody

1 The 'mockumentary', directed by Stephen Leslie, was first broadcast on BBC4 on 29 November 2005.
2 Gary Taylor, 'Afterword: The Incredible Shrinking Bard', in Christy Desmet and Robert Sawyer, eds, *Shakespeare and Appropriation* (London and New York: Routledge, 1999), pp. 198–9.
3 Richard Burt, '*Shakespeare in Love* and the End of the Shakespearean: Academic and Mass Culture Constructions of Literary Authorship', in Mark Thornton Burnett and Ramona Wray, eds, *Shakespeare, Film, Fin de Siècle* (Basingstoke: Macmillan, 2000), pp. 226, 227.
4 Douglas Lanier, 'Will of the People: Recent Shakespeare Film Parody and the Politics of Popularization', in Diana E. Henderson, ed., *A Concise Companion to Shakespeare on Screen* (Oxford: Blackwell, 2006), pp. 177, 195; Richard Burt, 'Shakespeare and Asia in Postdiasporic Cinemas: Spin-offs and Citations of the Plays from Bollywood to Hollywood', in Richard Burt and Lynda E. Boose, eds, *Shakespeare, the Movie, II: Popularizing the Plays on Film, TV, Video, and DVD* (London and New York: Routledge, 2003), p. 269.
5 Gérard Genette, *Palimpsests: Literature in the Second Degree*, trans. Channa Newman and Claude Doubinsky (Lincoln, NB and London: University of Nebraska Press, 1997), p. 14; Simon Dentith, *Parody* (London and New York: Routledge, 2000), pp. 183–4; Thaïs Flores Nogueira Diniz, 'Shakespeare Parodied: Romeo and Juliet', in Bernice W. Kliman and Rick J. Santos, eds, *Latin American Shakespeares* (Madison and Teaneck, WI: Fairleigh Dickinson University Press, 2005), p. 263.
6 Linda Hutcheon, *The Politics of Postmodernism*, 2nd edn. (London and New York: Routledge, 2002), pp. 89, 90.
7 See Anthony Kwame Appiah, 'Is the Post- in Postmodernism the Post- in Postcolonial?', *Critical Inquiry*, 17.2 (1991), pp. 342–3; Mike Featherstone, 'Global Culture: An Introduction', in Mike Featherstone, ed., *Global Culture: Nationalism, Globalization and Modernity* (London: Sage, 1990), p. 2; Michael Hardt and Antonio Negri, *Empire* (Cambridge, MA: Harvard University Press, 1999), p. 151.

190  Notes

8  In postmodernism, Jameson claims, 'parody finds itself without a vocation; it has lived, and that strange new thing pastiche slowly comes to take its place'. 'Pastiche', he continues, 'is ... a neutral practice of ... mimicry ... [it is] blank parody' (Fredric Jameson, *Postmodernism, or, the Cultural Logic of Late Capitalism* [London and New York: Verso, 1991], p. 17).
9  Arjun Appadurai, *Modernity at Large: Cultural Dimensions of Globalization* (Minneapolis, MN and London: University of Minnesota Press, 1996), p. 37.
10  McKenzie Wark, 'To the Vector the Spoils', in Thomas Y. Levin, Ursula Frohne and Peter Weibel, eds, *Ctrl [Space]: Rhetorics of Surveillance from Bentham to Big Brother* (Cambridge, MA: MIT Press, 2002), p. 400.
11  www.hm.com/uk (the film is available under the '&denim' menu option). All further references are taken from this website and appear in the text.
12  Judith Butler, *Gender Trouble: Feminism and the Subversion of Identity* (New York and London: Routledge, 1999), p. 41.
13  Victor M. Valle and Rodolfo D. Torres, *Latino Metropolis* (Minneapolis, MN and London: University of Minnesota Press, 2000), p. 20.
14  See Norman K. Denzin, *Reading Race: Hollywood and the Cinema of Racial Violence* (London: Sage, 2002), p. 10.
15  Manuel Castells, *The Information Age: End of Millennium* (Oxford: Blackwell, 1998), p. 138.
16  Dentith, *Parody*, p. 183.
17  Linda Hutcheon, *A Theory of Parody: The Teachings of Twentieth-Century Art Forms* (New York and London: Methuen, 1985), p. 116.
18  Thomas Cartelli, 'Shakespeare and the Street: Pacino's *Looking for Richard*, Bedford's *Street King*, and the Common Understanding', in Burt and Boose, eds, *Shakespeare, the Movie, II*, p. 196.
19  *Richard III*, in *The Norton Shakespeare*, ed. Stephen Greenblatt, Walter Cohen, Jean E. Howard and Katharine Eisaman Maus (New York and London: W. W. Norton, 1997), III.vii.92. Unless otherwise stated, all further references to the plays are taken from this edition and appear in the text.
20  See Hutcheon, *Politics of Postmodernism*, p. 94.
21  Hutcheon, *Theory of Parody*, pp. 32, 53, 101.
22  Cartelli, 'Shakespeare and the Street', p. 196; Carolyn Jess-Cooke, 'Screening the McShakespeare in Post-Millennial Shakespeare Cinema', in Mark Thornton Burnett and Ramona Wray, eds, *Screening Shakespeare in the Twenty-First Century* (Edinburgh: Edinburgh University Press, 2006), p. 167.
23  Typical are Willy Maley and Andrew Murphy, eds, *Shakespeare and Scotland* (Manchester and New York: Manchester University Press, 2004); Julie Sanders, *Novel Shakespeares: Twentieth-Century Women Novelists and Appropriation* (Manchester and New York: Manchester University Press, 2001).
24  Mark Pizzato, *Theatres of Human Sacrifice: From Ancient Ritual to Screen Violence* (New York: State University of New York Press, 2005), p. 114.
25  The title is, of course, adapted from Gertrude's response to the players in *Hamlet* (*The Norton Shakespeare*, III.ii.210).
26  Hutcheon, *Politics of Postmodernism*, pp. 91, 94.
27  Madhu Jain, 'The Happening City', in B. P. Singh and Pavan K. Varma, eds, *The Millennium Book on New Delhi* (Oxford: Oxford University Press, 2001), pp. 122, 138.

28 Gopal Guru, 'Dalits: Reflections on the Search for Inclusion', in Peter Ronald de Souza, ed., *Contemporary India – Transitions* (London: Sage, 2000), p. 59.
29 F. G. Savage, *The Flora and Folklore of Shakespeare* (London: Burrow, 1923), p. 183.
30 Thomas Babington Macaulay, *Prose and Poetry*, ed. G. M. Young (Cambridge, MA: Harvard University Press, 1957), p. 729; Paromita Chakravarti, 'Modernity, Postcoloniality and *Othello*: The Case of *Saptapadi*', in Pascale Aebischer, Edward J. Esche and Nigel Wheale, eds, *Remaking Shakespeare: Performance Across Media, Genres and Cultures* (Basingstoke: Palgrave, 2003), p. 41.
31 Appadurai, *Modernity*, p. 43.
32 Poonam Trivedi, '"It is the bloody business which informs thus": Local Politics and Performance Praxis, *Macbeth* in India', in Sonia Massai, ed., *World-Wide Shakespeares: Local Appropriations in Film and Performance* (London and New York: Routledge, 2005), p. 53.
33 Atom Egoyan and Ian Balfour, 'Introduction', in Atom Egoyan and Ian Balfour, eds, *Subtitles: On the Foreignness of Film* (Cambridge, MA: MIT Press, 2004), p. 21.
34 Ania Loomba, 'Shakespeare and the Possibilities of Postcolonial Performance', in Barbara Hodgdon and W. B. Worthen, eds, *A Companion to Shakespeare and Performance* (Oxford: Blackwell, 2005), p. 133.
35 Rustom Bharucha, *The Politics of Cultural Practice: Thinking through Theatre in an Age of Globalization* (London: Athlone, 2000), p. 67.
36 Claudia M. Milian Arias, 'New Languages, New Humanities: The "Mixed Race" Narrative and the Borderlands', in David Theo Goldberg and John Solomos, eds, *A Companion to Racial and Ethnic Studies* (Oxford: Blackwell, 2002), p. 362.
37 Rosa Linda Fregoso, 'Recycling Colonialist Fantasies on the Texas Borderlands', in Hamid Naficy, ed., *Home, Exile, Homeland: Film, Media, and the Politics of Place* (London and New York: Routledge, 1999), p. 172.
38 Lyn Di Iorio Sandín, *Killing Spanish: Literary Essays on Ambivalent U.S. Latino/a Identity* (New York: Palgrave, 2004), p. 105.
39 Andrew L. Barlow, *Between Fear and Hope: Globalization and Race in the United States* (Lanham, MD: Rowman and Littlefield, 2003), p. 69; Michael Peter Smith, 'Looking for Globality in Los Angeles', in Ann Cvetkovich and Douglas Kellner, eds, *Articulating the Global and the Local: Globalization and Cultural Studies* (Boulder, CO: Westview, 1997), pp. 56–7; Valle and Torres, *Latino*, p. 6.
40 Smadar Lavie and Ted Swedenburg, 'Introduction', in Smadar Lavie and Ted Swedenburg, eds, *Displacement, Diaspora, and Geographies of Identity* (Durham, NC and London: Duke University Press, 1996), p. 15.
41 Michael Bristol, *Shakespeare's America, America's Shakespeare* (London and New York: Routledge, 1990), p. 1; Lawrence W. Levine, *Highbrow/Lowbrow: The Emergence of Cultural Hierarchy in America* (Cambridge, MA: Harvard University Press, 1988), p. 43.
42 Michael Kimmel, *Manhood in America: A Cultural History* (New York: Free Press, 1996), p. 17.
43 Rodolfo O. de la Garza, Angelo Falcon and F. Chris Garzia, 'Will the Real Americans Please Stand Up? Anglo and Mexican–American Support of Core

American Political Values', *American Journal of Political Science*, 40.2 (1996), pp. 347–8.
44  Seán McLoughlin, 'Migration, Diaspora and Transnationalism: Transformations of Religion and Culture in a Globalizing Age', in John R. Hinnels, ed., *The Routledge Companion to the Study of Religion* (London and New York: Routledge, 2005), p. 534.
45  Roger Rouse, 'Mexican Migration and the Social Space of Postmodernism', *Diaspora*, 1 (1991), p. 15.
46  Mary C. Beltrán, 'The New Hollywood Racelessness: Only the Fast, Furious (and Multiracial) Will Survive', *Cinema Journal*, 44.2 (2005), pp. 56, 57, 59.
47  Ronald Niezen, *A World beyond Difference: Cultural Identity in the Age of Globalization* (Oxford: Blackwell, 2004), p. 40; Beltrán, 'New Hollywood Racelessness', p. 50.
48  Edwidge Danticat, 'Inspiration: Pictures with Meaning', *Guardian Weekend*, 5 November 2005, p. 122.
49  Ken Booth and Tim Dunne, 'Worlds in Collision', in Ken Booth and Tim Dunne eds, *Worlds in Collision: Terror and the Future of the Global Order* (Basingstoke: Palgrave, 2002), p. 20.
50  Here, again, *Romeo & Juliet* recalls Baz Luhrmann's *William Shakespeare's 'Romeo + Juliet'*, with the '&' of the design label self-consciously echoing the '+' of the earlier filmic title.
51  Hutcheon, *Politics*, p. 90.
52  Saskia Kossak, *'Frame My Face to All Occasions': Shakespeare's 'Richard III' on Screen* (Vienna: Braumüller, 2005), p. 167.
53  Mike Davis, *City of Quartz: Excavating the Future in Los Angeles* (London: Pimlico, 1998), p. 18.
54  Clara E. Rodríguez, 'Latinos on Television and in the News: Absent or Misrepresented', in Clara E. Rodríguez, ed., *Latin Looks: Images of Latinas and Latinos in the U.S. Media* (Boulder, CO: Westview, 1997), p. 15.
55  Loomba, 'Shakespeare and the Possibilities', p. 126; Bharucha, *Politics*, pp. 61, 62.
56  Poonam Trivedi, 'Reading "Other Shakespeares"', in Aebischer, Esche and Wheale, eds, *Remaking Shakespeare*, p. 66.
57  Anthony S. Mercatante, *The Facts on File Encyclopedia of World Mythology and Legend* (New York and Oxford: Facts on File, 1988), pp. 586–7.
58  Dentith, *Parody*, p. 36.
59  Walter Benjamin, *Illuminations*, trans. Harry Zohn (London: Fontana/Collins, 1973), p. 72.
60  Dan Harries, *Film Parody* (London: BFI, 2000), p. 43.
61  Harries, *Film Parody*, p. 21.
62  Hutcheon, *Theory of Parody*, p. 28.
63  Michael Cronin, *Translation and Globalization* (London and New York: Routledge, 2003), p. 1.

# Epilogue

1  Interview between Kenneth Branagh and Mark Thornton Burnett, 2 December 2005. All further Branagh quotations are taken from this interview and appear in the text.

2 Kenneth Branagh Archive [hereafter KBA], *Kenneth Branagh's The Shakespeare Film Company* (London: Intermedia, [2000]), unpaginated insert.
3 Ramona Wray, 'The Singing Shakespearean: Kenneth Branagh's *Love's Labour's Lost* and the Politics of Genre', in Pascale Aebischer, Edward J. Esche and Nigel Wheale, eds, *Remaking Shakespeare: Performance Across Media, Genres and Cultures* (Basingstoke: Palgrave, 2003), pp. 153, 162; all box office figures cited are taken from www.imdb.com.
4 Arthur De Vany, *Hollywood Economics: How Extreme Uncertainty Shapes the Film Industry* (London and New York: Routledge, 2004), p. 3.
5 KBA, *Kenneth Branagh's The Shakespeare Film Company*, unpaginated insert. On the hiatus in Branagh's Shakespeare film career, see also Samuel Crowl, *The Films of Kenneth Branagh* (Westport, CT: Praeger, 2006), p. 165; Mark White, *Kenneth Branagh* (London: Faber, 2005), p. 245.
6 Diana E. Henderson, 'Learning from Campbell Scott's *Hamlet*', in Diana E. Henderson, ed., *A Concise Companion to Shakespeare on Screen* (Oxford: Blackwell, 2006), p. 78.
7 Emma French, *Selling Shakespeare to Hollywood: The Marketing of Filmed Shakespeare Adaptations from 1989 into the New Millennium* (Hatfield: University of Hertfordshire Press, 2006), p. 1.
8 Russell Jackson, 'Introduction: Shakespeare, Film and the Marketplace', in Russell Jackson, ed., *The Cambridge Companion to Shakespeare on Film* (Cambridge: Cambridge University Press, 2000), p. 5.
9 Peter Holland, 'Foreword', in Mark Thornton Burnett and Ramona Wray, eds, *Shakespeare, Film, Fin de Siècle* (Basingstoke: Macmillan, 2000), p. xiii.
10 Mario Falsetto, *Personal Visions: Conversations with Independent Filmmakers* (London: Constable, 1999), p. 13.
11 *Hamlet* has been screened at the Nerve Centre, Derry (29 May 2005), at the British Shakespeare Association, Newcastle upon Tyne (1 September 2005) and at the Dublin International Film Festival (20 February 2006). For reviews, see Lisa Hopkins, rev. of *Hamlet*, *Shakespeare Bulletin*, 23.2 (2005), pp. 52–5; Aisling O' Donnell, rev. of *Hamlet* (www.dubliniff.com/content/review/22).

# Bibliography

## Archival and/or unpublished sources

Berthomieu, Pierre, Interview with Kenneth Branagh, 14 and 15 August 1997. Audio recording. Kenneth Branagh Archive, Queen's University, Belfast.

Branagh, Kenneth, *'Hamlet' by William Shakespeare: Adapted for the Screen by Kenneth Branagh*, 1st draft, September 1995. Screenplay. Kenneth Branagh Archive, Queen's University, Belfast.

Branagh, Kenneth, *'Much Ado About Nothing' by William Shakespeare: Adapted for the Screen by Kenneth Branagh*, 1st draft (1992). Screenplay. Kenneth Branagh Archive, Queen's University, Belfast.

Burnett, Mark Thornton, Interview with Stephen Cavanagh, 4 April 2003.

Burnett, Mark Thornton, Interview with Kenneth Branagh, 2 December 2005.

*Commemorative Programme: William Shakespeare's 'Hamlet' directed by Kenneth Branagh*. Belfast: Graham and Heslip, 1997. Kenneth Branagh Archive, Queen's University, Belfast.

*'Hamlet': Production Information* (1996). Kenneth Branagh Archive, Queen's University, Belfast.

Hoffman, Michael, *'A Midsummer Night's Dream' by William Shakespeare*, 1st draft (1997). Screenplay. Twentieth-Century Fox Film Archive, Los Angeles.

Hoffman, Michael, *'A Midsummer Night's Dream' by William Shakespeare: Shooting Script*, 3 March 1998. Screenplay. Shakespeare Institute, Stratford-upon-Avon.

*Kenneth Branagh's The Shakespeare Film Company*. London: Intermedia, 2000. Publicity package. Kenneth Branagh Archive, Queen's University, Belfast.

Letterman, David, *David Letterman: 'Much Ado About Nothing'*, 15 May 1993. Video recording. Kenneth Branagh Archive, Queen's University, Belfast.

*'Much Ado About Nothing': Day Breakdown* (1993). Shooting schedule. Kenneth Branagh Archive, Queen's University, Belfast.

*'Much Ado About Nothing': Day-Out-of-Days Schedule* (1993). Shooting schedule. Kenneth Branagh Archive, Queen's University, Belfast.

*'Much Ado About Nothing': Suggested Classroom Activities* (1993). Educational package. Kenneth Branagh Archive, Queen's University, Belfast.

Parker, Oliver, *'Othello': A Screenplay by Oliver Parker Based on the Play by William Shakespeare*, 3rd draft, February 1995. Screenplay. Kenneth Branagh Archive, Queen's University, Belfast.

Payne, Jamie, Interview with Kenneth Branagh, ABC Cinema, London, 7 June 1997. Audio recording. Kenneth Branagh Archive, Queen's University, Belfast.

Rose, Charlie, *Charlie Rose Interview: 'Much Ado About Nothing'*, 23 May 1993. Video recording. Kenneth Branagh Archive, Queen's University, Belfast.

*Voices from the Smithsonian Associates: Kenneth Branagh*, 21 December 1996. Audio recording. Kenneth Branagh Archive, Queen's University, Belfast.

Wallin, Pamela, *Pamela Wallin: Live*, 19 December 1996. Audio recording. Kenneth Branagh Archive, Queen's University, Belfast.

## Films, television productions and documentaries

*American Me* (dir. Edward James Olmos, 1992).
*American Psycho* (dir. Mary Harron, 2000).
*As You Like It* (dir. Kenneth Branagh, 2006).
*Beginner's Luck* (dir. James Callis and Nick Cohen, 2001).
*Being John Malkovich* (dir. Spike Jonze, 1999).
*Big Mac under Attack* (dir. Martin Small, 2003). Broadcast BBC2, 15 July 2003.
*Bottom's Dream* (dir. John Canemaker, 1983).
*Bound by Honour* (dir. Taylor Hackford, 1993).
*Braveheart* (dir. Mel Gibson, 1995).
*Cal* (dir. Pat O'Connor, 1984).
*Crouching Tiger, Hidden Dragon* (dir. Ang Lee, 2000).
*Dead Poets Society* (dir. Peter Weir, 1989).
*A Double Life* (dir. George Cukor, 1947).
*Escape from New York* (dir. John Carpenter, 1981).
*Escape from Sobibor* (dir. Jack Gold, 1987).
*The Fast and the Furious* (dir. Rob Cohen, 2001).
*Genocide and the Second Reich* (dir. David Olusoga, 2005). Broadcast BBC2, 15 August 2005.
*Get Over It* (dir. Tommy O'Haver, 2001).
*The Gingerbread Man* (dir. Robert Altman, 1997).
*Hamlet* (dir. Michael Almereyda, 2000).
*Hamlet* (dir. Kenneth Branagh, 1997).
*Hamlet* (dir. Stephen Cavanagh, 2005).
*Henry V* (dir. Peter Babakitis, 2004).
*Henry V* (dir. Kenneth Branagh, 1989).
*House of Flying Daggers* (dir. Yimou Zhang, 2004).
*In Othello* (dir. Roysten Abel, 2003).
*In the Bleak Midwinter* (dir. Kenneth Branagh, 1995).
*Indian Dream* (dir. Roger Goldby, 2003).
*The King is Alive* (dir. Kristian Levring, 2000).
*Life is Beautiful* (dir. Roberto Benigni, 1997).
*Looking for Richard* (dir. Al Pacino, 1996).
*Love's Labour's Lost* (dir. Kenneth Branagh, 2000).
*Macbeth* (dir. Michael Bogdanov, 1997).
*Macbeth* (dir. Gregory Doran, 2001).
*Macbeth* (dir. Jeremy Freeston, 1996).
*Macbeth in Manhattan* (dir. Greg Lombardo, 1999).
*The Magnificent Seven* (dir. John Sturges, 1960).
*Makibefo* (dir. Alexander Abela, 1999).
*A Midsummer Night's Dream* (dir. Peter Hall, 1969).
*A Midsummer Night's Sex Comedy* (dir. Woody Allen, 1982).
*Much Ado About Nothing* (dir. Kenneth Branagh, 1993).
*Nuit et Brouillard* (dir. Alain Resnais, 1955).
*'O'* (dir. Tim Blake Nelson, 2001).
*Othello* (dir. Oliver Parker, 1995).
*Othello* (dir. Stuart Burge, 1965).
*Peace is Every Step: Meditation in Action* (dir. Gaetano Kazuo Maida, 1998).

*Peter Pan* (dir. Hamilton Luske, 1953).
*The Pianist* (dir. Roman Polanski, 2002).
*Playing for Time* (dir. Daniel Mann, 1980).
*Romeo & Juliet* (dir. David Lachapelle, 2005).
*Romeo Must Die* (dir. Andrzej Bartkowiak, 2000).
*Schindler's List* (dir. Steven Speilberg, 1993).
*Scotland, PA* (dir. Billy Morrissette, 2001).
*Sen Noci Svatojánské* (dir. Jiří Trnka, 1959).
*Shakespeare in Love* (dir. John Madden, 1998).
*Shakespeare's Happy Endings* (dir. Stephen Leslie, 2005). Broadcast BBC4, 29 November 2005.
*Sophie's Choice* (dir. Alan J. Pakula, 1982).
*The Sound of Music* (dir. Robert Wise, 1965).
*The Street King* (dir. James Gavin Bedford, 2002).
*Taxi Driver* (dir. Martin Scorsese, 1976).
*The Tempest* (dir. Jack Bender, 1998).
*The Tempest* (dir. Derek Jarman, 1979).
*Triumph of the Will* (dir. Leni Riefenstahl, 1934).
*West Side Story* (dir. Robert Wise and Jerome Robbins, 1961).
*William Shakespeare's 'The Merchant of Venice'* (dir. Michael Radford, 2004).
*William Shakespeare's 'A Midsummer Night's Dream'* (dir. Michael Hoffman, 1999).
*William Shakespeare's 'Romeo + Juliet'* (dir. Baz Luhrmann, 1996).
*Zoot Suit* (dir. Luis Valdez, 1981).

## Soundtracks

*William Shakespeare's 'A Midsummer Night's Dream'* (Decca, 1999).

## Printed sources

Adorno, Theodor W., *The Adorno Reader*, ed. Brian O' Connor. Oxford: Blackwell, 2000.
—— and Max Horkheimer, *Dialectic of Enlightenment*, trans. John Cumming. London: Allen Lane, 1973.
Aebischer, Pascale, *Shakespeare's Violated Bodies: Stage and Screen Performance*. Cambridge: Cambridge University Press, 2004.
—— Edward J. Esche and Nigel Wheale, eds, *Remaking Shakespeare: Performance Across Media, Genres and Cultures*. Basingstoke: Palgrave, 2003.
Albanese, Denise, 'The Shakespeare Film and the Americanization of Culture', in Jean E. Howard and Scott Cutler Shershow, eds, *Marxist Shakespeares*. London and New York: Routledge, 2001, pp. 206–26.
Almereyda, Michael, *William Shakespeare's 'Hamlet': A Screenplay Adaptation by Michael Almereyda*. London: Faber, 2000.
Andrews, David L., 'The (Trans)National Basketball Association: American Commodity-Sign Culture and Global–Local Conjuncturalism', in Ann Cvetkovich and Douglas Kellner, eds, *Articulating the Global and the Local*. Boulder: Westview Press, 1997, pp. 72–101.

## Bibliography

Appadurai, Arjun, *Modernity at Large: Cultural Dimensions of Globalization*. Minneapolis, MN and London: University of Minnesota Press, 1996.

Appiah, Anthony Kwame, 'Is the Post- in Postmodernism the Post- in Postcolonial?', *Critical Inquiry*, 17.2 (1991), pp. 336–57.

Applbaum, Arthur Isak, 'Culture, Identity and Legitimacy', in Joseph S. Nye and John D. Donahue, eds, *Governance in a Globalizing World*. Washington, DC: Brookings Institution Press, 2000, pp. 319–29.

Arias, Claudia M. Milian, 'New Languages, New Humanities: The "Mixed Race" Narrative and the Borderlands', in David Theo Goldberg and John Solomos, eds, *A Companion to Racial and Ethnic Studies*. Oxford: Blackwell, 2002, pp. 355–64.

Arlidge, John, 'The Healthy Option from Mr McHamburglar', *The Sunday Times: Business*, 28 March 2004, p. 10.

Auslander, Philip, *Liveness: Performance in a Mediatized Culture*. London and New York: Routledge, 1999.

Balio, Tino, '"A major presence in all of the world's most important markets": The Globalization of Hollywood in the 1990s', in Steve Neale and Murray Smith, eds, *Contemporary Hollywood Cinema*. London and New York: Routledge, 1998, pp. 58–73.

Balizet, Ariane M., 'Teen Scenes: Recognizing Shakespeare in Teen Film', in James R. Keller and Leslie Stratyner, eds, *Almost Shakespeare: Reinventing his Works for Cinema and Television*. Jefferson, NC and London: McFarland, 2004, pp. 122–36.

Bardon, Jonathan, *A History of Ulster*. Belfast: Blackstaff, 1992.

Barlow, Andrew L., *Between Fear and Hope: Globalization and Race in the United States*. Lanham, MD: Rowman and Littlefield, 2003.

Barnouw, Erik, *Documentary: A History of the Non-Fiction Film*, 2nd edn. New York and Oxford: Oxford University Press, 1993.

Bartov, Omer, *The 'Jew' in Cinema: From 'The Golem' to 'Don't Touch My Holocaust'*. Bloomington and Indianapolis: Indiana University Press, 2005.

Baudrillard, Jean, *Selected Writings*, ed. Mark Poster. Cambridge: Polity, 1988.

Bauman, Zygmunt, 'Modernity and Ambivalence', in Mike Featherstone, ed., *Global Culture: Nationalism, Globalization and Modernity*. London: Sage, 1990, pp. 143–69.

Beck, Ulrich, *What is Globalization?* Cambridge: Polity, 2000.

Beltrán, Mary C., 'The New Hollywood Racelessness: Only the Fast, Furious (and Multiracial) Will Survive', *Cinema Journal*, 44.2 (2005), pp. 50–67.

Benbassa, Esther and Jean-Christophe Attias, *The Jew and the Other*, trans. G. M. Goshgarian. Ithaca, NY and London: Cornell University Press, 2004.

Benjamin, Walter, *Illuminations*, trans. Harry Zohn. London: Fontana/Collins, 1982.

Bennett, Susan, *Theatre Audiences: A Theory of Production and Reception*, 2nd edn. London and New York: Routledge, 1997.

Bergen, Doris L., 'Old Testament, New Hatreds: The Hebrew Bible and Anti-Semitism in Nazi Germany', in Leonard J. Greenspoon and Bryan F. LeBeau, eds, *Sacred Text, Secular Times: The Hebrew Bible in the Modern World*. Omaha: Creighton University Press, 2000, pp. 35–46.

Bernasconi, Robert, 'The Ghetto and Race', in David Theo Goldberg and John Solomos, eds, *A Companion to Racial and Ethnic Studies*. Oxford: Blackwell, 2002, pp. 340–7.

Berry, Philippa, 'Introduction', in Philippa Berry and Andrew Wernick, eds, *Shadow of Spirit: Postmodernism and Religion*. London and New York: Routledge, 1992, pp. 1–10.
Beyer, Peter, *Religion and Globalization*. London: Sage, 1994.
Bhabha, Homi K., 'DissemiNation: Time, Narrative, and the Margins of the Modern Nation', in Homi K. Bhabha, ed., *Nation and Narration*. London and New York: Routledge, 1990, pp. 291–322.
—— *The Location of Culture*. London and New York: Routledge, 1994.
Bharucha, Rustom, *The Politics of Cultural Practice: Thinking Through Theatre in an Age of Globalization*. London: Athlone, 2000.
*The Bible: Authorized King James Version with Apocrypha*, ed. Robert Carroll and Stephen Prickett. Oxford: Oxford University Press, 1997.
Bishop, Michael, 'Tournier, Simon, Hyvrard and Cixous', in David Bevan, ed., *Literature and Spirituality*. Amsterdam and Atlanta, GA: Rodopi, 1992, pp. 121–32.
Blandford, Steve, Barry Keith Grant and Jim Hillier, *The Film Studies Dictionary*. London: Arnold, 2001.
Bloom, Harold, *The Anxiety of Influence: A Theory of Poetry*. New York: Oxford University Press, 1973.
Boehrer, Bruce Thomas, 'Bestial Buggery in *A Midsummer Night's Dream*', in David Lee Miller, Sharon O' Dair and Harold Weber, eds, *The Production of English Renaissance Culture*. Ithaca, NY and London: Cornell University Press, 1994, pp. 123–50.
Booth, Ken, and Tim Dunne, 'Worlds in Collision', in Ken Booth and Tim Dunne, eds, *Worlds in Collision: Terror and the Future of the Global Order*. Basingstoke: Macmillan, 2002, pp. 1–26.
Bottinelli, Jennifer J., 'Watching Lear: Resituating the Gaze at the Intersection of Film and Drama in Kristian Levring's *The King is Alive*', *Literature/Film Quarterly*, 33.2 (2005), pp. 101–9.
Branagh, Kenneth, *In the Bleak Midwinter*. London: Nick Hern, 1995.
—— *'Much Ado About Nothing' by William Shakespeare: Screenplay, Introduction and Notes*. New York and London: W. W. Norton, 1993.
Breight, Curtis, 'Elizabethan World Pictures', in John J. Joughin, ed., *Shakespeare and National Culture*. Manchester: Manchester University Press, 1997, pp. 295–325.
Bristol, Michael D., *Shakespeare's America/America's Shakespeare*. London and New York: Routledge, 1990.
Brogan, Benedict, 'Is Labour Sinking towards Anti-Semitism as it Tries to Derail the Tory Challenge?' *Daily Mail*, 29 January 2005, p. 9.
Brown, Bill, 'The Dark Wood of Postmodernity (Space, Faith, Allegory)', *PMLA*, 120.3 (2005), pp. 734–50.
Brown, Brooks and Rob Merritt, *No Easy Answers: The Truth behind the Death at Columbine*. New York: Lantern, 2002.
Brown, Eric C., 'Cinema in the Round: Self-Reflexivity in Tim Blake Nelson's "*O*"', in James R. Keller and Leslie Stratyner, eds, *Almost Shakespeare: Reinventing his Works for Cinema and Television*. Jefferson, NC and London: McFarland, 2004, pp. 73–85.
Brown, John Russell, *New Sites for Shakespeare: Theatre, the Audience and Asia*. London and New York: Routledge, 1999.
—— *Shakespeare and the Theatrical Event*. Basingstoke: Palgrave, 2002.

Bruzzi, Stella, *New Documentary: A Critical Introduction*. London and New York: Routledge, 2000.
Bryman, Alan, *The Disneyization of Society*. London: Sage, 2004.
Buchanan, Judith, *Shakespeare on Film*. Harlow: Longman, 2005.
—— 'Virgin and Ape, Venetian and Infidel: Labellings of Otherness in Oliver Parker's *Othello*', in Mark Thornton Burnett and Ramona Wray, eds, *Shakespeare, Film, Fin de Siècle*. Basingstoke: Macmillan, 2000, pp. 179–202.
Bucker, Pat, 'The "Hope" *Hamlet*: Kenneth Branagh's Comic Use of Shakespeare's Tragedy in *A Midwinter's Tale*', *Shakespeare Yearbook*, 8 (1997), pp. 290–305.
Budra, Paul and Betty A. Schellenberg, 'Introduction', in Paul Budra and Betty A. Schellenberg, eds, *Part Two: Reflections upon the Sequel*. Toronto, Buffalo and London: University of Toronto Press, 1998, pp. 3–18.
Buhler, Stephen M., 'Shakespeare and Company: *The Lion King* and the Disneyfication of *Hamlet*', in Brenda Ayres, ed., *The Emperor's Old Groove: Decolonizing Disney's Magic Kingdom*. New York: Lang, 2003, pp. 117–29.
—— *Shakespeare in the Cinema: Ocular Proof*. New York: State University of New York Press, 2002.
—— 'Textual and Sexual Anxieties in Michael Hoffman's Film of *A Midsummer Night's Dream*', *Shakespeare Bulletin*, 22.3 (2004), pp. 49–64.
Burnett, Mark Thornton, 'The "very cunning of the scene": Kenneth Branagh's *Hamlet*', *Literature/Film Quarterly*, 25 (1997), pp. 78–82.
—— and Ramona Wray, eds, *Shakespeare and Ireland: History, Politics, Culture*. Basingstoke: Macmillan, 1997.
Burt, Richard, 'Shakespeare and Asia in Postdiasporic Cinemas: Spin-offs and Citations of the Plays from Bollywood to Hollywood', in Richard Burt and Lynda E. Boose, eds, *Shakespeare, the Movie, II: Popularizing the Plays on Film, TV, Video, and DVD*. London and New York: Routledge, 2003, pp. 265–305.
—— 'Shakespeare and the Holocaust: Julie Taymor's *Titus* Is Beautiful, or Shakesploi Meets (the) Camp', *Colby Quarterly*, 37.1 (2001), pp. 78–106.
—— 'Shakespeare, "Glo-cali-zation," Race, and the Small Screens of Post-Popular Culture', in Richard Burt and Lynda E. Boose, eds, *Shakespeare, the Movie, II: Popularizing the Plays on Film, TV, Video, and DVD*. London and New York: Routledge, 2003, pp. 14–36.
—— '*Shakespeare in Love* and the End of the Shakespearean: Academic and Mass Culture Constructions of Literary Authorship', in Mark Thornton Burnett and Ramona Wray, eds, *Shakespeare, Film, Fin de Siècle*. Basingstoke: Macmillan, 2000, pp. 203–31.
Burton-Carvajal, Julianne, '"Surprise Package": Looking Southward with Disney', in Eric Smoodin, ed., *Disney Discourse: Producing the Magic Kingdom*. New York and London: Routledge, 1994, pp. 131–47.
Butler, Judith, *Gender Trouble: Feminism and the Subversion of Identity*. New York and London: Routledge, 1999.
Caplan, Caren, *Questions of Travel: Postmodern Discourses of Displacement*. Durham, NC and London: Duke University Press, 1996.
Caputo, John D., 'Apostles of the Impossible: On God and the Gift in Derrida and Marion', in John D. Caputo and Michael J. Scanlon, eds, *God, the Gift, and Postmodernism*. Bloomington and London: Indiana University Press, 1999, pp. 185–222.
—— *Deconstruction in a Nutshell: A Conversation with Jacques Derrida*. New York: Fordham University Press, 1997.

—— 'Foreword: Of hyper-reality', in Ewan Fernie, ed., *Spiritual Shakespeares*. London and New York: Routledge, 2005, pp. xvii–xix.

—— and Michael J. Scanlon, 'Introduction: Apology for the Impossible: Religion and Postmodernism', in John D. Caputo and Michael J. Scanlon, eds, *God, the Gift, and Postmodernism*. Bloomington and London: Indiana University Press, 1999, pp. 1–19.

Carlisle, Carol J., 'Letter to the Editors', *The Shakespeare Newsletter*, 54.4 (2004/5), pp. 86, 100, 114.

Carmichael, Thomas, '"After the Fact": Marx, the Sequel, Postmodernism, and John Barth's *LETTERS*', in Paul Budra and Betty A. Schellenberg, eds, *Part Two: Reflections upon the Sequel*. Toronto, Buffalo and London: University of Toronto Press, 1998, pp. 174–88.

Caruth, Cathy, 'Trauma and Experience: Introduction', in Cathy Caruth, ed., *Trauma: Explorations in Memory*. Baltimore, MD and London: Johns Hopkins University Press, 1995, pp. 3–12.

Carroll, David, 'Foreword: The Memory of Devastation and the Responsibilities of Thought', in Jean-François Lyotard, *Heidegger and 'The Jews'*, trans. Andreas Michel and Mark S. Roberts. Minneapolis, MN and London: University of Minnesota Press, 1990, pp. vii–xxix.

Cartelli, Thomas, *Repositioning Shakespeare: National Cultures, Postcolonial Appropriations*. London and New York: Routledge, 1999.

—— 'Shakespeare and the Street: Pacino's *Looking for Richard*, Bedford's *Street King*, and the Common Understanding', in Richard Burt and Lynda E. Boose, eds, *Shakespeare, the Movie, II: Popularizing the Plays on Film, TV, Video, and DVD*. London and New York: Routledge, 2003, pp. 186–99.

—— and Katherine Rowe, 'Surviving Shakespeare: Kristian Levring's *The King is Alive*', *Borrowers and Lenders*, 1.2 (2005), pp. 1–28.

Cartmell, Deborah, *Interpreting Shakespeare on Screen*. Basingstoke: Macmillan, 2000.

Castells, Manuel, *The Information Age: End of Millennium*. Oxford: Blackwell, 1998.

Chakravarti, Paromita, 'Modernity, Postcoloniality and *Othello*: The Case of *Saptapadi*', in Pascale Aebischer, Edward J. Esche and Nigel Wheale, eds, *Remaking Shakespeare: Performance Across Media, Genres and Cultures*. Basingstoke: Palgrave, 2003, pp. 39–55.

Charnes, Linda, *Notorious Identity: Materializing the Subject in Shakespeare*. Cambridge, MA.: Harvard University Press, 1993.

Chedgzoy, Kate, *Shakespeare's Queer Children: Sexual Politics and Contemporary Culture*. Manchester and New York: Manchester University Press, 1995.

Cheru, Fantu, 'New Social Movements: Democratic Struggles and Human Rights in Africa', in James H. Mittelman, ed., *Globalization: Critical Reflections*. Boulder, CO and London: Lynne Rienner Publishers, 1997, pp. 145–64.

Cixous, Hélène and Catherine Clément, *The Newly Born Woman*. Minneapolis, MN and London: University of Minnesota Press, 1986.

Collins, Michael J., 'Sleepless in Messina: Kenneth Branagh's *Much Ado About Nothing*', *Shakespeare Bulletin*, 15.2 (1997), pp. 38–9.

*The Compact Edition of the Oxford English Dictionary*, 2 vols. London: Book Club Associates, 1979.

Cook, Pam, *Screening the Past: Memory and Nostalgia Cinema*. London and New York: Routledge, 2005.

Corrigan, Timothy, 'The Commerce of Auteurism', in Virginia Wright Wexman, ed., *Film and Authorship*. New Jersey and London: Rutgers University Press, 2003, pp. 96–111.
Coursen, H. R., *Shakespeare in Production: Whose History?* Athens, OH: Ohio University Press, 1996.
—— *Shakespeare in Space: Recent Shakespeare Productions on Screen*. New York: Peter Lang, 2002.
Cronin, Michael, *Translation and Globalization*. London and New York: Routledge, 2003.
Crowl, Samuel, *The Films of Kenneth Branagh*. Westport, CT: Praeger, 2006.
—— 'Looking for Shylock: Stephen Greenblatt, Michael Radford and Al Pacino', in Mark Thornton Burnett and Ramona Wray, eds, *Screening Shakespeare in the Twenty-First Century*. Edinburgh: Edinburgh University Press, 2006, pp. 113–26.
—— *Shakespeare at the Cineplex: The Kenneth Branagh Era*. Athens, OH: Ohio University Press, 2003.
Cvetkovich, Ann, and Douglas Kellner, 'Introduction: Thinking Global and Local', in Ann Cvetkovich and Douglas Kellner, eds, *Articulating the Global and the Local*. Boulder, CO: Westview Press, 1997, pp. 1–32.
da Vinci Nichols, Nina, 'Branagh's *Hamlet* Redux', *Shakespeare Bulletin*, 15.3 (1997), pp. 38–41.
Danticat, Edwidge, 'Inspiration: Pictures with Meaning', *Guardian Weekend*, 5 November 2005, p. 122.
Dawson, Anthony B., 'International Shakespeare', in Stanley Wells and Sarah Stanton, eds, *The Cambridge Companion to Shakespeare on Stage*. Cambridge: Cambridge University Press, 2002, pp. 174–93.
Davis, Mike, *City of Quartz: Excavating the Future in Los Angeles*. London: Pimlico, 1998.
de la Garza, Rodolfo O., Angelo Falcon and F. Chris Garzia, 'Will the Real Americans Please Stand up? Anglo and Mexican-American Support of Core American Political Values', *American Journal of Political Science*, 40.2 (1996), pp. 335–51.
de Man, Paul, *Blindness and Insight: Essays in the Rhetoric of Contemporary Criticism*, 2nd edn. Minneapolis, MN and London: University of Minnesota Press, 1983.
de Ruijter, Arie, 'Globalization: A Challenge to the Social Sciences', in Frans J. Schuurman, ed., *Globalization and Development Studies: Challenges for the 21st Century*. London: Sage, 2001, pp. 31–44.
De Vany, Arthur, *Hollywood Economics: How Extreme Uncertainty Shapes the Film Industry*. London and New York: Routledge, 2004.
Deane, Seamus, *Strange Country: Modernity and Nationhood in Irish Writing since 1790*. Oxford: Clarendon, 1997.
Deitchman, Elizabeth A., 'Shakespeare Stiles Style: Shakespeare, Julia Stiles, and American Girl Culture', in Barbara Hodgdon and W. B. Worthen, eds, *A Companion to Shakespeare and Performance*. Oxford: Blackwell, 2005, pp. 478–93.
Deleyto, Celestino, 'Men in Leather: Kenneth Branagh's *Much Ado About Nothing* and Romantic Comedy', *Cinema Journal*, 36.3 (1997), pp. 91–105.
Dentith, Simon, *Parody*. London and New York: Routledge, 2000.

Denzin, Norman K., *Reading Race: Hollywood and the Cinema of Racial Violence*. London: Sage, 2002.
Derrida, Jacques, *A Derrida Reader: Between the Blinds*, ed. Peggy Kamuf. New York and London: Harvester Wheatsheaf, 1991.
—— *Spectres of Marx: The State of the Debt, the Work of Mourning, and the New International*, trans. Peggy Kamuf. New York and London: Routledge, 1994.
Di Iorio Sandín, Lyn, *Killing Spanish: Literary Essays on Ambivalent U.S. Latino/a Identity*. New York: Palgrave, 2004.
Dickson, Andy, rev. of *William Shakespeare's 'The Merchant of Venice'*, *Sight and Sound*, February (2005), pp. 79–80.
Diniz, Thaïs Flores Nogueira, 'Shakespeare Parodied: Romeo and Juliet', in Bernice W. Kliman and Rick J. Santos, eds, *Latin American Shakespeares*. Madison and Teaneck, WI: Fairleigh Dickinson University Press, 2005, pp. 263–9.
Dollimore, Jonathan, *Sexual Dissidence: Augustine to Wilde, Freud to Foucault*. Oxford: Clarendon Press, 1991.
Donaldson, Peter, '"All which it inherit": Shakespeare, Globes and Global Media', *Shakespeare Survey*, 52 (1999), pp. 183–200.
—— 'Hamlet among the Pixelvisionaries: Video Art, Authenticity and "Wisdom" in Almereyda's *Hamlet*', in Diana E. Henderson, ed., *A Concise Companion to Shakespeare on Screen*. Oxford: Blackwell, 2006, pp. 216–37.
Dorval, Patricia, 'Shakespeare on Screen: Threshold Aesthetics in Oliver Parker's *Othello*', *Early Modern Literary Studies*, 6.1 (2000), pp. 1–11.
Eagleton, Terry, *The Ideology of the Aesthetic*. Oxford: Blackwell, 1990.
Egoyan, Atom, and Ian Balfour, 'Introduction', in Atom Egoyan and Ian Balfour, eds, *Subtitles: On the Foreignness of Film*. Cambridge, MA: MIT Press, 2004, pp. 21–32.
Falsetto, Mario, *Personal Visions: Conversations with Independent Filmmakers*. London: Constable, 1999.
Fanon, Frantz, *Black Skin, White Masks*, trans. Charles Lam Markmann. London and Sydney: Pluto, 1986.
Featherstone, Mike, 'Global Culture: An Introduction', in Mike Featherstone, ed., *Global Culture: Nationalism, Globalization and Modernity*. London: Sage, 1990, pp. 1–14.
Felman, Shoshana, 'Education and Crisis, or the Vicissitudes of Teaching', in Cathy Caruth, ed., *Trauma: Explorations in Memory*. Baltimore, MD and London: Johns Hopkins University Press, 1995, pp. 13–60.
—— and Dori Laub, *Testimony: Crises of Witnessing in Literature, Psychoanalysis and History*. New York and London: Routledge, 1992.
Fernandez, Ramona, 'Pachuco Mickey', in Elizabeth Bell, Lynda Haas and Laura Sells, eds, *From Mouse to Mermaid: The Politics of Film, Gender, and Culture*. Bloomington and Indianapolis: Indiana University Press, 1995, pp. 236–53.
Fernie, Ewan, 'Introduction: Shakespeare, Spirituality and Contemporary Criticism', in Ewan Fernie, ed., *Spiritual Shakespeares*. London and New York: Routledge, 2005, pp. 1–27.
—— 'Shakespeare and the Prospect of Presentism', *Shakespeare Survey*, 58 (2005), pp. 169–84.
Finkelstein, Norman, *The Holocaust Industry: Reflections on the Exploitation of Jewish Suffering*. London and New York: Verso, 2000.

Finkelstein, Richard, 'Disney Cites Shakespeare: The Limits of Appropriation', in Christy Desmet and Robert Sawyer, eds, *Shakespeare and Appropriation*. London and New York: Routledge, 1999, pp. 179–96.

Fischer-Lichte, Erika, *The Show and the Gaze of Theatre: A European Perspective*. Iowa City: University of Iowa Press, 1997.

Ford, David F., 'Holy Spirit and Christian Spirituality', in Kevin J. Vanhoozer, ed., *The Cambridge Companion to Postmodern Theology*. Cambridge: Cambridge University Press, 2003, pp. 269–90.

Fortier, Mark, *Theory/Theatre: An Introduction*, 2nd edn. London and New York: Routledge, 2002.

Foucault, Michel, *Language, Counter-Memory, Practice: Selected Essays and Interviews*, ed. Donald F. Bouchard. Oxford: Blackwell, 1977.

Fox, Judith, 'New Religious Movements', in John R. Hinnells, ed., *The Routledge Companion to the Study of Religion*. London and New York: Routledge, 2005, pp. 323–36.

Fraenkel, Peter, and Roger Murray, *The Namibians*, The Minority Rights Group Report No. 19. London: The Minority Rights Group, 1985.

Fregoso, Rosa Linda, 'Recycling Colonialist Fantasies on the Texas Borderlands', in Hamid Naficy, ed., *Home, Exile, Homeland: Film, Media, and the Politics of Place*. London and New York: Routledge, 1999, pp. 169–92.

Freinkel, Lisa, '*The Merchant of Venice*: "Modern" Anti-Semitism and the Veil of Allegory', in Hugh Grady, ed., *Shakespeare and Modernity: Early Modern to Millennium*. London and New York: Routledge, 2000, pp. 122–41.

French, Emma, *Selling Shakespeare to Hollywood: The Marketing of Filmed Shakespeare Adaptations from 1989 into the New Millennium*. Hatfield: University of Hertfordshire Press, 2006.

Friedman, Jonathan, 'Being in the World: Globalization and Localization', in Mike Featherstone, ed., *Global Culture: Nationalism, Globalization and Modernity*. London: Sage, 1990, pp. 311–28.

Gajowski, Eveyln, '"Sigh no more, ladies, sigh no more": Genesis Deconstructed in Kenneth Branagh's *Much Ado About Nothing*', *Journal of Theatre and Drama*, 5–6 (1999/2000), pp. 101–26.

Garber, Marjorie, *Quotation Marks*. New York and London: Routledge, 2003.

Gellner, Conrad, rev. of *The Merchant of Venice*, *Cineaste*, 30.2 (2005), pp. 48–50.

Genette, Gérard, *Palimpsests: Literature in the Second Degree*, trans. Channa Newman and Claude Doubinsky. Lincoln, NB and London: University of Nebraska Press, 1997.

Giddens, Anthony, *Runaway World: How Globalization is Reshaping Our Lives*. London: Profile, 2002.

Gilmore, Michael T., *Differences in the Dark: American Movies and English Theatre*. New York: Columbia University Press, 1998.

Girard, René, *Violence and the Sacred*, trans. Patrick Gregory. Baltimore, MD and London: Johns Hopkins University Press, 1977.

Goldman, Robert, and Stephen Papson, *Nike Culture: The Sign of the Swoosh*. London: Sage, 1998.

Greenhalgh, Susanne, '"Alas poor country!" Documenting the Politics of Performance in Two British Television *Macbeth*s since the 1980s', in Pascale Aebischer, Edward J. Esche and Nigel Wheale, eds, *Remaking Shakespeare: Performance Across Media, Genres and Cultures*. Basingstoke: Palgrave, 2003, pp. 93–114.

—— and Robert Shaughnessy, 'Our Shakespeares: British Television and the Strains of Multiculturalism', in Mark Thornton Burnett and Ramona Wray, eds, *Screening Shakespeare in the Twenty-First Century*. Edinburgh: Edinburgh University Press, 2006, pp. 90–112.

Grimal, Pierre, *The Dictionary of Classical Mythology*, trans. A. R. Maxwell-Hyslop. Oxford: Blackwell, 1986.

Guru, Gopal, 'Dalits: Reflections on the Search for Inclusion', in Peter Ronald de Souza, ed., *Contemporary India – Transitions*. London: Sage, 2000, pp. 59–72.

Halio, Jay L., *Shakespeare in Performance: 'A Midsummer Night's Dream'*, 2nd edn. Manchester: Manchester University Press, 2003.

Hall, Kim, *Things of Darkness: Economies of Race and Gender in Early Modern England*. Ithaca, NY and London: Cornell University Press, 1995.

Hall, Stuart 'New Ethnicities', in Linda Martín Alcoff and Eduardo Mendieta, eds, *Race, Class, Gender, and Nationality*. Oxford: Blackwell, 2003, pp. 90–5.

Halpern, Richard, 'An Impure History of Ghosts: Derrida, Marx, Shakespeare', in Jean E. Howard and Scott Cutler Shershow, eds, *Marxist Shakespeares*. London and New York: Routledge, 2001, pp. 31–52.

Hardt, Michael and Antonio Negri, *Empire*. Cambridge, MA: Harvard University Press, 1999.

Harries, Dan, *Film Parody*. London: BFI, 2000.

Hatchuel, Sarah, *Shakespeare, from Stage to Screen*. Cambridge: Cambridge University Press, 2004.

Hattaway, Michael, Boika Sokolova and Derek Roper, eds, *Shakespeare in the New Europe*. Sheffield: Sheffield Academic Press, 1994.

Heinze, Andrew R., *Jews and the American Soul: Human Nature in the Twentieth Century*. Princeton, NJ and Oxford: Princeton University Press, 2004.

Held, David and Anthony McGrew, 'The Great Globalization Debate', in David Held and Anthony McGrew, eds, *The Global Transformations Reader: An Introduction to the Globalization Debate*. Cambridge: Polity, 2000, pp. 1–45.

Henderson, Diana E., 'Learning from Campbell Scott's *Hamlet*', in Diana E. Henderson, ed., *A Concise Companion to Shakespeare on Screen*. Oxford: Blackwell, 2006, pp. 77–95.

Higgs, Eric, 'Nature by Design', in Eric Higgs, Andrew Light and David Strong, eds, *Technology and the Good Life?* Chicago and London: University of Chicago Press, 2000, pp. 195–212.

Hilberg, Raul, 'Ghetto Formation', in Simon Gigliotti and Berel Lang, eds, *The Holocaust: A Reader*. Oxford: Blackwell, 2005, pp. 124–42.

Hobson, Marian, 'History Traces', in Derek Attridge, Geoff Bennington and Robert Young, eds, *Post-structuralism and the Question of History*. Cambridge: Cambridge University Press, 1987, pp. 101–15.

Hodgdon, Barbara, 'Race-ing *Othello*: Re-engendering White-Out, II', in Richard Burt and Lynda E. Boose, eds, *Shakespeare, the Movie, II: Popularizing the Plays on Film, TV, Video, and DVD*. London and New York: Routledge, 2003, pp. 89–104.

—— 'Re-incarnations', in Pascale Aebischer, Edward J. Esche and Nigel Wheale, eds, *Remaking Shakespeare: Performance across Media, Genres and Cultures*. Basingstoke: Palgrave, 2003, pp. 190–209.

—— *The Shakespeare Trade: Performances and Appropriations*. Philadelphia: University of Pennsylvania Press, 1998.

—— 'William Shakespeare's "Romeo and Juliet"': Everything's Nice in America?' *Shakespeare Survey*, 52 (1999), pp. 88–98.

Hoffman, Michael, *William Shakespeare's 'A Midsummer Night's Dream'*. New York: HarperCollins, 1999.

Hole, Christina, *English Sports and Pastimes*. London: Batsford, 1949.

Holland, Peter, 'Foreword', in Mark Thornton Burnett and Ramona Wray, eds, *Shakespeare, Film, Fin de Siècle*. Basingstoke: Macmillan, 2000, pp. xii–xiv.

hooks, bell, *We Real Cool: Black Men and Masculinity*. London and New York: Routledge, 2004.

Hopkins, Lisa, rev. of *Hamlet*, *Shakespeare Bulletin*, 23.2 (2005), pp. 52–5.

Howlett, Kathy M., *Framing Shakespeare on Film*. Athens, OH: Ohio University Press, 2000.

Hozic, Aida, *Hollyworld: Space, Power, and Fantasy in the American Economy*. Ithaca, NY and London: Cornell University Press, 2001.

Hutcheon, Linda, *The Politics of Postmodernism*, 2nd edn. London and New York: Routledge, 2002.

—— *A Theory of Parody: The Teachings of Twentieth-Century Art Forms*. New York and London: Methuen, 1985.

Huyssen, Andreas, 'Present Pasts: Media, Politics, Amnesia', *Public Culture*, 12.1 (2000), pp. 21–38.

Innes, Duncan, 'South African Capital and Namibia', in Reginald H. Green, Kimmo Kiljunen and Marja-Liisa Kiljunen, eds, *Namibia: The Last Colony*. Harlow: Longman, 1981, pp. 59–86.

Iser, Wolfgang, *The Act of Reading: A Theory of Aesthetic Response*. London and Henley: Routledge & Kegan Paul, 1978.

Jackson, MacDonald P., '"A Wood Near Monte Athena": Michael Hoffman's *A Midsummer Night's Dream*', *The Shakespeare Newsletter*, 49.2 (1999), pp. 29, 37, 38, 44, 48.

Jackson, Russell, 'Actor-Managers and the Spectacular', in Jonathan Bate and Russell Jackson, eds, *Shakespeare: An Illustrated Stage History*. Oxford: Oxford University Press, 1996, pp. 112–27.

——'Introduction: Shakespeare, Film and the Marketplace', in Russell Jackson, ed., *The Cambridge Companion to Shakespeare on Film*. Cambridge: Cambridge University Press, 2000, pp. 1–12.

Jain, Madhu, 'The Happening City', in B. P. Singh and Pavan K. Varma, eds, *The Millennium Book on New Delhi*. Oxford: Oxford University Press, 2001, pp. 121–39.

Jameson, Fredric, 'Notes on Globalization as a Philosophical Issue', in Fredric Jameson and Masao Miyoshi, eds, *The Cultures of Globalization*. Durham, NC and London: Duke University Press, 1998, pp. 54–77.

—— *Postmodernism, or, the Cultural Logic of Late Capitalism*. London and New York: Verso, 1991.

—— *The Seeds of Time*. New York: Columbia University Press, 1994.

—— *Signatures of the Visible*. New York and London: Routledge, 1992.

Jess, Carolyn, '"The Barbarous Chronos": (Post)Colonialism, Sequelization, and Regenerative Authority in Kristian Levring's *The King is Alive*', *Shakespeare Studies in South Africa*, 15 (2003), pp. 11–20.

—— 'Newness, Sequelization, and Dogme Logic in Kristian Levring's *The King is Alive*', *New Cinemas: Journal of Contemporary Film*, 3.1 (2005), pp. 3–16.

Jess-Cooke, Carolyn, 'Screening the McShakespeare in Post-Millennial Shakespeare Cinema', in Mark Thornton Burnett and Ramona Wray, eds, *Screening Shakespeare in the Twenty-First Century*. Edinburgh: Edinburgh University Press, 2006, pp. 163–84.
Johnson, David, *Shakespeare and South Africa*. Oxford: Clarendon, 1996.
Jones, Nicholas, 'Bottom's Wife: Gender and Voice in Hoffman's *Dream*', *Literature/Film Quarterly*, 32.2 (2004), pp. 126–33.
Joughin, John J., 'Lear's Afterlife', *Shakespeare Survey*, 55 (2002), pp. 67–81.
Kaplan, E. Ann, *Trauma Culture: The Politics of Terror and Loss in Media and Literature*. New Brunswick and London: Rutgers University Press, 2005.
Kaplan, Jane, 'Introduction', in Jane Caplan, ed., *Written on the Body: The Tattoo in European and American History*. London: Reaktion, 2000, pp. xi–xxiii.
Kearney, Richard, 'Spectres of *Hamlet*', in Ewan Fernie, ed., *Spiritual Shakespeares*. London and New York: Routledge, 2005, pp. 157–85.
Kellner, Douglas, *Media Spectacle*. London and New York: Routledge, 2003.
Kennedy, Dennis, ed., *Foreign Shakespeare: Contemporary Performance*. Cambridge: Cambridge University Press, 1993.
—— 'Shakespeare and the Global Spectator', *Shakespeare Jahrbuch*, 131 (1995), pp. 50–64.
Kershaw, Baz, *The Radical in Performance: Between Brecht and Baudrillard*. London and New York: Routledge, 1999.
Kershaw, Ian, *Hitler 1889–1936: Hubris*. London: Allen Lane, 1998.
Kilfeather, Siobhán, 'The Gothic Novel', in John Wilson Foster, ed., *The Cambridge Companion to the Irish Novel*. Cambridge: Cambridge University Press, 2006, pp. 78–96.
Kiljunen, Kimmo, 'National Resistance and Liberation Struggle', in Reginald H. Green, Kimmo Kiljunen and Marja-Liisa Kiljunen, eds, *Namibia: The Last Colony*. Harlow: Longman, 1981, pp. 145–71.
Kimmel, Michael, *Manhood in America: A Cultural History*. New York: Free Press, 1996.
King, Richard, 'Mysticism and Spirituality', in John R. Hinnells, ed., *The Routledge Companion to the Study of Religion*. London and New York: Routledge, 2005, pp. 306–22.
King, Robert H., *Thomas Merton and Thich Nhat Hanh: Engaged Spirituality in an Age of Globalization*. New York and London: Continuum, 2001.
Kittler, Friedrich, *Gramophone, Film, Typewriter*, trans. Geoffrey Winthrop-Young and Michael Wutz. Stanford, CA: Stanford University Press, 1999.
Knowles, Caroline, *Race and Social Analysis*. London: Sage, 2003.
Kolker, Robert P., 'Algebraic Figures: Recalculating the Hitchcock Formula', in Andrew Horton and Stuart Y. McDougal, eds, *Play it Again, Sam: Retakes on Remakes*. Berkeley, Los Angeles and London: University of California Press, 1998, pp. 34–51.
Kossak, Saskia, *'Frame My Face to All Occasions': Shakespeare's 'Richard III' on Screen*. Vienna: Braumüller, 2005.
Kössler, Reinhart, 'Globalization and Human Rights: Some Developmental Reflections', in Frans J. Schuurman, ed., *Globalization and Development Studies: Challenges for the Twenty-First Century*. London: Sage, 2001, pp. 83–98.
Kreilkamp, Vera, *The Anglo-Irish Novel and the Big House*. New York: Syracuse University Press, 1998.

Kristeva, Julia, *Powers of Horror: An Essay on Abjection*, trans. Leon S. Roudiez. New York: Columbia University Press, 1982.
Laity, Sister Annabel, 'Introduction', in *Thich Nhat Hanh: Essential Writings*, ed. Robert Ellsberg. New York: Orbis, 2001, pp. 1–16.
Lampert, Lisa, *Gender and Jewish Difference from Paul to Shakespeare*. Philadelphia: University of Pennsylvania Press, 2004.
Langhorne, Richard, *The Coming of Globalization: Its Evolution and Contemporary Consequences*. Basingstoke: Palgrave, 2001.
Lanier, Douglas, '"Art thou base, common, and popular?" The Cultural Politics of Kenneth Branagh's *Hamlet*', in Courtney Lehmann and Lisa S. Starks, eds, *Spectacular Shakespeare: Critical Theory and Popular Cinema*. Madison and Teaneck, WI: Fairleigh Dickinson University Press, 2002, pp. 149–71.
—— 'Drowning the Book: *Prospero's Books* and the Textual Shakespeare', in James C. Bulman, ed., *Shakespeare, Theory, and Performance*. London and New York: Routledge, 1996, pp. 187–209.
—— 'Nostalgia and Theatricality: The Fate of the Shakespearean Stage in the *Midsummer Night's Dream*s of Hoffman, Noble and Edzard', in Richard Burt and Lynda Boose, eds, *Shakespeare, the Movie, II: Popularizing the Plays on Film, TV, Video, and DVD*. London and New York: Routledge, 2003, pp. 154–72.
—— 'Shakescorp *Noir*', *Shakespeare Quarterly*, 53.2 (2002), pp. 157–80.
—— 'Will of the People: Recent Shakespeare Film Parody and the Politics of Popularization', in Diana E. Henderson, ed., *A Concise Companion to Shakespeare on Screen*. Oxford: Blackwell, 2006, pp. 176–96.
Laub, Dori, 'Truth and Testimony: The Process and the Struggle', in Cathy Caruth, ed., *Trauma: Explorations in Memory*. Baltimore, MD and London: Johns Hopkins University Press, 1995, pp. 61–75.
Lavie, Smadar and Ted Swedenburg, 'Introduction', in Smadar Lavie and Ted Swedenburg, eds, *Displacement, Diaspora, and Geographies of Identity*. Durham, NC and London: Duke University Press, 1996, pp. 1–25.
Lehmann, Courtney, 'Crouching Tiger, Hidden Agenda: How Shakespeare and the Renaissance are Taking the Rage out of Feminism', *Shakespeare Quarterly*, 53.2 (2002), pp. 260–79.
—— 'Out Damned Scot: Dislocating *Macbeth* in Transnational Film and Media Culture', in Richard Burt and Lynda E. Boose, eds, *Shakespeare, the Movie, II: Popularizing the Plays on Film, TV, Video, and DVD*. London and New York: Routledge, 2003, pp. 231–51.
—— *Shakespeare Remains: Theater to Film, Early Modern to Postmodern*. Ithaca, NY and London: Cornell University Press, 2002.
—— 'Shakespeare the Saviour or Phantom Menace?: Kenneth Branagh's *A Midwinter's Tale* and the Critique of Cynical Reason', *Colby Quarterly*, 37.1 (2001), pp. 54–77.
Levine, Lawrence W., *Highbrow/Lowbrow: The Emergence of Cultural Hierarchy in America*. Cambridge, MA: Harvard University Press, 1988.
Leys, Colin and John S. Saul, *Namibia's Liberation Struggle: The Two-Edged Sword*. Athens, OH: Ohio University Press, 1995.
Li, David Leiwei, 'Introduction: Globalization and the Humanities', *Comparative Literature*, 53.4 (2001), pp. 275–82.

Lifton, Robert Jay, 'An Interview', in Cathy Caruth, ed., *Trauma: Explorations in Memory*. Baltimore, MD and London: Johns Hopkins University Press, 1995, pp. 128–47.

Livingstone, Paisley, 'Artistic Self-Reflexivity in *The King is Alive* and *Strass*', in Mette Hjort and Scott MacKenzie, eds, *Purity and Provocation: Dogma 95*. London: BFI, 2003, pp. 102–10.

LoMonico, Michael, '"Is all our company here?" An Interview with Michael Hoffman', *Shakespeare*, 3.2 (1999), pp. 9–13.

Loomba, Ania, 'Shakespeare and the Possibilities of Postcolonial Performance', in Barbara Hodgdon and W. B. Worthen, eds, *A Companion to Shakespeare and Performance*. Oxford: Blackwell, 2005, pp. 121–38.

Lyotard, Jean-François, *The Postmodern Condition: A Report on Knowledge*, trans. Geoff Bennington and Brian Massumi. Manchester: Manchester University Press, 1984.

Macaulay, Thomas Babington, *Prose and Poetry*, ed. G. M. Young. Cambridge, MA: Harvard University Press, 1957.

McCormack, W. J., *Dissolute Characters: Irish Literary History through Balzac, Sheridan Le Fanu, Yeats and Bowen*. Manchester: Manchester University Press, 1993.

—— 'Irish Gothic and After', in Seamus Deane, ed., *The Field Day Anthology of Irish Writing*, 5 vols. Derry: Field Day Publications, 1991–2002, II, pp. 831–54.

McGreal, Chris, 'We Must Rely on Ourselves, Says Sharon', *Guardian*, 27 January 2005, p. 17.

McLoughlin, Seán, 'Migration, Diaspora and Transnationalism: Transformations of Religion and Culture in a Globalizing Age', in John R. Hinnels, ed., *The Routledge Companion to the Study of Religion*. London and New York: Routledge, 2005, pp. 526–49.

Maguire, Laurie, *Shakespearean Suspect Texts: The 'Bad' Quartos and Their Contexts*. Cambridge: Cambridge University Press, 1996.

Mahon, John W., 'The Editors go to the Movies: Michael Radford's *The Merchant of Venice*', *The Shakespeare Newsletter*, 54.2–3 (2004), pp. 69–70, 76.

Malešević, Siniša, *The Sociology of Ethnicity*. London: Sage, 2004.

Maley, Willy and Andrew Murphy, eds, *Shakespeare and Scotland*. Manchester and New York: Manchester University Press, 2004.

Mallin, Eric S., 'Jewish Invader and the Soul of the State: *The Merchant of Venice* and Science Fiction Movies', in Hugh Grady, ed., *Shakespeare and Modernity: Early Modern to Millennium*. London and New York: Routledge, 2000, pp. 142–67.

Martinek, Jeffrey, '"An Ebullition of Fancy": *Othello*, Orenthal James Simpson, and the Play of the "Race Card"', *Studies in the Humanities*, 25.1–2 (1998), pp. 66–100.

Massai, Sonia, 'Defining Local Shakespeares', in Sonia Massai, ed., *World-Wide Shakespeares: Local Appropriations in Film and Performance*. London and New York: Routledge, 2005, pp. 3–14.

Matchinske, Megan M., 'Putting Bottom on Top: Gender and the Married Man in Michael Hoffman's *Dream*', *Shakespeare Bulletin*, 21.4 (2003), pp. 40–56.

May, Stephen, 'Multiculturalism', in David Theo Goldberg and John Solomos, eds, *A Companion to Racial and Ethnic Studies*. Oxford: Blackwell, 2002, pp. 124–44.

Mayo, Sarah, '"A Shakespeare for the People": Negotiating the Popular in *Shakespeare in Love* and Michael Hoffman's *A Midsummer Night's Dream*', *Textual Practice*, 17.2 (2003), pp. 295–316.

Mazur, Eric Michael and Tara K. Koda, 'The Happiest Place on Earth: Disney's America and the Commodification of Religion', in Eric Michael Mazur and Kate McCarthy, eds, *God in Details: American Religion in Popular Culture*. New York and London: Routledge, 2001, pp. 299–315.

Mercatante, Anthony S., *The Facts on File Encyclopedia of World Mythology and Legend*. New York and Oxford: Facts on File, 1988.

Miles, Steven, 'McDonaldization and the Global Sports Store: Constructing Consumer Meanings in a Rationalized Society', in Mark Alfino, John S. Caputo and Robin Wynyard, eds, *McDonaldization Revisited: Critical Essays on Consumer Culture*. Westport, CT: Praeger, 1998, pp. 53–65.

Milton, John, *John Milton*, ed. Stephen Orgel and Jonathan Goldberg. Oxford and New York: Oxford University Press, 1990.

Miller, Toby, Nitin Govil, John McMurria and Richard Maxwell, *Global Hollywood*. London: BFI, 2001.

Miller, William Ian, *The Anatomy of Disgust*. Cambridge, MA: Harvard University Press, 1997.

Moorehead, Caroline, *Namibia: Apartheid's Forgotten Children*. Oxford: Oxfam, 1989.

Nelson, Tim Blake, 'There's a Price You Pay for Getting Too Real: Delay', *The New York Times*, 26 August (2001), pp. B8, B15.

Newman, Karen, 'Portia's Ring: Unruly Women and Structures of Exchange in *The Merchant of Venice*', *Shakespeare Quarterly*, 38.1 (1987), pp. 19–33.

Nhat Hanh, Thich, *Essential Writings*, ed. Robert Ellsberg. New York: Orbis, 2001.

Nichols, Bill, *Representing Reality: Issues and Concepts in Documentary*. Bloomington and Indianapolis: Indiana University Press, 1991.

Niezen, Ronald, *A World beyond Difference: Cultural Identity in the Age of Globalization*. Oxford: Blackwell, 2004.

O'Byrne, Darren, 'Working-Class Culture: Local Community and Global Conditions', in John Earle, ed., *Living the Global City: Globalization as Local Process*. London and New York: Routledge, 1997, pp. 73–89.

Orkin, Martin, *Local Shakespeares: Proximations and Power*. London and New York: Routledge, 2005.

Partridge, Christopher, *The Re-Enchantment of the West: Alternative Spiritualities, Sacralization, Popular Culture, and Occulture*. London and New York: Continuum, 2004.

Pendleton, Thomas A., 'The Editors Go to the Movies: Michael Radford's *The Merchant of Venice*', *The Shakespeare Newsletter*, 54.2-3 (2004), pp. 69–70, 76.

Phelan, Peggy, *Unmarked: The Politics of Performance*. London and New York: Routledge, 1993.

Pizzato, Mark, *Theatres of Human Sacrifice: From Ancient Ritual to Screen Violence*. New York: State University of New York Press, 2005.

Poe, Edgar Allen, *The Poems*, ed. Killis Campbell. New York: Russell & Russell, 1962.

Puchner, Martin, *Stage Fright: Modernism, Anti-Theatricality, and Drama*. Baltimore, MD and London: Johns Hopkins University Press, 2002.

Read, Oliver and Walter L. Welch, *From Tin Foil to Stereo: Evolution of the Phonograph*. Bloomington and Indianapolis: Indiana University Press, 1959.

Ritzer, George, *The McDonaldization of Society*. London: Sage, 2000.

Robertson, Roland, 'Glocalization; Time–Space and Homogeneity–Heterogeneity', in Mike Featherstone, Scott Lash and Roland Robertson, eds, *Global Modernities*. London: Sage, 1995, pp. 23–44.

——*Globalization, Social Theory and Global Culture*. London: Sage, 1992.

Rodríguez, Clara E., 'Latinos on Television and in the News: Absent or Misrepresented', in Clara E. Rodríguez, ed., *Latin Looks: Images of Latinas and Latinos in the U.S. Media*. Boulder, CO: Westview, 1997, pp. 13–20.

Rothwell, Kenneth S., *A History of Shakespeare on Screen: A Century of Film and Television*, 2nd edn. Cambridge: Cambridge University Press, 2004.

Rouse, Roger, 'Mexican Migration and the Social Space of Postmodernism', *Diaspora*, 1 (1991), pp. 8–24.

Rowe, Katherine, '"Remember Me": Technologies of Memory in Michael Almereyda's *Hamlet*', in Richard Burt and Lynda E. Boose, eds, *Shakespeare, the Movie, II: Popularizing the Plays on Film, TV, Video, and DVD*. London and New York: Routledge, 2003, pp. 37–55.

Royster, Francesca T., *Becoming Cleopatra: The Shifting Image of an Icon*. New York: Palgrave, 2003.

Rutter, Carol Chillington, *Enter the Body: Women and Representation on Shakespeare's Stage*. London and New York: Routledge, 2001.

Sage, Victor, 'Irish Gothic: C. R. Maturin and J. S. Le Fanu', in David Punter, ed., *A Companion to the Gothic*. Oxford: Blackwell, 2000, pp. 81–93.

Salamone, Frank A. and Virginia A. Salamone, 'Images of Main Street: Disney World and the American Adventure', *Journal of American Culture*, 22.1 (1999), pp. 85–92.

Sanders, Julie, 'The End of History and the Last Man: Kenneth Branagh's *Hamlet*', in Mark Thornton Burnett and Ramona Wray, eds, *Shakespeare, Film, Fin de Siècle*. Basingstoke: Macmillan, 2000, pp. 147–64.

——*Novel Shakespeares: Twentieth-Century Women Novelists and Appropriation*. Manchester and New York: Manchester University Press, 2001.

Sassen, Saskia, *Globalization and Its Discontents*. New York: The New Press, 1998.

Savage, F. G., *The Flora and Folklore of Shakespeare*. London: Burrow, 1923.

Schirato, Tony and Jen Webb, *Understanding Globalization*. London: Sage, 2003.

Schohet, Lauren, 'The Banquet of Scotland (PA)', *Shakespeare Survey*, 57 (2004), pp. 186–95.

Scholte, Jan Aart, *Globalization: A Critical Introduction*. Basingstoke: Macmillan, 2000.

Sconce, Jeffrey, *Haunted Media: Electronic Presence from Telegraphy to Television*. Durham, NC and London: Duke University Press, 2000.

Scott-Douglass, Amy, 'Dogme Shakespeare 95: European Cinema, anti-Hollywood sentiment, and the Bard', in Richard Burt and Lynda E. Boose, eds, *Shakespeare, the Movie, II: Popularizing the Plays on Film, TV, Video, and DVD*. London and New York: Routledge, 2003, pp. 252–64.

Schwartz, Hillel, *The Culture of the Copy: Striking Likenesses, Unreasonable Facsimiles*. New York: Zone, 1996.

Shakespeare, William, *The Norton Shakespeare*, ed. Stephen Greenblatt, Walter Cohen, Jean E. Howard and Katharine Eisaman Maus. New York and London: W. W. Norton, 1997.

Shapiro, James, *Shakespeare and the Jews*. New York: Columbia University Press, 1996.

Shaughnessy, Robert, *The Shakespeare Effect: A History of Twentieth-Century Performance*. Basingstoke: Palgrave, 2002.

Sheppard, Philippa, 'The Castle of Elsinore: Gothic Aspects of Kenneth Branagh's *Hamlet*', *Shakespeare Bulletin*, 19.3 (2001), pp. 36–9.

Sher, Antony, *Beside Myself*. London: Hutchinson, 2001.

Silverman, Kaja, *The Acoustic Mirror: The Female Voice in Psychoanalysis and Cinema*. Bloomington and Indianapolis: Indiana University Press, 1988.

Smith, Michael Peter, 'Looking for Globality in Los Angeles', in Ann Cvetkovich and Douglas Kellner, eds, *Articulating the Global and the Local: Globalization and Cultural Studies*. Boulder, CO: Westview, 1997, pp. 55–71.

Somerville-Large, Peter, *Irish Eccentrics*. London: Hamish Hamilton, 1975.

Staiger, Janet, 'Authorship Approaches', in David A. Gerstner and Janet Staiger, eds, *Authorship and Film*. London and New York: Routledge, 2003, pp. 27–57.

Starks, Lisa S., 'The Veiled (Hot)Bed of Race and Desire: Parker's *Othello* and the Stereotypes of Screen Fetish', *Post Script*, 17.1 (1997), pp. 64–78.

Stewart, Susan, *On Longing: Narratives of the Miniature, the Gigantic, the Souvenir, the Collection*. Durham, NC and London: Duke University Press, 1993.

Sturrock, June, 'Sequels, Series and Sensation Novels: Charlotte Yonge and the Popular-Fiction Market of the 1850s and 1860s', in Paul Budra and Betty A. Schellenberg, eds, *Part Two: Reflections upon the Sequel*. Toronto, Buffalo and London: University of Toronto Press, 1998, pp. 102–17.

Suter, Jacqueline, 'Feminine Discourse in *Christopher Strong*', *Camera Obscura*, 3–4 (1979), pp. 135–50.

Svich, Caridad, 'Theatre in Crisis? Living Memory in an Unstable Time', in Maria M. Delgado and Caridad Svich, eds, *Theatre in Crisis? Performance Manifestoes for a New Century*. Manchester: Manchester University Press, 2002, pp. 15–19.

—— 'The Dynamics of Fractals: Legacies for a New Tomorrow', in Caridad Svich, ed., *Trans-global Readings: Crossing Theatrical Boundaries*. Manchester: Manchester University Press, 2003, pp. 1–14.

Taylor, Gary, 'Afterword: The Incredible Shrinking Bard', in Christy Desmet and Robert Sawyer, eds, *Shakespeare and Appropriation*. London and New York: Routledge, 1999, pp. 197–205.

Taylor, Mark C., 'Reframing Postmodernisms', in Philippa Berry and Andrew Wernick, eds, *Shadow of Spirit: Postmodernism and Religion*. London and New York: Routledge, 1992, pp. 11–29.

Tracy, David, 'Fragments: The Spiritual Situation of Our Times', in John D. Caputo and Michael J. Scanlon, eds, *God, the Gift, and Postmodernism*. Bloomington and London: Indiana University Press, 1999, pp. 170–84.

Traynor, Ian, 'The World Remembers', *Guardian*, 28 January 2005, p. 1.

Trivedi, Poonam, '"It is the bloody business which informs thus": Local Politics and Performance Praxis, *Macbeth* in India', in Sonia Massai, ed., *World-Wide Shakespeares: Local Appropriations in Film and Performance*. London and New York: Routledge, 2005, pp. 47–54.

——'Reading "Other Shakespeares"', in Pascale Aebischer, Edward J. Esche and Nigel Wheale, eds, *Remaking Shakespeare: Performance Across Media, Genres and Cultures*. Basingstoke: Palgrave, 2003, pp. 56–73.

Turner, Bryan S., 'The Possibility of Primitiveness: Towards a Sociology of Body Marks in Cool Societies', in Mike Featherstone, ed., *Body Modification*. London: Sage, 2000, pp. 39–50.

Valle, Victor M. and Rodolfo D. Torres, *Latino Metropolis*. Minneapolis, MN and London: University of Minnesota Press, 2000.

Vanhoozer, Kevin J., 'Theology and the Condition of Postmodernity: A Report on the Knowledge of God', in Kevin J. Vanhoozer, ed., *The Cambridge Companion to Postmodern Theology*. Cambridge: Cambridge University Press, 2003, pp. 3–25.

Walsh, Michael, 'Jameson and "Global Aesthetics"', in David Bordwell and Noël Carroll, eds, *Post-Theory: Reconstructing Film Studies*. Madison, WI: University of Wisconsin Press, 1996, pp. 481–500.

Wark, McKenzie, 'To the Vector the Spoils', in Thomas Y. Levin, Ursula Frohne and Peter Weibel, eds, *Ctrl [Space]: Rhetorics of Surveillance from Bentham to Big Brother*. Cambridge, MA: MIT Press, 2002, pp. 396–401.

Waters, Malcolm, *Globalization*, 2nd edn. London and New York: Routledge, 2001.

Wernick, Andrew, 'Post-Marx: Theological Themes in Baudrillard's *America*', Philippa Berry and Andrew Wernick, eds, *Shadow of Spirit: Postmodernism and Religion*. London and New York: Routledge, 1992, pp. 57–80.

White, Mark, *Kenneth Branagh*. London: Faber, 2005.

Williams, Linda, *Playing the Race Card: Melodramas of Black and White from Uncle Tom to O. J. Simpson*. Princeton, NJ: Princeton University Press, 2001.

Wilson, Rob and Wimal Dissanayake, 'Introduction: Tracking the Global/Local', in Rob Wilson and Wimal Dissanayake, eds, *Global/Local: Cultural Production and the Transnational Imaginary*. Durham, NC and London: Duke University Press, 1996, pp. 1–20.

Wistrich, Robert, 'From Weimar to Hitler', in Simon Gigliotti and Berel Lang, eds, *The Holocaust: A Reader*. Oxford: Blackwell, 2005, pp. 44–67.

Worthen, W. B., *Shakespeare and the Force of Modern Performance*. Cambridge: Cambridge University Press, 2003.

Wray, Ramona, 'The Singing Shakespearean: Kenneth Branagh's *Love's Labour's Lost* and the Politics of Genre', in Pascale Aebischer, Edward J. Esche and Nigel Wheale, eds, *Remaking Shakespeare: Performance Across Media, Genres and Cultures*. Basingstoke: Palgrave, 2003, pp. 151–71.

—— and Mark Thornton Burnett, 'From the Horse's Mouth: Branagh on the Bard', in Mark Thornton Burnett and Ramona Wray, eds, *Shakespeare, Film, Fin de Siècle*. Basingstoke: Macmillan, 2000, pp. 165–78.

Zarrilli, Philip B., Bruce McConachie, Gary Jay Williams and Carol Fisher Sorgenfrei, *Theatre Histories: An Introduction*. London and New York: Routledge, 2006.

Zeitlin, Michael, 'Donald Barthelme and the Postmodern Sequel', in Paul Budra and Betty A. Schellenberg, eds, *Part Two: Reflections upon the Sequel*. Toronto, Buffalo and London: University of Toronto Press, 1998, pp. 160–73.

Zhang, Xiao Yang, *Shakespeare in China: A Comparative Study of Two Traditions and Cultures*. Newark, DE: University of Delaware Press, 1996.

Žižek, Slavoj, *The Fragile Absolute: Or, Why is the Christian Legacy Worth Fighting For?* London and New York: Verso, 2000.
—— *The Puppet and the Dwarf: The Perverse Core of Christianity.* Cambridge, MA: MIT Press, 2003.
—— *Welcome to the Desert of the Real.* London and New York: Verso, 2002.
—— *The Žižek Reader*, ed. Elizabeth Wright and Edmond Wright. Oxford: Blackwell, 1999.

## Web sources

Anthony, Ross, 'Interviews with Actor Ethan Hawke and Director Michael Almereyda of *Hamlet*' (www.rossanthony.com/interviews/hawke.shtml).
Applebaum, Stephen, 'Al Pacino: *The Merchant of Venice*' (www.bbc.co.uk/films/2004/11/30/al_pacino_the_merchant_of_venice_interview.shtml).
International Movie Database (http://www.imdb.com).
Manifesto and 'vow of chastity' (www.dogme95.dk).
Moss, Stephen, 'Blacked up and proud', *Guardian*, 28 July 2005 (http://www.guardian.co.uk/arts/features/story/0153798300.html).
Murray, Rebecca, 'Interview with *The Merchant of Venice* director, Michael Radford' (romanticmovies.about.com/od/merchantofvenice/a/merchntmr122304.htm).
O' Donnell, Aisling, rev. of *Hamlet* (http://www.dubliniff.com/content/review/22).
*William Shakespeare's 'The Merchant of Venice': Press Pack* (www.sonypictures.com/classics/merchantofvenice/flash.html).

# Index

*Note:* Page references in italics indicate illustrations.

Abel, Roysten *see In Othello*
Abela, Alexander, *Makibefo*  164
acceptance, cultural  11–12, 21, 58, 67, 76, 85
Adorno, Theodor A.  105–6
Adorno, Theodor A. and Horkheimer, Max  97, 98
Aebischer, Pascale  72
aestheticization, as anaesthetization  88
affiliation  3, 5, 23–4, 124, 147
African-Americans, and *Macbeth in Manhattan*  123–4
Albanese, Denise  48, 123
Almereyda, Michael *see Hamlet*
*American Idol*  149
*American Me* (Olmos)  131–2
*American Psycho* (Harron)  52
anaesthetization, aestheticization as  88
Anderson, Laurie  168 n. 10
Anderson, Miles  125
Andrews, David L.  73
anti-Semitism
  institutionalized  89–90
  in *The Merchant of Venice*  87, 88–9, 92, 94, 97
  Nazi  91–2, 93
  in politics  87–8
*Antony and Cleopatra*  19
Appadurai, Arjun  64, 130, 140
Applbaum, Arthur Isak  100
appropriation  8, 48, 129–30
  in *Beginner's Luck*  25–6
  in *Get Over It*  24–5
  in *Indian Dream*  24
  in *The Street King*  134
Arias, Claudia M. Milian  144
*As You Like It* (Branagh)  165
  funding  161–3, 166
  and Japan  158–60, 161

Auschwitz, Day of Remembrance  87, 105
Auslander, Philip  10, 18
auteurship  15, 36–42, 43, 52, *53*, 131
authenticity, in *Beginner's Luck*  25
authority
  cultural  71
  of Shakespeare  12–13, 39, 129, 156
Babakitis, Peter, *Henry V*  164
Barlow, Andrew L.  86
Barlow, Patrick  129
Bartkowiak, Andrzej, *Romeo Must Die*  147
Bartov, Omer  104
Baudrillard, Jean  49
Bauman, Zygmunt  68
Beckinsale, Kate  34
Bedford, James Gavin *see The Street King*
*Beginner's Luck* (Callis and Cohen)  7–8, 9–11
  and appropriation  25–6
  and crisis of theatre  13
  and global domination  12
  and prejudice  16
  and professional stereotypes  23
  and retrospection  14
  and romance  20
  and self-discovery  14–15
  and theatre as community  20–1, 27
Beier, Karen  168 n. 9
*Being John Malkovich* (Jonze)  131
Belcher, Sarah  16
Bellini, Vincenzo, *Norma*  37
Beltrán, Mary C.  147
Bender, Jack *see The Tempest*
Benigni, Roberto, *Life is Beautiful*  103
Benjamin, Walter  36, 155
Bennett, Susan  24, 168 n. 7

213

# Index

Bergen, Doris L. 91
Berkhoff, Steven 9
Berteloot, Jean-Yves 13
Beyer, Peter 109
Bhabha, Homi K. 16, 71, 73, 80, 124, 169 n. 22
Bharucha, Rustom 141, 154
Bishop, Michael 122
Bisson, Christopher 8
Blandford, Steve, Grant, Barry Keith and Hillier, Jim 14, 169 n. 19
Blessed, Brian 57
Blige, Mary J. 148
blood motif
 in *Macbeth in Manhattan* 120
 in *The Merchant of Venice* 97–9
Boehrer, Bruce Thomas 169 n. 24
Bogdanov, Michael, *Macbeth* 49, 57–8
Bohringer, Romane 115
books
 burning 91–2, 98
 importance 36, 39–41
Booth, Ken and Dunne, Tim 149
Bottinelli, Jennifer J. 127
*Bottom's Dream* (Canemaker) 173 n. 41
*Bound by Honour* (Hackford) 132
Bradley, David 113
Branagh, Kenneth 19–20
 and American film acting 35
 *As You Like It* 158–60, 161–3, 165–6
 and *Henry V* 58
 and Ireland 61–2
 *Love's Labour's Lost* 160–1
 and *Othello* 75
 and Shakespeare as global property 47
 *see also Hamlet; In the Bleak Midwinter; Much Ado About Nothing*
*Braveheart* (Gibson) 58
Breight, Curtis 48
Briers, Richard 11, 41
Bristol, Michael 145
Brody, Adrian 93
Brown, Bill 110, 119
Brown, Eric C. 73

Brown, John Russell 25
Buchanan, Judith 77
Bucker, Pat 22
Buddhism, globalization 107–9, 111
Budra, Paul and Schellenberg, Betty A. 28
Buhler, Stephen M. 43, 79
Burt, Richard 48, 93, 129
Butler, Judith 131

Calder, David 113
Calf, Anthony 16
Callis, James and Cohen, Nick, *Beginner's Luck* 7–8, 9
Camastra, Danielle 152
capitalism
 and consumerism 3, 53, 108, 144, 150, 151
 and globalization 1, 13–14, 108
 and parody 6, 144, 150, 151
Caplan, Jane 70
Caputo, John D. 110–11, 121
Carlisle, Carol J. 104
Carmelo, Tonantzin 135
carnival
 and *A Midsummer Night's Dream* 32–3
 and *Much Ado About Nothing* 31–2
Carpenter, John, *Escape from New York* 52
Carr, Gus 136, 147
Carroll, David 88
Cartelli, Thomas 133
Cartelli, Thomas and Rowe, Katherine 126
Cartmell, Deborah 74, 180 n. 28
Caruth, Cathy 101
Castells, Manuel 132
Cavanagh, Stephen, *Hamlet* 62–4, 164–6
Cazenove, Christopher 9
celebrity, manufactured 149
Chaddha, Sheeba 138
Chakravarti, Paromita 140
Charnes, Linda 48
Charnley, Hetta 13
chorus, role 123–5

Christianity, and anti-Semitism 89–92, 96–8, 104
Chronos myth, and *The King is Alive* 122–3
Cixous, Hélène and Clément, Catherine 39
class
 in *In Othello* 139, 140
 in *The Street King* 134
Cohen, Rob, *The Fast and the Furious* 147
Collins, Michael J. 41
colonialism
 and *In Othello* 139, 141, 154
 and Namibia 126
colour
 and black and white 92–3
 and identity 91, 93, 95, 98
Columbine High School killings 66, 179 n. 6
commodification
 bodily 145
 global 108, 129, 151
 of the Orient 158
consumerism, and capitalism 3, 53, 108, 144, 150, 151
Cook, Pam 119
Corduner, Allan *90*, 95
corporations, global 1, 43–5, 163–4, 166
 and the local 59–60
 media 3–4, 13–14, 43–4, 64, 163
Corrigan, Timothy 36–7
Coursen, H. R. 41, 172 n. 20
Cox, Charlie 90
Cronin, Michael 157
*Crouching Tiger, Hidden Dragon* (Lee) 158
Crowl, Samuel 7, 36, 102, 105
Cukor, George, *A Double Life* 131
culture
 and acceptability 11–12, 21, 67, 76, 85
 border culture 6, 143–4, 146
 and doubling 9, 75, 77
 globalization 1–3, 5, 13, 48, 67–8, 101
 and Jewishness 88

Cvetkovich, Ann and Kellner, Douglas 72, 85

Danes, Claire 137
Davidtz, Embeth 94
Davis, Mike 152
Davison, Bruce *112*, 116
Day of Remembrance for Auschwitz 87, 105
De Man, Paul 27
De Vany, Arthur 161
*Dead Poets Society* (Weir) 7
deconstruction, and religion 110
Deitchman, Elizabeth A. 83
Deleyto, Celestino 173 n. 38
Delhomme, Benoit 95
Delpy, Julie 20
demythologizing of Shakespeare 6, 12–14, 34–5, 129
Derrida, Jacques 60, 64, 88, 117, 123, 127, 178 n. 43
Derry Film Initiative *see Hamlet* (Cavanagh)
desert motif, in *The King is Alive* 112–13, 114, 116, 119, 122, 124, 125
desire, same-sex
 and *The Merchant of Venice* 94–5, 97
 and *Othello* and *'O'* 69, 79–84, 86
difference
 and anti-Semitism 91
 and globalization 2, 68–9, 78
 and the local 4
 and race 71–2, 75, 77–9, 84, 85–6, 149
 and same-sex desire 80–4, 86
 and subtitling 140–1
Disney Corporation 3, 43–5, 163
displacement 5, 20, 26, 38, 100–1, 112–13
dissimulation
 and race 74–5
 and sexuality 90
diversity, and globalization 1–2, 68; *see also* localization
documentary, and authenticity 5, 49, 92–3

Dogme-95 movement   110
Dollimore, Jonathan   22
Donaldson, Peter   3, 107
Donato, Isabella   145
Doran, Gregory, *Macbeth*   49–50, 52
Dorval, Patricia   77
*A Double Life* (Cukor)   131
doubling, culture   9, 75, 77
Doyle, Patrick   159
Dunst, Kirsten   17

Eagleton, Terry   105, 184 n. 54
Edison, Thomas   37
Egoyan, Atom and Balfour, Ian   140–1
Eldon, Kevin   129
Elton, Ben   172 n. 18
Englishness
  and *Beginner's Luck*   23
  and *In the Bleak Midwinter*   11, 23
  and *In Othello*   140
  and *Indian Dream*   11, 16, 24
  and *Much Ado About Nothing*   35
epilogues   14–15, 19, 21
*Escape from New York* (Carpenter)   52
*Escape from Sobibor* (Gold)   103
Escobar Gaviria, Pablo Emilio   135
essentialism   16, 21, 47, 63, 64, 128, 131, 147–8
ethnicity
  and globalization   2, 68, 147–9
  performance   100
  and spirituality   123–4
Evans-Lombe, Harriet   21
Everett, Rupert   31, 35
exclusion
  and gender   38–9
  and race   66–7, 79, 85, 89–92
exoticism, racial   123
eyes *see* gaze

fairness, in *'O'*   82–3
Falsetto, Mario   163
*familia*, in *The Street King*   133–4, 146, 153
Fanon, Frantz   76
Farrell, Nicholas   13
fashion, and *Romeo & Juliet*   131, 137, 148, 150, 151

Featherstone, Mike   68
Felman, Shoshana   106
Felman, Shoshana and Laub, Dori   103
Fernie, Ewan   110, 127
Ferzetti, Gabriele   70
Fiennes, Joseph   90
Fiennes, Ralph   94
film
  and meta-theatricality   33–4
  and theatre   4, 7–27, 33
film industry, US, economic role   3
Fischer-Lichte, Erika   19
Fishburne, Laurence   69, 83
Fisher, Gregor   90
Flockhart, Calista   31, 35
Forced Entertainment   168 n. 9
Ford, David F.   109
Foster, Ben   8
Foucault, Michel   45, 122
Fox, Judith   109
Freeston, Jeremy, *Macbeth*   49, 57–8
Fregoso, Rosa Linda   144
Freinkel, Lisa   96
French, Emma   163
Friedman, Jonathan   68
Friel, Anna   31, 35
fundamentalism, and *The Merchant of Venice*   88, 98, 105

Ganatra, Nitin   11
gaze
  in *The Merchant of Venice*   95
  in *Much Ado About Nothing*   43
  in *'O'*   67, 76–7
  in *Othello*   75–7, 81
Geary, Karl   54, 188 n. 61
gender, and auteurship   38–42, 43
Genette, Gérard   28, 29, 130, 171 n. 3
genocide, in Namibia   126;
  *see also* Holocaust
*Get Over It* (O'Haver)   8, 9–11, 18, 24–5
  and homoeroticism   16–17
  and impenetrability   12
  and improvization   24–5
  and parody   17
  and prejudice   16–17

and professional stereotypes 22–3
and recuperation 16–17
and retrospection 14
and romance 17–19, 23
and self-discovery 14–15, 18, 169 n. 24
and theatre as community 27
ghetto
 in *The Merchant of Venice* 90, 91, 95, 99
 in *Romeo & Juliet* 149, 152
 in *The Street King* 132, 144
ghosts *see* spirituality
Gibson, Mel, *Braveheart* 58
Gilmore, Michael T. 23, 170 n. 41
Girard, René 97
globalisation
 and capitalism 1, 13–14, 108
 of culture 1–3, 5, 13, 48, 67–8, 101
 definition 1–2
 and film and theatre 7–27
 and global flows 6, 130, 133, 140, 147, 153
 and identity 2, 48, 63, 68, 73–4, 78, 85–6, 101, 160
 and language 141
 and migration 1, 143–4, 147, 152–3, 160
 and multinationals 14, 59
 and nostalgia 27
 and parody 130, 156–7
 and postmodernity 130
 and power 2, 140
 and race 2, 5, 68–9, 78, 150
 and reflexivity 125
 and Shakespeare 3–6, 13–14, 33, 47–65, 67, 110, 140, 147–8
 and spirituality 107–9, 128
 and technology 1, 3
 *see also* homogeneity; localization
Glover, John 114
Goebbels, Joseph 91–2
Gold, Jack, *Escape from Sobibor* 103
Goldby, Roger, *Indian Dream* 8, 9
Gray, Tamyra 136, 147, 149
Greenhalgh, Susanne 49
Greenhalgh, Susanne and Shaughnessy, Robert 21

Gregory, Nick 113–14
Grupo Galpão 168 n. 9
Guru, Gopal 139

H&M, and *Romeo & Juliet* 131, 147–8, 150
Hackford, Taylor *see Bound by Honour*
Hadfield, Mark 15
Hall, Kim 82
Halpern, Richard 122
*Hamlet*
 allusions to 19
 in film 8, 11, 15, 20, 22, 23, 48, 64–5
 as recuperative 15
*Hamlet* (Almereyda)
 and auteurship 52, 53
 and global homogeneity 4, 50–2
 and Ireland 4, 54, 56, 60, 62
 and New York landscape 52–3, 161
 and *Romeo & Juliet* 137
 and spirituality 107–8, 188 n. 61
*Hamlet* (Branagh) 44, 55, 61, 163
 design sheet 51
 European première 61–2
 and global homogeneity 4, 50–1
 and Ireland 4, 54, 57, 61–2
 and nostalgia 4, 54
*Hamlet* (Cavanagh)
 and global corporations 164, 166
 and Ireland 62–4
hand imagery 19, 69, 78, 79, 80, 98
Harries, Dan 156
Harron, Mary, *American Psycho* 52
Hartnett, Josh 66
Harvey, Tim 158–9
Hatchuel, Sarah 75
Hawke, Ethan 52, 53, 107
HBO company, and *As You Like It* 161–3
Heard, John 78
Heinze, Andrew R. 104
Henderson, Diana E. 161
*Henry IV*, and sequels 28–9
*Henry V* (Babakitis) 164
*Henry V* (Branagh) 58
*Henry VI*, and sequels 28–9
Henson, Elden 66

218 *Index*

heterogeneity 4, 48
Higgs, Eric 109
Hobson, Marian 33
Hodgdon, Barbara 69, 75, 78, 84, 123
Hoffman, Michael *see A Midsummer Night's Dream*
Holland, Peter 163
Hollywood
 influence 2–4, 44
 and professional stereotypes 22–4
 and Shakespeare 3, 8, 13, 45, 47
Holocaust
 commemoration 5, 87
 and *The Merchant of Venice* 87–94, 96, 98–9, 101, 103–4, 105–6
 and Shakespeare 93–4
homoeroticism
 in *Get Over It* 16–17
 in *The Merchant of Venice* 97
 in *'O'* 69, 79–80, 81–3, 86
 in *Othello* 69, 80–1, 83–4, 86
homogeneity, global 59, 68–9, 72, 85, 147, 157
 and diversity 1–2, 68
 and *Hamlet* 4, 49–52
 and *Macbeth* 49–52
hooks, bell 84
Horan, Gerard 32
*House of Flying Daggers* (Yimou Zhang) 158
Howard, Michael 87–8
Howlett, Kathy M. 11
Hughes, Richard 165
Hussain, Adil 138–9, 140–2
Hutcheon, Linda 130, 134, 156
Huyssen, Andreas 8, 168 n. 2
hybridity
 and global identity 2, 68–9
 in *'O'* 5, 71–3, 85, 86
 in *Othello* 5, 71, 77, 81, 86

identity
 communal 134–5
 and ethnicity 147
 and gender 38–42
 and globalization 2, 48, 63, 68, 73–4, 78, 85–6, 101, 160
 multiple 2, 68–9, 72–3, 86

and performance 69, 73–6, 86, 100
and race 5, 66–86, 143–4
and sport 67, 72, 73–4, 76, 78–9
*see also* hybridity
ideoscapes 64
imperialism
 American 6
 electronic 1
 and *In Othello* 139
impersonation 3
imprisonment imagery 39, 69, 79, 81
improvisation 24–5
Imrie, Celia 24
*In the Bleak Midwinter* (Branagh) 7–8, 9–11
 and demythologizing of Shakespeare 12–14
 and Englishness 11, 23
 and parody 13
 and professional stereotypes 23–4
 and retrospection 14
 and self-discovery 14–16
 and theatre as community 20, 27
 and theatre as redemptive 21–2
 and theatre as unrepeatable 169–70 n. 28
*In Othello* (Abel) 6, 7, 130–1, *142*, *154*
 endings 153–5
 and global corporations 164
 globalization and localization 140–2
 *Kathakali* style 138, 139, 141, 154
 and multiculturalism 138–9, 140, 154
 and parody 133, 137–40, 141–3, 147, 151–5, 156–7
 and subtitles 140–1
 and textuality 139–40
India
 and globalization 141
 and *In Othello* 138–40, 153–5, 156
 languages 141
*Indian Dream* (Goldby) 8, 9–12
 and Englishness 11, 16, 24
 and global corporations 164

and postcolonialism 11, 16, 19, 21, 24
and prejudice 19
and recuperation 16
and romance 19
and self-discovery 15
and Shakespeare and acceptability 11–12, 21
and theatre as community 27
individualism, American 146, 153
inequity, cultural 16–17, 132–3
interrelatedness
  and *Hamlet* 107–9
  and *The King is Alive* 117–20, 122–3, 128
intertextuality 3, 94, 123
  and localization 58
  and sequelization 29, 33, 42
  and spirituality 107–8
  and *The Street King* 145–6
Ireland 64–5
  and Almereyda's *Hamlet* 4, 54, 56, 60, 62
  and Branagh's *Hamlet* 4, 54, 57, 61–2
  and Cavanagh's *Hamlet* 62–4
Irish Gothic 54, 57
Irons, Jeremy 89
Iser, Wolfgang 15

Jackson, Russell 11, 163
Jacob, Irène 69
Jain, Madhu 138
James, Brion 118
Jameson, Fredric 2, 27, 43, 53, 57, 130
Japan, and *As You Like It* 158–60, 161
Jarman, Derek 170 n. 44
Jess, Carolyn 113, 118
Jess-Cooke, Carolyn 4, 135
Jessica (*The Merchant of Venice*)
  elopement 95–6, 100
  and guilt 102, 105
  and Jewishness 95, 102–5, 106
  and redemption 5, 89
Jesurum, John 168 n. 10
Jewesbury, Edward 36
Jews

exclusion 89–92
in global culture 88
as scapegoats 97
see also Holocaust; Shylock
John, Barry 139
Johnson, Anthony 72
Jonze, Spike, see also *Being John Malkovich*
Jordan, Michael 72
Joughin, John J. 117
Juste, Carl, 'Mask' 149

Kaplan, Caren 20, 26–7
*Kathakali* style 138, 139, 141, 154
Kearney, Richard 127–8
Keaton, Michael 34–5, 172 n. 17
Keegan, Andrew 76
Kennedy, Dennis 13
Kershaw, Baz 9
Khubeke, Peter 120
Kilfeather, Siobhán 54
Kimmel, Michael 146
*The King is Alive* (Levring) 5, *112*
  chorus 124–5
  and desert theme 112–13, 114, 116, 119, 122, 124, 125
  and displacement 112–13
  and emotion and relationships 117–20, 122–3
  ending 125, 126–7
  and *King Lear* 115–16, 117–19, 121–3, 124, 127
  and redemption 119–20, 123, 125, 126
  and spirituality 5–6, 110–11, 118–20, 121–3, 127–8
*King Lear*
  and displacement 113
  and *The King is Alive* 115–16, 117–19, 121–3, 124, 127
  mixed-media production 168 n. 9
King, Richard 109
Kittler, Friedrich 38, 41–2
Kline, Kevin 35, 37
Kolker, Robert P. 33–4
Kosenkova, Veronika A. 165
Kossak, Saskia 152
Kössler, Reinhart 78
Kozintsev, Grigori 7

Kristeva, Julia 86
Kunene, Vusi 126–7
Kurosawa, Akira 7

Lachapelle, David *see Romeo & Juliet*
*The Lady Doth Protest* 136–7
Lampert, Lisa 102
Langhorne, Richard 2
Lanier, Douglas 22, 28
Lansbury, David 116
Laub, Dori 105
Lavie, Smadar and Swedenburg, Ted 144
Lee, Ang, *Crouching Tiger, Hidden Dragon* 158
Lehmann, Courtney 13, 23, 48, 49, 59, 171 n. 10, 172 n. 21
Leigh, Jennifer Jason 116
Leonard, Robert Sean 32
Levine, Lawrence W. 145
Levring, Kristian *see The King is Alive*
Li, David Leiwei 114
*Life is Beautiful* (Benigni) 103
liveness, and theatre 13, 18–19, 36
Livingstone, Paisley 115
localization 1–2, 6, 47–65, 68, 124–5, 166
 and difference 4
 and *Hamlet* 4, 50–2, 54, 56–7, 60–4
 and *In Othello* 140–2
 and *Macbeth* 4, 49–50, 57–8
 and patriotism 59, 145–6, 149
location, in *Much Ado About Nothing* 30
Locke, Philip 71
Lombardo, Greg *see Macbeth in Manhattan*
*Looking for Richard* (Pacino) 15
Loomba, Ania 141, 154
López, Mario 146, 153
Los Angeles, as location 132, 144, 152
*Love's Labour's Lost* (Branagh) 160–1
Luhrmann, Baz *see Romeo + Juliet*
Lynch, Tertia 114

Macaulay, Thomas Babington 140
*Macbeth*, in film 48, 49, 64–5; *see also* Scotland, PA

*Macbeth* (Bogdanov)
 opening 49
 and regional signifiers 49, 57–8
*Macbeth* (Branagh) 52, 161, *162*
*Macbeth* (Doran)
 and global homogeneity 49–50
 and location 52
 and self-discovery 52
*Macbeth* (Freeston) 49, 57
 and intertextuality 58
 regional markers 57, 58
*Macbeth in Manhattan* (Lombardo) 5, 52
 chorus 123–4, 125
 and global corporations 164
 and New York 111, 113–15
 and satire 113–14
 and spirituality 5–6, 110–11, 120–1, 128
McConachie, Bruce 3
McDonaldization 59–60
Mackichan, Doon 19
McLachlan, Kyle 56
McLoughlin, Seán 146
McTeer, Janet 116
Madden, John, *Shakespeare in Love* 26, 44, 163
Mahon, John W. 89–90
*Makibefo* (Abela) 164
Malešević, Siniša 100
Mallin, Eric S. 98
Maloney, Michael 11, 75
Mann, Daniel, *Playing for Time* 103
Mansukhani, Vivek 138, 141
Marceau, Sophie 35
market, global 1, 2
 and religion 109, 111
 and Shakespeare 3, 4–6, 33, 34, 59, 64, 105, 111, 160, 163–6
 and theatre 9
Marshall, Kris 90
masculinity, in *The Street King* 134–5, 144–5, 152
masks 32, 39, 74, 90
Massai, Sonia 48
maternity
 in *The Merchant of Venice* 103
 in '*O*' 82, 84
 in *The Street King* 145

May, Stephen   68, 179 n. 12
Mayo, Sarah   33, 48
media
  corporations   3–4, 13–14, 43–4, 64, 163
  mass   13, 73–4
  in *The Street King*   152–3
Mendelssohn, Felix   41
*The Merchant of Venice*, quoted in *Romeo & Juliet*   150
*The Merchant of Venice* (Radford)   5, 87
  and ambiguity   96, 102
  and anti-Semitism   87, 88–9, 92, 94, 97
  and blood motif   97–9
  and difference   91
  and displacement   100–1
  and documentary realism   5, 89, 92–3, 99
  and exploitation   94–5
  and ghetto   90, 91, 95, 99
  'Hath not a Jew eyes?' speech   92–5, 98, 99, 103
  and Holocaust   87–94, 96, 98–9, 101, 103–4, 105–6
  loss of paradise motif   100–1
  opening   88, 89, 100
  and remembering   105–6
  scapegoat motif   96–7
  and subjectivity   95–6, 106
  *see also* Jessica; Shylock
meritocracy   67, 148
*A Midsummer Night's Dream*
  in film   7, 8, 11–12, 14, 16–18, 22, 24–5
  multi-cultural production   168 n. 9
*A Midsummer Night's Dream* (Hall)   173 n. 41
*A Midsummer Night's Dream* (Hoffman)   4, 169 n. 25
  and antiquity   31
  and auteurship   36–9, 42
  and books   36
  and carnival   32–3
  ending   43–5
  and location   30
  and meta-theatricality   33
  and *Much Ado About Nothing*   28, 29, 30–1, 37–8, 41
  and nostalgia   45
  opening   41–2
  as sequel   28–35, 43–6
*A Midsummer Night's Sex Comedy* (Allen)   173 n. 41
migration, and globalization   1, 143–4, 147, 152–3, 160
Miller, William Ian   82
Milton, John, *Paradise Lost*   100–1
Miramax   8, 44, 163
misogyny, in *The Street King*   145
monstrosity, and *The Street King*   133, 134
Morrissette, Billy, *Scotland, PA*   58–60
*Much Ado About Nothing* (Branagh)   28, 29, 30, 40, 47
  and antiquity   31, 32, 33
  and auteurship   36–41, 43
  and books   36, 39–41
  and carnival   31–2
  ending   42–3
  location   30
  and meta-theatricality   34
  and nostalgia   44
  opening   39–41
  and parody   172 n. 17
  profitability   163
multiculturalism   17, 132
  performative   10, 19, 138–9, 140, 141
multinationals *see* corporations, global
music   36, 37, 41, 43, 80, 84
  in *As You Like It*   159
  in *In Othello*   138
  in *Macbeth in Manhattan*   115
  in *The Merchant of Venice*   100–2, 104–5
  in *A Midsummer Night's Dream*   37, 41
  in *'O'*   73
  in *Romeo & Juliet*   148, 149
  in *The Street King*   132

names   85–6
Namibia, as location   112–13, 125–6
Nazism *see* anti-Semitism; Holocaust

Nelson, Tim Blake *see* 'O'
New York
  and *Hamlet* 52–3, 161
  and *Macbeth in Manhattan* 111, 113–15
  and *Romeo & Juliet* 136, 148
Newman, Karen 102
Nhat Hanh, Thich 107, 109, 188 n. 61
Niezen, Ronald 148
nostalgia 8, 11, 24, 27
  and Bogdanov's *Macbeth* 57–8
  and Branagh's *Hamlet* 4, 54
  and Disney 44–5
  and Freeston's *Macbeth* 57
  and parody 130
  and sequels 29
*Nuit et Brouillard* (Resnais) 93, 106

'O' (Nelson) 66–7, 164
  bird images 78
  and gaze 76–7
  and global homogeneity 72
  hand images 69, 78
  and homoeroticism 69, 79–80, 81–3, 84, 86
  and hybridity 5, 71–3, 85
  maternal imagery 82, 84
  and performance 73–4, 74, 76
  and racial identity 68–9, 72–3, 76, 78, 85
  and racialized sexuality 69–70
  and state power 71
  and subjectivity 70–1, 85
objectification, and race 70, 78, 81, 83
O'Byrne, Darren 58
O'Connor, Pat, *Cal* 56
O'Haver, Tommy, *Get Over It* 8, 9
Olivier, Laurence 7, 153
Olmos, Edward James 136
  *American Me* 131–2
Orkin, Martin 48
*Othello*
  in film 7, 153
  *see also In Othello*; 'O'
*Othello* (Parker) 66, 67
  and chess imagery 79
  and dissimulation 74–5
  and gaze 75–7, 81
  and global homogeneity 72
  hand imagery 69, 79, 80
  and homoeroticism 69, 80–1, 83–4, 86
  and hybridity 5, 71, 77, 81, 86
  and imprisonment imagery 69, 79, 81
  opening 74
  and racial identity 68–9, 74–5, 77–8, 85
  and racialized sexuality 69–70
  and state power 79, 81
  and subjectivity 70–1, 83
otherness *see* difference

Pacino, Al
  *Looking for Richard* 15
  *The Merchant of Venice* 89, 90, 96
Pakula, Alan J., *Sophie's Choice* 103
*Paradise Lost* (Milton) 100–1
Parker, Nathaniel 76
Parker, Oliver *see Othello*
parody
  and ideology 156
  and *In Othello* 133, 137–40, 141–3, 147, 150–5, 156–7
  post-millennial 13, 129–57
  and *Romeo & Juliet* 133–4, 136–7, 147–50, 151, 156–7
  and *The Street King* 133–6, 144–7, 151–4, 156–7
Partridge, Christopher 108
past, and nostalgia 11
Patrick, Anne 80
patriotism, American 59, 145–6, 149
*Peace is Every Step: Meditation in Action* 107, 109
Pendleton, Thomas A. 96
Perez, Manny 145
performance 3, 7–8, 10
  and chorus 124
  and community 20–1
  and ethnicity 100, 147
  and identity 14–15, 69, 73–6, 86, 100
  live 13, 18–19, 36
  multicultural 10, 19, 138–9, 141
  and theatre-based films 7–8, 10, 15

Perrez, Timothy Paul 133
Perrineau, Harold 123
*Peter Pan* 43
Pfeiffer, Michelle 31, 43, 47
Phelan, Peggy 18
Phifer, Mekhi 66
*The Pianist* (Polanski) 94–5
Pizzato, Mark 136
*Playing for Time* (Mann) 103
Poe, Edgar Allen, 'Bridal Ballad' 104
Polanski, Roman, *The Pianist* 93–4
Pook, Jocelyn 104
postcolonialism
  and *Indian Dream* 11, 16, 19, 21, 24
  and *The King is Alive* 5, 126–7
  and *Romeo & Juliet* 147
postmodernity
  and globalization 130
  and parody 134
  and religion and spirituality 109–10
  and sequels 29
  and Shakespeare 16, 24, 27, 36, 46, 49, 64, 66, 114
power
  female 38–9, 153
  hierarchies 140, 143–4
  of Shakespeare 12–13
prejudice
  and *Beginner's Luck* 16
  and *Indian Dream* 16
  and *The Merchant of Venice* 105
productions, mixed-media 10
professionals, stereotypes 22
prologues 15
prostitution, and *The Merchant of Venice* 94–5
Puchner, Martin 124

race
  and cultural authority 71
  and exoticism 123
  and globalization 2, 5, 68–9, 78, 149–50
  and homogeneity 147, 150
  and identity 5, 66–86
  and imprisonment 81
  markers 5

  and ownership 70
  and same-sex desire 69, 79–84, 86
  and sexuality 69–70, 75, 127
racism, *see* anti-Semitism
Radford, Michael *see The Merchant of Venice*
realism, and *The Merchant of Venice* 92–3, 99
recuperation
  and *In the Bleak Midwinter* 15
  and *Indian Dream* 16
  and *The King is Alive* 119, 124
  and *The Merchant of Venice* 105–6
  and *'O'* 84–5
  and theatre 15–17, 20, 26–7, 42
redemption
  and *In the Bleak Midwinter* 21–2
  and *The King is Alive* 119–20, 123, 125, 126
  and *The Merchant of Venice* 5, 105
  and *'O'* 84–5
  theatre as redemptive 8, 21–2, 24
Reese, Roger 35
Reeves, Keanu 32
reflexivity, and globalization 125
relationships, and *The King is Alive* 117–20, 122–3
relevance
  of Shakespeare 6, 8, 12–15, 24, 26–7, 47
  of theatre 9
religion, and globalization 2, 109, 111
remembering
  and Auschwitz 5, 87, 105
  and *The King is Alive* 119–20, 127
  and *The Merchant of Venice* 105–6
representation
  global 58
  and parody 130, 148, 156
  of race 5, 70–1, 75–7
reproduction, and sequelization 35–7, 41
Resnais, Alain, *Nuit et Brouillard* 93, 106
Reuben, Gloria 116

*Richard III*
  and American individualism 145, 146
  and *The Street King* 132, 133–5, 143, 153
  and subordination of women 134, 153
  in USA 145–6
Riefenstahl, Leni, *Triumph of the Will* 92
Ritzer, George 59
Robinson, Zuleikha 95
Rodríguez, Clara E. 153
romance
  in film 65
  and theatre 17–19, 23
*Romeo & Juliet* (Lachapelle) 6, 130–1
  endings 151
  and ethnicity 147–9
  and fashion 131, 137, 148, 150, 151
  and homogeneity 147
  and parody 133–4, 136–7, 146–50, 151, 156–7
*Romeo + Juliet* (Luhrmann) 47, 123, 137, 147, 163, 191 n. 50
*Romeo and Juliet*, multivocal production 168 n. 9
*Romeo Must Die* (Bartkowiak) 147
Rothwell, Kenneth 80
Rouse, Roger 147
Rowe, Katherine 52
Royal Shakespeare Company
  and Branagh 45
  'Complete Shakespeare' season 10
  *Macbeth* 49

Sagemiller, Melissa 8
St Sebastian, iconography of 104
Salaman, Toby 21
Sassen, Saskia 64
Saunders, Jennifer 23
Sawalha, Julia 20
scapegoat motif, in *Merchant of Venice* 96–7
*Schindler's List* (Speilberg) 93–4, 99
Schohet, Lauren 59
Scholl, Andreas 101
Scholte, Jan Aart 1–2, 68

schools, and racial conflict 66–7
Schwartz, Hillel 36
Scorcese, Martin, *Taxi Driver* 52
Scotland 64–5
  and America 58–9
  and Bogdanov's *Macbeth* 4, 49, 57–8
  and Freeston's *Macbeth* 4, 57, 58
*Scotland, PA* (Morrissette) 58–60
Scott, Alex 44
Scott-Douglass, Amy 118, 119, 187 n. 40
Seda, Jon 133
seeing, in *The King is Alive* 125;
  *see also* gaze
self
  multiple 2, 68–9, 72–3, 86
  self-creation 73, 145
  *see also* identity
self-discovery
  and film 52, 67
  in *The Street King* 144
  and theatre 8, 14–16, 18, 22, 24, 169 n. 24
*Sen Noci Svatojánské* (Trnka) 173 n. 41
sequel, Shakespearean 6, 25, 28, 29, 30, 32–46
Sessions, John 11, 90
sexuality
  'Bollywood' conventions 143
  and dissimulation 90
  female 72, 82–3
  as property 145
  racialized 69–70, 75, 127
  same-sex 79–82
  and technological innovation 41–2
Shakespeare Association of America 164–5
*Shakespeare in Love* (Madden) 26, 44, 163
Shakespeare, William
  accessibility 36
  authority 12–13, 39, 129, 156
  commodification 129, 151–2
  comprehensibility 8, 12, 17
  demythologizing 6, 12–14, 34–5, 129

essentialist views   3, 16, 21, 47, 63, 64, 128, 131, 147
and film and theatre   4, 7–27
and globalization   3–6, 33, 47–65, 67, 110, 140, 148
and Holocaust   93–4
Indian adaptations   140
and multiculturalism   10, 19, 132
parodic versions   6, 9, 129–57
and particularity see localization
as passport to acceptability   11–12, 21
as performative property   10
portrait   134–5
and postmodernity   6, 16, 24, 27, 36, 46, 49, 110
relevance   6, 8, 12–15, 24, 26–7
and revisionism   34, 47–8
social utility   26–7
and spirituality   110–12, 124–5, 128
see also individual plays
Shakespeare's Happy Endings   129, 133
Shankar, Dilip   138
Shapiro, James   183 n. 40
Shaughnessy, Robert   10
Sheen, Martin   70
Shepard, Sam   188 n. 61
Shiva/Shivite   154–5
Short, Martin   22
Shuttleworth, Andy   42
Shylock
  'Hath not a Jew eyes?' speech   92–5, 98, 99, 103
  identification as Jew   91, 93, 96, 100
  as martyr   99, 104–5
  as outsider   90–1, 94–6, 98–101
  as victim   88, 96–7, 99
Silverman, Kaja   41
Simpson, O. J., trial   66, 67
Slings and Arrows   116
Sophie's Choice (Pakula)   103
The Sound of Music (Wise)   42
soundtrack
  As You Like It   159
  In Othello   138
  Macbeth in Manhattan   114–15

The Merchant of Venice   100–2, 104–5
A Midsummer Night's Dream   37, 41
'O'   73
Othello   69–70
Romeo & Juliet   148, 149
The Street King   132
Speilberg, Steven, Schindler's List   93–4, 99
spirituality
  and globalization   107–9, 128
  and Hamlet   107–8, 188 n. 61
  and In the Bleak Midwinter   21–2
  and The King is Alive   5–6, 110–11, 118–20, 121–3, 127–8
  and Macbeth in Manhattan   5–6, 110–11, 118, 120–1, 128
  and postmodernity   109–10
  and Shakespeare   5–6, 110–12, 124–5, 128
sport
  and acceptance   67, 78
  and identity   67, 72, 73–4, 76, 78–9
Starks, Lisa S.   69
stereotypes
  gangland   135, 149
  national   57–8
  of professionals   22–4
  racial   67, 69–70, 71–2, 84, 85, 96, 127
  of terrorists   149
Stewart, Colin   165
Stewart, Susan   44
Stiles, Julia   72
Stoppard, Ed   93
Strahairn, David   36
The Street King (Bedford)   6, 130, 131–2
  and American individualism   145–6, 152
  and border culture   6, 143–4, 147
  endings   152–3
  and familia   133–4, 146, 153
  and media   152–3
  misogyny   144–5
  and monstrosity   133, 134
  opening   134–5

*The Street King* (Bedford) – *continued*
and parody 133–6, 144–6, 150–3, 156–7
and self-made man 145
and subjectivity 132
writing and rewriting in 134–6, 151–2
Sturges, John *The Magnificent Seven* 172 n. 18
subjectivity
in *Merchant of Venice* 95–6, 106
in *Much Ado About Nothing* 38–41
in *'O'* 70–1, 85
in *Othello* 70–1, 83
in *The Street King* 132
subtitling 124, 140–1
Suter, Jacqueline 42
Svich, Caridad 9

tattoos
in *Othello* 70, 83–4
in *The Street King* 135, 144
*Taxi Driver* (Scorcese) 52
Taylor, Gary 129
Taylor, Mark C. 113
technology
and globalization 1, 3, 13
and sexuality 41–2
*The Tempest*, in film 8, 9–10, 12, 14–16, 20, 25
*The Tempest* (Bender) 123
terrorism, global war on 149
textuality, and *In Othello* 139–40
*The Fast and the Furious* (Cohen) 147
theatre
'alternative' 10
as aspirational realm 9–10, 17
as community 19–22, 27
crisis of 9, 13–14, 26, 34
and film 4, 7–27, 33
and professionals 22
as redemptive 8, 21–2, 24
and romance 17–19, 23
and self-discovery 14–16, 18, 22, 24, 169 n. 24
as site of recuperation and possibility 15–17, 20, 26–7, 42

as unrepeatable 18–19, 169–70 n. 28
theology, negative 110, 128
Thompson, Emma 32, 39
torture 81, 83
Tracy, David 120, 128
trade, and Japan 159–60
Trivedi, Poonam 140, 154
Turner, Bryan S. 83–4
*The Two Gentlemen of Verona*, quoted in *Romeo & Juliet* 150

universalism *see* essentialism
USA
and ethnicity 147–8
foreign policy 149
and global culture 48
globalization and the local 48, 59–60
hegemony 6, 160
and manufactured celebrity 148
and multiculturalism 17
reception and use of Shakespeare 145
and Scotland 49, 58–60, 64–5
usury, and anti-Semitism 91

Valdez, Luis, *Zoot Suit* 136
Valle, Victor M. and Torres, Rodolfo D. 131
values, Shakespearean 8, 22, 48, 50
Vanhoozer, Kevin J. 110
Venice, and exclusion of Jews 89–92
Verdi, Guiseppe, *Otello* 84–5
victim, Jew as 5, 88, 96, 99, 104

Walken, Christopher 59
Walker, Chris 117
Walsh, Michael 2
Walter, Harriet 52
Washington, Denzel 32, 34–5
Weir, Peter, *Dead Poets Society* 7
Welles, Orson, as director 7
Werner, Jules 89
West, Dominic 31
West, Shane 16
*West Side Story* (Wise and Robbins) 136–7, 147
Westenra, Hayley 104

whiteness, and purity  83
Williams, Gary Jay  1, 16
Williams, Lia  117
Williams, Linda  77
willow, in Shakespeare  139–40
Wilson, Rob and Dissanayake, Wimal  2
Wilson, Robert  168 n. 10
*The Winter's Tale*  20
Wise, Robert, *The Sound of Music*  42
women
   and *A Midsummer Night's Dream*  43
   and *Much Ado About Nothing*  38–41, 42–3
   and *Richard III*  134, 153
   and *The Street King*  135, 144–5
Wooster Group  168 n. 10
Worthen, W. B.  11

Wray, Ramona  160
writing and rewriting
   in *Get Over It*  24–5
   in *A Midsummer Night's Dream*  41–2
   in *Much Ado About Nothing*  39–41
   in *The Street King*  134–6, 151–2
   *see also* parody

Yuill, Jimmy  36

Zeffirelli, Franco  7, 30
Zeitlin, Michael  45
Zhang, Yimou, *House of Flying Daggers*  158
Žižek, Slavoj  49, 91, 94, 108, 125, 127
*Zoot Suit* (Valdez)  136